# HUMAN MOTIVATION

*A Social Psychological Approach*

# HUMAN MOTIVATION

## *A Social Psychological Approach*

**RUSSELL G. GEEN**
*University of Missouri*

**BROOKS/COLE PUBLISHING COMPANY**
PACIFIC GROVE, CALIFORNIA

**I(T)P** ™  The trademark ITP is used under license.

Brooks/Cole Publishing Company
A Division of Wadsworth, Inc.

Printed in the United States of America

10   9   8   7   6   5   4   3   2   1

**Library of Congress Cataloging-in-Publication Data**

Geen, Russell G., [date]
    Human motivation : a social psychological approach / Russell G. Geen.
        p.   cm.
    Includes bibliographical references and index.
    ISBN 0-534-23850-5 :
    1. Motivation (Psychology)   2. Incentive (Psychology)   3. Goal (Psychology)   I. Title.
    BF503.G428   1995
    153.8 — dc20                                        94-2432
                                                          CIP

Sponsoring Editor: *Vicki Knight*
Marketing Representative: *Susan Hays*
Editorial Associate: *Lauri Banks Ataide*
Production Coordinator: *Fiorella Ljunggren*
Production: *Greg Hubit Bookworks*
Manuscript Editor: *Carol Reitz*
Permissions Editor: *Lillian Campobasso*
Interior Design: *John Edeen*
Cover Design: *E. Kelly Shoemaker and Laurie Albrecht*
Cover Photo: *Kai Chiang / SuperStock, Inc.*
Art Coordinator: *Greg Hubit*
Interior Illustration: *Susan Benoit*
Photo Coordinator: *Greg Hubit*
Photo Researcher: *Sarah Bendersky*
Typesetting: *University Graphics, Inc.*
Cover Printing: *Phoenix Color Corporation, Inc.*
Printing and Binding: *Arcata Graphics / Fairfield*
(Credits continue on p. 336.)

*TO SEBASTIAN*

# Brief Contents

# CONTENTS

# 7 AROUSAL 163

# 8 EMOTION 192

## 9 PROSOCIAL AND AGGRESSIVE MOTIVATION 218

## 10 MOTIVATING EFFECTS OF SOCIAL SETTINGS 243

**11   STRESS AND MOTIVATION   *271***

**12   CONCLUDING COMMENTS   *302***

# PREFACE

Questions about why people do the things they do have been asked since the beginning of time and are still being asked today. Examples of such questions are: Why do we go to great lengths to obtain some things but are relatively indifferent to others? How much control do we have over our actions? To what extent is our behavior driven by the pursuit of pleasure? Why do we set out to do something important but fail to make the effort necessary to see it through?

These enduring questions are indicators of what forms the basis of the psychology of motivation, as we call it today. Theories of motivation vary widely. Some emphasize physiological mechanisms in the brain and other organs of the body. Others pay particular attention to overt behavior, seeking to relate the behavior to processes of classical conditioning or operant learning. Still others are organized around people's reactions to their social environment. All of them seek to explain behavior through some process going on inside the person, and they differ from one another primarily in terms of how they interpret and define that internal activity. But what they all have in common is the three basic concepts of *origins, intensity,* and *persistence* of behavior (see Chapter 1). To answer the questions listed above, as well as others also related to the "why" of behavior, motivational psychologists will employ concepts and variables linked to these three characteristics. The particular answers any given psychologist will offer depends on the theory of motivation that he or she follows.

The material included in this book is presented within the framework of a theoretical model based on my own interpretation of human behavior. According to this model, motivation arises when a basic *motive,* or *need,* interacts with events in the person's *environment* to produce a condition within the person that we call an *incentive.* It also assumes that most of the time the person's "working" environment—that is, the immediate environment that has the greatest impact on the person—is *social* in that it involves people, groups, and institutions that are important to the individual. An incentive, once formed, determines the *goals* that the person is going to pursue. In turn, the selection of a goal necessitates the formulation of a *strategy* for action, as well as the *intentional control* of action, so that the strategy can be employed to attain the goal. This model of human motivation is developed in detail in

Chapters 2–4 of the book, and it underlies most of the substantive material that appears in subsequent chapters.

In this context, what do we mean by needs, situations, incentives, and goals? The most basic human needs arise from conditions of deprivation in the body—such as hunger, thirst, hypothermia, and the quest for sexual activity. However, our behavior is often driven not by these fundamental biological needs but by others, which we learn through our social development. It is on these other motives that we concentrate in this book. People need food, water, and the other necessities of life, but they also need to feel important, to experience the love and respect of others, to believe that what they do has an impact on the world in which they live, to achieve meaningful goals, and to avoid embarrassment. These are just a few of the most common social motives that animate human behavior.

This book maintains that social needs become activated and translated into inner states of incentive when they are combined with conditions in the environment that involve people or collectives that are important to the person. The immediate result of the activation of a motive by a situation is the creation of an incentive—for example, making money, having many good friends, or becoming a powerful leader. Once the incentive has been created, the person sets some specific goals through which the incentive can be satisfied, such as getting a good job, joining a sorority, or running for office. The entire process from needs/motives to incentives, to the setting and pursuit of goals constitutes what, in this book, I refer to as motivation.

I think that this approach will provide the student of motivation with a usable framework on which to develop a particular application of interest. Most of the readers of *Human Motivation* will someday embark on a professional career that involves psychology. Whatever their field, they will find that the concept of motivation plays a crucial role in their work. Those who choose industrial or organization work, for example, will find that motivation is a key factor in business and industry. Much of the material on goal setting, commitment to goals, acceptance of goals, and goal-directed activity presented in Chapters 2 and 3 is based on research in industrial/organizational psychology carried out in natural settings in the workplace. People working in industry may also find that a knowledge of such basic motives as the need for achievement and the need for power will help solve certain types of personnel problems (see Chapter 6).

Other students may go on to careers in clinical or counseling psychology. A knowledge of how people choose their life goals may contribute to an understanding of why they sometimes develop emotional or adjustment problems. Chapters 4 and 5 deal with motivational issues regarding self-esteem, personal freedom and control, helplessness, and other variables that are central to much of clinical and counseling psychology today. In addition, the concept of motivation can shed light on the ways in which people deal with the stress they experience in everyday life (Chapter 11).

Those interested in social or public service will also find that a knowledge of the fundamentals of motivation can be of help in discharging their responsibilities. Both those acts carried out for the benefit of others and those directed against other people make up important areas of study. Much of the current interest in these topics is directed toward understanding prosocial and violent behavior in real-life settings and toward being able to answer questions such as, How may we increase people's willingness to support charitable causes? and, How may we control the level of violence so prevalent in our society? These are important practical issues, and, as shown in Chapter 9, exploring the motivational basis of prosocial and aggressive behavior may provide important ideas for approaching them. Finally, in Chapter 10 we examine some of the motivational processes involved in some common face-to-face social situations, touching on a variety of everyday concerns such as the effects of an audience on performance, the effects of supervisor surveillance on productivity, the tendency of members of a group to become less productive the larger the group becomes, and the processes by which people present themselves to others in order to make a desired impression.

## *Acknowledgments*

It is customary to conclude the preface by acknowledging the help and support the author has received in writing the book. I am very glad to follow that tradition by, first of all, expressing my appreciation to the following reviewers for their valuable comments and suggestions: William Calhoun of the University of Tennessee at Knoxville, Caran Colvin of San Francisco State University, Edmund Fantino of the University of California at San Diego, Randy Fisher of the University of Central Florida, Richard O. Straub of the University of Michigan at Dearborn, and Merry West of California State University–Fresno. I am deeply grateful to Vicki Knight for recognizing the potential of my idea of what a book on human motivation should be and for offering advice and support throughout its development. I also wish to acknowledge how pleasant it has been to deal with the production staff at Brooks/Cole. Thanks to the professional acumen of these people, I have had virtually no problems during the entire production process. I also appreciate the nice interactions I have had with Greg Hubit about many of the technical and not-so-technical details of production. Finally, I wish to thank the students in my graduate class in motivation at the University of Missouri, who helped me stay focused with their collegial feedback and who did me the great service of spotting several typographical errors that originally marred the text.

*Russell G. Geen*

## CHAPTER 1

# INTRODUCTION TO THE STUDY OF MOTIVATION

## CHAPTER OUTLINE

## THE DOMAIN OF MOTIVATION

People who go to movies or watch television are probably familiar with some version of the following scenario: The defense lawyer rises to address the jury. Her client is on trial for first-degree murder and the evidence against him is compelling. He was seen near the site of the murder shortly before it happened. A handkerchief stained with blood of the same type as the victim's was found in his car. His fingerprints were on the murder weapon. Acknowledging this, the lawyer reminds the jury that in spite of the evidence that tends to incriminate her client, the state has failed to explain *why* he supposedly committed the murder. "What," she asks, "was his ostensible *motive* for the crime?"

Absence of a demonstrable motive has long been recognized as grounds for reasonable doubt in criminal trials. This fact reflects some common assumptions of our culture: that people are generally *aware* of the meanings of their actions, that they behave in ways that serve their *purposes*, that they are able to *control* their behavior. These assumptions form the basis for judgments of why people do the things they do, and this is what motivation is about: the *why* of behavior.

In this book several psychological processes are examined and explained, and every one of these processes pertains to the question of why people behave as they do. A number of theoretical orientations are considered, and an attempt is made to integrate these orientations into a general model for human motivation.

## What Is Motivation?

In order to understand what is meant by motivation, we need only observe people as they go about their everyday activities. We note first that human behavior is constantly changing in direction. People frequently stop doing what they are doing and move on to something else, so that new actions are regularly *initiated*. Next we observe that behavior varies in its *intensity*. People sometimes work vigorously at whatever they are doing, and at other times they perform in a slower and more relaxed manner. Finally, we observe that people show great *persistence* in some of the things they do, whereas in others they are less likely to show such tenacity and may be likely to give up when the going becomes difficult. These are simple and common aspects of human life, and they exemplify the basic dimensions of what we describe when we use the word *motivation*—namely, *the initiation, intensity, and persistence of behavior.*

Like many words that psychologists use, the term *motivation* originated in common speech. We hear it used by people in all three of the senses noted above. For example, someone may ask, "Whatever motivated him to say such a thing?," thereby indicating that some verbal action was initiated by a process of motivation. Sometimes the initiatory properties of motivation are manifested in decisions that involve a choice among alternatives. An example is "This player is no longer part of his team but is motivated only to seek personal glory." Motivation-as-intensity is the basis for statements like "She certainly is a highly motivated student," meaning that she studies hard and attends class regularly. Motivation-as-persistence can be used to describe the same fictitious student: "She must be highly motivated to tolerate the rigors of graduate study the way she does." Think about how these observations reflect the things that people normally do, and you will begin to understand why motivation is such an important concept for understanding human behavior. If we were all robots, carrying out programmed sets of acts in the same monotonous way every time, we would not need such a concept. The fact that we are not robots is the reason that we do need it.

In this book the term *motivation* will be used in the context of a complex process. It is an important element in the process but not the only one. This process involves three steps:

1. Defining a goal to which the person aspires.
2. Choosing a course of action that leads to attainment of the goal.
3. Carrying out the chosen course of action.

The first question to be answered is, Why does the person need to have a goal in the first place? Obviously, motivated behavior must begin with some situation or condition that requires the person to adopt a goal. Such antecedents are of two kinds. One is some *need* that a person experiences and that animates action consistent with that need. For example, a mother who feels a strong sense of nurturance for her infant who lies sleeping in the next room may suddenly go to the baby's crib, look lovingly at the child, and kiss her. The mother's need to nurture the child initiates a spontaneous act of goal setting—to be near the infant—and motivates the simple and direct course of action by which the mother expresses her love.

The other type of antecedent of choosing a goal is some *demand* on the person that arises in the environment and interacts with one or more needs to motivate action. For example, if the young mother we have observed saw smoke coming from under the door to her baby's bedroom, she would react instantly by rushing to the child and carrying her from the dangerous situation. The goal in this case is clearly defined by the situation: to get the baby to safety. The mother's nurturance need is, of course, heavily involved in such action, but the major impetus comes not from the need but from the situational demand. Years ago the great personality psychologist Henry Murray (1938) called these two pressures on the person *needs* (personal demands) and *press* (situational demands). These terms still evoke a sense of the forces that a person experiences in such situations: needs from inside and pressure from outside.

The second step in the process we have described involves commitment to a course of action, or an *intention,* that will give the person a good chance of reaching the goal. Certain variables go into this decision (as will be noted in greater detail later in this chapter and in Chapter 2). One is the likelihood that a given course of action in fact leads to the goal. Another is the person's belief about how capable he or she is of carrying out the course of action. Still other variables are the complexity of the problems that the person faces and any barriers to activity that the environment may present.

After a goal has been selected and an intention for attaining it has been chosen, the person must devise and enact a *strategy*. This strategy is a plan for the initiation of the required behavior. If the goal is even moderately difficult to attain, the person will be forced to expend some effort in this process. In addition, he or she will have to assess the situation periodically to discover how much progress has been made toward the goal. If the person

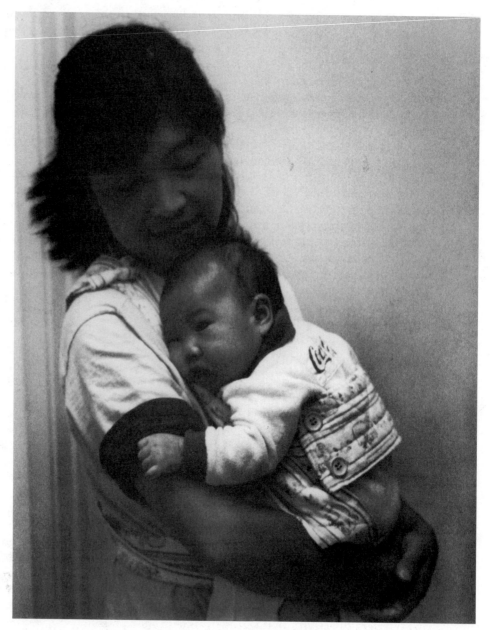

*The need to nurture the young is a powerful human motive.*

thinks that progress is too slow, the amount of effort expended may be increased. It is in this expenditure of effort that the intensity of the behavior is seen. Of course, it is also possible that at some point the person may decide that no further effort is worth the trouble and give up pursuing the goal. However, if the person thinks that more effort is worthwhile, he or she will persist. The variables that go into the actual enactment of goal strategies will be described more fully in Chapter 3, but for now we are content to define the outlines of the process and to locate behavioral initiation, intensity, and persistence within it.

### Motivation in Context

Note that in this scheme of motivated behavior, variables other than motivation per se are involved. For example, cognitive processes play an important role in assessing available goals, in devising strategies, and in evaluating the degree of progress that the person has made at any time. Affect and emotion may be involved in the process at various stages. For example, the person may feel pleasantly challenged by the thought of pursuing an attainable goal, and he might experience disappointment and disillusion if repeated failures are encountered. Motivation, in the broad sense that we are using the word, is just one process that occurs in behavior in concert with other processes.

# THE SOCIAL NATURE OF MOTIVATION

A major assumption in this book is that most human motivation takes place in social settings. We begin our exposition of this position with a truism: *Homo sapiens,* the human being, is a social animal. Most people would agree with this statement; hermits are relatively rare. Human beings, whether loving or hating, helping or hurting, dominating or deferring, spend most of their time with one another. Humans evolved as a social species in small packs or groups of people who lived together for mutual protection and collective hunting and gathering. Today people live in physical surroundings different from those of their distant ancestors and the nature of the social bonds that tie them together have changed, but human nature is still basically *social.*

To say that human beings are social animals does not mean that they are always group-loving, sociable, and cooperative individuals who respect the rights of others. Sometimes social settings are the occasions for crime, hatred, exploitation, and abuse. However, whether a person is in a group, against it, or merely isolated from it, the context of action and the motivation involved are still social. Motivated acts by human beings are almost always carried out within a social environment. Moreover, such action usually *requires* a social environment, regardless of whether the motive is to approach others or to set oneself against them. We will return to this theme in Chapter 10, where it will be proposed that human motives can be divided into two classes: those that promote the welfare of the individual vis-à-vis other people and those that integrate the individual within a larger social community.

# THE HISTORICAL BACKGROUND OF MOTIVATIONAL PSYCHOLOGY

One might think that a concept as central to understanding human activity as motivation would be ensconced within a well-articulated theoretical structure and expressed in clear and forceful statements on the nature of behavior. Furthermore, one might expect that psychologists would often invoke motivational explanations for behavior. At one time in the history of psychology, motivation did occupy such a position, but it no longer does. Other constructs, especially cognition, have become far more accepted in explaining behavior. Theoretical development on the subject of motivation has become fragmented and piecemeal, which no doubt contributes to its lack of influence. Some of the reasons for all of this can be traced to specific developments in psychology. By paying attention to these developments, we may be able get some idea of not only how motivational theory fell into disuse but also how it can be brought back into the mainstream of modern psychology. A few observations on the historical background of the construct of motivation are therefore in order.

## Classical Conceptions of Motivation

Depending on how broadly one defines the term, motivation is either one of the oldest or one of the newest constructs in psychology. As a formal construct within the theory of behavior, it is a product of the 20th century (Cofer, 1980). In a more general sense, however, the idea of motivation as most people understand it—as a word describing the initiation of action, the choice of goals for behavior, and the expenditure of effort—is very old. It is reflected, for example, in the viewpoints on the basis of human conduct held during classical antiquity. One such viewpoint was *hedonism*, the doctrine that human behavior is animated by the search for pleasure. A major hedonic doctrine was *Epicureanism*, which taught the importance of pleasure but also held that an important cause of activity is the avoidance of pain. Still another was *Stoicism*, which taught the virtue of voluntarily bringing one's life into conformity with the laws of nature. The idea of *self-actualization* and the fulfilling of one's potential, a concept that appears to be quite modern, can be found in the writings of Aristotle (Waterman, 1984). Other classical philosophers taught the importance of civic virtue and the obligation of citizens to discharge certain responsibilities to the community. In these various classic ideas we can discern the outlines of certain modern themes that underlie our contemporary approaches to motivation: pleasure seeking, will, commitment to goals, and social responsibility. In the sense that ideas such as these have been with us since the dawn of Western civilization, we may say that motivation has always been recognized as a variable in human behavior.

The decline of classical antiquity, which began during the third century A.D., had important implications for theories of human motivation. Gradually, the philosophical academies and the religions of the ancient world were replaced in the West by a single source of moral authority: the Christian church. The early Christian fathers taught that the human being is a sinful creature in need of divine redemption and that the pleasures of the body—those pleasures so central to a hedonic theory of motivation—are innately evil. Thus, the tradition of Epicureanism, which had been a major viewpoint on human motivation, became an untenable position for anyone who wished to remain in the good graces of the church.

## Voluntarism

The official Christian dogma on motivation was a blending of the teachings of Judaism with a Roman philosophy called Neoplatonism. The latter, an extension of the classical tradition of Plato, held that the physical world is corrupt and degenerate and that we should rise above it to seek fulfillment on a higher, more ideal level. Rejection of the world meant, of course, rejection of bodily pleasures. This doctrine, which undoubtedly appealed to early Christian moralists, ultimately became fused to Christian theology in the fifth century by St. Augustine, a converted Neoplatonist and the church's first great philosopher. Augustine, in proclaiming the evils of sensual pleasure, made the will central to all human behavior. A fundamental teaching of his great book, *The City of God,* is that the soul is eternal, and that to save the soul one must transcend the demands and wishes of the body in which the soul is, during one's life on earth, briefly housed. We have free will to make our own choice: whether to subordinate the body to the soul and choose the way to salvation offered by the church, or to give in to the lusts of the flesh and thereby choose the road to everlasting damnation. This doctrine became the prevailing one on human motivation throughout the Middle Ages.

The medieval view of the human being was characterized by two assumptions. The first was that human beings are conscious and aware of what they are doing. The second was that the natural processes of the consciously aware person, processes to which we today would give such labels as cognition, affect, and emotion, are under the control of the will. Such was the legacy of Augustine. A person was required not only to behave in accordance with the doctrines of the church but also to think orthodox thoughts. To do otherwise was to invite condemnation as a heretic. Even emotional states were considered to be under conscious control. What we today call depression, for example, was regarded as a sin by the medieval church on the grounds that Christians should be happy and rejoice in their redemption (Jackson, 1986). One might say, therefore, that the concept of motivation, defined as simple volition, was the cornerstone of the medieval approach to behavior. Moreover, even though the Renaissance and the Protestant Reformation of the 16th century brought many changes to Christian doctrine and practice, the central role of volition continued to be accepted by Protestants and Catholics alike.

The hedonic approach to motivation did not return as a major alternative to voluntarism until the 17th century, and when it returned it had acquired a new conceptual language: the language of science, natural law, and empiricism. We are all more or less familiar with the scientific revolution that took place in the 17th and 18th centuries. During this time, great scientists like Copernicus, Galileo, and Newton made the discoveries that led to our understanding of the universe and formulated physical laws to explain its functioning. In such an atmosphere it was inevitable that somebody would attempt to explain the behavior of living organisms in terms of natural law. The attempt began in France in the 17th century. The French philosopher Rene Descartes proposed that animate motion is ultimately founded on the *reflex,* a natural and innate reaction to external stimulation that requires no conscious mediation or will. In fact, Descartes taught that in all animals below human beings, behavior consists of nothing but such reflexive motor patterns. He was not prepared to explain all human behavior in the same way, however, and he therefore retained a belief in the human soul and the conscious will.

## Materialism

Whereas Descartes was unwilling to reduce human behavior to reflexology, others who came after him in his native country were less constrained. One was Pierre Gassendi, who advocated the position, quite radical at the time, that consciousness plays no role in evoking or guiding human behavior but is merely an incidental by-product, or epiphenomenon, of physical and material processes. And what are these processes? Quite simply, they are the reflexes that Descartes had described. All human behavior consists of only blind and unconscious reactions to stimuli from the environment. These reactions are physical and chemical; they obey the laws of nature in the same way as do plants, the weather, and the stars. Everything that happens is a result of matter in motion, and there is no such thing as a conscious will causing anything.

Another important figure of this period of French thought was Julian Offray de la Mettrie, whose viewpoint can be readily understood from the title of his major book: *Man the Machine.* In likening the human being to a machine, la Mettrie was using what is called a *metaphor:* a device by which something that is relatively unknown is described in reference to something that is known. At about this time, Europeans were becoming familiar with mechanical gadgets like clocks and music boxes, so the mechanical metaphor was readily at hand. The point of the metaphor was obvious: human beings can initiate nothing on their own, just as a machine cannot go into motion until it is activated by some outside force. This doctrine, which became known as *mechanistic materialism,* would exert a powerful influence on psychology in the 19th century. It is today the ultimate basis for the field of physiological psychology.

## British Empiricism and Kant

The French thinkers who rejected the philosophy of Descartes all believed, as did the great scientists of the age, that the only way human beings can obtain knowledge is through experience. Galileo, for example, knew that the moons of Jupiter existed because he had seen them through his telescope. He did not have to take them on faith, nor did he have to figure out their existence through logical reasoning. This belief that experience is the basis of knowledge is called *empiricism*. It was a viewpoint that flourished during the 17th and 18th centuries not only in France but also in Great Britain. The movement called British empiricism, though rejecting some of the more radically materialistic conclusions of its French counterpart, nevertheless placed a premium on experience. The first of the great figures in this school, John Locke, advanced the metaphor of the *tabula rasa,* the idea that each of us is born like a blank sheet of paper and that whatever we are is a result of what experience, gained though our interactions with the environment, inscribes upon us. An even more radical form of empiricism was that of David Hume, who dismissed the concept of a soul entirely, arguing that what we call the soul (and would today characterize as the self) is only a fleeting and ever-changing array of sense impressions and simple ideas.

Given this empiricist view of human functioning and this dismissal of the soul, how did the empiricists account for the motivation of action? They did it by anchoring motivation, as they had anchored knowledge, in experience. The ultimate basis for why we do some things and avoid doing others, they reasoned, must lie in our experience of the consequences of our behavior. Quite simply, we do certain things because they bring us pleasure, and we avoid doing other things because they bring us pain. Only by first doing something can we ascertain whether it is a "good" act or a "bad" one, and we make this determination on the basis of how the action affects us. In this way, the hedonic approach to human motivation came back into the mainstream after its long exile. Once returned, it exerted a strong influence on the development of psychology, finding its modern expression in Thorndike's Law of Effect (the principle that pleasurable outcomes strengthen behavior whereas painful ones stamp it out). The hedonic principle is therefore the basis for those modern behavioral theories that explain behavior in terms of reward and punishment contingencies.

The coming of materialism and hedonism did not signify the demise of the traditional voluntarist approach to motivation. The radical empiricism of Hume, and the assumptions about the soul that characterized it, were the principal targets of the German philosopher Immanuel Kant. In his argument that the soul is nothing more than a name we give to fleeting and imperманent sensations, Hume denied the existence of any central consciousness— that is, a mind—that transcends immediate experience. For reasons that need not detain us here, Kant rejected this notion and proposed instead that each person possesses a transcendent and central self that is capable of understanding and acting upon moral imperatives—that is, voluntarily making behavioral choices. Thus, whereas the British empiricists had moved the causes of human behavior from inside the person to the external environment, Kant moved them back inside the person by linking them to the person's rational understanding and the actions of the will. We will return to the concept of the will in Chapter 3, where we will observe its application to a modern theory of human motivation.

## The 19th Century

Although some scientists of the 19th century followed the materialistic approach to human behavior that had been advocated by the French mechanists (the British philosopher Herbert Spencer is an example), most people of that period continued to believe that behavior is largely under rational and conscious control. Two challenges to this popular belief arose in the last half of the century, however, and both had important effects on the psychology of motivation. One challenge came from the slowly developing concept of the *unconscious,* an idea with a long history that became especially salient with developments in the study and use of hypnosis by French physicians like Jean-Martin Charcot and Hippolyte Bernheim (Ellenberger, 1970). Interest in the unconscious culminated in the work of Sigmund Freud, whose theory of psychoanalysis introduced a new version of materialism. Freud assigned the motives for human behavior to deep and unconscious drives and needs. Like the radical empiricists of the 18th century, he conceded no role to the conscious mind, stating instead that the "reasons" we intuit for our actions are not reasons at all but merely after-the-fact rationalizations.

The other development that challenged 19th-century assumptions about motivation was Charles Darwin's theory of *evolution.* The basic idea of evolution—that living beings evolve from lower and simpler to higher and more complex forms—had existed since the days of the earliest Greek philosophers. Darwin's contribution to the concept was his explanation of evolution in terms that were entirely biological and purely in accord with natural law. In doing this, he ruled out any idea of purpose in evolution. Evolution is a competitive process. Species do not evolve according to some grand design, but because the stronger, more adaptable members of the species survive and reproduce, while the weaker members perish.

*Sigmund Freud's theory of psychoanalysis traced human motives to unconscious, instinctual forces.*

What both Freud and Darwin brought to the idea of human motivation was the concept of *instinct.* By obscuring the distinction between human beings and lower animals, Darwin (1859) opened the door to the study of instincts in humans. It had generally been assumed until then that instincts are restricted to subhuman animal forms. In an evolutionary system, however, it made little sense to imagine that the possession of instincts stopped with the great apes. Freud also built instinct into his theory as a natural consequence of his idea of unconscious drives (Freud, 1915, 1920). Early in the 20th century the idea of human instinct was widely accepted, and many psychologists drew up long lists of specific instinctual states. For example, William James (1890), whose list was shorter than most, included such instincts as pugnacity, sympathy, acquisitiveness, curiosity, modesty, and love. These terms were not used, as we use them today, merely to describe human behavior; they were invoked as the actual *causes* of behavior.

Instinct theories were of two general types. Some simply described organizations of behavior of varying complexity similar to reflexes. This is the sense in which most people would define instinct today. Under certain conditions, specific behaviors simply happen because they are "wired into" the person. These behaviors were considered to be invariant, much like the "fixed action patterns" described by ethologists today (e.g., Eibl-Eibesfeldt, 1970; Lorenz, 1966). Except that they were thought to arise spontaneously within the person, they bore all the characteristics of reflexes.

*Charles Darwin set forth a theory of evolution that opened the way to the study of human instincts.*

The other viewpoint on instinct was far different. Advocated mainly by the English psychologist William McDougall (1908), this theory defined instinct in terms of an innate set of emotions that is activated by a wide range of conditions in the environment. A central emotion, once activated, elicits certain internal cues that prompt a particular type of response. The specifics of that response may take a wide variety of forms. For example, McDougall would have argued that some conditions in our environments—the actual number and range depend largely on the person's previous experiences—elicit an emotional state of fear. This emotion, in turn, initiates internal cues, prompting a flight response that serves the *purpose* of getting the person to a safer place. Some of the actual movements made to effect this flight are innate, but others are learned by the person in the course of his or her life. The only element in the sequence that is not subject to modification through experience is the central emotion of fear itself. This is fixed and innate. McDougall's approach to instinct is motivational; the central emotion sets up what McDougall called a state of *striving* to reach some goal. In our example the goal was safety. Every emotion has as its end the attainment of some such goal. McDougall is often dismissed by modern psychologists as an outmoded instinct theorist. He was, in fact, primarily an advocate of the purposiveness of behavior and an early forerunner of contemporary goal theorists (see Chapter 2).

Instinct theory did not survive the rise of behavioral psychology. In the 1920s the behaviorists had little trouble terminating the psychology of human instincts. By doing so, they opened the door to the rise of a new concept: motivation. Before we move on to discuss that development, however, we must pause to consider a concept that arose in the preceding discussion at several points and that plays an important role in what will follow. This is the metaphor.

## METAPHORS OF MOTIVATION

Although the idea of the metaphor has been around for a long time (Aristotle, for instance, was familiar with it), its importance for psychology has only recently been recognized by historians of the field. A good definition of the term has been provided by one of those historians:

> *Metaphor consists in giving to one thing a name or description that belongs by convention to something else, on the grounds of some similarity between the two (Leary, 1990, p. 4).*

This assignment of a name from one thing to another is done for a purpose. One wishes to describe or explain something about which relatively little is understood by comparing it to something else about which relatively much is known. For example, suppose that one wished to tell another person that so-and-so is a sloppy and gross person in his eating habits. To do so one might say that "so-and-so is a pig," hoping to convey to the listener some sense of so-and-so's eating behavior by comparing it to that of an animal notorious for just such behavior. Note that the similarity between the person (called the *object* of the metaphor) and the pig (called the *source*) is assumed to be limited to certain features or characteristics of the two (in this case to the characteristic of eating). In calling the person a pig, it is understood that you do not mean that he has hooves and a snout. Metaphors are always used in such a limited way to explain certain specific characteristics of the object.

In current psychology the word *metaphor* is used in a generic sense to include such variations as analogies, similes, and models. In each case we use a device that involves a comparison in order to explain some unknown or poorly understood idea. The word *motivation* is itself based on a metaphor: the metaphor of motion. It is derived from the Latin *movere,* meaning "to move." The idea of motion has the connotation of the expenditure of effort and the conversion of potential energy to actual energy. It is this connotation that one wishes to convey by the words *motive* and *motivation*: a connotation of intensity, activation, and expenditure of force that results in either the initiation of behavior or the switch from one ongoing activity to another.

The history of the concept of motivation is a history of changing metaphors (McReynolds, 1990). Let us consider some developments in the history of American psychology in light of this idea. At one time, around the beginning of the 20th century, psychology addressed itself mainly to the structure and content of human experience, as revealed through the method of introspection. This approach, which incorporated such processes as memory, association, and consciousness, was the basis, in the United States, of the theoretical viewpoint called *structuralism*. This point of view had much in common with what we today think of as cognitive psychology (Bolles, 1972). The metaphor on which this approach was built was an architectural one: conscious experience was likened to a building in which simple elements were combined according to some plan to form a complex and multichambered edifice. This metaphor lives on today in theories of "cognitive structure" and conceptualizations of memory in terms of discrete compartments in which different memorial units are stored. During the earlier period of emphasis on structure, if the question ever arose of how behaviors originate and are sustained, it was commonly answered in terms of certain processes that arise spontaneously within the person. These innate processes that gave the "force" to behavior were usually attributed to instincts. As we noted earlier, the definition of instinct varied widely; the word was used to account for everything from innate motor patterns to complex sets of emotions. What the theories had in common was the assumption that behaviors could arise and be maintained endogenously—that is, from inside the person—and did not have to be elicited by external causes. This was, in effect, a general theory of motivation. It was common for psychologists in those earlier times to account for a considerable part of human action and experience in terms of the concepts of instinct and mental structure (e.g., James, 1890).

Both the structural metaphor and the concept of human instinct declined in influence during the second and third decades of the 20th century. The demise of each can be attributed to the same cause: the emergence of behaviorism. The behaviorists, at least in their early years, tended to simplify the subject matter of psychology by eliminating any variables that could not be directly observed or measured and by explaining action in terms of a simple functional unit: the observable association between a stimulus and a response. They were especially at pains to eliminate mentalism (hence, cognitive structure) in their explanations of behavior and to define all behavior as the result of conditioning and learning, thereby banishing instinct as a cause. Behaviorists also tended to reject the concept of purposiveness in behavior (Silver, 1985). The only intervening state in behavior was a hypothetical stimulus-response (S-R) bond, presumably established in the nervous system through associations between behaviors and the situations in which they occur. This concept, which had been formulated first by Thorndike (1898), became a central construct in behavioral psychology.

The S-R bond proved to be an unappetizing substitute for the older and more familiar variables, however, and psychologists soon began to look about for other constructs that could be plugged into the gap between the observed stimuli and responses. The first construct to emerge from this search was *drive,* which more or less took the place that had previously been occupied by instinct (Herrnstein, 1972). The term had been introduced by Woodworth (1918) to describe an energizing or activating force in the person that initiates and intensifies activity. Functionally, drive differed little from instinct. Unlike instinct, however, it was considered to be a reaction to external conditions and not an innate process.

The most elaborate and influential drive theory of motivation was that of Hull (1943). Because of the great influence that this theory once had, its main premises are worth noting. Drive is defined in Hull's theory as a direct response to either deprivation of some necessary commodity (such as food or water) or strong stimulation (such as a painful stimulus). Once aroused, drive influences the intensity of behavior, but not the direction, by "energizing" all behaviors in the given situation. Because some behaviors are more likely to occur than others as a result of having been more heavily reinforced in the past, these habitual, or dominant, responses are energized to a greater degree than are less dominant, or subordinate, ones. The actual relationship between drive and habit strength, or relative response dominance, is considered to be multiplicative. This means that as drive increases, dominant responses become more likely to occur and subordinate ones become relatively less likely. Whatever behavior is activated by increased drive, it persists until a response is made that reduces the level of the drive that motivated the behavior in the first place. For example, a hungry animal finds food or a frightened one finds a way out of a situation that elicits fear. Drive reduction reinforces the responses that preceded and led up to it, thereby increasing their habit strength on future occasions. In this way, Hull's theory became one of not just motivation but also instrumental learning.

More important than the details of drive theory is the underlying metaphor on which it is based. The whole theory is premised on the related assumptions that behavior is driven in a mechanistic way, with no intervening thought or volition guiding the action, and that reinforcement is also a mechanical strengthening of response tendencies. The metaphor is that of the *machine.* Just as a machine performs specific actions after being activated by some outside force (ultimately no machine turns itself on), so too does the living animal or person carry out specific habitual acts after the drive mechanism has been activated by external conditions.

During the 1950s drive theory began to lose its influence. It was replaced in part by another theory that stressed the dynamic or activational side of behavior: *arousal theory.* This approach is based on the assumption that behaviors can be ordered along a continuum of intensity, from sloth and lethargy at one end to frenzy on the other. Usually, but not always, theorists relate the arousal process to activity in the central and/or autonomic nervous system. From this arises the concept of general arousal, a loosely defined construct that implies that the several parts of the body innervated by the arousal process (e.g., the heart, the skeletal muscles, the viscera, the cerebral cortex) all respond to stimulation in roughly the same way: with increases proportional to the intensity of the stimulus.

It is assumed that people feel their best and perform most efficiently when their arousal levels are somewhere in the intermediate range of this continuum. This assumption is expressed in two basic premises of arousal theory. One is that behavior is motivated by a need to attain an optimal level of activation or arousal and that people will expend effort to reach such a level, whether they are too highly aroused or not aroused enough. The other premise is usually stated in the form of the Yerkes-Dodson Law, an empirical statement that performance on any task is better when the person is moderately aroused than when arousal is above or below this intermediate level. Both of these will be discussed more fully in Chapter 9.

## MOTIVATION AND COGNITION

Drive theory and arousal theory created some of the problems that have beset traditional approaches to motivation and that probably have contributed to the relative disuse into which the concept has fallen in recent years. One of these problems is the tendency to define motivation in terms of intensity of behavior independent of direction. This distinction may make some sense at a theoretical level, but in terms of explaining actual behavior it is difficult to comprehend. It is virtually impossible to imagine a real person "behaving intensely," for example, without also imagining *what* the person is doing with such vigor. Another problem is that the mechanistic drive and arousal theories of motivation have ruled out intention and will as important elements in motivation, emphasizing instead a mechanistic determinism that is inconsistent with the experiences of most people. Still another problem with the mechanistic theories is their tendency to split off motivation from other concepts, especially cognition, in describing what people actually do. Human behavior is complex, and in describing it psychologists invent and invoke many different explanatory terms. Actually, these terms really describe processes that work together. None alone can possibly describe the totality of human action in the best possible way. People think, they feel, they experience emotional ups and downs, they make judgments, they increase and decrease the amount of effort that they expend, they persist at some things and give up on others. No single concept of psychology can account for the richness of all this, but several constructs together, with each supplying a part of the picture, can.

Consider three constructs that have been considered basic by psychologists for hundreds of years, so basic in fact that they tend to be thought of as the subject matter of psychology. They are *cognition,* which involves thinking, judging, interpreting, and understanding; *affect,* which involves feeling; and *conation,* which involves willing, striving, and expending effort. This tripartite division of psychology has been generally accepted since the 17th century (Hilgard, 1980). Obviously, most if not all behavior can be subsumed in a general way by these three concepts. Unfortunately, however, we have tended to regard them as separate processes rather than mutually complementary ones and, sometimes, to treat them as alternative or even rival explanations of behavior. The "cognitive revolution" that has been going on for two decades, and still manifests exceptional vigor, provides a clear example of how one construct has come to the fore and virtually driven the others from the field.

Human behavior, however, especially behavior of any complexity, always involves many processes. To illustrate this, consider a typical experiment on vigilance in which a subject is instructed to spend a long period of time watching a screen on which various stimuli are presented in rapid order, and to report the occurrence of a particular stimulus whenever it occurs. The target stimulus occurs infrequently, and these occurrences are separated by long periods in which the subject must inhibit responding in order to avoid making a false report. The subject is further told that each time a correct detection is reported, a reward will be given, but that false reports will be punished. This procedure is usually used to study sustained *attention.* What is involved in this experiment? Is it cognition, affect, or conation? Obviously cognition is involved because the person holds a belief: "If I pay attention and do not act impulsively, I will have a good chance of winning something." The procedure also involves affect because it is boring and unpleasant; the subject will remain attentive only if he or she anticipates a pleasurable outcome to offset the unpleasantness. And, finally, conation is involved. The subject must exercise internal control and effort to stay attentive. Motivation, in the broad sense that we are conceptualizing it, includes elements of all three processes.

This brings us to the last of the great theories of motivation from the past: the incentive, or expectancy-value, theory of Tolman (1932). This theory describes the impetus toward a goal that is experienced by a person in a state of need. What is unique about this theory, relative to other motivational theories from the same historical period, is that it combines a cognitive element, the person's _expectancy_ of reaching a goal, with a motivational-affective element, the *value* of that goal for the person. Both of these elements are necessary if the person is to have motivation to strive for the goal.

Whereas drive theory can be thought of, to use still another metaphor, as a "push" theory of motivation, with drive supplying a "prod" that moves the individual to action, Tolman's was a "pull" theory, according to which behavior is drawn out of the person by attractive goals and incentives in the environment. The major variables of this theory still play a role in some of the modern incentive models of motivation, as will be shown in Chapter 2. The theory has been applied most often to behavior in choice situations, where a person has an array of possible goals from which to choose. Simply stated, the theory predicts that the person will choose the one that yields the highest payoff in terms of value and probability of attainment (e.g., Atkinson, 1974; Hamilton, 1974; Chapter 6). Attainment of a goal serves as reinforcement for the relevant behavior. Reinforcement, however, does not strengthen any responses, as claimed by the drive theorists. Instead, reinforcement increases the expectancy of future reinforcement for the same behaviors. For example, a child who is praised for cleaning his room does not acquire a stronger "room-cleaning" habit as a result of this social reinforcer; what he acquires is a stronger belief that keeping his room clean will bring additional praise.

This theory deals with deprivation and strong stimulation, not as causes of drive, but as antecedents of value. Tolman postulated certain "energizing conditions" that are similar in some ways to drive. These conditions are necessary preconditions to the formation of judgments of goal value: "only if animals are . . . energized (motivated) in some specific way, do goal stimuli . . . have possible positive or negative values and hence lead to expected valences and bring about actual performances" (Tolman, 1959, p. 130). This reflects a common human experience: food, for example, takes on greater and greater attractiveness the more hungry one gets. This process, presumably, requires no deep thinking. It just happens, automatically and mechanically.

The expectancy-value approach to motivation is, therefore, not an entirely mechanistic one. In fact, Tolman's theory, though having certain mechanistic features, fits another metaphor more closely than that of the machine. This metaphor is *homeostasis,* a term discussed at length by biologists such as Walter Cannon (1939). Homeostasis in biology is a reflex process by which the body adjusts to changing conditions with offsetting physiological changes. A common example is a person's perspiring when he or she is overheated; evaporation of sweat promotes cooling and a return to a more nearly normal temperature. Note that this concept involves an original state (normal body temperature) that is displaced by a higher temperature. The discrepancy between the normal state and the existing state initiates activity that reduces that discrepancy. The normal state is therefore the one that the body "desires" and "works for." In incentive theory, the human being who strives after goals resembles a biological system making adjustments to restore a previously existing situation. The goal is the desired state, and existing conditions are at some distance removed from the goal. Incentive motivation produces the activity by which this discrepancy is reduced and finally eliminated. Both homeostasis and incentive motivation are discrepancy-reducing and goal-seeking processes, hence the metaphoric comparison of the two. These ideas will be discussed at length in Chapter 3.

# NEW DIRECTIONS IN THE STUDY OF MOTIVATION

To repeat a statement made earlier in the chapter, the context within which human motivation is manifested in behavior is almost always social. The study of social motives and social motivation has, unfortunately, suffered the fate of the study of motivation in general. A leading authority on motivation, writing in 1980, observed that, at that time "the field of social motivation appears excessively fragmented, theoretically incoherent, and isolated from other specialties within psychology" (Brody, 1980, p. 165). Indeed, until very recently the prospects for a revived psychology of motivation, especially one with a social psychological emphasis, did not appear good.

During the 1980s, however, several developments caused a renewed interest in motivation, and many of these came about as a result of the efforts of social psychologists. The study of the motivating effects of causal attributions, which had been among the few programs within social psychology to keep the concepts of motivation alive during the 1970s, was expanded (Weiner, 1985) and made an integral part of a new model of goal-setting behavior (e.g., Klein, 1989). These developments will be described in Chapter 2. In addition, within both social and organizational psychology important investigations were made of the ways in which people set and pursue goals (e.g., Wright & Brehm, 1989; Locke, Shaw, Saari & Latham, 1981). These studies and the theories that they supported went beyond the early models of expectancy, value, and incentive by showing specific processes in goal-directed action (Hyland, 1988; Kuhl & Beckmann, 1985a). Finally, research in social cognition began to find growing evidence of the importance of the self concept. The self became described increasingly as a central element in experience, an entity that allows a person not only to understand his or her past behaviors but also to predict future actions (e.g., Markus, 1977). It also became apparent that self-esteem and self-validation are important affective outcomes for the person, and that these outcomes are sought-after goals.

These developments tended to break down the older conceptions of motivation that were rooted in mechanistic metaphors, which conceptualized motivation primarily in terms of arousal or the intensity of behavior, and which separated motivation from other processes in behavior. What has emerged from all this is a newer approach that places motivation within a larger framework, along with cognition, affect, and emotion, with these processes working jointly in voluntary, effortful, directed action. The chapters that follow will make this theme and the developments that underlie it more explicit.

# BRIEF OVERVIEW
# OF THE BOOK

This book is organized, roughly, in three sections. In the first (Chapters 2–6) a general theoretical model is described. This model is organized around the concepts of basic needs and situations that interact with those needs to generate incentives. Incentives, in turn, are the basis for the setting of goals for behavior. Several topics are covered in these five chapters, including variables that influence the setting of goals and the expenditure of effort in goal-striving, attributional processes that mediate goal-related behavior, the strategies that people follow in pursuing goals, and the role of the will in maintaining control over action. The importance of the self in controlling action and of perceptions of personal competence is also discussed. A chapter is devoted to a review of the development and operation of three well-known needs: achievement, affiliation, and power.

The second section (Chapters 7 and 8) covers two topics that are involved in the model discussed in the preceding chapters but are not central to it. These topics—arousal and emotion—have a long history in the psychology of motivation. Arousal theory addresses primarily questions about the intensity of behavior, whereas theories of emotion deal with the affective side. Given the integrative approach taken in this book, it is important that we know something about these processes. The final section of the book (Chapters 9–11) reviews three areas of research in which the social emphasis of the book is most clearly presented. Some of the premises of the model presented in the first part of the book are applied to the study of social motivation, including prosocial behavior, aggression, social anxiety, and stress. A final short chapter summarizes some of the major points of the book and presents some conclusions about human motivation.

# CHAPTER SUMMARY

**1.**  The construct of motivation refers to the initiation, intensity, and persistence of behavior; it addresses the question of why people do the things that they do. Motivation is embedded within a complex process that consists of choosing a goal, devising a strategy for reaching the goal, and carrying out the planned course of action. This process also involves the operation of cognitive and affective variables. Goals for action are chosen to the extent that they satisfy either personal needs or situational demands.

**2.**  Most human motivation takes place in social settings. Regardless of whether a person is actually in a group, working against a group, or isolated from a group, most human action and the motivation behind it are social in nature.

**3.** Broadly defined, the concept of motivation can be traced back to classical antiquity, where it was found in such doctrines as hedonism and Stoicism. Hedonism held that the purpose of action was the pursuit of pleasure and the avoidance of pain. With the passing of the classical era and the ascendancy of the Christian church, the orthodox theory of motivation became voluntarism. According to this viewpoint, which dominated thinking for more than a thousand years, all action was placed under the control of the will, the body was subordinated to the soul, and pleasure seeking was held to be sinful.

**4.** The classical hedonic approach to motivation reappeared at the beginning of the modern era in philosophy in the 17th century. Both the British empiricists and the post-Cartesian materialists in France held that human action was motivated by the search for pleasure. The German idealists, following Kant, maintained the voluntarist approach.

**5.** Toward the end of the 19th century the concept of unconscious motives arose out of both the evolutionary theory of Darwin and the psychoanalytic approach of Freud. Under the influence of these viewpoints, psychology adopted the concept of human instincts, which served the purpose of a theory of motivation for many years. Instinct theory was refuted by the behaviorists in the 1920s, but many of the functions of instincts reappeared in the newer concept of drive in the 1920s and 1930s.

**6.** Drive theory is based on a metaphor that likens human action to that of a machine activated by external influences. As such, it is one of a long list of metaphors that have been used to explain human consciousness and behavior since classical times. The history of the concept of motivation is a history of the metaphors that have been used to describe it.

**7.** The theory that explained motivation in terms of expectancy and value was related to another metaphor: biological homeostasis. This theory assumed that the setting of goals establishes incentives to action, a view that presupposes that the individual is motivated to reduce a discrepancy between his or her present state and the desired state represented by the goal. This model became a basis for more modern conceptualizations of motivation based on discrepancies between existing and idealized conditions, which form the basis for Chapters 2–4 of this book.

# GOALS IN MOTIVATION

The word *goal* is a common one in everyday speech, and most people have at least some idea of what it means. We may hear a young person say that his goal is to make several million dollars and retire, whereas another may reveal that her great goal in life is to become a surgeon. In general, what these people mean is that they have defined for themselves a desirable state that they hope someday to attain and for which they are willing to expend some effort. Although this definition of a goal lacks a few specifics that will be considered below, it is basically useful in approaching the subject.

How goals affect behavior is not, however, spelled out in the everyday use of the term. To understand the role played by goals in human life, we must construct some links between the goal that the person sets and the actual behavior invested in working for that goal. In this chapter we will investigate some variables involved in those links. We begin with the assumption that "goals are immediate regulators of human action" (Locke, Shaw, Saari & Latham, 1981). The important word here is *regulator*. It implies a *process,* or a number of processes, set in motion by the formation of a goal. A goal does *not* regulate behavior in some automatic or mechanical way, in the manner of an accelerator pedal on an automobile regulating the flow of gasoline to the engine. After a goal has been decided upon, certain processes are set in action, and these processes move the person along the path toward fulfillment of the goal.

A number of variables, many of which involve volition and self-control on the part of the person, are involved in these processes. Goal theory is addressed to a large extent to a description of the conditions that mediate the relationship between goals and performance. In the pursuit of such goals, people utilize their cognitive abilities, they respond to affective conditions, and they expend effort. These psychological processes act in concert to promote functional behavior that helps the person move toward the goal. How these processes actually produce goal-directed behavior will be explained in Chapter 3. For now, however, we must first define a goal and then explain how goals are related to some other important constructs of motivation, such as need and incentive.

## GOALS, NEEDS, AND REFERENCE PERSONS

The first point we must make is that goals have a certain element of wishfulness about them. But a goal is more than merely a wish; it is also an end state that is considered to be attainable given some level of ability and some expenditure of effort. A wish, by contrast, does not necessarily have this feature of attainability. An aspiring junior league baseball player, for example, may wish that he was the current right fielder of the Oakland Athletics, or a young and infertile couple may wish that they could become the biological parents of a child, but in neither case would the desired outcomes be called goals.

A goal, then, is a wished-for end that is considered to be attainable. We usually assume that attainment is contingent upon some expenditure of effort. Some degree of difficulty must be overcome in reaching the goal. One way in which we infer a person's level of motivation is to erect obstacles for the person to overcome and observe how much effort the person is willing to expend. Initiation rituals are an example of this practice.

We should not confuse effort with awareness or consciousness of effort, however. People often seek and reach goals without being fully aware of what they are doing. A woman may, for example, leave her apartment in the morning, get into her car, drive through traffic to her parking garage, and walk to her office, all the while thinking mostly of a dinner party that she plans to give that evening. Her performance of the well-learned and often-rehearsed actions that get her to work is largely automatic and "mindless," yet we would still say that getting to work was her goal when she left home, and nobody would deny that she has put forth effort in doing so.

Another point that must be made is that any person's goals form a *hierarchy* that extends from simple discrete acts at the bottom to large, complex, and global aims at the top. This brings us to a matter that will require clarification as we go along. Strictly speaking, the word *goal* can refer to any end state that the person has in mind while putting out effort to reach that state. A goal can be identified in any discrete act, like changing a tire, buying a ticket to a movie, or ordering a hamburger at a fast-food restaurant. We can

*Success in business requires the formulation of clear goals and the expenditure of effort to attain them.*

say, for example, that while the person is in the process of changing the tire, his immediate goal is to get the new tire put on the car.

The word loses much of its meaning when we do this, however, because it becomes virtually synonymous with behavior. Ordinarily, we reserve the word *goal* to apply to larger processes than simple functional acts. We apply it to events higher in the hierarchy of purposeful actions. To go back to the man changing a tire, we might learn that his goal in doing this is to get back on the highway so that he may drive to the nearby town where he intends to attend a piano recital. Driving to town and hearing a recital are therefore goals that rank just above changing a tire in the man's hierarchy.

This brings us to still another question: What is at the top of the hierarchy? To answer this, we must try to find a still higher goal that is served by attainment of the lower ones, and we must do this at each successive level. To return again to the man changing a tire, we must ask: Why does he want to attend the concert? The answer might be that he wishes to be a cultivated and artistic person. Again we must ask why. Possibly because he wishes to impress a certain young woman, a wish that could lead us still further to some basic "goals" like a need to be intimate with others. In doing this, we may notice that we have stepped across another borderline and are now dealing not with goals, as we usually define the word, but with what we commonly call "needs."

The point of this discussion is that the words we use in motivational analysis do not usually have clear and obvious referents and are often used more or less interchangeably. At what point does an act or set of acts become a goal? At what point in the hierarchy does a goal become a need? Most systems of classifying and analyzing motivation use their own schemes of classification for answering these questions. In this spirit, one such scheme will be outlined below.

The last point to be made about goals before we turn to our definitional classification is that the setting of any goal always rests upon two antecedent conditions. One is a condition of need in the person; the other is a condition that arises in the environment. These conditions work together to activate goal setting. Consider the simple example of a person who has not eaten for several hours and who passes a hamburger restaurant from which the aroma of food is coming. The combination of a need (hunger) and an environmental condition (the presence of food, along with salient food-related cues) produces a potential goal in the mind of the person: to enter the restaurant and to order and eat a hamburger. If the person is not currently entertaining any stronger and more compelling goals (like rushing to make an appointment or skipping lunch as part of a diet), the potential goal may become a real one. A word that is often used to describe the joint operation of a need and a situational condition is *incentive,* and we will use that term to describe goals that arise from this joint operation.

In social motivation, the situational condition that contributes to this process involves certain expectations and demands made upon the individual by other people. Socially mediated incentives, therefore, are the product of some socially relevant need and some socially conditioned demand. Such demands take their character from the particular person or persons to whom the individual refers in such settings. A crying infant, for example, makes demands on the person different from those made by an employer. One's Saturday night drinking partners make demands different from those made by one's in-laws (in most cases, at least). Thus, when we spell out the nature of the demands made by the social situation, we must bear in mind the salient *reference person or persons* within that environment.

As noted above, the immediate outcome of the interaction of need with situational demand is the creation of an incentive, which is actually a higher-order goal. This, in turn, subsumes some lower-order goals that extend downward until we reach specific actions that, for reasons of convenience, we do not usually refer to as goals. This scheme is illustrated in Table 2-1, which lists the various goal options open to a fictitious college student who has a strong need to seek the approval of others and who must choose how to spend a weekend. In making her decision, she must appraise her available options. Four of these options are listed for the four reference persons or sets of persons she is most interested in pleasing. Her parents expect her to get the highest grades possible in her courses. Her employer in her part-time job expects her to complete an assignment that he has given her. The professor for whom she is doing a research project is waiting for a paper that reports her findings. Her friends hope that she will go to a party with them. The combination of a need for approval and each of the reference persons creates four alternative incentives. Each incentive may, in turn, give rise to several lower-order goals; only one is given for each incentive in the example. We could have generated other levels of goals below these. In addition, the student may

**TABLE 2-1**

***Example of Relationships among Needs, Reference Persons, Incentives, Goals, and Actions***

| | Need for Approval | | | |
|---|---|---|---|---|
| Reference | Parents | Employer | Professor | Peers |
| Incentive | High grades | Productivity | Scientific achievement | Popularity |
| Goal | Get "A" on next test | Finish job | Write paper | Socialize |
| Action | Study on weekend | Work on weekend | Organize paper on weekend | Attend party on weekend |

carry out lower-level actions that are subsumed by the general "actions" listed in the table. "Study on weekend," for example, may involve such components as finding a quiet place in which to study, reading some assigned chapters in the textbook, and borrowing some missing lecture notes from a friend.

# INCENTIVE AND MOTIVATIONAL STRIVING

The word *incentive* is used here to denote a *broadly defined desired outcome that subsumes several classes of lower-order goals*. In the example given in Table 2-1, getting an "A" on one test in one course contributes to the incentive of "high grades" but does not define it; many more "A"s must be obtained on many more tests before the incentive is attained. The word *incentive,* used in this way, is fairly commonplace in everyday speech. Most people would, for example, probably agree with the following statements:

> The prospects of future profits give businesspersons an *incentive* to invest more capital.

> The hope of obtaining academic honors is an *incentive* for serious students.

> Paying a worker for the number of pieces produced creates an *incentive* for a high level of production.

> In many Third World countries, the fear of poverty is an *incentive* to have large families.

In each of these statements, the "incentive" is not some specific goal but a complex goal state that can be realized by attaining a number of smaller goals. The underlying meaning of each of these statements involves some commonly held suppositions: the people involved are aware of some goal, they think that the goal is reachable with some effort, and the goal is worth the effort expended. Incentives thus lead to *striving* that involves movement toward goals at every level (see Emmons, 1986).

The strength of motivational striving depends on a number of variables associated with goals (e.g., Little, 1983; Wadsworth & Ford, 1983). When people are faced with a decision about whether to choose and work for a goal, they ask several questions that reveal these variables: Is the goal worth the effort? How well have I done in trying for this or similar goals in the past? Do I have the necessary abilities to undertake a serious effort to reach the goal? If I make a serious effort, is the environment such that I can expect to have a reasonable chance of reaching the goal, or will the environment contain obstacles that negate my efforts? The ways in which these questions have been answered make up most of the remainder of this chapter.

# EXPECTANCY AND VALUE

In Chapter 1 a brief mention was made of the expectancy-value theory of motivation advocated by Tolman and his associates in opposition to the dominant mechanistic drive theory of the time. Expectancy-value theory is a version of the utilitarian approach to behavior, which holds that human acts are rational and motivated by a desire to seek the greatest possible *utility*, which in turn is defined as the product of the expectancy of success and the value of the outcome. The meaning behind this multiplicative relationship (i.e., that utility equals expectancy times value) is that if either of the two variables has a strength of zero, then the behavior in question has zero utility and will not be carried out. To a student who lacks mathematical aptitude, for example, the value of a Ph. D. in nuclear physics may be great, but the student will still probably not choose physics as a major because actually getting the degree will appear to be impossible.

The expectancy-value approach formed the basis for a considerable amount of work on achievement motivation during the 1950s and 1960s (Atkinson, 1974). Some of this will be described in Chapter 6. The theory was also applied to work motivation, beginning with the ideas of Vroom (1964), who theorized that both performance in one's occupation and job satisfaction vary as a function of the expectancy of being rewarded for work done and the value of the rewards received. Subsequent extensions and refinements of Vroom's propositions were made by Porter and Lawler (1968).

In time, however, criticisms of this theoretical approach began to appear. It must be remembered that the utilitarian approach to behavior assumes a high level of rationality and facility for accurately processing information about expectancy and value. Stahl and Harrell (1981) and Zedeck (1977) have argued that whereas some people do process information about expectancy and the value of success in the way stated by the theory, others are less likely to do so. Some people find the rational expectancy-value approach to decision making to be difficult (Slovic, Fischoff & Lichtenstein, 1977) and prefer to use other means. The expectancy-value approach to motivation may therefore have some validity, but it is not a simple and sovereign theory.

# GOAL SETTING AND PERFORMANCE

After a goal has been set, several processes move the person toward the goal, and each of these processes involves the operation of several variables. Three of these processes that are especially important are (1) effort, which is affected by task difficulty and specificity, (2) strategy formation, which is influenced by goal complexity, and (3) commitment to the goal, which is influenced by several situational and personal variables.

## Goal Difficulty and Specificity

Research on goal setting and performance has shown in most cases that the adoption of difficult goals leads to better performance than the adoption of easier ones (Mento, Steel & Karren, 1987; Tubbs, 1986). Thus, for example, a realtor who sets a goal for herself of selling eight houses in a week will have greater success than she would have if she had set a goal of just four sales. Obviously, this effect has limits. The setting of unrealistically high goals (i.e., goals that outstrip a person's ability and/or exceed constraints imposed by the situation) will ordinarily not be followed by success. If eight sales per week are not consistent with the realtor's ability as a saleswoman or with the demand for houses in her area, she will not meet her high goal. When goals are in the range of attainability, however, difficult ones are generally more likely to lead to success than are easy ones.

The specificity of a goal denotes how clearly the goal is defined by the person or, in the case of an assigned goal, the supervisor. Studies on goal specificity usually involve three conditions: one in which the goal is clearly stated (e.g., "You should produce 30 units per hour"), one in which the goal is less clear (e.g., "Do your best on this task"), and one in which no goal is stated. Specificity as such has not been found to have much effect on task performance, but specificity in combination with difficulty plays an important role in how well people perform. A large number of studies have shown that performance is significantly superior when people are given difficult and specific goals than when they are given difficult goals with instructions to "do their best" or no goals at all (Mento et al., 1987). Superiority under these conditions is manifested in both higher quality and a greater quantity of output (Latham & Lee, 1986).

Why do these effects occur? At least four specific mechanisms are set in place once a goal has been set, and any or all of these may explain why difficult and specific goals are associated with maximum performance (Locke et al., 1981). These mechanisms are (1) effort expended in pursuit of the goal, (2) persistence, which is actually effort expended in a certain direction over time, (3) focusing of attention on the goal, and (4) adoption of strategies for striving. The mechanisms most likely to account for the effects of difficulty and specificity are the first two. When faced with a difficult, challenging, and clearly defined goal, a person elevates her or his level of effort and persistence. Increasing the amount of effort expended can also make a goal more attractive and valuable (e.g., Matsui, Okada & Mizuguchi, 1981; see also the next section of this chapter), thereby adding another reason for improved performance. Although attentional focusing and strategy formation are also important, it is more likely that they account for the effects of variables other than difficulty and specificity of goals. This will be discussed later.

Another important variable in determining performance of a goal-related task is the knowledge of results. After people have set goals for themselves, they check periodically to find out whether their behavior has enabled them to make progress toward the goal. The process whereby performance is evaluated following such feedback, a process critical to many approaches to motivation, will be described at length in Chapter 3. For now we need only note its importance in goal-related action. By itself, feedback of results has little effect on performance. If a person is engaged in some idle and unimportant activity, knowing the outcomes of his actions will not necessarily cause any appraisal or change. However, when feedback is given after action in pursuit of specific and difficult goals, it takes on considerable importance as a motivator and guide of future activity (Erez, 1977).

## Goal Attractiveness and Effort

In a major program of research, Brehm and his associates have suggested another link between goal difficulty and performance by showing that goal difficulty not only produces increased effort but also makes the goal more valuable to the person (Brehm & Self, 1989; Wright & Brehm, 1989). The theory that guides this research rests on three major premises:

1. The difficulty of a task determines the amount of motivational energy (i.e., effort) that must be mobilized for performance.
2. The attractiveness of success on a task is a direct function of the amount of energy mobilized. Thus, applying the relationship of task difficulty to mobilization of energy noted in premise 1, we find that task success is attractive to the degree that the task is difficult. In general, the more difficult the task, the greater is the attractiveness of doing well at it.
3. Two conditions limit the generality of the direct relationship between task difficulty and effort:
   a. When the *potential motivation* (defined below) for reaching a goal is low, relatively little effort is mobilized, even on a difficult task.
   b. When a task is so difficult that success is considered impossible regardless of effort, no effort is mobilized.

Potential motivation, referred to in premise 3a, is the highest level of motivation that a person can experience in a given situation. It is a function of what we have called expectancy and value, and it can vary independently of task difficulty. The more valuable an outcome and/or the greater the person's expectancy of attaining it, the higher the potential motivation for a task will be. A person with high potential motivation to carry out a task will mobilize more effort for the task than will a person with low potential motivation.

Before considering an example of this drawn from everyday life, let us consider premise 3b in greater detail. Task difficulty will engender effort only as long as the person considers the effort to be worthwhile—that is, likely to lead to realization of the goal. If the person thinks that a task is impossible to perform regardless of the effort expended, he or she will stop trying.

An example of these ideas is two students who are taking the same course in psychology, one a psychology major who plans to go on to graduate school and the other a student who is taking the course only because it fits into his schedule. Independent of how difficult the course may be to the two students, it is clear that the former has higher potential motivation, in terms of both the value of the course and the expectancy of success, than the latter. The case of the two students is shown graphically in Figure 2-1. These two figures spell out the implications of the theoretical premises given above.

Figure 2-1 shows that for student A (the psychology major), effort will increase in direct relationship to how difficult the student finds the course, up to the point at which, should this ever occur, the student considers the course to be impossible to pass. Only at that point will the student give up and stop trying. Student B, on the other hand, will work as hard as student A only if the course proves to be an easy one. This student's low level of potential motivation places a relatively low ceiling on the level of effort mobilized. Note that both students will give up trying beyond a certain level of task difficulty, but that the level of difficulty at which this occurs (high for student A and moderate for student B) depends on the individual student's potential motivation.

The theory of effort and goal attractiveness proposed by Brehm and his colleagues has stimulated a number of interesting experiments. In general, they support the predictions from the premises stated above. Some studies have tested the hypothesis that the mobilization of motivational energy varies directly with task difficulty up to the point at which the task is considered impossible. Mobilization of energy in these studies is defined as increased psychophysiological arousal. These studies have shown that systolic blood pressure, a commonly used indicator of arousal, is higher among subjects who

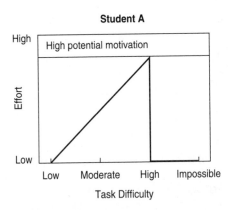
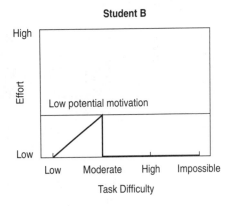

*Figure 2-1.* Example based on Brehm's theory.

are performing a difficult task than among subjects performing either an easier one or an impossible one (e.g., Wright, Contrada & Patane, 1986; Wright, Brehm & Bushman, 1989).

It has also been shown that when potential motivation is low, systolic blood pressure is no higher among subjects who are doing a hard task than among those performing an easier one (Wright & Gregorich, 1989). In this study subjects were told that successful task performance would earn them only an *opportunity* to win a prize and that the actual probability of winning, even after becoming eligible, was either high or low. Perceiving one's chances of winning to be low should make potential motivation likewise low, so in that condition task difficulty would be irrelevant to arousal levels. On the other hand, when potential motivation is high, Wright and Gregorich reasoned, there should be a direct relationship between task difficulty and effort mobilization. Thinking that one has a good chance of winning should elevate potential motivation and make task difficulty pertinent to arousal in the direction predicted by the theory: arousal (in this case blood pressure) would be higher when the task is moderately difficult than when it is easy. This is what Wright and Gregorich (1989) found (Figure 2-2).

Evidence supporting the prediction of a positive relationship between task difficulty and goal attractiveness has also been reported, with subjects given difficult tasks assigning higher ratings of attractiveness to the reward

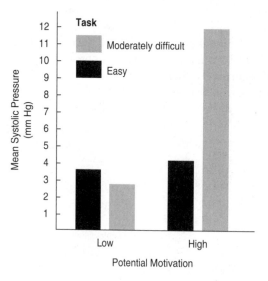

**Figure 2-2.** Mean increase in systolic blood pressure above baseline as a function of potential motivation and task difficulty. (Drawn from data reported in "Difficulty and Instrumentality of Imminent Behavior as Determinants of Cardiovascular Response and Self-Reported Energy" by R. A. Wright and S. Gregorich, *Psychophysiology,* 1989, *26,* 586–592.)

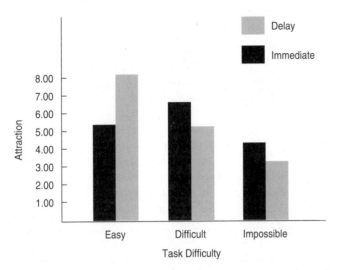

***Figure 2-3.*** Goal attractiveness as a function of task difficulty and length of delay between ratings and performance. (Adapted from "Effects of Task Difficulty and Interruption on Goal Valence" by P. M. Biner and S. Hammond, *Journal of Research in Personality,* 1988, *22,* 496–512.)

than those given easy or impossible tasks (Wright et al., 1986; Brehm, Wright, Solomon, Silka & Greenberg, 1983). When subjects are given a task to perform in order to avoid some aversive stimulus like loud noise, they rate the stimulus as worse (so that avoidance of it is better) when the necessary task is difficult than they do when it is easy (Biner, Hua, Kidd & Spencer, 1991).

It must be emphasized that the relationship between task difficulty and the attractiveness of the goal is mediated by a mobilization of energy for performance. Thus, the theory says that the predicted relationship between the two variables will be found only when energy is building—that is, *just before* the person begins working at the task. If ratings of goal attractiveness are made after the task has been completed, the relationship of attractiveness to difficulty is not found (Brehm et al., 1983). In addition, if a long delay is interposed between the rating of the goal and the beginning of task performance, the expected relationship between task difficulty and attractiveness is not found. Biner and Hammond (1988) carried out an experiment in which subjects had to rate the attractiveness of a $1.00 prize for doing either an easy, difficult, or impossible task. When ratings were made immediately before the task, the expected relationship was found (Figure 2-3). When a 20-minute delay was imposed, the attractiveness of the dollar fell off as the difficulty of the task increased. When the mobilization of energy is no longer a factor in goal attraction, the value of a fixed goal *declines* the harder one must work for it.

## Goal Complexity

Less is known about the effects of goal complexity on performance than is known about specificity and difficulty. There is some reason to believe that complexity may influence the type of mechanism that operates following the establishment of a goal: when goals lack complexity, the motivational effects of goal setting—effort and persistence—may be the most likely to affect action, whereas when goals are complex, the cognitive effects, especially the development of strategies, may predominate (Wood, Mento & Locke, 1987). Chesney and Locke (1991), in a test of this possibility, used a complex computer simulation of a business problem in which goals at two levels of difficulty were established, after which subjects reported using different types of strategy in attempting to reach the goal of selling the products manufactured by the business. The subjects' eventual performance was also measured. The results of the study were (1) that people with difficult goals used better strategies than those with easier goals, (2) that both goal difficulty and strategy were positively related to performance, and (3) that the effects of strategy on performance were stronger than those of goal difficulty. Because the task was a complex one, this study supports the hypothesis that goal complexity increases the importance of strategy development over more motivational processes as a mechanism by which goal difficulty is related to performance. Possibly, when goals are relatively low in complexity, they are most easily attained through increased effort or persistence because complex strategies are not needed. With increasing complexity, however, effort and persistence become less important than the devising of suitably complicated plans.

In daily life we encounter many situations in which successful performance requires the proper use of effective strategy more than simply the application of more effort. For example, football coaches often say after games in which their team lost that the defeat was due more to "poor execution" than to lack of a desire to win. Modern football is a complicated game that requires the orchestration of several different activities on each play, all of them guided by an overall strategy for either gaining points or preventing the other team from scoring. Without good strategies that are well executed, simply trying hard to win is often not enough.

## Commitment to Goals

A goal motivates a person to the extent that the person accepts and is committed to that goal. The importance of commitment in goal theory is indicated in the large amount of attention that researchers have devoted to studying it. Commitment is a highly important moderator of goal effects. As will be shown in Chapter 3, one of the critical questions of motivation theory is why people sometimes persist in pursuing a goal despite great difficulty and even failure, whereas at other times they cease their efforts and abandon a goal. In the context of the current discussion, we could say that when a person is highly

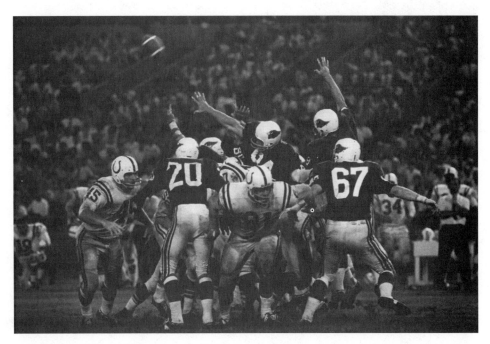

*Modern football provides an example of how striving to reach a goal involves the use of strategies.*

committed to a goal, he or she will persist in expending effort to pursue it despite difficulties, whereas when commitment is weak, no such effort will be mobilized. The reader will recall that a similar point was made by Brehm and his associates in discussing their concept of potential motivation.

If commitment is directly linked to effort and persistence, it should moderate the relationship between goal difficulty and performance. This moderating effect has been shown in an experiment by Erez and Zidon (1984). Subjects worked at a series of seven tasks that represented an ascending order of difficulty. The subjects expressed the extent to which they accepted each of the tasks before proceeding to work at it. The subjects were also instructed to perform the tasks as well as they could. The results of the study, which are shown in Figure 2-4, clearly indicate that over the range of tasks that were judged acceptable by the subjects, performance improved as task difficulty increased. When subjects stopped accepting the task, however, starting on task 4, increasing task difficulty was matched by a steady decrease in performance.

Several variables contribute to commitment to goals (Hollenbeck & Klein, 1987; Locke, Latham & Erez, 1988). One condition under which people become committed to goals is when the person's goal choice is known to others. Making a public announcement of one's intent places some pressure on

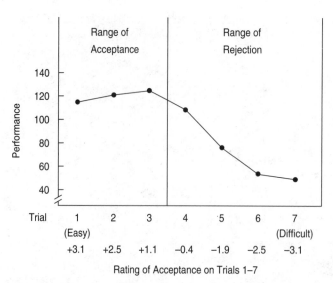

**Figure 2-4.** Performance as a function of acceptance or rejection of easy and difficult tasks. (Adapted from "Effect of Goal Acceptance on the Relationship of Goal Difficulty to Performance" by M. Erez and I. Zidon, *Journal of Applied Psychology*, 1984, *69*, 69–78.)

the person to produce results consistent with that intent or otherwise risk embarrassment. Hollenbeck, Williams, and Klein (1989), for example, found that students were more committed to reaching their goals for grade point averages when those goals were revealed to other persons than when they remained known only to the students themselves. A public declaration of a goal probably influences commitment by making attainment of that goal relatively attractive in comparison to nonattainment, which, as we have noted, could be humiliating.

Rewards such as money or perquisites may have at least two effects on performance, according to Locke and others (e.g., Lee, Locke & Latham, 1989). One is the establishment of higher goals, which can maximize the amount of money or other rewards that are earned. The other is commitment. When a goal is made more attractive, the promise of reward can increase acceptance of, and commitment to, that goal.

The importance of participation in goal setting has been debated extensively. It is commonly assumed by laypersons, and by some psychologists as well, that people are more committed to goals that they set themselves, or have some part in setting, than to goals that are assigned by managers. Although this idea appears to make sense, there is relatively little support for it in controlled studies (e.g., Tubbs, 1986). Most of the time, people in such studies commit themselves to goals that are given to them and make these assigned goals their own personal ones (e.g., Wagner & Gooding, 1987).

One important factor in the acceptance of assigned goals is the amount of legitimacy that people perceive in the assignment. If the authority figure, such as a supervisor, is seen to be making a legitimate demand in setting the goal, people will usually accept it (Locke et al., 1988). Another important factor is the way in which the supervisor assigns the goal. If goals are laid down in a peremptory and demanding way, they are less likely to be accepted by others than if they are "sold" through persuasion and reason (Latham, Erez & Locke, 1988). In addition, having the support of one's supervisor in seeking to carry out goals may be more important than whether one sets the goals or is assigned them (Locke et al., 1981).

Finally, we should note that commitment to goals is affected in large part by judgments of personal ability. People often succeed or fail at tasks because they either do or do not believe that they have the ability to carry out the necessary behaviors. One may fully believe that a course of action leads to a valued goal, but unless one also believes in a personal ability to execute that course of action, it is unlikely that the action will follow. The sense of one's ability to attain a goal not only influences the choice of goals that one makes but also helps to determine the amount of effort that will be expended. It should be noted in this connection that studies carried out in actual work settings generally show that although expectancy and value of success are good predictors of job satisfaction, they are poor predictors of actual effort (Mitchell, 1974). One reason for this is that workers may recognize the incentive value of a goal yet feel that conditions beyond their control render them unable to perform the necessary activity. A sense of personal ability, therefore, is a vital element in motivation. In addition, the whole issue of perceived

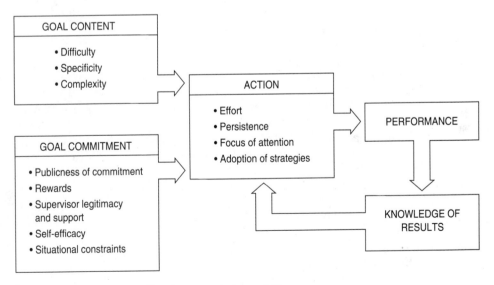

**Figure 2-5.** Summary of basic concepts in goal theory.

control over the environment and the role that it plays in motivation and performance requires extensive attention. This subject will be taken up in Chapter 5.

### Summary of Goal Setting

In this section we have observed a few of the processes involved in the setting of goals and striving for them. A simple schematization of these processes, all of which have been explained in the text, is given as a summary in Figure 2-5. This figure is a simplified version of a more complex process that will be detailed in the next chapter.

# GOAL CONFLICT
# AND AMBIVALENCE

In a simple, trouble-free life, a person's various goals would all be relatively isolated from one another and not likely to clash and conflict. In real life, of course, such is not the case. We all have many incentives and goals in our lives, and sometimes they do evoke motivational strivings that are mutually incompatible. An adolescent, for example, may place high value on being independent, yet may at the same time value the comfort and security that come from being protected and supported by his parents. Striving to reach incompatible goals leads to *goal conflict*. In turn, a state of conflict causes the person to be less than certain in his or her acceptance or rejection of any goal. The conflict experienced by the adolescent in our illustration may cause him to become less certain of the value of both independence and parental protection as he comes to see good and bad points in both. This feeling of simultaneous acceptance and rejection of a goal is *goal ambivalence*, and it is often a result of goal conflict.

Goal conflict and ambivalence are unpleasant conditions. Emmons and King (1988) have shown that these two states are associated with tendencies toward neuroticism, depression, negative affect, and psychosomatic problems. Subjects who experienced a high level of goal conflict also showed a greater incidence of physical illness over a one-year period following the initial study than did subjects who experienced less conflict. In addition, Emmons and King found that subjects who experienced high levels of goal conflict acted out fewer behaviors related to the conflicting goals but thought about those goals more than about goals over which no conflict existed. The overall picture that we get from this research is that goal conflict causes people to inhibit behavior related to the conflict and to ruminate over this state of affairs. These reactions in turn lead to emotional distress, negative affect, and eventual medical problems.

Goal conflict has taken on increased importance as a result of recent developments in research on women who must play multiple roles simultaneously. A role (e.g., mother, professional person, caregiver to elderly relatives) can be thought of as a loose collection of specific goals oriented toward a common incentive. Thus, a woman who must fill several such roles may experience some conflict among them. Although it has been shown that a woman can experience well-being even while occupying multiple roles provided she derives satisfaction from each (Barnett & Baruch, 1985), problems may arise when the demands created by goals conflict and lead to role overload. The result may be strain, depression, and even stress-related physical illness (McBride, 1990). There is no reason, of course, to suppose that role overload and the same consequent problems do not occur among men.

## ATTRIBUTIONS AND GOALS

As we have noted, one of the major contributors to the expectancies that people have of reaching their goals is past experience. In general, being successful in attaining a goal on one occasion increases one's expectation of future success in reaching the same goal. The process is not a simple or automatic one, however. Between the past experience and the future expectation comes the person's interpretation of the reason for the previous outcome. Understanding consists of attributing causes to events. People engage in processes of cognitive attribution in order to understand why things happen.

Why do we do this? In a major theory of cognitive attributions, Weiner (1986) has proposed that two reasons are common to human experience. By understanding why things happen we acquire some degree of control and mastery over our surroundings, a generally desired state of affairs (White, 1959). In addition, knowing the reason for events is functional. By having some theory of why events came about in the past, we can better predict what will happen in the future. This not only reduces uncertainty, but also gives us information that can guide future choices and plans of action. In the context of motivation and the pursuit of goals, attributions mediate and connect feedback from our successful and unsuccessful actions with subsequent goal-directed behavior. They do this in two ways. One is by influencing the formation of expectancies of future performance. The other is by eliciting an affective response that, in combination with the expectancy, activates and guides action. To understand this, we must first understand the structure and organization of attributional processes.

The attributions of cause that we make can be organized along certain relatively independent dimensions. In the simplest possible case, Weiner (1985, 1986) describes three such dimensions: *locus*, *stability*, and *controllability* of cause. The first refers to whether the cause is something that the person has done or whether it is attributable to persons or events external to the person. The second refers to whether the cause is something that happens with regularity or sporadically. The third describes whether the cause is under the control of the person or other persons or whether it is due to

*The effects of success or failure on a test depend to a large degree on the causes to which we attribute these outcomes.*

uncontrollable forces. To state briefly what will be shown below: attributions of stability influence the formation of expectancies of future outcomes, whereas attributions of locus and controllability influence the development of affective responses. These ideas may be best explained by means of an illustration.

Consider a college senior who has taken the Graduate Record Examination as part of the process of applying for graduate work in psychology. He has just learned that his scores are too low for admission to any of the universities that he wishes to attend. He must now decide whether to take the examination again the next time it is given. He must decide, in other words, whether to set for himself a goal of performing better in another attempt. His decision will depend in part on the causes to which he attributes his poor performance. Among the many attributions that are possible, let us consider just four for purposes of our illustration.

**1.** He failed because he lacks the aptitude necessary to get a higher score. The cause of his failure is therefore internal because it represents a defect in the student himself. It is uncontrollable because there is really little that the student can do about his lack of aptitude. It is stable because aptitude does not change much, if at all.

**2.** His failure was caused by <u>overconfidence</u> and insufficient effort. This cause is also internal because it follows from his own lack of initiative, but it is controllable because he could have tried harder if he had wanted to. Furthermore, it is unstable because the student can presumably increase his level of effort quickly if he so desires.

**3.** He failed because he had an <u>attack of test anxiety</u> as soon as he saw the questions, and by the time he had calmed down he had insufficient time to complete many items. This cause is obviously internal. It is also largely uncontrollable once it starts, and unstable because it does not always happen on tests.

**4.** He failed because he was <u>distracted</u> by the agitated behavior of the student sitting next to him. This person's muttering, nervous coughing, and constant movement were an annoyance that prevented the student from concentrating on the test. This cause is clearly external, uncontrollable, and unstable.

In the first scenario, the student will probably feel embarrassed and inadequate. This is the most likely *affective* response to failure, and it has internal and uncontrollable causes. In addition to this, the stability of the cause will lead the student to conclude that his chances of passing on a second try are realistically no better than they were on the first; that is, his *expectancy* of future success will be low. His most likely decision, therefore, will be to give up and not try again.

In the second scenario, the affective response should be guilt because this is the most common reaction to failing when the failure is one's own fault (internal) and could have been avoided (controllable). Because the cause is also unstable, the student has no reason to think that it will necessarily occur again. (He can, if he wishes, try harder.) Motivated by this desire to overcome his guilt, and thinking that he still has a chance to succeed, the student will probably decide to try again.

In scenario 3, the student will probably feel embarrassed (as he would have if the failure had been due to lack of aptitude). However, because an occasional anxiety attack on a test is a less stable occurrence than lack of aptitude, the student will not have a low expectancy of future success. In this case, he will probably choose to take the test again, hoping not to have another attack and maintaining some optimism about his chances.

In the last scenario, because the cause of the student's failure is external and uncontrollable, the student should not experience much negative emotion over the incident. Because the cause was also unstable, the expectancy of doing well on another try should not be adversely affected by the failure. All things considered, the student will be motivated to try again.

This simple example outlines just a few of the attributions that people may make after failing at a task, but it illustrates how the facets of attributions—locus, stability, and control—combine in complex ways to generate both affective states and expectancies of future outcomes. It would be possible to outline other possible dimensions of causality. It would also be possible to generate a parallel set of successful outcomes, showing how the student might behave after having scored well on the test. The same rules would apply: locus and control define the affective component of the motivated behavior, and stability contributes the expectancy component.

# OTHER EFFECTS OF GOAL SETTING AND COMMITMENT

## Goals and Cognitive Activity

Once a goal has been set and the person makes a commitment to it, the goal influences many aspects of the person's life. This is especially true of the person's cognitive system. We tend to think about our goals, to remember them and to attend to them, to feel badly when we contemplate not reaching them. Commitment to goals sets up a state inside the person that has several effects on cognitive activity. This hypothetical state of the person has been called by many names. One of the most familiar comes from Kurt Lewin (1935), who named it a *tension system*. Lewin described a set of psychic "forces" created by goal commitment that motivate goal-directed behavior and that have the same compelling influence on people as basic needs such as hunger and thirst. These forces were accordingly called "quasi-needs," and Lewin believed that they affect not only behavior, but also such processes as thinking and remembering (see Klinger, Barta & Maxeiner, 1980). Lewin's theory is remembered today primarily because of the well-known "Zeigarnik effect": the common finding that memory for tasks that have not yet been completed is better than memory for finished tasks. The reason for this is that after the task has been completed, the tension that it generated simply dissipates. More recently, Klinger (1977) has given the name *current concern* to what Lewin called the tension system. This is a good descriptive name because it emphasizes the fact that goals have a pervasive effect on a person only when the person is concerned about outcomes. The presence of concern, in turn, implies that the person is highly committed to the goal. A current concern is a state that is produced by commitment to a goal and that remains active until the goal is either reached or abandoned.

Klinger (1977) has reported a series of experiments showing that a person's current concerns make the person sensitive to stimuli in the environment that pertain to those concerns and, as a result, more likely to attend to those stimuli. For example, in one study subjects listened to a presentation of two simultaneous narratives, with one delivered to each ear. One narrative gave material relevant to the subject's current concerns, and the other presented irrelevant material. Subjects not only attended to concern-related passages more than to irrelevant ones, but afterward also recalled more of the former than of the latter. Other studies have suggested that material relevant to current concerns may be attended to more than other material because it is more affectively arousing (Bock & Klinger, 1986). This idea is corroborated by evidence from a study by Nikula, Klinger, and Larson-Gutman (1993) in which subjects listened to recordings of words that had been chosen so as to be closely associated with the subjects' current concerns or not so related. Words associated with current concerns elicited significantly greater increases in skin conductance than did the unrelated words.

## Goal-Directed Activity and Social Perception

Goals and motives influence not only the thoughts that people have but also the ways in which they perceive the world around them, especially the social world. In the late 1940s a number of psychologists proposed that there was a close link between motivation and perception. The main emphasis in this approach was on the role of motivational factors in the defensive repression of potentially threatening material. This research led to a movement known at the time as the "new look" viewpoint. Eventually this approach was criticized for a number of shortcomings, although later it was reformulated along somewhat different theoretical lines (Erdelyi, 1974).

More recently the motivational approach to perception has been cast in terms of situational *affordances* (McArthur & Baron, 1983), which are defined as opportunities for goal-directed action that are provided by events or situations. For example, to a person with intellectual aspirations, a club that meets to discuss great books may provide the affordance of meaningful intellectual activity and growth. To another person whose main interests lie outside intellectual activities, the same club would probably give no affordances at all. This raises the possibility that the ways in which the two people perceive the club may be a joint function of the characteristics of the club and those of the person. In other words, affordances, which are closely related to personal goals, may play a role in social perception.

This sort of interaction of the person with the situation, in a goal-directed context, is illustrated by an experiment reported by Assor, Aronoff, and Messé (1981). Subjects who had previously scored high or low on measures of need for dominance and need for dependency were shown a videotape of a person with whom they would later interact. The person on the tape was said to have either a high social status or a low status. When subjects were asked to evaluate the person prior to interacting with him or her, subjects who were high in need for dominance gave more favorable evaluations of low-status persons than of high-status ones, whereas subjects who were high in need for dependency gave the opposite evaluations. What did this mean? To a highly dominant person, the upcoming interaction afforded a better chance for goal-directed behavior (i.e., dominance of another person) if that person were of low status than if a high-status person were to be the interaction partner. In the same way, for a dependent subject the forthcoming interaction would afford a better opportunity for being dependent with a high-status person than with one of low status. The target people were therefore perceived by the subjects in ways that maximized the affordances of the anticipated situation. In a related experiment, Battistich and Aronoff (1985) showed that highly dominant subjects had a more pleasant interaction with another person if the interaction promised to be competitive than if it was expected to be cooperative. Highly dependent subjects foresaw greater pleasure in a cooperative interaction. In this study it was the perception of the situation itself that was influenced by the affordances it was expected to provide.

## Goals as Sources of Behavioral Cues

The state of the person who is committed to a goal, whatever we may call it, is the primary link between goals and actions. Lewin (1935) held that the state of tension in the individual remains unrelieved until either the original goal or some satisfactory substitute has been reached. The tension state may be thought of, therefore, as the source of certain specific cues for behavior that is relevant to the goal state. For example, when a person desires the company of other people, the person's goal is to find companionship. This goal then generates specific behaviors that bear a "natural" relationship to seeking and finding friends, such as going where other people congregate or using the telephone to contact acquaintances. As we have already observed in other contexts, some of these acts may be relatively effortless and hence involve only a low level of motivated activity. Should the person encounter difficulties, like receiving no answers to any phone calls, then a measure of her motivation would be how much persistence she shows in seeking companions through other means. Should all such attempts fail, the person may try to substitute an alternative goal, such as putting on a favorite videotaped movie.

Whenever internal cues to behavior do not lead to satisfactory goal-related action, the person experiences some discomfort, and this state increases as interference with the relevant action increases. In our example, the less able the woman is to find social companionship, the more unpleasant her situation will become. The same process will occur when a person is motivated to carry out some action but, for some reason, deliberately refrains from doing so. In recent years the effects of inhibiting one's responses to inner cues for behavior have been seen in a wide range of behaviors related to several types of goal. One example is the inhibition of emotional expression. Pennebaker (1985) has observed that such inhibition, whether deliberate and intentional or the result of personal inability to be expressive, is often associated with the symptoms of stress. Persons who manifest regular tendencies to inhibit emotion through a repressive style of coping with their problems show higher rates of cancer, hypertension, and various other psychosomatic problems. On the other hand, expressing and talking about the stresses of life lead to a relatively better state of health (Pennebaker & O'Heeron, 1984).

Another type of behavioral inhibition that is relatively common is found among people on diets. Among those who restrain their impulse to eat, distress is often a result. Chronic restraint of eating has been shown to produce emotionality and distractability and heightened sensitivity to provocation. The effects of inhibited eating may reach more extreme physiological levels as well, such as coronary problems, gall bladder disease, fatigue, and even death. Finally, chronic restrainers are likely to go on eating "binges" when they consume excess amounts, especially of highly fattening foods. This latter finding suggests that strong inner cues for eating, by being suppressed, may develop in strength until the point is reached at which they can no longer be held in check. An excellent and more thorough review of this whole subject has been made by Polivy (1990).

## CONCLUSION

This chapter has introduced the subject of goals as a central element in motivation. It has been proposed that the selection and setting of a goal are the first step in a complex behavioral process that includes motivation. The term *motivation* itself applies to the component of need that interacts with situations to produce incentives, and also to the expenditure of effort that is involved in striving for goals that serve those incentives. This effort is embedded in a complex of other processes that are related to the thoughts and feelings that go into purposeful and directed behavior.

We have come only part of the way, however. After a goal has been set and a commitment has been made (and, we might suppose, those "inner cues" discussed in the preceding section have come into play), the person must still do something. The goal will never be reached without action. It is to this that we must now turn our attention and, as we will see in the next chapter, the connection between commitment and action is not a simple one.

## CHAPTER SUMMARY

1. Goals are the immediate regulators of behavior. The setting of a goal initiates processes that direct and impel behavior along a path toward the goal. Goals are states that a person desires and considers attainable, and for which the person is willing to expend effort.

**2.**   Desired states are organized in hierarchies that range in complexity from specific acts to relatively broadly defined needs. Needs are activated by situations to create incentives for action, which, in turn, are expressed in the formation of specific goals. In interpersonal settings, the situation that activates a need usually includes one or more persons to whom the individual refers in setting his or her goals.

**3.**   The strength of striving for goals depends on the person's expectancy of reaching the goal and the goal's value. Expectancy and value combine multiplicatively to determine the subjective utility of a goal to the person. The multiplicative relationship indicates that if either expectancy or value equals zero, the goal will be of no utility and the person will not work for it. Although it has been criticized for not providing the total explanation for goal striving, expectancy-value theory has been applied successfully to the study of achievement and work motivation.

**4.**   Performance is generally better when people work for difficult and specific goals than when goals are either easy or ambiguous. Superiority of performance under conditions in which goals are difficult and specific is manifested in both a higher quality of performance and greater quantitative output. This superiority is due to any or all of four mechanisms set in motion by clear and difficult goals: (1) a high level of effort, (2) a high level of persistence, (3) focusing of attention on the goal, and (4) development of strategies for striving.

**5.**   Good performance in working for a goal is enhanced by knowledge of the results. When people can check their progress toward a goal periodically, especially if the goal is important, they perform more effectively than if they receive no feedback.

**6.**   The attractiveness of a goal varies directly with the amount of effort that must be expended in striving for it, which in turn is a direct function of the goal's difficulty. However, when potential motivation is low, the maximum effort expended will be less than when potential motivation is high, regardless of the task difficulty. In addition, effort will be spent on a task only as long as the person considers performance of the task to be possible. When the task is regarded as so difficult that it cannot be completed, no effort will be invested in it.

**7.**   When highly complex goals are set, the development and enactment of strategies for striving become important. Although both goal difficulty and strategy are positively related to performance, the effects of good strategy outweigh those of increased effort when tasks have a high level of complexity.

**8.**   Commitment to a goal is necessary before effort will be spent in striving. Several variables contribute to commitment to a goal; among them are (1) a public declaration of intent to work for the goal, and (2) rewards such as money or perquisites. Although participation in goal setting has sometimes been thought to be a condition for personal commitment, research evidence now indicates that this is probably not the case. A high level of commitment may be made even to an assigned goal if certain conditions are met, such as (1) the assignment is considered to be legitimate, (2) the assignment is made reasonably, and (3) the person believes that he or she has the support of the immediate supervisor.

9.   When a person strives for multiple goals that are not compatible with one another, goal conflict results. Goal conflict leads to ambivalence and uncertainty about one's goals. It can also cause people to inhibit behaviors that are involved in the conflict, to think excessively about the conflicting goals, and, possibly, to experience emotional distress.

10.   Causal attributions of previous successes and failures mediate both motivation and emotional responses to subsequently experienced task situations. The analysis of causal attributions allows us not only to interpret past events but also to predict, to some extent, future behavior in similar situations. Attributions vary along several dimensions, three of which are locus, stability, and controllability. Attributing a success or a failure to stable causes increases the expectancy that the same outcome will occur again under similar conditions. Attributing an outcome to internal and/or controllable causes elicits positive affect following success and negative affect following failure. Future behaviors can be predicted from the combination of expectancy and affect that follows any given attribution.

11.   After a person has made a commitment to a goal, the presence of the goal influences many aspects of the person's life. The goal becomes a current concern for the person and, as such, has a pervasive effect on cognitive processes. A person's current concerns make the person more sensitive to stimuli related to those concerns, more affectively aroused by those stimuli, and more likely to attend to such stimuli and to recall them later.

12.   Goals may also play a role in the ways in which individuals perceive and respond to each other. One person may react to another on the basis of not only the latter's personal characteristics, but also the way in which those characteristics interact with certain dominant motives in the perceiver.

13.   Commitment to a goal brings about a state of inner tension that provides specific cues for behavior related to the goal. When the behavior that is prompted by such inner cues is blocked or inhibited, the person experiences stress and discomfort. The eventual result of suppressing or inhibiting behaviors animated by inner cues can be an "explosion" or "binge" of such behaviors.

# ACTION CONTROL IN MOTIVATION

### CHAPTER OUTLINE

Being able to identify a person's goals can help us know what the person's behavior is most likely to be with respect to those goals. In the end, however, all that we get from such information is an understanding of the person's beliefs, feelings, and degree of commitment to the goal. To learn how the person actually goes beyond commitment and performs the behavior necessary to attain the goal requires an understanding of some other concepts and processes. In this chapter two such concepts will be introduced and incorporated into a general model of voluntary activity and effort. Our concern will be with the nature of the *action* that is generated by commitment to a goal.

The first of these concepts is a *discrepancy* between the state of things as they are and some desired state represented by a goal. This is an old concept that has spawned a number of specific theories. We may say that there is always a discrepancy when a person has some goal that has not yet been reached. The other concept that will be introduced is *will*, which describes a human capacity to engage in conscious and purposeful behavior, sometimes in the face of great difficulty. The two concepts merge in motivated action: commitment to a goal creates a discrepancy between the person's present and desired states, and this discrepancy is removed through purposeful and willful action.

## DISCREPANCY AND MOTIVATION

### Early History of the Concept

The idea that motivation arises from a discrepancy between a desired and an existing state is an old one. A reference to it from the late 19th century can be found in the writings of the American philosopher and psychologist John Dewey. In 1897 Dewey published an article entitled "The Psychology of Effort," in which he outlined the rudiments of a theory of motivation. This paper is worth considering in detail because it anticipated certain modern

*Philosopher John Dewey's theory of effort was an early attempt to explain human motivation.*

theories of action in several respects. The central motivational concept for Dewey was effort, which he defined as a conscious state produced by a "rivalry" between the sensations we have of sensorimotor adjustments and concomitant sensations arising from the idea of some desired end. In other words, when the feedback we receive from the environment does not conform to the idea that we have in mind of the goal state, we experience a conflict.

Like many psychologists of his day, Dewey placed great emphasis on the role of habits in behavior. These he tended to think of as "natural," and essentially effortless, responses that a person makes in pursuing a goal. Much of the time the habitual responses are sufficient to bring about attainment of the goal, but sometimes they are inadequate. The failure of habitual behavior to allow goal attainment is, Dewey believed, accompanied by a state of displeasure. The person reacts to this unpleasant state by mobilizing effort for subsequent behavioral adjustments. Thus Dewey concluded, "it is the rivalry, with the accompanying disagreeable tone due to failure of habit, that constitutes the sense of effort"; and "effort is nothing more, and also nothing less, than tension between means and ends in action" (Dewey, 1897, pp. 49, 51).

The basic conditions that Dewey described in his theory of effort are still the major elements in action theories of motivation. The person perceives a discrepancy beween a desired goal state and his or her present condition. Initial reactions to this discrepancy are most often responses that have been efficacious in reducing discrepancy in the past. These may be relatively effortless and possibly even not fully in awareness. Failure of these responses to bring the person to the goal creates negative affect. The person's reaction to this condition is to increase effort and to strive for the goal more vigorously.

## Homeostasis as a Discrepancy Model

In Chapter 1 we noted that the biological concept of homeostasis has served as a metaphor for human motivation in several theories. What all of these theories have in common is the idea of a discrepancy between some normal or "steady" state of the person and an existing state that is induced by some event or situation. People react to these discrepancies either by attempting to eliminate the cause of the existing state or by adapting to it and thereby creating a new steady state that is closer to the one elicited by conditions. For example, a person who has gone to a party may find aversive the noise level and the necessity of making small talk to people he hardly knows. He may respond to this by leaving the party or by making an adjustment, getting into the spirit of the occasion and chatting with others at a level of intensity that can be heard above the din. If he does the latter, he may in time reach a new steady state in which noisy parties are tolerated or even enjoyed.

Discrepancy theories can be classified into two groups. One proposes that the immediate consequence of a discrepancy between two states is the mobilization of energy or *arousal,* which powers the effort necessary to change the situation or to adapt. According to some versions of this model, discrepancy may also generate negative affect (e.g., Berlyne, 1967). The other type of theory is based on the concept of *feedback loops*. Discrepancies between existing states and steady states activate a feedback process to which the person automatically reacts with adaptation or problem-solving activity (e.g., Hyland, 1988). The end result is the same in both types of theory; the difference is that theories of the first type involve arousal, a biological concept, as a necessary mediating condition and those of the second type do not. In fact, theories of the second type are based on a different metaphor from those of the first. Whereas the metaphor for theories of affective mediation is biological adaptation, the metaphor for those of the other type is a modern and updated version of the machine. We will return to this.

## Discrepancy, Arousal, and Affect

Cannon's (1939) principle of homeostasis was entirely biological. It provided for the existence of automatic mechanisms in living beings that maintain certain physiological characteristics (such as body temperature and blood pressure) at constant levels. It is interesting to note that Cannon thought that the general principle behind homeostasis could be extended in a metaphoric sense to an inclusive approach to human motivation:

> It seems not impossible that the means employed by the more highly developed animals for preserving uniform and stable their internal economy (i.e., for preserving homeostasis) may present some general principles for the establishment, regulation, and control of steady states, that would be suggestive for other kinds of organization (Cannon, 1939, p. 25).

Cannon went on to suggest that one type of organization that could be explained in this way is social organization.

An explicit extension of the principle of homeostasis to social motivation was formulated by Stagner (1977), who proposed that a discrepancy between an existing state and an "established or preferred" steady state activates an *arousal system that is common to all motives*. It is biological in origin, involving activation of the nervous system. The initiation of activity in this arousal system is automatic, physiological, and unlearned. The discrepancies that activate the system initially are biological ones. It is this system that Cannon described in his original concept of homeostasis. However, Stagner (1977) proposed that through experience and learning we come to associate other discrepancies of a nonbiological nature with the original biological ones. "This means," Stagner concluded, "that a system activated originally by a metabolic (discrepancy) can be, after learning, triggered by social (discrepancies)" (p. 113). In this way a purely social discrepancy, such as one that arises from a social goal, can come to elicit activity in the arousal system. The end result is the effort that the person expends in working for socially relevant outcomes.

As we have seen in this section on historical background, the principle of homeostasis was extended metaphorically to nonbiological motivation in the way that Cannon foresaw in 1939. The early homeostatic models involved arousal as an operative mechanism, as befit models based on a biological concept. These models proposed that a discrepancy between an existing state and some preexistent or desired state generates increased arousal, which may be experienced as negative affect and which in turn generates effort aimed at reducing the discrepancy. As time went by, however, such biological models began to lose popularity. In part this was because the concept of arousal itself was found to be inadequate to explain the complex activities of the body's various physiological systems. The decline of the biological homeostatic metaphor was also associated with a rising interest in the role of cognition in behavior, stimulated in large part by theoretical models of information processing and artificial intelligence (Gardner, 1985). This interest, in turn, was largely the product of the development and extensive use of a new type of information-processing device: the computer.

## Discrepancies and Feedback

In the early 1960s a new discrepancy model appeared, one that took its conceptual terminology not from the biological organism but from the machine. In this case the machine was, in its simplest form, a cybernetic feedback mechanism. Such mechanisms are equipped with internal sensors that detect deviations in the situation from some prearranged and set value. Deviations are read as "error," which feeds back to an operating mechanism that initiates action to remove the error. A simple example of this sort of device is an automatic thermostat that detects discrepancies between a set temperature and the actual temperature, and then switches on either a furnace or an air conditioner.

An early model of behavior patterned after the cybernetic machine was the TOTE unit of Miller, Galanter, and Pribram (1960). TOTE is an acronym for Test-Operate-Test-Exit, which represent the operative terms in the model. The initial "test" is a comparison between the existing situation and some desired one. If a discrepancy results from this comparison, the person does something ("operates") to reduce it, and then tests again to discover how successful the operation has been. This continues until the discrepancy is removed ("exit"). The system is illustrated in Figure 3-1. An example of a TOTE unit may be a person who places some change in a soda machine, pushes the button for his favorite brand, and receives nothing. This "test" reveals that some "operation" must be performed to make the machine work properly. The person therefore "operates" by punching the machine and pushing the button again, but still no can of soda is delivered. A second test shows that another operation must be carried out. Finally the person jiggles the coin return before pushing the button again, and this time the soda is delivered. At this point the goal is reached and the system "exits." In this series of simple motivated acts aimed at

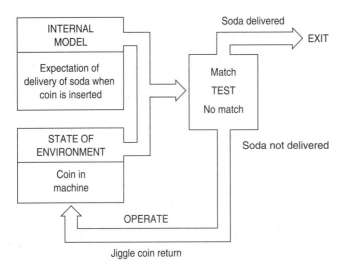

**Figure 3-1.** The TOTE unit. (Adapted from *Plans and the Structure of Behavior* by G. A. Miller, E. Galanter, and K. H. Pribram, 1960, New York: Holt.)

attaining a goal, the successive reactions are guided by feedback from a comparison between the goal state and the ever-changing existing states.

One of the first theorists to draw a specific connection between the cybernetic type of control mechanism and human motivation was Powers (1973). The model that he proposed was a general explanatory scheme for all behavior, and it involved the feedback loop as the central construction. Because Powers's model contained several elements that were important parts of later discrepancy theories, it is worth attending to in detail. The key to the model is that it accounts for the *regulation* of behavior through mechanisms that keep behavior running smoothly and in the service of immediate goals and purposes. These mechanisms can best be understood as automatic responses built into the person. Where motivation enters into this we will see in a moment.

Figure 3-2 illustrates the model in its simplest form. The major input to the system is a "reference signal," which, in human behavioral terms, is best defined as a purpose or a desired state. This signal is matched with a "sensor signal" that comes from outside and indicates stimuli in the environment. If the match, which occurs at a "comparator," shows a discrepancy ("error") between the two signals, a behavioral mechanism called an "effector" initiates action that creates a revised environment, stimuli from which enter into the "sensor function" to create a new sensor signal. This signal is compared to the reference signal and either a match is obtained or a new round of effector activity is begun to remove any new discrepancy that may have arisen. The function of the entire system is to keep the amount of error (discrepancy) as close to zero as possible. It must be repeated that this happens in a routine way and with as little effort as possible.

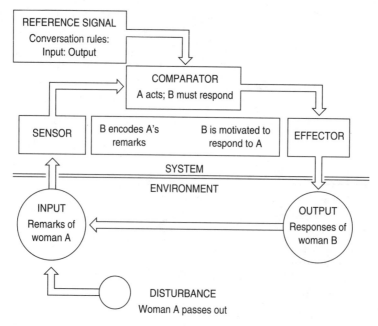

**Figure 3-2.** Schematic of a basic action control system. Items above the double line represent activities inside the processing system. Items below the double line represent observable events in the environment. (Adapted from "Feedback: Beyond Behaviorism" by W. T. Powers, *Science,* 1973, *179,* 351–356.)

The interesting element in the model for our purposes is what Powers calls a "disturbance." This can be any event that occurs in the environment while ordinary behavior is going on and that adds to the input certain stimuli that are not related to the normal input from the feedback process. The immediate result is that the entire process slows down to handle the newly enlarged stimulus volume. This is what happens in goal-seeking behavior. Behaviors that normally kept the system regulated and functioning in a fairly automatic way no longer suffice when something in the situation introduces a new goal into the system. This is a disturbance that slows down the process and makes it appear "sluggish" (Powers, 1973, p. 353).

An example may illustrate what this means. Suppose two people meet in a supermarket and stop to have a friendly chat. Each has a general sort of purpose in mind: to carry on the conversation, to avoid saying anything offensive to the other person, to listen attentively, and so on. All of this runs smoothly because each person is constantly comparing what she is doing and saying with a built-in reference signal that prescribes the required behaviors and establishes the goal or purpose of the conversation. Now suppose that one of the women suddenly begins to choke, rolls up her eyes, and falls unconscious to the floor. The other woman will be, to put it mildly, disturbed. How will she react? Certainly not by continuing to chat with her now-comatose friend. Instead, she will become excited, call others for help, and try to assist her friend in whatever way she can with emergency procedures. Her behavior will lose its automaticity and become effortful, it will be intense, and it will be prolonged for the amount of time the crisis continues. Effortful, *motivated* behavior begins when relatively effortless behavior is inadequate to new demands, and to new goals, that intrude upon the person.

Several theoretical models of behavior now incorporate the concept of a discrepancy between existing and desired states (e.g., Scheier & Carver, 1988; Klein, 1989; Hyland, 1988; Kanfer & Hagerman, 1987; Wicklund, 1975). Figure 3-3 illustrates a general model of human motivation that contains elements from these various approaches. It is a simple working model that can be used to analyze social motives in general and will, in fact, be used as a reference in later chapters of this book. It contains six general classes of action beginning with the thinking and deliberating that go on prior to goal setting, and ending with attainment of the goal or with responses to nonattainment, in which case the process cycles back to an earlier stage. The four stages that lie between these end points are: (1) intention, (2) action, (3) comparison, and (4) attribution.

The behavioral sequence begins when the person is required, by virtue of some demand in the environment or some inner need often associated with his or her past history, to take action. Whatever the person is doing must yield to something else that must be done, and this requires the formulation of a new goal for behavior. For example, a young lawyer may decide that she wishes to move ahead in her profession and decides to begin by making an impression on the senior partners in her firm. Obvious social and environmental forces impinge upon her to demand this course of action (the need for a higher salary, the wish to be regarded as a competent member of the profession), as well as personal needs (to maintain self-esteem). To put matters in the terminology used in Table 2-1 (see Chapter 2), we say the lawyer has an incentive—professional success. She must now find a goal or goals for which she can work in order to attain the incentive.

The question usually becomes a choice from among an array of possible goals. This requires the person to deliberate among his or her choices, to consider the good and bad points of each, and, finally, to settle on one goal. This process of decision and commitment is determined by factors discussed in Chapter 2: the perceived probability of reaching the goal, the value of the goal, and the person's appraisal of his or her ability to pursue the goal. The young lawyer in our example may decide that her best chance of getting the attention of the senior partners is by presenting an outstanding argument in court as part of a case on which she is working. She therefore commits herself to this goal.

Now, commitment must be translated into intention. The person must prepare for action by formulating a plan that will render his or her eventual actions efficacious for reaching the goal. In short, a *strategy* must be devised.

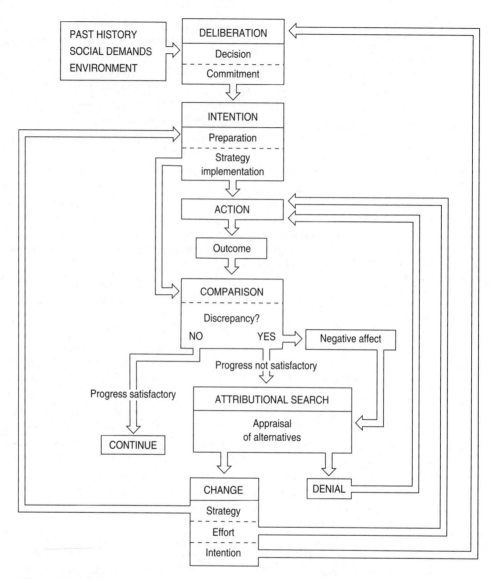

**Figure 3-3.** Schematic of an action control system showing all intervening processes. This schematic is derived from the theoretical models of several investigators.

This involves an appraisal of current options as well as a retrospective consideration of what has worked in the past and a projected guess about how various alternatives will work in the future. The attorney in our example must not only recall strategies that have led to success in the past, but also try to anticipate the effect that certain acts might have on a judge or a jury should she carry them out. This may require her to devise some elaborate mental scenarios of possible future events. It is at this stage that cognition and motivation come together in a particularly important way. More will be said about the strategic side of goal-directed behavior later in the chapter.

Finally, the person acts by initiating his or her strategic behavior. At some point the person will stop to consider whether the strategy is working and whether he or she is making progress toward the goal. To do this the person must compare the existing state of affairs with the state defined by the intention that had been formed prior to action. If satisfactory progress is being made toward the goal, the person will continue in the current course of action. If the result is unsatisfactory, so that either no progress is being made toward the goal or the rate of progress is too slow, the person will begin to search the situation for reasons for the lack of progress. This attributional search will lead the person to assign failure to make satisfactory progress to causes that are relatively personal, stable, and controllable (see Chapter 2). A number of outcomes are possible from this search. The person may simply deny that there is a problem and continue to behave in exactly the same way (Janoff-Bulman & Timko, 1987). As we know from Chapter 2, this outcome is most likely when the person thinks that failure has unstable causes. The young lawyer in our example may find that the brilliant legal brief she has prepared has little effect on a tired and bored jury, but she may think that this is because she had to present it late in the day and that her arguments the next morning will have a better effect.

The person may, on the other hand, react to the lack of progress by changing strategies and adopting a new course of action addressed to the same goal. The lawyer, for example, may drop her carefully crafted arguments and decide to use rhetoric to sway the jury. Or the person may recognize the discrepancy, maintain the same strategy, and simply try harder. This course of action comes closest to describing the purely motivational side of action, where motivation is defined as an increase in effort mounted in pursuit of a goal. It is most likely, as we saw in Chapter 2, when failure is attributed to unstable and personal causes. Finally, the person may give up trying to reach the goal and change his or her intention. This brings the person back to the beginning of the process, to the stage of deliberation, where a new goal must be found. Our young lawyer may concede that she has lost her big case but that she can have a better future practicing law outside the courtroom.

One final feature of the model in Figure 3-3 should be noted. Lack of satisfactory progress toward a goal may result in an increase in negative affect. To the extent that such an affective state does occur, its main influence is probably to facilitate the processes being carried out as a result of the attributional search. Thus, if denial, or a change in strategy, or increased effort is the means chosen by the person to reduce the discrepancy between the goal and the existing state, that particular course of action will be pushed along by a strong negative affect.

The phase of the sequence shown in Figure 3-3 that pertains most directly to motivation is the one labeled "action," which begins after the intention has been formed and ends when the person compares his or her progress to that point with the desired ideal state. As noted above, the person will, after the comparison has been made, either continue with the ongoing action or make some change in intention, strategy, or intensity of effort. If satisfactory progress is being made, the person will continue. Such progress may indicate that tried and true methods of going after goals are still working and that little difficulty is being encountered. From the standpoint of motivational psychology, this activity is of little interest. What is of interest is behavior under conditions of unsatisfactory progress because this activity involves effort.

At this point we must ask certain questions. What makes a person persist in seeking a goal even when little or no progress is being made toward it? Why should a person continue to pursue a goal when certain other more attractive goals may become recognized after pursuit of the original one has begun? When will a person react to the knowledge that little progress is being made by increasing effort, and when will the person respond to such knowledge by giving up? All of these questions touch upon one common theme, which can be stated as another question: what does a person do to *protect an intention* to strive for a goal so that the intention may be acted upon until the goal has been attained? To answer this question as well as the ones before it, we must first turn to the second of the two major themes of this chapter and discuss the concept of the *will*.

## THE PLACE OF WILL IN MOTIVATION

### The Distinction Between Will and Intention

Much of what was discussed in Chapter 2 involved, at least implicitly, an assumption that people exert volitional control over their actions in seeking to reach goals. In the preceding section of this chapter, volition was again implicit in much that was said. Reducing a discrepancy between a present state and a desired one is usually thought of as something that requires determination and the willful exertion of effort.

The problem of what volition means is an old one in psychology. In traditional expectancy-value theory it tends to be assumed that once a person has formed a goal and has some incentive to reach it, he or she will undertake the action necessary for the task. Volition is usually subsumed by other concepts, like commitment. But it is not obvious why choosing a goal and making a commitment to it *necessarily* assure that the necessary actions will be carried out. This was the point upon which some of the major arguments over the nature of will took place early in the 20th century. The viewpoint that action requires something beyond intention was the basis for a theoretical orientation called *will psychology*.

The theory of volition as developed by will psychologists need not be discussed at great length. (See Kuhl & Beckmann, 1985b, for an extended discussion.) It is important to note a few of its major premises, however, because they form the basis for some contemporary conceptions of will that will be discussed later. The first of these premises is that volition refers to processes that take place *after* a decision has been made to seek some goal and after the person has formed a commitment. All of the processes that we have observed so far—analysis of the expectancy of success and goal value, judgments of ability and self-efficacy, commitment—are *preliminaries* to willful action. They set the stage for acts of will but do not define them. The second premise is that volition is involved in action only if there is some level of difficulty in reaching the goal that must be overcome by effort. Will is what causes action to be first initiated and then maintained in the face of difficulties. The third premise is that willful action includes certain procedures and strategies that keep the intention alive and protect it until the goal is successfully attained. These acts include selective attention and encoding (e.g., ignoring thoughts or events that distract from goal striving). In addition, the occurrence during goal-directed action of emotions connected to the outcomes of action can strengthen the will to carry out the intended behaviors. For example, if a person fails to attain a goal because of some difficulty in the situation, the anger that results from that failure can arouse the person to put out the effort necessary to overcome the problem.

## Stages of Action

By drawing a distinction between volition and the processes that precede it, like decision and commitment, will psychologists made volition a part of a larger process that begins in the early stages of goal setting and ends with either success or failure in reaching the goal. A statement of the complete process is found in a theory proposed by Heckhausen and Gollwitzer (1987; Gollwitzer, 1990). This theory describes a four-stage scheme beginning with a *predecisional* phase and followed, in sequence, by *postdecisional* (preactional), *actional,* and *postactional* stages.

We already know a great deal about what happens in the predecisional stage from matters discussed in Chapter 2. During this stage the person is confronted by an array of possible goals from which a choice must be made. This is a time for deliberation and decision. It involves wishing, hoping, attempting to foresee the consequences of various courses of action, and weighing the expectancies and values of goal attainment. The phase ends when a decision has been made to seek one of the goals.

The postdecisional, or preactional, phase follows, during which the person's concerns shift away from deliberation and focus on the formation of strategies for implementing the decision. The person inhibits thoughts about alternative goals and concentrates on how he or she may best strive for the goal that has been chosen.

Several conditions must exist before intentions are translated into actions, thereby initiating the actional phase of the process. Obviously, the situation must be favorable; if insurmountable barriers stand in the way, action is unlikely even with the strongest of intentions. In addition, the intention must be sufficiently greater than competing intentions associated with alternative, and recently rejected, goals. Furthermore, the intention must be stronger than any intentions that may arise from future opportunities. To put it simply, action is taken and maintained when the goal of that action is seen to be clearly more attainable or more valuable than any viable alternative, and when it is also considered to represent a better bet for a valued outcome than any alternatives that may become available in the future.

The postactional stage begins after either the goal has been attained or striving for the goal has ended. In this phase of the process the person asks two questions: (1) Was the goal reached? and (2) If so, was it worth the effort? If the answer to either of these questions is no, the person will either form a new set of intentions and plans or lower the standards related to the quality and attractiveness of the outcome. For example, a student who fails a course that is required for graduation in a science will either adopt a new strategy with the same goal in mind (e.g., plan to repeat the failed course at a nearby college where competition is weaker) or change his or her major to some subject that is less demanding.

## Processes Within the Stages

Knowing the four stages in action helps us understand the broad context of motivated activity, but it does not answer the fundmamental question of how intentions are translated into acts. To answer that question we must turn to a model of action proposed by Kuhl (1985), which defines specific processes that occur within the four stages. Kuhl's is a model of action control. It describes ways in which a person initiates strategies and enacts goal-directed intentions, and how the person regulates action voluntarily. Action control begins only after a commitment to a goal has been made. Whereas a person will formulate an intention to carry out an act on the basis of how much ability the person *thinks* that she has, action control begins after the intention and reflects how well the person uses the ability that she actually *possesses* to strive for the goal. A person who has action control is likely to reach his goals because he uses good voluntary strategies and exercises good control over his emotions.

Figure 3-4 describes the processes in Kuhl's model of action control. The process begins just after an intention to carry out some act has been formed. Immediately two questions arise: (1) Is the task required to fulfill the intention sufficiently difficult to require effort? and (2) If it is, do I have sufficient control over the situation that my efforts will be rewarded with goal attainment?

The first of these questions, as we have already observed, lies at the heart of will psychology. If a task is so easy that the person can perform it

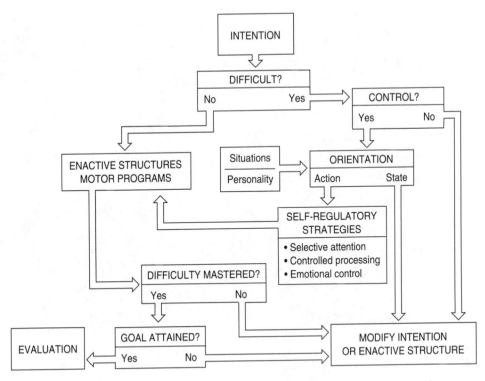

***Figure 3-4.*** Diagram of Kuhl's action control model. (Adapted from "Volitional Mediators of Cognition-Behavior Consistency: Self-Regulatory Processes and Action Versus State Orientation" by J. Kuhl in *Action Control: From Cognition to Behavior,* edited by J. Kuhl and J. Beckmann, 1985, New York: Springer-Verlag.)

with routine, well-learned, "automatic" behaviors, no great act of the will is required to carry it out. A large portion of human behavior does manifest just such a routine and "mindless" quality (e.g., Taylor & Fiske, 1978; Langer, 1989). In fact, it is because so much behavior is outside voluntary control that people often experience difficulty carrying through on voluntarily controlled actions. This happens in cases in which the person wishes to do one thing but feels a stronger urge to do something else. Such behaviors, often called "unconscious" (Jacoby & Kelley, 1990), represent responses to situations and past associations of which the person may not be entirely aware at the time (e.g., Bargh, 1990). For example, a person who desires to quit smoking may find that by going to places where she used to smoke and by associating with smoking friends, she requires great willpower to overcome the habitual urge to smoke again. In general, whenever goals are especially important to a person, voluntary and strategic behavior overrides automatic responses (Showers & Cantor, 1985). Finally, if a person believes that he has no control over the outcomes of his actions, volition will not come into play and no effort will be

*People who wish to stop smoking must exercise willpower to overcome old habits in familiar surroundings.*

expended. As we have noted, belief in the lack of control may involve a feeling that one has little ability to do the task or a low level of self-efficacy, or it may reflect a perceived lack of affordances for action in the situation, or it may be due to some other element in the attributional process (see Chapter 2). In general, feelings of lack of control and helplessness lead to a cessation of goal-directed behavior, as will be shown in Chapter 6 of this book.

If the task is difficult and the person feels a sense of control over the outcomes of action, then the person may adopt an *action orientation*. This is a state of mind characterized by concentration on the various alternatives for action that the person has, preparatory to exercising one or more of them. The person who is action oriented avoids attending to or processing information that does not pertain to striving for the goal and instead processes mainly goal-related information. The person also tends to experience emotional and affective states that support goal-directed action. For example, difficulties experienced in reaching the goal may inspire feelings of challenge and optimism.

Sometimes, however, people do not adopt an action orientation but instead their attention is diverted to certain features of the situation or of their own thoughts and feelings. For example, a person may make a commitment to carry out a plan of action yet be distracted by thoughts related to other matters such as personal problems or plans for other activities. Another example is a person who has trouble doing a difficult task and, instead of concentrating on what must be done, starts thinking about how stressful the situation is or how much disappointment he is experiencing. These examples characterize a *state orientation* that is inimical to action and works against it. As we can readily see, a state orientation can be one of the many difficulties that must be surmounted by effort.

Whether a person develops an action orientation or a state orientation depends on four factors. An action orientation comes about only if the person has a clear understanding of (1) the present state of events, (2) some future state of events that represents the goal, (3) a discrepancy between the present and future states, and (4) alternative actions available to reduce the discrepancy. If any of these conditions is lacking, the person will adopt a state orientation (Kuhl, 1982). These conditions describe the variables of the discrepancy model of motivation outlined earlier in the chapter. A state of action orientation is therefore a necessary condition for the operation of the feedback process in motivation.

To some degree the person's orientation following commitment to a goal

## TABLE 3-1
## Sample Items from an Action Control Scale

When I really want to finish an extensive assignment in an afternoon,

_____ S* _____ it often happens that something distracts me.

_____ A* _____ I can really concentrate on the assignment.

When I know that something has to be done soon,

_____ S _____ I often think about how nice it would be if I were already finished with it.

_____ A _____ I just think about how I can finish it the fastest.

When I have to study for a test,

_____ S _____ I think a lot about where I should start.

_____ A _____ I don't think about it too much; I just start with what I think is most important.

When I have a hard time getting started on a difficult problem,

_____ S _____ the problem seems huge to me.

_____ A _____ I think about how I can get through the problem in a fairly pleasant way.

*S = state-oriented response; A = action-oriented response
*Source:* Adapted from *Action Control: From Cognition to Behavior,* edited by J. Kuhl and J. Beckmann, 1985, New York: Springer-Verlag.

is determined by environmental stimuli that draw attention toward or away from goal-related actions (e.g., Kuhl, 1981; Kuhl & Helle, 1986). In the course of everyday behavior people alternate between action and state orientations (Kuhl, 1984). Nevertheless, there are individual differences in the relative balance between the two states. Some people tend to be action oriented most of the time and others to be state oriented. Thus action and state orientations are determined by both situational and personal variables. The personal aspect of the two orientations is assessed by means of a self-report scale developed by Kuhl (1985). A few items from the scale are shown in Table 3-1 to illustrate how action and state orientations are operationally defined.

## Effects of Action and State Orientations

As noted, people who have adopted an action orientation utilize three strategies to implement their intentions: selective attention, processing, and emotion control. Thus state-oriented subjects in a study reported by Kuhl (1982) showed a stronger tendency during a word memorization task to recall words that they had been instructed to ignore than did action-oriented subjects. State orientation apparently interfered with subjects' ability to attend selectively. The effects of action orientation on the processing of information have been shown in a study by Beckmann and Kuhl (1984) in which students who were looking for apartments were asked to rank order 16 apartments on their desirability. Later, after having chosen an apartment from among the 16, each subject again rated the entire set for attractiveness. Action-oriented subjects increased the attractiveness rating of their chosen alternatives relative to the others in the set. In other words, following a commitment to one of the apartments, the action-oriented people protected this intention by processing information selectively.

State orientation has been shown to play a role in depression and depression-related behaviors. It would make sense to suppose that becoming preoccupied with one's state rather than looking for action alternatives might make a person less active and engaged. If failure or other negative events should befall the person under such conditions, the person could become ruminative and morose. A connection between state orientation and depression has been shown by Rholes, Michas, and Shroff (1989), who also found that high stress in a person's life is more likely to cause depression if the person is highly state oriented than if he or she is relatively less state oriented (Figure 3-5). Kuhl (1981) also found that persons who are action oriented are less likely to show degenerated performance following uncontrollable failure than are state-oriented people. Kuhl and Helle (1986) have supplied further evidence that depressives show a tendency toward state orientation by ruminating on unfulfillable intentions and, as a consequence, missing opportunities to enact other, fulfillable ones. This is a theme that comes up in some other theories of depression, which also propose that the depressive is a person who becomes locked into unproductive thought about past failures or other states, and is relatively incapable of taking the action necessary to get out of his or her dysphoric mood (e.g., Hyland, 1987; Psyzczynski & Greenberg, 1987).

The remainder of Kuhl's action control model in Figure 3-4 is similar to the overall scheme shown in Figure 3-3. After an action orientation has been adopted and the proper self-regulatory strategies implemented, the person makes use of appropriate cognitive and motor programs to carry out the goal-directed action, and then observes whether or not difficulty that had been experienced in striving for the goal has been mastered. If it has, the next question is whether the goal has been reached or more effort is needed. If the latter is the case, the person will either modify the enactive structure (i.e., make another attempt to reach the goal by either trying harder or using a different strategy) or drop that goal and choose another (i.e., modify the intention). If, however, the person has formed a state orientation earlier, the likelihood of his or her dropping the original goal and switching to another one occurs much sooner, before much effort has been invested in pursuing the original goal.

Following the flow of events described in Figure 3-4 may be easier if a simple example is used. Imagine two roommates who set about working at the same task: preparing a two-page report on a psychology experiment that they completed earlier in the day in a lab. As they sit down to their word processors, they both realize that the task before them, though difficult, is

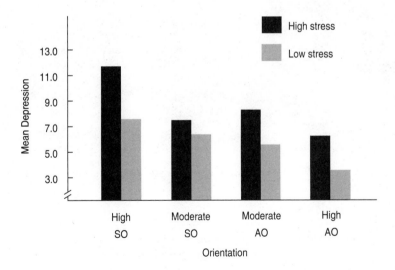

***Figure 3-5.*** Action and state orientation as moderator variables in the relation of stress to depression: AO = action orientation; SO = state orientation. (Drawn from data reported in "Action Control as a Vulnerability Factor in Dysphoria" by W. S. Rholes, L. Michas, and J. Shroff, *Cognitive Therapy and Research*, 1989, *13*, 263–274.)

*The action-oriented person focuses on completing a task at hand and tries to shut out distracting thoughts.*

something that they can perform with some effort. The first student, for various reasons having to do with his personality and his appraisal of the situation, takes an action orientation and concentrates only on writing the report. After writing a draft of his report, he checks it over and decides that, although he has overcome the difficulty of writing the report, the finished product is still not good enough (i.e., his goal has not yet been reached), so he revises the report and reads it again. This time he is satisfied with his work and judges it to be ready to be turned in. The second student is state oriented. After writing a few lines of his report, he begins to get restless and nervous about the pressure of having to finish the project that night. Concentrating more on his discomfort than on the quality of the paper, he decides not to do the careful report that he had planned to do, but dashes off a barely adequate one in a single draft, and then heads for the lounge to relax and watch television.

## Motivational Change

We still have not dealt sufficiently with the question of why intentions must be protected in the course of striving for a goal. Why do our intentions sometimes appear to waver and weaken before we have successfully carried them out? One answer, of course, is that often we do not have a single clear goal in mind, but instead entertain a number of goals that may be fairly near to each other in importance (see Table 2-1). In such cases, goal conflict is a strong possibility (see Chapter 2), and striving for one goal may eventually weaken as one thinks about alternatives. But this still does not explain how a tendency to strive for alternative goals may actually displace a tendency to strive for the original one unless strategies for protecting the original one are enacted. To understand this we need a theory of motivational change.

An answer to our question is provided by the dynamics of action theory of Atkinson and Birch (1970). This is a theory of how motivation and motivated action change over time. Unlike most theories of motivation, which freeze action in a relatively short time frame, the dynamics of action theory analyzes the ongoing "stream" of behavior over long periods. What characterizes behavior over long periods is fluctuation and change. Thus the disposition toward interference among goal tendencies that sometimes underlies the need for the protection of intentions is rooted in the variable nature of motives themselves.

The theory of the dynamics of action describes the interplay among actual and potential motivational "forces" in ongoing behavior. Any particular action is initiated by an instigating force ($F$) that arises in response to some condition of the person or the environment. This, roughly speaking, is what we usually mean by goal-directed behavior: a number of interrelated and directed actions with some common purpose. The instigating force will, theoretically, persist indefinitely as long as no other force comes into play to weaken it. An example might be performing all of the coordinated acts required to paint the wall of a room. These actions are instigated by the condition of the unpainted room and the person's desire to paint it. The person doing the painting will continue to paint until some competing force arises to stop the action. The most obvious of these forces is completion of the task. After the action begins, a consummatory force ($C$) begins to develop as a reaction to the behavior itself. The strength of the overall tendency ($T$) to carry out the action is equal to the strength of $F$ minus the strength of $C$. The longer the person performs the act, the greater the strength of $C$ becomes until it exceeds the strength of $F$. This will happen when either the wall is painted or the person becomes tired of painting. The point to note in this theory is that *the weakening of the overall tendency to carry out the act begins as soon as force C begins to build*. (This is shown as behavioral tendency $T_A$ in Figure 3-6.) Thus, under normal conditions every action carries the seeds of its own extinction in the consummatory force that it creates.

A potential behavior that is not carried out has an instigating force behind it but, because there is no action, it creates no consummatory force. Prolonged exposure to the conditions that elicit this initiating force will therefore cause the strength of the force to build without opposition. This is shown in the progressive development of tendency $T_B$ in Figure 3-6. The person who is painting the wall may early in his work entertain the thought of stopping work to watch television but not do so because the desire to paint is too strong. As this desire weakens with growth in the relevant consummatory force, however, the relative desire to watch TV instead of painting increases. Eventually, the tendency to watch TV exceeds the tendency to paint, and motivational change occurs. This is shown in the period following time $t$ in Figure 3-6.

Putting the Atkinson-Birch model into the context of action control theory, we see that what Kuhl and others have called "protecting an intention" involves keeping the dominant behavioral tendency ($T_A$) stronger than any

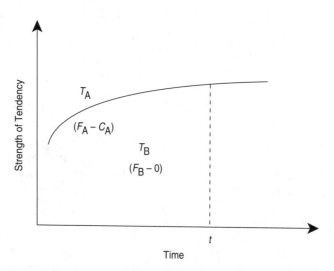

*Figure 3-6.* Hypothetical strengths of action tendency for ongoing behavior ($T_A$) and potential behavior ($T_B$). The strength of $T_A$ is equal to the strength of the instigating force ($F_A$) minus the strength of the consummatory force ($C_A$). The strength of $T_B$ is equal to the strength of the growing instigating force ($F_B$) only because no consummatory force accrues without action. The two action tendencies will be equal in strength at time $t$. (Adapted from *The Dynamics of Action* by J. W. Atkinson and D. Birch, 1970, New York: Wiley.)

competing tendency such as $T_B$ until the final goal served by tendency $T_A$ has been reached. One way in which this can be done is to replenish the strength of the instigating force for the desired behavior. If the magnitude of this force can be increased to offset the growing strength of the consummatory force, this could keep the tendency going and perhaps even increasing. This may be done by concentrating on the desired action and rehearsing one's commitment to it. At the same time, the person can try to ignore thoughts about the alternative tendency, thereby limiting the rate of growth of the instigating force for that act. As we have already seen, the combination of the two—concentrating on the importance of what one is doing and avoiding thoughts of alternatives—is an important part of action orientation.

## Protective Strategies

PLAYING THROUGH AND INHIBITION.    In addition to selective attention and processing and emotion control, people use other cognitive strategies to protect their intentions to work for certain goals. One such strategy is "playing through" to a goal, in which the person constructs a script of imagined events and actions (Showers & Cantor, 1985). Anyone who has awaited an interview for an important job has probably had the experience of trying to foresee what questions the interviewer will ask, and trying to frame some responses mentally in anticipation of those questions. Forming mental images of goals and goal-related acts has been shown to facilitate goal attainment (Sherman, Skov, Hervitz & Stock, 1981).

Another successful protective strategy, a variation of playing through, involves inhibiting the mental images of chosen and alternative goals. In a series of studies with children, Mischel and his associates (e.g., Mischel & Mischel, 1983) have shown that children are better able to wait for delayed but preferred rewards if they control their thoughts about more immediate but less desirable rewards. For example, Mischel and Moore (1980) found that young children who were given a choice between waiting 20 minutes for a preferred food treat or having a less preferred treat immediately were more able to wait the required length of time if they had been instructed to think about food items *different* from those involved in the choice than if they had been told to think about the relevant items. Thus the intention to wait for 20 minutes was protected by inhibiting thoughts about the possibility of not waiting.

MIND-SETS.    In their model of stages in the motivation process, Heckhausen and Gollwitzer (1987) suggested that the person goes through a series of stages of cognitive activity that exactly parallel the four stages of action. These cognitive stages represent a series of "mind-sets" adopted by the person to facilitate the activity going on at each particular stage. In this way, mind-sets work in harmony with motivation and action.

The predecisional stage is matched by the *deliberative* stage of mind-set, during which the person is particularly sensitive and open to any information that can help in decision making. Information on the probability of attaining goals, on goal values, and on personal ability is of great importance to the person who is trying to decide what to do. The person is impartial and objective in weighing information at this stage because impartiality is adaptive.

After a decision to act has been made, but before the decision has been implemented (i.e., during the preactional stage of motivation), the person is in an *implemental* mind-set. During this phase, the person's attention shifts away from gathering information and fixes upon ways and means of striving for the chosen goal. The person now ceases to be objective and impartial, becoming instead closed-minded and sensitive only to information that promotes goal-related striving. It is during this stage that cognitive activity is addressed to protecting the intention to act.

This state of closed-mindedness is maintained throughout the *actional* stage of motivation, which is what the corresponding stage of mind-set is also called. The person resists processing information that could lead to rethinking his or her decision or the strategy that has been adopted. The person also tries not to think about the self, such as how he or she feels, during this period, thereby avoiding the adoption of a state orientation. Attention is directed toward cues, both in the person and in the environment, that guide the goal-directed activity.

When action has stopped, because either the goal or some other outcome has been reached, the *evaluative* stage of mind-set begins (paralleling the postactional motivational phase). Once again the person becomes open-minded and sensitive to information in the hope that he or she can evaluate the outcome of the action. The person asks two questions: Was the goal attained or not? and If the goal was attained, was it worth the effort?

The entire model of Heckhausen and Gollwitzer's (1987) approach to decision making, action, and mind-sets is summarized in Figure 3-7.

Evidence for changing mind sets has been presented in a series of studies by Heckhausen, Gollwitzer, and their associates. Heckhausen and Gollwitzer (1987) instructed subjects to choose among different sets of stimuli to be used in a test to be taken later; then they interrupted the subjects either before or after they had made their choices in order to assess their thoughts. These thoughts were subsequently classified as being "deliberative" (i.e., concerned with weighing options and reaching a decision) or "volitional" (i.e., oriented toward voluntarily carrying out a course of action). When thoughts were assessed before the decision was made, they tended to be primarily deliberative and not volitional. This fits the pattern we would expect in the first stage of the process shown in Figure 3-7.

Gollwitzer, Heckhausen, and Steller (1990) have described a process of "cognitive tuning" that arises from the mind-set in which a person happens to be. This process refers to a tendency to "tune in" on, and be sensitive to, thoughts that are congruent with the motivational stage in which one happens to be. In their study, Gollwitzer and colleagues (1990) induced a deliberative mind-set in some subjects by asking them to concentrate on some unresolved personal problem. A second group of subjects was given an

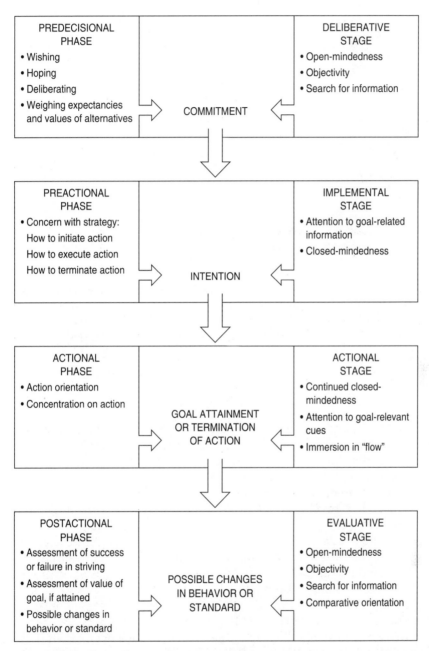

***Figure 3-7.*** Summary of the model of Heckhausen and Gollwitzer. (Boxes on the left side of the diagram represent action stages in motivation, boxes on the right side represent corresponding phases in mind-sets, and boxes in the center represent the behavior associated with each level of action and mind-set.)

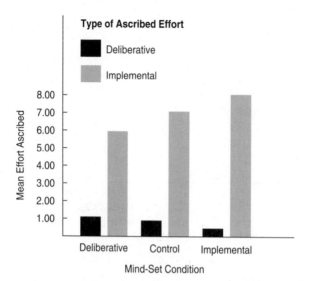

*Figure 3-8.* Ascription of efforts in story to deliberation or implementation as a function of prior establishment of deliberative or implemental mind-set in subject. (Drawn from data reported in "Deliberative and Implemental Mind-Sets: Cognitive Tuning Toward Congruous Thoughts and Information" by P. M. Gollwitzer, H. Heckhausen, and B. Steller, *Journal of Personality and Social Psychology,* 1990, *59,* 1119–1127.)

implemental mind-set by being asked to concentrate on how they might carry out some planned personal project. Subjects in a control condition merely watched slides during this time. Later all subjects were given the task of writing the ending to short and incomplete stories; the themes of their story endings were subsequently classified as either deliberative or implemental in substance. The results of the study, illustrated in Figure 3-8, showed that even though subjects preferred to use implemental themes to deliberative ones (i.e., most stories stressed action rather than thought), the greatest incidence of deliberative stories came from subjects who had been put in a deliberative mind-set and the greatest number of implemental ones came from subjects in an implemental mind-set.

Being in an implemental mind-set can also have some subtle effects on thoughts and actions during goal striving. For example, Gollwitzer and Kinney (1989) found that subjects who carried out a task over which they had little control nevertheless believed that they had more control when they were in an implemental mind-set than when they were in a deliberative one. An implemental mind-set, by causing the person to concentrate on what must be *done,* may enable people to focus on their abilities with respect to situational demands, and may as a consequence foster an illusory optimism in situations in which the person has no real power.

# CHAPTER SUMMARY

**1.** The process of motivation originates in a discrepancy between a goal and one's existing state. If habitual behavior fails to reduce the discrepancy, effort must be expended for that purpose. This idea, which was expressed by John Dewey in the 19th century, is the basis for all modern discrepancy models of motivation.

**2.** Another concept that underlies the discrepancy models is homeostasis, a term used to describe a reflex process by which the body adapts to changing conditions. In a similar manner, people react to discrepancies between normal or "steady" states and states that are induced by situational events. It has been suggested that systems that are originally activated only by biological discrepancies can come, through learning, to be activated by more complex social discrepancies.

**3.** Whereas earlier discrepancy models of motivation involved a hypothesized increase in arousal as the immediate antecedent of effort, later models did not. These newer models were based, not on the metaphor of biological homeostasis, but on the metaphor of the computer. Thus they described responses to discrepancies in terms of innate feedback loops and control mechanisms. The TOTE system was one such model. Another was Powers's cybernetic model, which describes effortful and motivated behavior as the consequence of a disturbance that interrupts the normal flow of behavior.

**4.** Modern models of motivation based on the concept of discrepancy describe a process that begins with (1) the formation of an intention to strive for a chosen goal and the development of a strategy for implementing that intent, (2) specific actions aimed at attaining the goal, (3) a comparison between the outcome of the actions and the goal state, in order to detect any discrepancy, and (4) the attribution of cause for any discrepancy that is detected. Depending on the attribution, the person increases the amount of effort expended, changes the strategy or intention, or denies the discrepancy.

**5.** Simply having an incentive to strive for a goal does not guarantee that the person will actually undertake the effort that is required. Goal striving also requires an act of will that comes after commitment. Will is manifested in conscious effort if two conditions are met: (1) the task must be sufficiently difficult that effortless behavior will not result in attainment of the goal, and (2) the person must believe that he or she has sufficient control over the outcome to be assured of reaching the goal with the required effort.

**6.** Striving for a goal also requires that the person adopt an *action orientation,* a state of mind characterized by focusing attention on the goal and having a high level of control over the emotions. A state orientation, on the other hand, is a turning of attention away from the goal and toward one's own thoughts and feelings. Adoption of a state orientation is inimical to goal-directed action and tends to undermine it. Action and state orientations are also due in part to stable individual differences in the tendency to adopt one or another of these dispositions.

**7.**   One's intention to reach a goal must be protected from other motives and intentions; will serves this protective function. The theory of dynamics of action describes one way in which intentions to carry out activities weaken and become supplanted by other behaviors. According to this theory, an action generates an accumulation of a consummatory force that subtracts from the instigating force behind the action. Other *potential* actions do not generate consummatory forces because they are not actually carried out. Thus any action in progress loses strength, relative to alternative actions, until it is finally weaker than the latter.

**8.**   Various cognitive strategies can be used to protect one's intentions to act. Planning a sequence of actions in the mind before acting ("playing through") facilitates attaining the goal of the action. Inhibiting the formation of mental images of alternative goals may likewise enhance goal striving and attainment. Forming mind-sets that are consistent with the stage of goal striving in which the person happens to be (e.g., predecisional, actional) can also help the person carry through the cognitive and emotional strategies necessary to successfully complete that stage. Deliberative mind-sets are consistent with the decisional processes required in choosing and committing to a goal, whereas implemental mind-sets are more functional when the person forms a strategy for reaching the goal and then carries it out.

# THE SELF IN MOTIVATION

Up to this point we have been defining goals as desired outcomes that guide and energize effortful, voluntary action. Ordinarily we think of goals in terms that are either material, such as goods and services, or interpersonal, like achievement, esteem and love. On a slightly more general level, however, these goals may be considered instrumental to the attainment of a still higher-order one: a desired state of the *self*. Landing a good job, scoring the winning goal in a game, and graduating with honors are examples of hoped-for outcomes, to be sure, but much of their value is derived from the fact that they enable the person to assume a desired *identity* as a worker, an athlete, or a scholar. In general, people want to think well of themselves and to have a high level of self-esteem. One way in which people maintain their self-esteem is by working for valued social goals and attaining them. An appropriate state of the self, or identity, is desirable, and the reason the person works at various activities like studying, developing social skills, training for sports, and

*Intensive training for athletic competition is one way in which people can enhance and maintain self-esteem.*

practicing musical skills is to become the person characterized by that identity.

We will start out this chapter by assuming that every person has at least some idea of the sort of person he or she wants to be, which we call the *ideal self*. We also assume that everyone has some idea of the kind of person that she or he actually *is* at the present time and in the present setting, and we call this the *actual self*. If we now assume that every person has the ability to make comparisons between their actual and ideal selves, then we have at least the rudiments of an application of the discrepancy model of motivation (see Chapter 3) to the principle of self-esteem. People usually want to have high levels of self-esteem, and they achieve this by keeping the degree of negative self-discrepancy (i.e., a discrepancy caused by the actual self falling short of the standards embodied in the ideal self) as small as possible. Detection of a negative discrepancy motivates attempts to reduce that discrepancy. Of course, it is possible for people to judge that they are living up to the standards of their ideal selves, and possibly even exceeding those standards on occasion. In such cases, consistent with the discussion in Chapter 3, there is no need for motivated effort.

In this chapter we will review some of the ways in which people deal with negative discrepancies between their ideal and actual selves. In the first part we will consider two models of discrepancy reduction that can serve as prototypes of how negative discrepancies can motivate the person to bring the actual self closer to the ideal by changing his or her behavior. Next we will consider some modern constructs that elaborate on ideas contained in those models: (1) the *self-schema,* which is a key to understanding how people become aware of their actual selves; (2) *possible selves,* which allow us to describe how people conceptualize their ideal selves; and (3) the distinction between the ideal self and the *ought self,* which is a self that is enjoined upon a person by other parties. We will then review studies that support our assumption of a basic need for self-esteem, noting some of the normal cognitive activities in which people indulge to maintain high levels of this variable. Finally, we will consider some of the ways in which people respond to negative discrepancies between actual and ideal selves without changing their actual selves, through the use of various *self-defensive strategies.*

# THEORIES OF ACTUAL–IDEAL SELF DISCREPANCIES

## Self-Awareness and Negative Affect

A theory of objective self-awareness developed by Duval and Wicklund (1972) describes certain conditions under which people become, literally, "objects" of their own attention. When these conditions are present, people become highly self-conscious and look at their behavior in the same way as they usually observe the behavior of other people. The theory states that at any given time we give our total attention either to what is going on outside ourselves (i.e., in our environment) or to what is going on "inside ourselves" (i.e., our conscious state, thoughts, feelings, and other aspects of our person). Attention shifts, sometimes rapidly, between the external and internal focus, and the directions of these shifts are caused by stimulus events around us. For example, a loud explosion a few blocks away may rivet our attention firmly on the environment. Other stimuli may make us more aware of, and sensitive to, our selves as objects of attention. Hearing one's own voice played on a tape recorder can enhance the feeling that one is observing one's own behavior in an objective sense and, accordingly, direct attention away from the environment and toward the self (Ickes, Wicklund & Ferris, 1973). Seeing one's reflection in a mirror may have a similar effect. Research on self-focusing has involved the use of several stimuli of this type (Wicklund, 1975).

The theory goes on to propose that "the objectively self-aware person will not simply react to himself impartially and in a neutral manner, but that he will come to evaluate himself as soon as the objective state occurs." This evaluation consists of the person's comparing his or her ongoing behavior, as observed during the state of heightened self-awareness, with "a psychological system of standards of correctness that is possessed by each person" (Duval & Wicklund, 1972, p. 3). Thus the theory assumes that when people become self-aware, they immediately undertake a process of comparing the actual self with an ideal self defined in terms of correct or sanctioned behavior. The ideal, or standard of correct behavior, depends on the situation. If, for example, the person is in a situation that calls for altruistic behavior toward other people, then increasing the person's self-awareness should bring to mind *ideal* altruism (e.g., Duval, Duval & Neely, 1979). If the situation calls for aggression, then increased self-awareness should facilitate a "proper" level of aggressive behavior (e.g., Carver, 1974), and so forth.

When the person is aware of both the ideal self and the actual self, the two selves will either match each other or show a discrepancy. If an intraself discrepancy is observed and if it is positive (i.e., if one's behavior matches the ideal or even exceeds it), the person will experience a sense of well-being and will, as a result, continue what he or she is doing. If, however, a comparison of the real self with the ideal reveals that the person has fallen short of her or his ideal, the person will feel uncomfortable and seek ways to reduce the discomfort. The person will therefore try either to get away from or otherwise avoid the stimuli that are causing the increased self-awareness or to change his or her behavior to bring it closer to that dictated by the standard of correctness. The end state produced by the new behavior is then compared with the ideal and, depending on the result, is found to produce either positive or negative affect. The cycle is repeated, if necessary, until there is no longer a discrepancy. The reader will notice numerous similarities between this model and the discrepancy models outlined in Chapter 3.

## *Self-Focus and Action Control*

Carver and Scheier have developed a model of self-focus based on the initial assumption that behavior is "the consequence of an *internal guidance system* that is *inherent* in the way humans are organized" (Carver & Scheier, 1990b, p. 3; emphasis added). This guidance system adjusts behavior to the implicit demands of certain standards that are invoked by situational conditions (this will be discussed below). Note that this adjustment is not motivated by a need to reduce negative affect, as was the case in Duval and Wicklund's (1972) model. Instead, the adjustments needed to remove discrepancies between ongoing behavior and the invoked standards are assumed to be innate and "wired in." (The reader familiar with Chapters 1 and 3 will recognize the use of two different metaphors in the Duval-Wicklund and the Carver-Scheier approaches. Both models describe a process of discrepancy and discrepancy reduction, but whereas the first uses a metaphor from biological homeostasis, the second uses one based on the computer.) In most other respects, the two models make virtually identical predictions about behavior.

Carver and Scheier's complete model includes several steps.

**1.** The process begins with stimuli in the environment, which feed into the model in two ways. First, they make salient a *behavioral reference standard* for that situation. For example, walking into a funeral home during a service confronts a person with stimuli that make silence and decorum the standard behaviors. The adequacy of one's actions in that setting will be judged according to how well she or he matches this standard. Second, the environment provides other stimuli that increase the person's *self-focus*. As noted, any stimulus that draws the person's attention to the self has this effect.

**2.** The immediate consequence of self-focus is a heightened *awareness of ongoing behavior*. A person may be engaged in some action of which she is barely aware, but if something happens to cause her to focus on herself, she will suddenly become very conscious of what she is doing. The ongoing behavior and the reference standard are then compared.

**3.** The comparison process has two consequences. The first has to do with the amount of desire for information that self-focused people show. They become especially interested in receiving information from the environment that will allow them to check on how closely their behavior matches the reference standard. Thus they *monitor* their behavior to judge its appropriateness. Scheier and Carver (1983), for example, gave subjects the task of copying complex figures from a photoslide, allowing them to see the slide for five seconds at any time they wished. In addition, some of the subjects were exposed to conditions designed to increase their self-focus: in one case a mirror was present, and in the other the experimenter watched the subject during the task. The results are shown in Figure 4-1. Subjects who were in one of the two conditions that contained cues for self-focus asked to see the slides more often (presumably so that they could check on how closely they were coming to reproducing it) than did subjects who performed in the absence of such cues.

The other consequence of heightened self-awareness is an effort to change behavior to bring it into line with the reference standard. Numerous studies have shown the enhancing effects of the presence of a mirror on normative behavior across a broad range of settings. For example, Carver (1975) found that subjects who were opposed to the use of physical punishment were less likely to use such punishment during an experiment when they could see their reflections in a mirror than when they could not. Self-focus has also been shown to influence clinically relevant behaviors. Scheier, Carver, and Gibbons

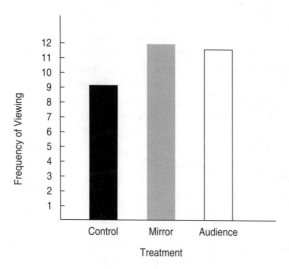

**Figure 4-1.** Frequency of viewing slides as a function of mirror presence and audience presence. (Drawn from data reported in "Self-Directed Attention and the Comparison of Self with Standards" by M. F. Scheier and C. S. Carver, *Journal of Experimental Social Psychology,* 1983, *19,* 205–222.)

(1981), for example, observed that snake-phobic subjects showed less tendency to approach a snake when a mirror was present than when no mirror was in evidence. The presence of a mirror therefore exacerbated the normal tendencies of these people to avoid snakes.

**4.** If attempts to match the standard are not interrupted (i.e., if the situation does not present real difficulties), the matching proceeds smoothly. If difficulties are encountered and the process is interrupted, the person stops, evaluates the situation, and assesses his chances of matching the standard. If the result of the assessment is favorable, so that the person thinks the chances of matching are good, the attempt proceeds. If the assessment yields an unfavorable expectancy of success, the person will withdraw from any further attempts. Carver, Blaney and Scheier (1979) found that self-focus interacts with the person's expectancy of being able to match the standard, so that *persistence is enhanced by self-focus when the expectancy is high but is hurt by self-focus when the expectancy is low.* Subjects in this study were first informed that they had performed poorly on a test of verbal ability. Some were then given a second task with instructions that encouraged optimism about success, whereas others were given the task with instructions that encouraged a low expectancy of success. The second task was actually unsolvable. The number of minutes that subjects spent on the second task are shown in Figure 4-2. When the expectancy of success on task 2 was high, the presence of a mirror motivated persistence; when the expectancy of success was low, the presence of the mirror led to withdrawal from the task.

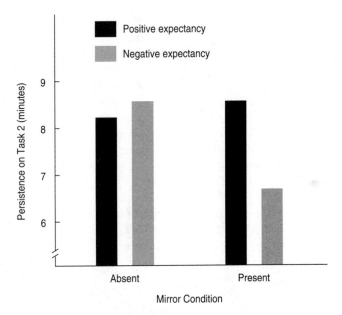

**Figure 4-2.** Persistence at unsolvable task as a function of outcome expectancy and self-focus. (Drawn from data reported in "Reassertion and Giving Up: The Interactive Role of Self-Directed Attention and Outcome Expectancy" by C. S. Carver, P. H. Blaney, and M. F. Scheier, *Journal of Personality and Social Psychology,* 1979, *37,* 1859–1870.)

**5.** The person who has a low expectancy of success will withdraw physically from the situation if this is possible. If this is not possible, the person will withdraw mentally by turning to distracting thoughts, fantasy, inattention, and other such expedients. When a person disengages in this way, either physically or mentally, she attempts to avoid information from the environment that would be a reminder of the discrepancy between the standard and the ongoing behavior. In a study by Greenberg and Musham (1981), for example, subjects were required to voice opinions that were either consistent with or contrary to their own. Those who expressed opinions with which they disagreed expressed less desire to sit facing a mirror than subjects who expressed opinions that they shared. By avoiding the mirror's cue for self-focus, subjects could escape some of the discrepancy between behavior and a standard that was produced by the experiment. Avoidance of information related to a discrepancy between behavior and a standard by self-focused subjects has also been reported by Carver, Antoni, and Scheier (1985).

**6.** If the person thinks that there is a reasonable probability that the behavioral standard can be matched by a change in behavior, and if, as a result, behavioral change is initiated, the person checks periodically to discover whether in fact the change is successful. At this point, the *rate of reduction* of the discrepancy between the reference standard and the ongoing behavior becomes critical. If the rate of discrepancy reduction is greater than the rate that the person wishes to attain, the person will experience positive affect. If the rate is lower than the person desires, negative affect will be felt. A rate of discrepancy that equals the hoped-for rate will have no affective consequences. Carver and Scheier (1990a) refer to this process of assessing the rate of discrepancy reduction as a *metamonitoring* process that is one step beyond the lower-order monitoring of the relationship between ongoing behavior and the reference standard. While the person's monitoring system is detecting discrepancies, the larger metamonitoring system is detecting the rate at which the discrepancies are being reduced or eliminated.

The "ideal rate" at which the discrepancy is reduced can be determined by a number of factors. In general these are either internal or external in origin. An example of setting an internally determined rate is a student's informing himself at the beginning of his freshman year in college that he will spend four years in getting the bachelor's degree. He will then periodically count his credit hours to determine whether he is on target for that goal. An example of an externally set rate is a mandate from an employer that an employee has a week to complete an important report.

The model described here is a complex one involving several steps that occur in a sequence. Figure 4-3 summarizes this flow of events in terms of a simple example: a nightclub comedian doing his comedy routine in front of an audience. The relevant environmental conditions are found in the ambience of the club, especially an audience waiting to be entertained. This ambience has the dual effect of (1) creating a reference standard or ideal (an amused and laughing audience) and (2) making the comedian more focused on his role (i.e., increasing his awareness of what he must do). He then begins to deliver his routine. If the audience laughs at his jokes, he will detect no discrepancy between his behavior and the reference standard, and he will continue as he started. If the audience is not amused, the comedian will consider making some changes in his routine, perhaps by throwing in some risqué or scatological material that he knows. Suppose, however, that before he can do this, an inebriated person in the audience begins to heckle him, thereby interrupting his routine. If the comedian has a few put-down lines to silence the heckler, he will figure his chances of making the necessary adjustments to be favorable. He will make the changes and then reevaluate: Does the new material get laughs or doesn't it? If the audience reacts quickly to the new routine and starts to laugh, the comedian will feel relieved, but if the audience responds to the new jokes slowly, he will continue to feel apprehensive.

If the comedian had been unable to stop the heckler from bothering him, he might have assessed his chances of doing a successful act to be unfavorable. At this point he would want only to withdraw from the impossible situation. If he were close to the end of the act, he might cut it short, finish with a couple of one-liners, and exit quickly (i.e., withdraw physically). If he could

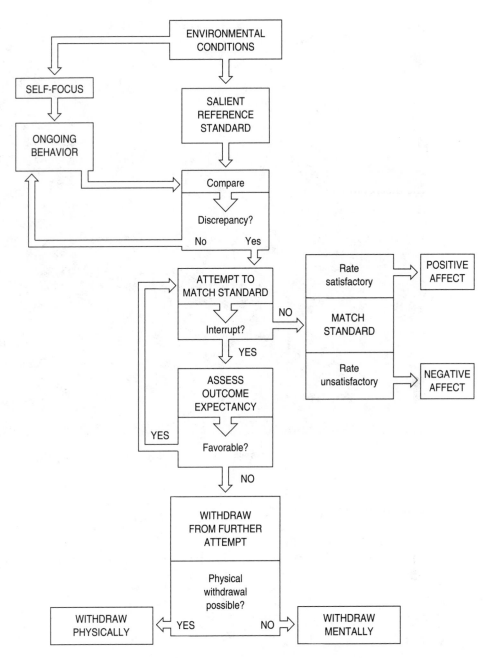

***Figure 4-3.*** General model of processes in self-focus.

*A performer such as a comedian provides an everyday example of how people use feedback from others to guide their actions.*

not do this, as might be the case early in his performance, he might withdraw mentally by deciding that the audience is no good, that they are not worthy of his efforts, and that he does not care whether they laugh or not. In this way he will be able to finish his act and leave.

## GOAL STATES RELATED TO THE SELF

### The Self as a Schema

One of the fundamental principles of the cognitive approach to behavior is that we organize information about the environment into categories. After a category has been formed, we form a mental picture of the various attributes that go into that category, and we refer to the mental structure by which we enumerate and organize these attributes as a *schema*. A schema is defined as "a cognitive structure that contains knowledge about the attributes of a category and the links among those attributes" (Fiske & Pavelchak, 1986).

To cite a simple example, suppose we see a large number of young people dressed in common uniforms and we form from this information the category of "soldier." Immediately we know certain things about these people—that they can fire a rifle accurately, they they can do the manual of arms and close-order drill, that they can follow orders—without ever seeing any one of them do these things. From the category "soldier" we build a "soldier schema" that not only lists the attributes of such a person but links them together meaningfully. We draw inferences about people on the basis of the schematic categories to which we assign them, and we follow these inferences with predictions about how the people will act in certain situations. A schema, therefore, is an important aid in organizing and utilizing social information.

In a similar way each of us builds up a number of *self-schemata* that consist of the various attributes by which we define ourselves. These schemata allow us to make certain cognitive generalizations about ourselves, to organize events from our past, and to predict what we are likely to do in the future. For example, Markus (1977) investigated the effects of self-schemata for independence on the self-perceptions of college age women. She found that women who were schematic for independence (i.e., who regarded independence as one of their central attributes) not only recalled a greater number of instances of being independent than did women who were not schematic for independence, but also predicted that they would behave more independently in the future. Thus, when we speak of a person's actual self as the person understands and perceives it, we are referring to the person's self-schema. When a person observes his or her behavior, that behavior is seen in the context of the various self-schemata that the person holds.

## Possible Selves

People are capable of not only organizing their actual self in schematic terms but also conceptualizing various alternative self-schemata. We are, in other words, capable of imagining a number of various *possible selves* (Markus & Nurius, 1986; Markus & Ruvolo, 1989). Each person has several possible selves that correspond to the goals for which he is working at any time. These identities can be obtained with some effort, and they may be highly desired. To a large extent it is these possible selves that give meaning to the goals for which we strive. A gangling adolescent girl, for example, may have a picture of herself in mind as a graceful ballerina and, given the talent and enough hard work, she may reach the goals that will confer that identity upon her when she is an adult.

People also have some potential selves that they wish *not* to become. We usually think of goals in terms of what the person wishes to be; indeed this bias has been present throughout this book. However, people sometimes expend more effort in avoiding *undesired* selves than in working for alternative desired ones. Ogilvie (1987) showed this in a study in which the subjective "distances" between the subject's real self, the ideal self, and the undesired self were assessed. It was found, as expected, that the subjects' satisfaction with life was negatively correlated with the magnitude of the distance between their real and ideal selves: as expected, the closer their real selves were to the ideal, the greater was the satisfaction. Satisfaction with life was positively related to the magnitude of the distance between the real and the undesired self: the farther they saw themselves being from this aversive self, the happier they were. The latter correlation was greater than the former. This means that the subjects derived greater satisfaction from avoiding an undesirable identity than from approximating a desirable one.

When we consider the effects of possible selves on motivation, it is therefore necessary to consider that both desired selves and undesired selves can sometimes have roughly parallel effects. They may also reinforce each others' influences. For example, a young man who is seeking a job may expend considerable effort at finding one because he pictures himself, ideally, as being employed. At the same time, he may work hard at finding a job in order to avoid picturing himself out of work. Following this line of reasoning, Oyserman and Markus (1990) have argued that motivation will be maximally effective when the person's desire to attain the ideal desired self is approximately balanced by fear of attaining the undesired one. In a study to test this idea, they found that delinquent youths from inner city schools tended to be dominated by their undesired selves, whereas nondelinquent adolescents were guided by both desired and undesired self-images. If we assume that adolescents as a whole aspire to socially desirable lives and to the traditionally accepted symbols of success, these findings suggest that students who tended to achieve these goals were the ones influenced by both their desired and undesired selves. On the other hand, students who failed to attain these goals reacted mainly to just their undesired selves.

## Ideal Self and Ought Self

What exactly is the "desired" self? Sometimes it is a personal ideal to which people aspire, but at other times it is an identity that is enjoined upon the individual by others. In Chapter 2 we described these others as "reference persons" whose wishes help to determine the various social incentives that motivate goal-seeking actions. Sometimes people "swim against the current" by choosing to do things strictly on their own and, possibly, in defiance of what others want them to do. But this is not always the case. Very often individuals choose their identities from among several that are defined for them by other people. Recall the fictitious student who was required to choose how to spend her weekend in Chapter 2 (see Table 2-1). She may have done none of the four things listed in the table but instead spent the weekend reading a novel for her own enjoyment. On the other hand, the self that she chose as her goal may well have been one of the four "social" selves created by the expectations of others.

It is helpful to distinguish between a personally chosen ideal self and one that is accepted only to meet a social demand, because the consequences of the two types of choice are quite different. Higgins (1987, 1989) addressed this dual sense of the aspired-to self by making a useful distinction among (1) an *ideal* self, defined as the representation of those attributes to which the person aspires, (2) an *actual* self, which is the self as it is perceived, and (3) an *ought* self, which is defined in terms of the demands made on the person. In addition, Higgins distinguishes among the three selves in terms of whether the person or someone else is making the judgment. Thus one's actual self can be defined either by the person or by some significant other such as a friend, spouse, boss, or parent. The two actual selves (one self-determined and one other-determined) need not be identical and probably seldom are. Likewise, one's own image of his or her ideal self may be different from what others perceive to be the ideal, nor is one's ought self always the same as that defined by others. A young person may, for example, feel pressures to join a gang (i.e., he feels that he ought to belong), whereas his parents may think that he ought to avoid bad company at all costs.

Either the ideal or the ought self may serve as a standard of reference with which the actual self is compared. In either case the person is motivated to reach a state in which the actual self matches the relevant personal guide, whether it be the ideal self or the ought self. The two types of discrepancy have different outcomes in terms of the emotion produced by the discrepancy. When a person experiences a discrepancy between his or her actual self and an ideal self, *some positive outcome that was sought after is absent.* For example, the student who fails in a pre-medicine major loses the opportunity to attend medical school, which would have been a positive outcome. A discrepancy between the actual self and an ought self, by contrast, produces *a negative result.* A student who is majoring in pre-medicine only to satisfy parental demands will lose nothing positive by failing but may incur disapproval. As a result, Higgins (1989) proposes that a discrepancy between the ideal and the actual self will produce emotions related to *dejection* over the loss of a valued outome, whereas an actual–ought discrepancy will produce emotions related to *agitation,* such as fear, guilt, and anxiety.

The type of self-discrepancy that a person experiences is in part a function of individual differences. For some people the most common discrepancy is between the actual and the ideal, whereas for others the actual–ought discrepancy is more typical. Which of the two discrepancies is experienced is determined largely by which is the more readily retrieved from memory, and this, in turn, is partly a function of how often such discrepancies have existed in a person's past. Still other people tend to experience the two types of discrepancy about equally. This individual difference variable determines in part how people react to failure to attain a goal. In a study to show this, Higgins,

Bond, Klein, and Strauman (1986) first measured which of the two types of self-discrepancy each person in a group of students typically experienced; then they asked each student to describe how he or she would feel after receiving a grade of "D" in a course. Those students whose predominant tendency was to compare their actual selves with some ideal selves reacted to the grade with feelings of dejection, unhappiness and discouragement, whereas students whose predominant tendency was to compare the actual self with an ought self reacted to the low grade with feelings of agitation, fear, and anxiety. These are the outcomes that Higgins and his associates predicted.

After an actual–ideal or actual–ought discrepancy has been detected, regardless of the cause, the ideas will engender the emotional states associated with them. Any cue that "primes" such ideas will have the effect. Strauman and Higgins (1987), for example, gave subjects a list of trait adjectives that supposedly described strangers and instructed the subjects to make up sentences from these terms. The words had actually been selected from earlier descriptions of their own ideal and ought selves given by the subjects. It was predicted that these self-relevant terms would activate ("prime") predominant actual–ideal or actual–ought discrepancies in the subjects and that the subjects' moods caused by exposure to this list of words would show either increased dejection or increased agitation. The latter effects, of course, would vary as a function of whether the subjects' normal tendencies were to experience actual–ideal or actual–ought discrepancies. The results of the study, shown in Figure 4-4, are exactly in line with this expectation. For subjects who typically experience actual–ideal discrepancies, dejection-relevant emotions were higher after the priming treatment than before; for subjects who typically experience actual–ought discrepancies, the words produced an increase in agitation-related feelings. Strauman and Higgins (1987) also showed that activation of the actual–ought discrepancy led to increased physiological arousal typical of an agitated emotional state, whereas the priming of the actual-ideal discrepancy was not accompanied by increased arousal.

How do these emotional states influence motivation? We might expect that subjects who are dejected over failure to match their actual behavior to an ideal standard might show an overall motivational deficit, whereas subjects who are agitated because of failure to meet some demanded standard would show an overall increase in activity level. The two studies cited above each give some evidence that such motivational effects do occur. Higgins and colleagues (1986) gave subjects a writing task both before and after they were asked to imagine receiving a "D" and found that subjects whose typical self-comparison was between the actual and the ideal showed a decrease in speed of writing after imagining the low grade. Subjects who characteristically made actual–ought comparisons showed an increase in writing speed over the same period. The study by Strauman and Higgins (1987) showed similar effects when the total output of verbal activity by the subjects was the variable of interest. Thus dejected and agitated moods are paired with appropriately matching depressed and increased activity.

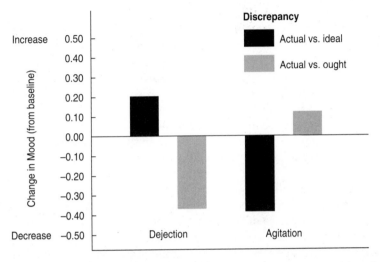

**Figure 4-4.** Mean mood change (dejection and agitation) as a function of priming manipulation and predominant self-discrepancy. (Drawn from data reported in "Automatic Activation of Self-Discrepancies and Emotional Syndromes: When Cognitive Structures Influence Affect" by T. J. Strauman and E. T. Higgins, *Journal of Personality and Social Psychology,* 1987, *53,* 1004–1014.)

We have seen, therefore, that people are motivated to reduce or eliminate discrepancies between the actual self and some desired self, and that such discrepancies bring about unpleasant and aversive emotional states. These motivational and affective processes are, in turn, the result of a broader and more comprehensive need: the need that people have to think well of themselves and to have high levels of self-esteem. To say that people desire self-esteem is neither original nor remarkable, and yet we cannot understand human motivation without accepting this basic premise. This fundamental need underlies many, if not all, of the commonly defined social motives. Two such motives, dating from an earlier era of thinking on motivation, are social comparison and cognitive dissonance.

# SELF-ESTEEM AS A BASIC NEED

## The Self in Social Comparison

**DOWNWARD SOCIAL COMPARISON.**    The theory of social comparison processes, as originally formulated by Festinger (1954), stated that people have a need to understand their levels of ability and the correctness of their opinions. The theory assumed the existence of a need for valid information about oneself to promote self-understanding. When objective information about the self is available, the original theory went, people will use it; when such information is not available, people seek self-information by looking to other people who are similar to themselves. For example, a person who plays tennis at her club on weekends and who wishes to determine how good a tennis player she is will not choose a leading professional as her comparison model. She will choose another woman who has been playing for about as long as she has and against a comparable level of opposition. In much the same way, Festinger (1954) argued, people decide whether their opinions are correct or incorrect by referring to the opinions of people who are generally similar to themselves.

In a major extension of social comparison theory, Schachter (1959) described situations in which people compare themselves with others in order to judge the appropriateness of their emotional states. He reported that when people are placed in a situation in which fear and uncertainty have been engendered, they tend to define their emotional states by observing how other people in the same condition are reacting.

The original theory explained all of these findings by asserting that people have a "drive" to know about themselves. For the most part, however, social comparison theorists have now abandoned this theoretical approach. Instead, social comparisons are now explained as part of a process whereby people learn that it is useful and adaptive to know how well they can do various things and how valid their beliefs on certain matters are (Goethals & Darley, 1987). In another refinement of the original theory, it is now held that when people desire self-information, they seek as objects of social comparisons not those who are generally similar to themselves, but those who have similar background attributes that are related to the ability or opinion in question (Wheeler & Zuckerman, 1977; Wheeler, Koestner & Driver, 1982). Another development in the theory pertains to the desire for self-improvement. When a person is motivated to improve his or her performance or ability level, there may be a motive to compare the self with someone who is better at the ability in question (e.g., Seta, 1982), a process called *upward social comparison*.

Still another change in social comparison theory is especially relevant to the purposes of this chapter. It is now recognized that people sometimes engage in social comparisons not to obtain accurate information about themselves but to obtain information that bolsters their self-esteem and sense of well-being. This phenomenon has been called *self-validation* (Goethals, 1986), and it leads to a tendency to compare oneself with others who are less fortunate. This tendency to make *downward social comparisons* (Wills, 1981, 1991) has been shown to have several effects on behavior. Gibbons (1986), for example, found that subjects who were mildly depressed chose to read self-evaluative statements from others who were also experiencing negative feelings more than statements from people who were in happier moods. A similar finding by Psyzczynski, Greenberg and LaPrelle (1985) was that subjects who had just done poorly at a task preferred to learn about similarly failing others than about others who had been successful. It has also been shown that depressed people tend to experience more unpleasantness when talking with nondepressed persons than when talking with people who are also depressed, and they tend to have best friends who are also depressed (Rosenblatt & Greenberg, 1991). Taken together, these studies suggest that when people are unhappy, they are motivated to compare themselves with others who are similarly unhappy and not with others whom they perceive as being better off than themselves.

Moreover, making downward comparisons can improve a person's mood under some conditions. Gibbons (1986) found that depressed subjects experienced an increase in positive affect after reading about someone else who was having troubles. This effect is not limited to people who are depressed. Gibbons and Gerrard (1989) have shown that people who are low in self-esteem experience a greater increase in positive affect after learning about someone who is having trouble coping with personal problems than after hearing about someone who is coping successfully. Subjects high in self-esteem showed the opposite, by experiencing the larger increase in positive affect after learning of someone who was coping successfully (see Figure 4-5). Thus people who are low in self-esteem, like those who are depressed, may be likely to make downward comparisons. This is not surprising, given that depression and low self-esteem are positively related (Kernis, Granneman & Mathis, 1991; Tennen & Herzberger, 1987).

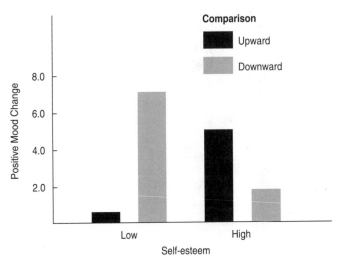

***Figure 4-5.*** Positive change in mood as a function of self-esteem and upward and downward social comparisons. (Drawn from data reported in "Effects of Upward and Downward Social Comparison on Mood States" by F. X. Gibbons and M. Gerrard, *Journal of Social and Clinical Psychology,* 1989, *8,* 14–31.)

Does this mean that people who have high self-esteem never make downward social comparisons? Not necessarily. What it may indicate is that people who have low self-esteem feel more threatened by everyday occurrences, are more motivated to seek out as objects of comparison persons who are worse off than they are, and feel relieved when they compare themselves with such others. If people who are high in self-esteem ever find themselves in a potentially threatening situation, they may be likely to make downward comparisons also. When they do make such comparisons, however, the comparisons may be of a different type from those made by people low in self-esteem. Gibbons and McCoy (1991) found that when people were threatened by failure at a task, those with low self-esteem experienced increased positive affect after learning of others who were going through some difficult problems in adjustment, whereas subjects with high self-esteem did not (see Gibbons & Gerrard, 1989). However, subjects high in self-esteem made downward comparisons in a more active way, by derogating the unfortunate victim. Men high in self-esteem did this by judging the target person to be incompetent, and women high in self-esteem did it by rejecting the target person and rating him or her as less likeable (see Figures 4-6 and 4-7). Thus, threatened people who had high self-esteem made downward comparisons—that is, they judged the object of comparison as worse off than themselves—by *actively constructing* a picture of that person as someone of a relatively low and undesirable station.

Before leaving the subject of social comparisons, we must note that the process does not apply to only behavior in achievement-related situations.

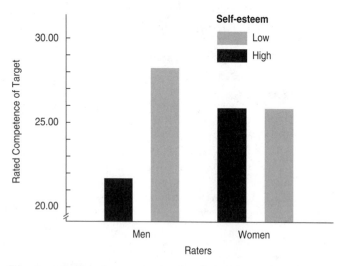

***Figure 4-6.*** Rated competence of unfortunate target person as a function of gender and self-esteem of rater. (Drawn from data reported in "Self-Esteem, Similarity, and Reactions to Active Versus Passive Downward Comparison" by F. X. Gibbons and S. B. McCoy, *Journal of Personality and Social Psychology,* 1991, *60,* 414–424.)

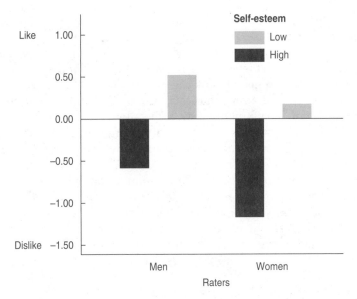

***Figure 4-7.*** Liking for unfortunate target person as a function of gender and self-esteem of rater. (Drawn from data reported in "Self-Esteem, Similarity, and Reactions to Active Versus Passive Downward Comparison" by F. X. Gibbons and S. B. McCoy, *Journal of Personality and Social Psychology,* 1991, *60,* 414–424.)

Taylor and Lobel (1989) have used the revised theory to explain the social behavior of people who are suffering from cancer. In findings that reflect those reported above, they have found that cancer patients tend to evaluate their status as patients by comparing themselves with other patients who are worse off than they are, but they prefer to affiliate with others who are better off. These findings indicate that downward social comparison helps people protect themselves from stress by thinking of others who are worse off, whereas upward social comparison in actual affiliation gives them hope and information that may help them in their battle with the disease.

***Esteem Maintenance.*** The importance of maintaining self-esteem and the ways in which the desire for esteem may motivate action have been described in a multifaceted theory by Tesser (1988). This theory describes social comparisons. It is based on two premises: (1) people act in ways that maintain or increase their self-esteem, and (2) relationships with other people play a role in the esteem-maintenance process. In turn, three major variables are involved in the process: (1) the closeness of the relationship to the other (i.e., the comparison) person, (2) the performance of the other, and (3) the degree to which the other person's performance is relevant to the person's self-definition. For example, success at sports would be a relevant activity to a person who considers herself an athlete.

Certain combinations of these variables cause us to have high self-esteem, whereas others cause us to have low self-esteem. To understand Tesser's approach and what it predicts, consider an example. Suppose that one has a close friend who achieves some important goal. There may be a normal tendency for one to feel good about the other's success to the extent that the friendship allows one to gain some esteem through association with the other. This phenomenon is commonly seen in people who like to refer to their connections with rich or powerful people. By stressing that they know important people, they may "bask in the reflected glory" of the others (Cialdini & Richardson, 1980). What would happen, however, if the friend achieves success in some way that invites an unfavorable comparison with oneself? Suppose, for example, that a person's best friend has just been admitted to a prestigious university but that the person has been denied admission to the same school. When the achievement of the other has been superior in some area that is highly relevant to the subject's performance, there will be no basking in reflected glory but instead a painful sense of rivalry, perhaps mixed with envy.

This theory has implications for emotional behavior and for social motivation. One is that people feel worse when a friend outperforms them on a task of high relevance than when the friend is superior on a task of low relevance (Tesser, Millar & Moore, 1988). In such a situation, the need to maintain self-esteem can also have implications for behavior. Thus, when close friends compete on a task that is important for both of them, the motives of each person will be such that neither will want to peform less well than the other. Tesser and Smith (1980) conducted an experiment in which one member of a pair of friends was caused to perform badly on a task that was said to measure important verbal skills and that member was then given an opportunity to help his friend on the same task. Subjects did not help their friends under these conditions, tending instead to take actions that might hinder the friend's performance. On the other hand, when subjects had failed at a task that was described as unimportant, they did help their friends when given the chance to do so. Thus the combination of closeness and high relevance made the friend's success aversive to failing subjects. Subjects protected their self-esteem following failure by working against being "shown up" by a friend.

The self-esteem maintenance theory also accounts for other social behaviors, such as approaching and avoiding other people. From the theory we would expect a person to be most likely to avoid others when outperformed by the others on some task that is relevant to the person's self-definition. This was shown in a study by Pleban and Tesser (1981), who first informed subjects that they had performed at the 50th percentile on a test and that another person had performed at either the 60th percentile or the 80th. The theory predicts that when the task is relevant for the subject, being outperformed by 80–50 would be harder on the subject's self-esteem than being outperformed by 60–50. Accordingly, subjects would try to put as much distance as possible between themselves and the person at the 80th percentile. When

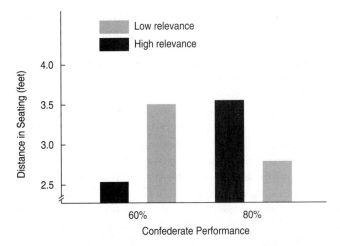

**Figure 4-8.** Distance between self and confederate maintained by subject as a function of confederate's success and relevance of activity for subject. (Adapted from "The Effects of Relevance and Quality of Another's Performance on Interpersonal Closeness" by R. Pleban & A. Tesser, *Social Psychology Quarterly,* 1981, *44,* 278–285.)

subjects were later instructed to sit in the same room as the other person (who was actually a confederate of the experimenter), and when the task had been relevant, they sat farther away from that person when his performance had been at the 80th percentile than when it had been at the 60th. When the task had been irrelevant, the opposite was found (Figure 4-8). Taken together, this finding and the other ones cited above indicate that the need for self-esteem can motivate a number of actions that follow from social comparisons. The major variables are the performance of others, the degree of closeness to the others, and the relevance of the others' performance for the person's self-identity. If we know two of these three variables, the theory allows us to predict the third.

## *The Self and Cognitive Dissonance*

The theory of cognitive dissonance originally proposed by Festinger (1957) was a discrepancy theory of human motivation similar to those discussed in Chapter 3. The main elements of the theory may be summarized briefly (for reviews of the theory, see Aronson, 1969; Cooper & Fazio, 1984; Wicklund & Brehm, 1976):

  **1.**  Whenever a person does something with consequences that are contradictory to the person's beliefs, self-interests, or rationality, the possibility exists of a state of inconsistency or dissonance.

2.  For dissonance to occur, the person must have carried out the behavior willingly and by choice.
3.  The person must also be committed to acceptance of the belief and the inconsistent behavior and must be able to foresee the negative consequences of his or her inconsistency.

A common type of experiment that creates these conditions is one in which a subject is induced to express voluntarily and publicly an opinion that contradicts his or her own belief. It is presumed that when this happens, there is a state of dissonance because of the discrepancy between (1) the person's cognition that he or she has made the statement and (2) the cognition that his or her opinion is inconsistent with the statement. Dissonance is assumed to create increased arousal, which in turn produces negative affect. To reduce or eliminate this affect is what motivates subsequent behavior, which most often takes the form of an attitude change (i.e., the person changes the belief to make it more consistent with the behavior).

Newer approaches to cognitive dissonance interpret the phenomenon in terms of its relationship to the maintenance of self-esteem in behavior. The conditions of the typical dissonance study that uses counterattitudinal behavior create a situation in which self-esteem may be threatened (e.g., Greenwald & Ronis, 1978; Steele, 1988). The implicit scenario for the person is one in which she or he holds the following cognitions: "I have just said or done something freely and with no real justification that flies in the face of what I really believe. I am also an intelligent, moral, and honest person who does not lie or otherwise represent himself falsely." The first cognition follows naturally from the person's behavior in the experiment. The second follows from his sense of self-worth. The dissonance in the cognitive dissonance experiment does not arise from a clash between beliefs and behavior, but from a discrepancy between what the person has actually done and an ideal image of the self. If the person changes her attitude under such conditions, it is because she wishes to bring her ideal self (i.e., what she believes) into harmony with her behavior.

# MOTIVATION AND SELF-DEFENSIVE STRATEGIES

Because people need to think well of themselves, they typically use cognitively mediated strategies to maintain self-esteem. Some of these strategies are used *before* actions are carried out and serve thereby to insulate or defend the person against the consequences of possible failure. An example is downward social comparison, which we considered earlier in this chapter. People sometimes buffer themselves against the consequences of anticipated failure by comparing themselves with others who are worse off than themselves, hoping thereby to put themselves in a relatively good light. Another such antici-patory approach to expected failure is self-handicapping, which will be dis-cussed below. Other strategies are invoked *after* failure or other esteem-threatening consequences of action occur, so that the full impact of those consequences for the self does not have to be faced. Some of these will be dis-cussed later. The role of all of these strategies within the general motivational scheme of the individual is the same: to remove some of the negative affect that normally accompanies a discrepancy between the ideal self and the actual self, either before or after the discrepancy is realized.

## Self-Handicapping

One strategy that people use in anticipation of a negative outcome is *self-handicapping,* which is the deliberate creation of conditions by which failure can be attributed to causes outside the person's control. In introducing this concept, Jones and Berglas (1978) observed that

> *(B)y finding or creating impediments that make good performance less likely, the strategist nicely protects his sense of self-competence. If the person does poorly, the source of the failure is externalized in the impediment (p. 201).*

One means of self-handicapping is to ingest performance-blocking drugs prior to activity at which the drug user expects to perform badly. By taking drugs under such conditions, users take on a self-imposed handicap that then serves as a convenient excuse when things go wrong. Berglas and Jones (1978) found evidence to support this idea among men but not women. In their study, men who were uncertain and anxious about an upcoming task self-handicapped more than men who were less anxious about the task. Uncertainty concerning the task was induced by giving the subjects noncon-tingent feedback of success on an earlier task (i.e., telling them they had done well when it was obvious that the task had been unsolvable). Subjects were then given a choice between two drugs prior to performing the second task: one that would supposedly enhance performance and one that would inhibit performance. Among the male subjects, those who had been given noncontin-gent success feedback following the first task chose the performance-*inhibit-ing* drug more than the performance-enhancing one. In other words, they opted for a self-handicapping strategy. Men who had enjoyed success on the earlier task that was contingent on their performance tended to choose the performance enhancer. Why this effect was not found for women could not be explained from the data.

Although the original conception of self-handicapping traced the origin of the practice to a desire for a good self-image (as the quotation above implies), others have argued that the self-handicapper is really trying to maintain a good image in the eyes of other people. As we will observe later, the distinction between private and public images is not always clear. However, some students of self-handicapping have stressed the socially protective nature of the process, insisting that self-handicapping is essentially a strategy for presenting oneself to others and not for fooling oneself (e.g., Kolditz & Arkin, 1982).

Numerous tactics can be used in the pursuit of self-handicapping. Drug use has been noted. Other devices include reduced effort (Psyzczynski & Greenberg, 1983), the choice of unfavorable settings (Shepperd & Arkin, 1989), and even the assumption of symptoms of disorders to which failure can be attributed (Smith, Snyder & Perkins, 1983; Smith, Snyder & Handelsman, 1982). Self-handicapping can be an efficacious strategy for protecting the self. It has been shown, for example, to help people preserve a high level of self-esteem following failure (Rhodewalt, Morf, Hazlett & Fairfield, 1991).

## Excuse Making

Everyone, at some time, makes excuses for certain things that he or she does without really thinking about it much. Making excuses for failure or other negative outcomes is another attempt to attribute the undesired outcomes to external and uncontrollable causes rather than to internal and controllable ones. This is done in an attempt to avoid the loss of esteem and the negative affect that would result from attributing negative outcomes to the latter. It may also be done to avoid incurring the anger of other people who may be caused inconvenience by our failures. Weiner, Amirkhan, Folkes, and Verrette (1987) found that when people seek to explain why they miss important appointments, they tend to make excuses based on attributions of uncontrollability and unintentionality. For example, a person may explain missing an important appointment with the excuse "I was sick" or "I had car trouble." When subjects were asked whether such an excuse would be accepted without anger by the other party to the appointment, they expressed the belief that it would. Thus excuse making involves the same self-protective attributional processes after the fact as those used in self-handicapping before the fact.

In excuse making, people make any or all of three types of judgment about their failures (Snyder, Higgins & Stucky, 1983). One is a *consensus* judgment, in which blame for failure is attenuated by arguing that failure is consensual (e.g., "I failed on the task, but so did most of the other people who performed it"). Such a judgment tends to shift the blame for failure away from the person and on to the situation (the difficult task). A second judgment in excuse making is *distinctiveness* of the failure ("I failed on this task because it is unusual; on other tasks I would have done well"). Again, the failure is laid at the feet of the task rather than the person, not because of its difficulty but because of something peculiar in its nature. Finally, *consistency* judgments may be made: the person has failed, but the failure is not typical and must be attributed to unusual circumstances ("I just had a bad day"). In this way the failure is made specific to the particular case and is not treated as typical of the person.

People select excuses with specific audiences in mind, and they tailor their excuse making to make it plausible to the chosen recipient. Sometimes the audience is the excuse maker, and the result is what is usually referred to as "kidding oneself." The process usually goes on below the level of awareness; the self-deluding person is not conscious and deliberate in this practice. In fact, the "self-kidder" usually considers his or her excuses, which would be correctly labeled as such if other people gave them, as "reasons" for behavior (Snyder, 1989). Excuse making sometimes involves external audiences, of course, and then the process tends to be more deliberate and conscious. It involves a give-and-take in which the audience's reactions to the excuses shape and direct the level of excuse giving until a tacit agreement between the person and the audience is reached regarding the extent to which the person is responsible for the outcome.

Does excuse making have any utility? Apparently it does. Snyder and Higgins (1988) reviewed a number of studies involving the effects of excuse making on several outcomes and concluded that the practice leads to reduced anxiety and negative affect, to increased self-esteem, to less depression and improved general health, and to relatively good performance on several laboratory and real-world tasks. In general, therefore, the excuse-making strategy allows one to maintain one's sense of being a competent individual with control over his or her life outcomes, and this translates into direct benefits for the person.

## Attributional Bias

Most people are familiar with the typical politician's tactic of taking full credit for everything good that happens during her or his term of office but denying all responsibility for the bad events. This self-serving approach to assigning causes to events applies to more than just elected officeholders, however. It is a commonly used method for the protection of self-esteem after failure or other negative consequences of action. That people are motivated to make *self-serving attributions* of causality (i.e., attributing successes to internal and personal causes and failures to external ones) has been documented in several major reviews (e.g., Bradley, 1978; Zuckerman, 1979). The self-serving attributional bias is a common phenomenon that has been shown in studies both inside and outside of the laboratory setting. In one interesting example of the latter, Smith and Manard (1980) asked applicants for medical school to indicate the amount of importance they assigned to several reasons for the acceptance or rejection of an application. They found that controllable factors, such as the personal interview, the applicant's desire, and work and research backgrounds, were considered keys to acceptance, whereas the relatively uncontrollable factors of lack of personal connections and ethnic background were regarded as prime reasons for rejection.

An interesting facet of the self-serving bias is that men practice it more than women on tasks that are typically considered to be masculine, whereas women engage in it more than men on typically feminine tasks. In one study

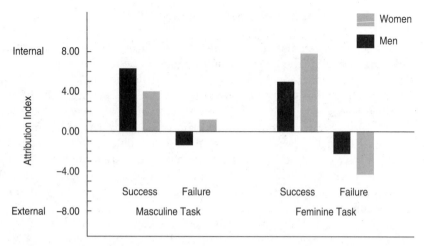

**Figure 4-9.** Internal and external attributions for success and failure as a function of gender typing of task and gender of subject. (Drawn from data reported in "Sex Differences in Attributions for Sex-Typed Tasks" by D. Rosenfield and W. G. Stephan, *Journal of Personality,* 1978, *46,* 244–259.)

that showed this, Rosenfield and Stephan (1978) arranged for male and female subjects to either fail or succeed on a task that supposedly assessed either a "masculine personality" or a "feminine personality." Each subject was then asked to describe the degree to which success or failure was due to (1) skill, (2) effort, (3) the difficulty of the test, and (4) luck. Ratings on the first two dimensions indicate the attribution of success–failure to internal causes, and ratings on the third and fourth indicate attribution of the outcome to external factors. When the overall magnitude of the two external ratings was subtracted from the overall magnitude of the internal ratings, an attribution index was obtained, so that positive numbers indicate internal attributions and negative numbers external ones. The results of the study (Figure 4-9) show that men made more self-serving attributions (internal for success, external for failure) than women on the masculine task, whereas women made more self-serving attributions than men on the feminine task. The findings suggest that persons of both genders feel a strong need to maintain feelings of competence on gender-relevant tasks and therefore attribute successes and failures at such tasks in such a way as to maintain these feelings.

## Alcohol Use and Avoidance of Self-Focus

When people wish to avoid facing the consequences of failure, they may attempt to retreat into an altered state of consciousness. In a series of studies, Hull and his associates have shown that consumption of alcohol varies as a function of self-awareness and personal success or failure. Highly self-aware people have been found to drink more following failure than following successful experiences, whereas less self-aware people do not. This finding has been reported in both laboratory experiments in which success and failure were manipulated and studies outside of the laboratory involving persons with alcohol problems (Hull, Levenson, Young & Sher, 1983; Hull & Young, 1983; Hull, Young & Jouriles, 1986). Hull and his colleagues have concluded that alcohol is used as a means of blocking self-awareness, which is especially painful after failure.

## Symbolic Self-Completion

People project their sense of identity to others in terms that are largely symbolic. Those who have amassed wealth display their fortunes by purchasing symbols like expensive homes and automobiles. Adolescents show that they are in touch with their culture by wearing symbolically valued articles of clothing, like name-brand athletic shoes or designer jeans. University students often seek social status by affiliating with the right sororities and fraternities. Every person actively constructs a social identity built of symbols that are recognized by people whose approval is important.

In the same way, threats to one's social identity involve the threatened or actual loss of important symbols. For example, an athlete whose skills become diminished with advancing age will often experience a crisis as he or she realizes that a valued part of the self is being lost. What do people do in such circumstances? Experience tells us that they often try to compensate for the loss of some symbols by accentuating and calling to attention alternative ones. This process has been called *symbolic self-completion* (Wicklund & Gollwitzer, 1982). The basic assumption behind the process is that the various symbolic indicators of a person's self-definition may be substituted for one another. If, for example, a person loses self-esteem for some reason, he or she may attempt to regain it by referring to other aspects of life that confer esteem.

In a study designed to test this possibility, Gollwitzer, Wicklund, and Hilton (1982) instructed one group of subjects to write down at least six mistakes that they had made while carrying out activities in some area of achievement with which they were closely identified. Other subjects were asked to list mistakes that they had made in areas outside their main interest. All subjects were then allowed to write essays describing themselves with respect to their areas of interest. The results showed that subjects who had first acknowledged errors in their interest areas spent more time writing self-descriptive essays than did those who had listed errors in irrelevant areas. Admitting mistakes in self-relevant characteristics apparently created a need to assert other strong points through the written essays.

The strength of people's need to maintain esteem through symbolic self-completion has been suggested in a study by Gollwitzer and Wicklund (1985)

*Affiliation with groups such as sororities and fraternities can provide a desired social status for some students.*

in which self-completing subjects were shown to be highly insensitive to the feelings of others with whom they were interacting. Male subjects in this study were first informed either that they had personalities that were ideal for success in activity areas that were important to them, or that they had personalities that were not ideal. Later each man interacted with a young woman who was said to prefer either men who were modest in talking about themselves or men who were self-assertive and who liked to emphasize their strong qualities. Men who had been told that they possessed a nonideal personality talked about their qualities more than those who had been told that their personality was ideal for success in their areas of interest. This repre-

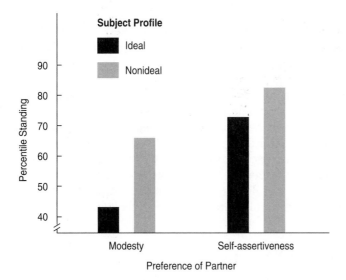

**Figure 4-10.** Positivity of self-descriptions as a function of prior feedback and preference of partner for self-descriptions. (Drawn from data reported in "Self-Symbolizing and Neglect of Others' Perspectives" by P. M. Gollwitzer and R. A. Wicklund, *Journal of Personality and Social Psychology,* 1985, *48,* 702–715.)

sented self-completing behavior. Moreover, they engaged in this self-completion even after having been been informed specifically that their interaction partners preferred men who were more modest and less self-assertive. Figure 4-10 illustrates this by showing how the subjects assessed their standing (in percentile terms) relative to other men on the abilities in question. Thus men who were engaging in self-completing behaviors (i.e., the ones with nonideal profiles) described themselves as superior to 66% of all men on the self-relevant attributes in question, even when they had been told that the young woman listening to them did not approve of such boasting. This suggests that the need for symbolic self-completion is a powerful motive that can override other social motives, such as receiving approval from others in normal interaction.

## Self-Defensive Behavior as Denial and Withdrawal

To understand how the various kinds of self-protective behavior described above fit into the overall motivational scheme that we are following, refer back to Figures 3-3 and 4-1. Recall that when one's attributional search reveals that the discrepancy between a goal and one's actual position while striving to reach that goal is such that little or nothing can be done to reduce it (see Figure 3-3), denial of the discrepancy is the likely outcome. We can now see that when some self-ideal is the goal, denial may consist of self-protective strategies to minimize the distance between the ideal and the actual self. To use the conceptual language of Figure 4-1, we might say that when the person is convinced that the probability of being able to match the real self to the ideal is extremely low, he or she will "mentally withdraw" from any more comparisons. Self-defensive behavior can be regarded as a sort of mental retreat from facing the discomfiting lack of fit between the self that is desired and the self that really exists. Thus we might speculate that self-protective devices such as those described in the preceding sections are most likely to occur when (1) the person feels threatened and (2) other types of motivated behavior are considered unlikely to alleviate the problem.

# ESTEEM: PERSONAL OR SOCIAL?

The reader may have noticed something about the studies and theories reviewed in this chapter: concepts like "esteem," "self-concept," and "self-defensiveness" have been used in a somewhat ambiguous way. At times they have referred to a process of personal and private *self-esteem*—that is, a good feeling that a person has about herself or himself that arises from performing at or near the idealized goal level. At other times the concepts have indicated *social esteem*—that is, a good feeling derived from the realization that one's performance is approved of by other people. This ambiguity does not arise through carelessness on the writer's part. Often in social psychological research it is virtually impossible to distinguish between the two and know the real source of a person's affect following success or failure. One reason is that experiments are often not designed to separate the two, so that at the experiment's end we may have grounds for assuming that the subject really has increased self-esteem, but we also may be unable to rule out the possibility that social approval is driving at least some of the affect. A second reason is that in life the two probably occur simultaneously much of the time. Actions that lead to increased self-esteem do not usually take place in a complete social vacuum, and both types of reward may therefore follow good performance. A third possibility is that the two sources of esteem are inextricably bound together and subsumed by a higher motivational synthesis. Part of the self-esteem that one sometimes experiences may be valued because the sort of competence and personal achievement that produce it are themselves socially valued. We may, in other words, derive a large part of our self-esteem from knowing that we have carried out certain social responsibilities and earned a place of respect in the community. This matter will be considered in greater depth in a subsequent chapter.

We must at least note it now, however, because in the two chapters to follow a distinction will be made between two types of motivational states: (1)

states that appear to be under internal control and are aimed at the accomplishment of personal and idiosyncratic ends and (2) states that appear to be based on accomplishing social ends. In Chapter 6 this distinction will arise in connection with the matter of personal control over the outcomes of behavior. We will turn to that problem next.

## CHAPTER SUMMARY

1.   The various goals for which people work may be regarded as means to the attainment of the larger goal of a desired identity or *self*. Material and interpersonal goals may be sought largely because they allow the person to gain the esteem of others or to enhance his or her self-esteem.

2.   People become self-aware when certain stimuli cause their attention to become focused inward rather than on the environment. Self-focus leads people to become aware of any existing discrepancy between the self-as-is and the desired or ideal self. Recognition of such a discrepancy motivates behavior designed to reduce or eliminate it. People monitor their behavior to judge both the existence and the extent of discrepancies and whether they are reducing such discrepancies at a desired rate.

3.   The actual self as perceived is a cognitive *schema* by means of which the person understands his or her attributes and the relationships among them. The person is also aware of several possible selves that he or she is capable of becoming; some of these are desired and others are avoided as undesirable. Motivation to attain a desired self is augmented by motivation to avoid undesired selves.

4.   A person may choose as a desired self either one that is fashioned after a personal *ideal* or one that is enjoined upon him or her by others (an *ought* self). Discrepancies between the actual self and an ideal self result in feelings of dejection, whereas actual–ought discrepancies result in feelings of agitation. These affective states motivate associated depressed or agitated behaviors.

5.   People need and seek self-esteem. One way in which they do this is through reacting to failure by comparing themselves with others who are worse off than themselves. Such *downward social comparison* is more typical of people who are depressed or low in self-esteem than of those who do not show these characteristics. People also work to maintain esteem by adjusting the social distance between themselves and successful others. Social distance is minimized when close associates perform well on tasks that are irrelevant to the person, but it is increased when those associates perform well on tasks that are relevant to the subject's performance.

**6.** Cognitive dissonance, once described as the product of a discrepancy between strongly held beliefs and behavior, is now held to be the result of a discrepancy between an actual self that behaves inconsistently with beliefs and an ideal self that does not. The discrepancy leads to loss of self-esteem and a consequent change in beliefs or behaviors; the underlying motivation is the restoration of self-esteem.

**7.** A sense of failure to realize a sought-after self is guarded against through the use of several self-protective strategies. *Self-handicapping* is the creation of conditions prior to performance that facilitate failure and hence are readily available as an impersonal cause to which the expected failure can be attributed. Several such handicaps have been identified, such as ingesting performance-inhibiting drugs, selecting surroundings that do not allow good performance, and assuming debilitating symptoms. *Excuse making* and using *self-serving attributions* also help to protect self-esteem. In both cases, as in self-handicapping, failures are attributed to causes that are outside the person and beyond the person's power to control. People may also compensate for failure or loss in one sphere of life by emphasizing and displaying symbols of success from other areas, a process called *symbolic self-completion*.

**8.** Distinguishing between self-esteem and social esteem is often difficult. The two tend to occur together in many situations. In addition, self-esteem may to a large extent be a product of social esteem.

## CHAPTER 5

# MOTIVATION FOR COMPETENCE AND CONTROL

## CHAPTER OUTLINE

A belief in individual freedom has long been a cardinal element of faith in the Western democratic tradition of government. Freedom presupposes a large measure of personal control over the conditions and the outcomes of one's behavior. To be free is to make choices, to exercise individual responsibility, to act with at least some liberty from external constraint, and, finally, to reap the rewards or punishments of one's actions. Given the centrality of these notions in our culture, it is not surprising that psychologists have paid a great deal of attention to the question of personal control and its effects.

The experimental study of the role played in behavior by having control over outcomes was originally carried out in animal psychology laboratories. In an early experiment, Mowrer and Viek (1948) demonstrated that when rats were shocked while eating, they became immobile and ceased their consumption of food unless they were able to terminate the shock by jumping up and down. Animals that could make such a response soon learned to do so and continued to eat, even though the situation was arranged so that they received as much shock overall as did the animals that were helpless. Merely having some control over the stressful stimulus reduced the power of that stimulus to induce stress.

That different levels of stress are induced by making punishment controllable or uncontrollable was verified in a later experiment by Weiss (1971). Pairs of rats were run in adjacent chambers and wired together in such a way that both received the same series of electric shocks. One rat could terminate the shocks for both itself and its yoked mate by making a simple response, but the mate was totally helpless. After 48 hours of this treatment, the animals were subjected to biopsies, which revealed that the helpless rats had a higher incidence of gastrointestinal ulcers than did those that had been in control.

Early studies also found that control over stressors affects stress levels in human subjects. One of the earliest demonstrations came from a study by Staub, Tursky, and Schwartz (1971), who discovered that humans manifested greater tolerance for pain in response to electric shocks if they could determine both the time of onset and the amount of increment from one shock to the next in a series than if such control was impossible. At about the same time Geer, Davison, and Gatchel (1970) found that humans manifested less stress in response to shock if they merely believed that they had control than they did if they were helpless, even though they actually had no control at all. At least some of the effects of control thus appear to be mediated by cognitive mechanisms.

Other research showed that among both humans (e.g., Pervin, 1963) and animals (e.g., Furedy & Biederman, 1976) controllable stressors were preferred to uncontrollable ones, thereby strengthening the conclusion that control is a desirable state at least most of the time and for most organisms. This has engendered the idea that people are motivated to achieve control over the outcomes of their behavior. Since the time of the studies cited in this historical introduction, theory and research on the role of control in human motivation and behavior have been extensive.

In this chapter we will review some of the current contributions to conceptualizations of control motivation. These contributions reflect two broadly defined viewpoints. One emphasizes a fundamental motive for mastery, manifested in a need to feel competent and effective in dealing with the events of everyday life. This viewpoint assumes that our desire for control arises out of this mastery motive. In the first part of the chapter, this position and some of the constructs that it has produced will be examined and reviewed. Not everyone traces the desire for control to such a motive, however. Several investigators have sought to explain the importance of control by proposing only that it is useful and adaptive and that it can lead to valuable outcomes. This more utilitarian approach will be reviewed in the second section of the chapter.

# MOTIVATION FOR COMPETENCE

The idea that people follow some basic motive to achieve control over their environments is usually traced back to the theorizing of Robert White. In a now-classic paper, White (1959) concluded that the single most important motive is one that he called *effectance,* defined as "an innate need to manipulate the environment" (p. 318). This motive was said to dominate the ongoing behavior of all living organisms, including humans, at all times except during brief periods, called "homeostatic crises," when basic needs like hunger, thirst, and avoidance of danger must be satisfied. Once these crises have been met and overcome, the person goes back to mastery-oriented behavior. The goal of the effectance motive is the desirable state called *competence,* which is marked by control and mastery of the personal environment.

## Socialization of the Mastery Motive

COMPETENCE AND APPROVAL AS BASIC MOTIVES. What White (1959) called the effectance motive is now usually referred to as the motive for mastery on the grounds that successful manipulation of the environment leads to personal control. White speculated that this motive is at least partly inherent, and some recent evidence tends to lend indirect support to that idea. It has been shown, for example, that there is a heritability component in the level of activity that children manifest within their surroundings (Buss & Plomin, 1984), suggesting that some children may actively interact with their environments more than others as a result of some genetic factor in their personalities. In addition, Kagan and his colleagues have found that children reveal differential levels of inhibition in approaching novel persons or situations from a very early age, and that these temperamental tendencies remain stable as the child develops. Some children are open and fearless in interacting with their social environments, whereas others are inhibited and fearful. Kagan and his colleagues have suggested that these differences may be at least partly due to genetic inheritance (e.g., Kagan, Reznick & Snidman, 1988).

Despite suggestions of genetic influences on the person's level of interaction with the environment, however, most subsequent research on effectance motivation has treated it as something that is learned through the process of socialization. In a major extension and refinement of White's theory, Harter (1981) proposed that children learn two different motives from their parents, or other socializing agents, as they develop. One is for mastery and the other is for dependence on other people. The key to which of these motives will be predominant in the child's life is how the major socializing agents react to the child's independent attempts at mastery. These attempts take the forms of different domains of mastery; the most important for children are cognitive, physical, and social (e.g., taking on intellectual or academic challenges, attempting to have physical attractiveness or prowess, seeking social acceptance and peer support).

The child's socializing agents may approve of and reinforce these mastery attempts or they may not. If they do, and especially if they combine this reinforcement with a relative lack of reinforcement for dependent behaviors, the child will be steered on a course of developing motivation for mastery. It should be noted that what is reinforced is the *attempt* at mastery, not only the successful attainment of it. Even failed attempts must be reinforced if mastery motivation is to be developed.

This process, which is shown schematically in Figure 5-1, goes through two critical intervening steps. First, the child who has been rewarded for mastery attempts comes to *internalize* the approval that the socializing agents deliver. This process, which emerges as the child develops and attains maturity, involves the transfer of reinforcement from the adult to the child and is manifested in self-reward for attempted mastery. After the child has developed the capacity for self-reward, the acceptance of mastery-related goals, such as achievement and independence, is likewise internalized and made part of the child's value system. The upshot of this is that the child comes to feel competent and in control of her or his environment. Challenging activities now become a source of anticipated pleasure, and success at these activities increases the mastery motive that had originated the process. In this way, a cycle in motivated activity is completed.

Nonreinforcement or disapproval of independent mastery attempts creates a pattern of development that is the mirror image of what has just been described. Such nonreinforcement, especially when it is paired with reinforcement for dependency on adults, leads to development of a chronic need for social approval and an acceptance of goals that are defined or assigned by other people. This eventually causes the child to develop a sense of incompetence and of being controlled by his or her environment. Instead of eliciting the anticipation of pleasure, challenging activities foster anxiety and fear, which decrease the original level of mastery motivation.

In a study related to Harter's model of internalization, Ryan and Connell (1989) distinguished between *internalization* of social values, a process by which a person takes in these values and accepts them as part of his or her own value system, and *introjection*, in which values are taken in because society demands it. The study involved social and academic achievement behavior in school children. Ryan and Connell proposed that children could be motivated to perform well in school and to be prosocial in their behavior toward others either because they had internalized such values or because they accepted their obligation to conform and had therefore introjected them. It was found that children who identified with academic values had higher levels of mastery motivation than those who introjected. Identifiers also expended greater effort in school and enjoyed school more. In the prosocial

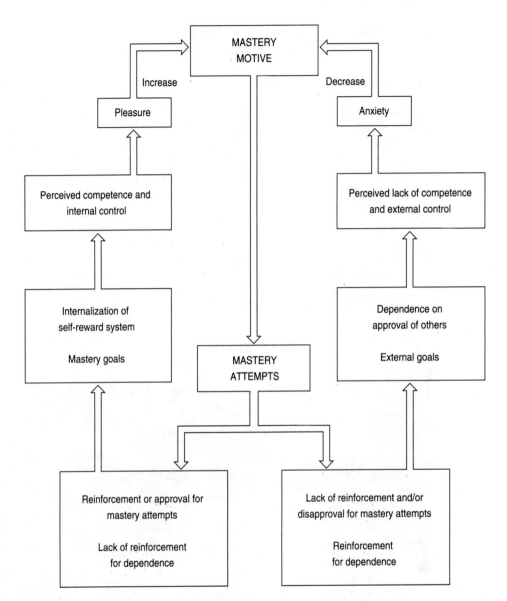

**Figure 5-1.** Development of mastery motivation and dependency motivation. (Adapted from "A Model of Mastery Motivation in Children: Individual Differences and Developmental Change" by S. Harter in *Aspects of the Development of Competence: The Minnesota Symposia on Child Psychology,* Vol. 14, edited by W. A. Collins, 1981, Hillsdale, NJ: Erlbaum.)

domain, those who identified were superior to those who introjected in terms of empathy, moral reasoning, prosocial attitudes, and relatedness to significant others.

The distinction that Harter (1981) made between the person who internalizes mastery goals and the one who becomes dependent on goals approved of by others has also been emphasized by Dweck and her associates (Dweck & Leggett, 1988). Dweck defines two types of goals that people are motivated to seek. They are similar to the ones that Harter defined: *performance* goals, which are met through gaining the approval of others and avoiding disapproval, and *learning* goals, the purpose of which is to increase the person's sense of competence.

***THE MASTERY-ORIENTED PATTERN.*** The type of goal typically adopted by a child is associated with a dominant pattern of affect, cognition, and behavior. The *mastery-oriented pattern* is usually associated with the adoption of learning goals, and the *helpless pattern* is associated with the adoption of performance goals. There is one exception to this rule, however: when a person has a positive idea of his or her ability, even the adoption of performance goals leads to mastery motivation. Elliott and Dweck (1988) discovered this in an experiment in which children's perceptions of their ability levels were manip-

*Students who identify with academic values tend to develop strong motives to master the subjects they study.*

ulated with bogus information. In addition, the children were led by the experimenter's instructions to adopt either a learning or a performance goal. When a learning goal was set, children behaved in a mastery-oriented way regardless of their perceived level of ability. However, when a performance goal was set, children who thought themselves to be high in ability behaved in a mastery-oriented way, whereas children with low perceived ability fell into a helpless pattern of behavior. This study therefore establishes the strong link between mastery motivation and the adoption of goals pertaining to self-improvement.

Dweck and her colleagues argue that whether a person adopts performance or mastery goals is related to the implicit theory of intelligence and ability that a person holds. People who believe that intelligence is fixed and unchangeable have the greatest tendency to adopt performance goals because they believe that the attainment of mastery is constrained by limited ability. Those who adopt the view that intelligence is fluid and can be increased tend to set learning goals for themselves because they believe that such goals can be reached with sufficient effort (Dweck & Leggett, 1988).

Mastery and helplessness orientations influence more than the effectiveness of behavior. Diener and Dweck (1978) showed that children whose orientation is basically helpless manifest cognitive and affective responses to failure that are different from those of mastery-oriented children. In particular, helplessness-oriented children form negative cognitions about themselves, such as by attributing their failure to deficiencies in memory, intelligence, and problem-solving ability. They also experience high levels of negative affect and engage in verbalizations during failure, often of a boastful and self-aggrandizing nature (Elliott & Dweck, 1988). Clearly, then, the helpless orientation, which is an outgrowth of the adoption of performance goals and, before that, of the assumption of a fixed level of ability, has a number of harmful effects on the person and on his or her performance.

**STANDARDS OF COMPETENCE.**    In order to understand the nature of mastery motivation, it is also necessary to know something about the standards that people use to determine whether or not they are performing competently. These vary considerably over the course of a person's development from childhood to adulthood. Harter (1990) has identified four basic domains in which people judge themselves throughout their life span: *cognitive competence, physical competence, peer acceptance,* and *behavioral conduct.* We have already encountered the first three of these (see pages 109–110). The last encompasses such activities as living morally, maintaining a sense of humor, and providing for oneself and one's family. These domains are defined relatively simply in very young children, but they form the basis for a widening circle of more complex competence judgments later on in life.

People of all ages examine the extent to which they fit idealized models of competence in each of these domains (the nature and origin of these models will be described below). In doing this, they are comparing their actual selves (or at least that part of their selves that pertains to abilities) with the idealized level of competence (see Chapter 4). When such comparisons are made in domains that are considered important by the person, a negative discrepancy between perceived and ideal levels of competence may cause the person to lose some self-esteem. The larger the perceived negative discrepancy, the more self-esteem the person may lose.

In several studies, Harter (1990) has investigated the magnitude of correlation between competence-discrepancy judgments in important domains of life and the person's sense of self-worth. She has shown that children as young as those in the lower grades of elementary school make such discrepancy judgments and that their ratings of self-worth are correlated with those judgments. The same correlations are found in persons at all later age levels as well. Across all age groups, a large discrepancy between the real and the ideal selves is associated with low ratings of worth. The domain in which discrepancies between the actual and the ideal correlate most highly with feelings of self worth is *physical appearance*. This is true at all ages. The greater the discrepancy between actual and idealized appearance, the more likely a person is to have a low sense of self-esteem. This is not to say, however, that physical appearance is the only important source of self-worth. Among college students, for example, social acceptance, job competence, scholastic achievement, and competence in romantic relations all contributed significantly to overall self-worth. Among adults, competence as a provider, personal morality, and ability to manage a household were also found to be important contributors.

One question remains, however: What constitutes the standard by which the ideal is defined? When we say that a person recognizes that she or he is not performing at some ideal level of competence, what do we mean? Standards may come from two sources. One is the person's autonomous and internalized set of values, and the other is the norm for the activity set by other people. To take a simple example, suppose a man who competes in long-distance races wants to determine how good a runner he is. He may use a standard derived from his own past performance, so that, for example, if he ran a race in a certain time last year, he expects to run it in even less time this year. If he fails to attain the new standard, he will be disappointed and may suffer some loss in self-esteem.

This sort of process, involving a comparison within the person's life at different times, is called a *temporal comparison* (Albert, 1977). It is to be contrasted with *social comparison,* which involves comparing one's performance with that of other people (see Chapter 4). The relative use of temporal versus social comparisons in setting standards for competence and mastery is influenced by development. Very young children tend to use autonomous nonsocial standards (e.g., Dweck & Elliott, 1983), but as children mature they shift to make more use of social comparisons. This shift coincides with the beginning of school and probably reflects the use of social reinforcement in the classroom setting (Veroff, 1969). As development proceeds further, however, some children—those who have a relatively high level of ability—return to the use of autonomous standards. Ruble and Flett (1988) gave children from second-, fourth-, and sixth-grade classes a set of mathematics problems along with an option of obtaining information that either (1) provided an evaluation of the child's performance or (2) provided information on how well other children had performed. Regardless of their ability level, second-graders preferred social comparisons to autonomous ones. The choices of fourth- and sixth-graders were different. At those age levels, children with high ability preferred autonomous comparisons over social ones, whereas children of low ability continued to opt for social comparisons. Thus, as the children grew older, the brighter ones became less interested in what other children did and more interested in testing their own levels of mastery and success.

At the opposite end of the development continuum, we find among older adults a liking for social comparisons similar to that of younger children. To some extent this is because of a declining level of skills. For example, a woman who as a 30-year-old had always judged her ability as a golfer in terms of how good a score she could attain may find when she is 65 that temporal comparison of her present ability with that of past years reveals a decline. When this happens, she may begin to judge her competence by comparing her game to that of other 65-year-old women whose skills have likewise deteriorated. This was shown in a study reported by Frey and Ruble (1990), who asked long-distance runners between 20 and 77 years of age to describe their target goals in running a race. The results, shown in Figure

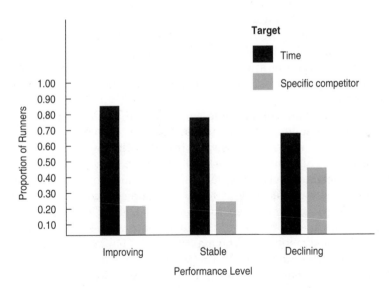

***Figure 5-2.*** Proportion of runners reporting comparison target as time or another runner. (Drawn from data reported in "Strategies for Comparative Evaluation: Maintaining a Sense of Competence Across the Life Span" by K. S. Frey and D. N. Ruble in *Competence Considered,* edited by R. J. Sternberg and J. Kolligian, Jr., 1990, New Haven, CT: Yale University Press.)

5-2, reveal that among runners of all ages who were still improving, a greater proportion preferred comparison with an ideal running time rather than with other runners. Runners whose skills were declining also preferred comparison with an ideal time, but not as much as those who were still improving.

We can summarize briefly what we have reviewed in this section. The mastery (or effectance) motive described by White is determined, at least in part, by the person's history of reinforcement for early attempts at mastery. It is, moreover, pervasive across the important domains of life, and it provides a goal—the desired state of competence—that guides behavior according to the principles of action control that we reviewed earlier. People are motivated to attain competence by reducing discrepancies between current performance and ideal performance, regardless of by what standard the latter is determined, and failure to do so results in loss of self-esteem. We are ready now to consider motivation for competence in an applied context by examining the role that it plays in interest for tasks and intrinsic motivation.

# COMPETENCE AND INTRINSIC MOTIVATION

## Effects of Rewards on Interest

One important aspect of the distinction between mastery and approval motivation is the effect that each has on the amount of interest that people take in activities. Interest is commonly referred to as *intrinsic motivation* (Deci, 1975) because it refers to the motive to carry out some course of action when there is no external reward, such as material goods or the approval of others. One of the more interesting findings to come out of studies of the interplay of the two motives is that external reinforcers sometimes weaken or destroy intrinsic interest.

The initial study on this problem was reported by Deci (1971), who gave subjects a puzzle to solve. After an initial baseline period in which subjects worked on the puzzle, some subjects were told that they would be given a payment in money for continuing to perform the same task. Following the task phase of the experiment and payment of the money to those who were to receive it, a free period was provided in which subjects could either continue to play with the puzzle or switch to other activities. Figure 5-3 shows the number of minutes spent on the puzzle during each of the three phases of the experiment. Obviously, subjects who expected to be paid worked at the puzzle longer than those who did not until the payment was actually made. During the third period of the experiment, however, unpaid subjects showed a slightly greater tendency to play with the puzzle, whereas paid subjects showed a dramatic loss of interest in it.

At about the same time as he was observing this loss of intrinsic motivation following a money reward, Deci (1971) made another interesting discov-

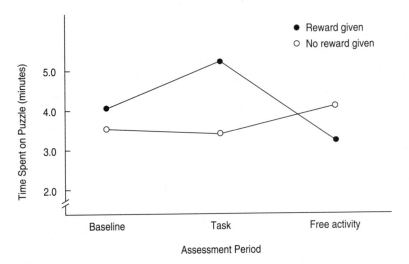

***Figure 5-3.*** Time spent on puzzle during baseline, task, and free activity periods. (Drawn from data reported in "Effects of Externally Mediated Rewards on Intrinsic Motivation" by E. L. Deci, *Journal of Personality and Social Psychology,* 1971, *18,* 105–115.)

ery. When he gave subjects verbal approval for performing the puzzle, their intrinsic interest in the task did not diminish. Verbal reinforcement took the form of statements such as "Very good. That's the fastest this one has been done yet." Instead of producing a decrease in intrinsic motivation, this sort of praise increased such interest relative to that shown by unrewarded subjects. The most obvious feature of the verbal reinforcers given by Deci (1971) was the message that they gave to the subjects: that the subjects' performance was superior and that they were manifesting a high level of competence on the task.

Praise and encouragement of this sort need not be limited to verbal statements. Material rewards are often given less as payments for work done than as tokens of appreciation for work that is done well. For example, an employee may be given a raise by her supervisor because she has exceeded expectations. This sort of "merit" raise is likely to cause the recipient to take a greater interest in her job than she had previously taken. Thus the key to whether or not a reward decreases interest in a task lies not in the characteristics of the reward but in the *information* that it conveys. If the information raises the recipient's sense of competence, it will engender more interest. If it causes the person to perceive that rewards are nothing more than payment for a job done, it will lead to less interest. The reason for the latter is that when payment is made only for services rendered, it detracts from perceptions of competence by focusing attention on the economic aspect of the payment.

## Cognitive Evaluation Theory

From these original observations and other empirical findings on the relationship of rewards to intrinsic interest, Deci and Ryan (1985, 1987) formulated a general *cognitive evaluation theory* to describe the effects of certain environmental events on motivation. The environmental events in question are those that are "relevant to the initiation or regulation of behavior" (p. 62), or, in other words, anything that causes people to begin and sustain activity. Rewards, direct orders, self-administered commands, surveillance, and threats are all examples of such events. Deci and Ryan assert that if such events promote the belief that the person is in control of outcomes and also foster a sense of competence, intrinsic motivation for the activity will thereby be increased. If, on the other hand, these events promote the person's beliefs that he or she is incompetent and not in control, intrinsic motivation will be weakened by them. Note the similarity between these conclusions and those of Harter (see Figure 5-1). Any event, Deci and Ryan conclude, can convey both types of information and thereby can be thought of as having both a *controlling* function and an *informational* function. The former weakens interest, whereas the latter strengthens it.

As we have noted, a reward will either increase or decrease interest in a task depending on whether its informational function or its controlling function is dominant and salient. Other environmental events that *diminish* intrinsic interest are surveillance (Pittman, Davey, Alafat, Wetherill & Kramer, 1980), competition (Deci, Betley, Kahle, Abrams & Porac, 1981), and deadlines for performance (Amabile, DeJong & Lepper, 1976). In each of these cases, someone sets conditions and makes demands on the person, thereby controlling the person's actions to some extent.

Sometimes the relative salience of the informational and controlling aspects of events is quite subtle, as has been shown in a study by Harackiewicz, Manderlink, and Sansone (1985), in which evaluation by the experimenter was found to cause decreased interest on the part of the subject, but evaluation combined with a reward contingent on performance *increased* subsequent interest. Before beginning to play a pinball game, some of the subjects had been told that their performance would be judged. Of these, some were told that a reward would be given for good performance and some were not. After the game was completed, all subjects were told that they had performed adequately and were then observed in a free play period during which they could continue to play pinball or switch to some other activity. One measure that was assumed to indicate interest in the game was the number of balls that subjects played during the free play period (Figure 5-4). Compared with subjects who were neither evaluated nor rewarded, those who received only evaluation showed a low level of interest, whereas those who were *evaluated and rewarded* showed a relatively high level. The combination of being judged and then pronounced adequate obviously produced feelings of competence at the task. It would appear that the negative effects of being evaluated can be offset by converting the evaluation into a vehicle for the transmission

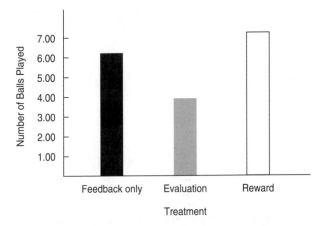

**Figure 5-4.** Number of balls played in a pinball game as a function of evaluation and performance-contingent reward. (Drawn from data reported in "Rewarding Pinball Wizardry: Effects of Evaluation and Cue Value on Intrinsic Interest" by J. M. Harackiewicz, G. Manderlink, & C. Sansone, *Journal of Personality and Social Psychology,* 1985, *47,* 287–300.)

of competence information. There is no reason to suppose that the same may not be true of the other environmental events listed above as typical precursors of decreasing intrinsic interest (see Harackiewicz, Abrahams & Wageman, 1987).

## Competence Valuation

The influence of environmental events on intrinsic interest in a task also depends to some extent on personal factors. Some people are more likely to be affected by such events than others. An important variable in all of this is how important people consider competence and mastery to be. This variable, which has been called *competence valuation,* is a complex one that is determined by both individual and situational conditions (Harackiewicz & Manderlink, 1984). The theory behind this concept is interesting because it treats extrinsic rewards in a way slightly different from the way in which Deci and Ryan do.

The basic model of competence valuation is shown in Figure 5-5. It is assumed that when a high value is placed on competence, interest in an activity will be high. In turn, this level of value is decided by an interplay of situational factors, such as extrinsic rewards, and individual factors related to intrinsic standards, such as achievement motivation. Where Harackiewicz and Manderlink differ from Deci and Ryan is in their assumption that extrinsic rewards may sometimes be stimuli for competence valuation. They concede that rewards often convey information about control (i.e., that the recipient is being controlled by the reward giver), but they also argue that when

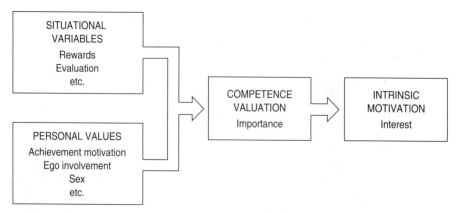

**Figure 5-5.** Scheme of the mediating function of competence valuation in task interest. (Adapted from "A Process Analysis of the Effects of Performance-Contingent Rewards on Intrinsic Motivation" by J. M. Harackiewicz and G. Manderlink, *Journal of Experimental Social Psychology*, 1984, *20*, 531–551.)

rewards are particularly attractive, they may elevate the value of competence because competent performance is the means of obtaining the reward. Thus competence may have instrumental value as well as intrinsic value.

At this point the interaction of reward and achievement motivation becomes critical. If a person has a high level of achievement motivation—that is, if he or she values achievement for its own sake—then competence at a task will be highly valued even if no reward is given. If, however, the person is low in achievement motivation, an attractive reward may be necessary to stimulate a valuation of competence (in the instrumental sense as described above). This means that when a reward is offered, people low in achievement motivation may value competence as much as high achievers do when no reward is offered. This leaves only one remaining question: How will high achievers respond to the offer of a reward? In this case, the reward is not needed to stimulate the competence value and may instead be seen as a con-trolling tool. Thus high achievers may value competence *less* when a reward is offered than when one is not. In an experiment designed to test these pre-dictions, Harackiewicz and Manderlink (1984) found support for all of them. Competence valuation did predict interest in the task, and the expected inter-action did occur between achievement motivation and the presence or absence of a reward.

What began as a relatively simple observation—that providing a reward for an activity may weaken interest in that activity—has been shown to be only part of a more complicated picture. As we have noted in this section, a number of environmental events, rewards among them, can convey informa-tion about a person's level of competence, or they can simply be a means by which the person's behavior is controlled by others. The person's interest in the activity depends on the value placed on competence, and this, in turn, depends on (1) whether the informational or controlling aspect of events is salient in a given situation and (2) certain individual variables such as achievement motivation.

# ILLUSION OF CONTROL, DESIRE FOR CONTROL, AND CONTROL MOTIVATION

The hypothesized need for mastery and control has been the basis for certain concepts in social and personality psychology that extend the boundaries of the original premise. One is the *illusion of control* (Langer, 1975). Because people have a motive to master the environment, they sometimes imagine that they have greater control over events than is actually the case. This illusory sense of control leads people to make judgments about the outcomes of situations that are actually determined by chance as if they were decided by human skill and ability. For example, Langer showed that people had a higher expectancy of winning a lottery if they selected the ticket themselves than they did if the ticket was selected for them, even though in either case the probability of the ticket's being the winner was the same.

The need for control that supposedly engenders such an illusory belief is also the basis for the personality variable *desire for control,* which has been extensively studied by Burger and his associates. This variable, which is measured by means of a 20-item self-report scale, has been shown to be related to a number of behaviors (see Burger, 1991a, for a review). A few are especially relevant for motivation. For example, people who score high on the desire for control scale are more likely than low scorers to succumb to the illusion of control. Burger (1991b) tested a sample of people who had just bought tickets in a state-sponsored lotto game in which participants had the option of choosing the numbers to go on their tickets or having this done by a computer. Those who had chosen their numbers had a higher average score on the desire for control scale than did those who had asked for computer-generated numbers.

Burger (1985) has also shown that high levels of desire for control are associated with several dimensions of achievement-related behavior, such as setting difficult and challenging goals, holding high expectations of personal success, and manifesting effort and persistence on a difficult task. Taking on challenges and working hard to overcome them prove to the person that he or she is competent and in control. Findings such as these point to the existence of a basic *control motivation* in humans (Pittman & Heller, 1987).

What elicits control motivation? Presumably, any event that reduces or threatens the person's sense of being in control. A sudden and unexpected event, for instance, may catch a person unprepared to respond and thus make

*Under certain conditions, people who take part in lotteries feel that they have control over the outcome even though they do not.*

the lack of control, for the time being at least, especially salient. Receiving outcomes from one's behavior that are independent of the behavior may likewise foster a sense of being out of control (compare this with the phenomenon of learned helplessness discussed in a subsequent section of this chapter). Whatever the case, any event that promotes uncertainty and feelings of lack of control may trigger control motivation.

In addition, Burger and Hemans (1988) showed that people with strong desires for control attribute causes for events more than do people with weaker desire for control. Because the attribution process is the outcome of a need to understand, predict, and control the environment (Heider, 1958; Weiner, 1985; see Chapter 2), it is to be expected that people who have a high need for such control will engage in it extensively. The study by Burger and Hemans (1988) is important because it shows that *desire for control can initiate cognitive activity,* thereby illustrating one of the links between cognition and motivation that we are seeking to describe in this book. In several studies to test this idea, Pittman and his associates studied cognitive activity following the experimental manipulation of control motivation. They have shown, for example, that people who are first subjected to a "helplessness" treatment later process information more carefully than do those who have not been deprived of control over the outcomes of their behavior (Pittman & D'Agostino, 1985).

# EPISTEMIC MOTIVATION

A concept that is related to what we have been discussing here is *epistemic motivation,* defined as the motive to seek and obtain information or knowledge (e.g., Kruglanski, 1989). The search for information serves the more basic need to be able to predict and control our surroundings. Epistemic motivation has been the subject of numerous investigations. In the past it has been described by such names as need for certainty, need for cognitive consistency, need for structure, and intolerance of ambiguity. All of these constructs refer to a need that people have to understand their environments through cognitive organization and structuring, and all are indirectly linked to the larger and more inclusive need for control.

Each of these theories rests on the premise that people are limited in their capacity to process stimuli that emanate from the complex environment in which they live. We cannot possibly use all the information that we take in, so the environment is capable of overwhelming the person with information. Being overloaded by information reduces one's personal control over events. In order to avoid being overloaded, the person adopts certain strategies for processing information that give structure to the environment and thereby simplify it.

Kruglanski (1989) has proposed that at some times, such as when they work under time pressures, people experience a need (called the *need for closure*) to come up with definite answers, to avoid ambiguity and confusion, and to resist information that might "muddy the waters." To a person in this frame of mind, once a feasible solution to the problem has been found, he or she becomes closed-minded and resistant to all further information. At the same time, however, the person experiences a countervailing need to avoid making errors; the person is said to be motivated also by a *fear of invalidity.* This fear tends to make people open-minded and ready to process any information that helps them avoid errors. Actual behavior is a tradeoff between these two antagonistic motives and is largely determined by the nature of the situation. Need for closure should be the dominant motive in problem-solving situations when time pressures are great and fear of failure is weak; fear of invalidity should be the stronger of the two motives when the reverse is true.

The tendency to simplify the environment is a function of a high need for closure and relatively low fear of failure. This tendency may animate several types of social and cognitive activity. For example, it may influence the way in which people form impressions of one another. Kruglanski and Freund (1983) found that when subjects were asked to form an impression of another person's ability, they were disproportionately influenced by their first impressions of that person when they worked under time pressure and were told that their performance would not be evaluated. Thus, with high time pressure and low fear of failure (because failure would not be detected), subjects took in some information about the person, formed a quick impression, and then did not process information that came later. By contrast, subjects who worked without time pressure and who had been told that their work would be evaluated showed the least tendency to base ther judgments on first impressions. Need for closure was therefore related to cognitive processing that rendered the situation simpler and easier to handle. One can imagine a personnel officer in a business, interviewing job candidates according to a tight schedule and under pressure to hire someone soon, reacting in exactly this way.

Another epistemic motive that has received considerable attention is the need for cognition, which has been defined as simply "the tendency for an individual to engage in and enjoy thinking" (Cacioppo & Petty, 1982, p. 116). This need was first investigated in studies of persuasion and attitude change, in which it was shown to be an important moderator of the ways in which people process information. For example, Cacioppo, Petty, Kao, and Rodriguez (1986) found that people who had a high need for cognition were more favorably influenced by strong arguments in favor of an issue, and less favorably influenced by weak arguments, than subjects who were low in need for cognition. Need for cognition, therefore, apparently enhances the degree to which people process arguments in a rational and thoughtful way. Other studies have shown that a high need for cognition is also associated with a greater amount of attributional and explanatory processing in situations unrelated to persuasion and attitude change (Lassiter, Briggs & Slaw, 1991).

What accounts for the need for cognition? One interesting possibility is that the need for cognition is related to a more general need for control. Thompson, Chaiken, and Hazlewood (1993) have reported a covariation of need for cognition with Burger's (1992) construct of desire for control. They have suggested that the latter variable may cause at least some of the effects of the former. If this is so, then the need for cognition could be another epistemic motive in the service of personal organization and control over the environment.

## SELF-EFFICACY

Belief in one's ability to exert control over one's surroundings is central to the concept of *self-efficacy* described by Bandura (1977, 1982). This concept arose in the context of clinical therapy; Bandura (1977) argued that therapeutic interventions are effective only to the extent that they foster a sense of self-efficacy in the person—a sense that the person can do what is necessary to overcome whatever symptoms are involved. As it has been developed, however, the concept now applies more generally to goal-related behavior and is, in fact, virtually synonymous with the ability to carry out a desired behavior.

### Origins of Self-Efficacy

Feelings of self-efficacy come from information that a person receives in the context of relevant actions. Bandura (1982) has identified four sources of this information: performance outcomes, vicarious outcomes, verbal persuasion, and physiological feedback. The first is the most common and the most powerful. In general, success in past performance of the activity being practiced will produce feelings of ability to succeed in that activity, whereas recollections of past failures should produce feelings of relative inability. Vicarious feedback, such as observing another person enjoying success at the task that one faces, may also convey some sense of self-efficacy (Bandura, Adams, Hardy & Howells, 1980), but not to the same extent as performance outcomes. In the same way, verbal persuasion, such as "pep talks" and other confidence boosters, may have some effect on self-efficacy, but less than direct experience would have. Finally, the feedback sensations that one receives from one's body during performance can influence self-efficacy. Although self-efficacy has been found to be unrelated to actual physiological arousal, it is influenced by *perceptions of arousal* (Feltz & Mugno, 1983). A person will probably feel less confident and capable when anticipating a task if she feels her heart racing and experiences tension in her muscles than if she is feeling relaxed.

Self-efficacy may also originate in certain cognitive judgments that a person makes when facing a task. The person must, in such a situation, utilize whatever information is available in order to decide whether he or she has the necessary ability to carry out the actions necessary to reach the goal. To some extent everybody uses information like the difficulty of the task, recollection of past performances, environmental drawbacks to success, and so forth. Sometimes, however, particularly when they are uncertain about the situation, people who are making a decision do not engage in extensive and detailed searches for information. Instead, they react to certain conditions, either in themselves or in the environment, and thereby make relatively simple and uninformed judgments. Such heuristic processes have been shown to operate in the formation of self-efficacy judgments.

For example, people sometimes make judgments simply on the basis of a stimulus or a thought that just happens to be salient and available at the time. A person may be thinking in an abstract way about failure, and this thought may become a decisive cue for judgments that he makes about how likely he is to succeed or fail at an upcoming task. This has been shown in an experiment by Cervone (1989). Subjects were told about a psychomotor task and instructed to think about either what makes that task difficult or what makes it easy. Self-efficacy for the task was then assessed by subjects' self-reports. Finally, subjects were given the task, which had been structured in such a way that it became progressively more difficult until finally becoming impossible. The main performance variable was how long the subject persisted at the task. Persistence indicates sustained effort and is therefore a measure of motivation to keep working toward the goal of successful performance.

Cervone (1989) found that those subjects who had been instructed to focus on what makes the psychomotor task difficult later showed lower ratings of self-efficacy than both those who focused on what makes the task easy and those given no instructions to focus on the task at all (Figure 5-6). Judgments of self-efficacy were based, in other words, largely on a cognition (difficulty versus ease of task) that was available simply because of a preceding treatment. Other studies have shown that feelings of self-efficacy may be heightened in a subject merely by exposing her to the idea of a high performance standard as compared to the idea of a lower standard (Cervone & Peake, 1986). It would appear, therefore, that self-efficacy is susceptible to a number of conditions that pertain to success and failure in the person's immediate environment.

## Effects of Self-Efficacy

Whatever its origins, self-efficacy, once aroused, has a motivating effect on performance. In Cervone's (1989) study, the subjects' persistence on the task varied as a function of pretask focus on the difficulty or ease of the task in the same way as did self-efficacy judgments (see Figure 5-6). In addition, persistence and self-efficacy ratings were positively correlated in most conditions of the study, indicating that self-efficacy was an important contributor to motivation. Self-efficacy has been shown to have a positive effect on motivation in research from several areas.

**ACHIEVEMENT MOTIVATION.** The experiment by Cervone described above is one of several (e.g., Cervone & Peake, 1986; Peake & Cervone, 1989) showing that a high level of self-efficacy produces a motive to achieve success. It can

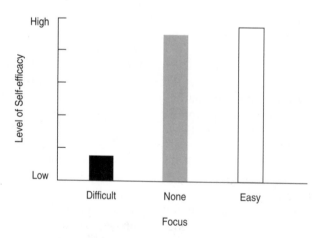

***Figure 5-6.*** Effects of focus on future activities on judgments of self-efficacy and persistence. (Drawn from data reported in "Effects of Envisioning Future Activities on Self-Efficacy Judgments and Motivation: An Availability Heuristic Interpretation" by D. Cervone, *Cognitive Theory and Research*, 1989, *13*, 247–261.)

also lead to improved performance on such tasks. For example, Schunk (1984) found that increasing self-efficacy for mathematics in underachieving school children produced increased mathematical skills. In part, self-efficacy had a direct influence on performance, perhaps by making the children more confident and more willing to take on the challenge of solving problems. In addition, increased self-efficacy motivated the children to be more persistent in working on problems.

**CAREER CHOICES.**  Self-efficacy is also closely related to the career choices that people make. People who lack a sense of self-efficacy tend to be less decisive in making a career decision than are more self-efficacious people (Betz & Hackett, 1984), and a strong feeling of self-efficacy for a particular type of activity is a good predictor of the likelihood that people will choose careers involving such activity. It has also been shown that much of the reluctance that women sometimes have about specializing in mathematics relative to men arises from socially learned feelings of low self-efficacy where mathematics is concerned (Betz & Hackett, 1983).

**HEALTH-RELATED BEHAVIOR.**  As has been noted, the concept of self-efficacy originated in studies of clinical treatment (Bandura, 1977). It is not surprising, therefore, that the concept has been shown to apply to health-related behaviors. Bandura, Reese, and Adams (1982) showed that after phobic patients acquired strong feelings of self-efficacy for approaching the object of their fears, their heart rate and blood pressure reactions in the presence of those objects were considerably diminished. Increased self-efficacy has also been associated with lowered levels of epinephrine and norepinephrine in the blood during phobia-related tasks; these two hormones are usually indicators of high stress (Bandura, Taylor, Williams, Mefford & Barchas, 1985). High levels of self-efficacy for coping with stressors have also been shown to increase tolerance for pain (Bandura, O'Leary, Taylor, Gauthier & Gossard, 1987) and to increase activity in the body's immune system (Weidenfeld, O'Leary, Bandura, Brown, Levine & Raska, 1990).

In addition to conferring resistance to stressful situations, self-efficacy affects behaviors related to health by engendering positive attitudes about the person's ability to adopt good health-related practices. An interesting study by Ewart, Taylor, Reese, and DeBusk (1984) has shown that people who are recovering from heart attacks are more likely to engage vigorously in rehabilitating exercise if they have a high level of self-efficacy for such activity than if they do not. This same study revealed a "snowball" effect, in that the intensity of exercise was positively correlated with subsequent self-efficacy for exercise, so that self-efficacy led to greater effort, which in turn elevated self-efficacy even more. Self-efficacy has also been found to be a good predictor of the extent to which people adhere to medical regimens that are advised for them (O'Leary, 1992).

*A strong sense of self-efficacy can motivate people to be diligent in doing rehabilitative exercise following illness.*

# THE USES OF CONTROL, NONCONTROL, AND ILLUSORY CONTROL

As we noted early in this chapter, having control over one's environment can bring benefits other than those associated with mastery motivation and competence. Control over outcomes may be valuable because of its practical utility and instrumentality. For example, many studies have shown that stressful conditions produce less stress when the persons subjected to them believe that they have some degree of control over them (Miller, 1980; Thompson, 1980). Such outcomes may, of course, be mediated by increased feelings of competence and control, but they need not be. One possible product of having control over the outcomes of a situation may simply be a reduction in uncertainty regarding those outcomes. When a person controls an event, he or she can also predict what the outcome of that event will be, and it has long been recognized that predictability of an event helps to reduce its stressful impact (Mineka & Hendersen, 1985). Possession of control may also facilitate the development of coping strategies that may mitigate the effects of stressors.

Another result of having control that has practical value is the increased likelihood of a desirable state of affairs. In a series of studies, Rodin and her associates have presented evidence showing that people choose control over events only when they are convinced that having control will allow them to obtain the best possible outcome (Rodin, Rennert & Solomon, 1980). For example, when subjects were given a choice between having control and not having it in a situation in which a good outcome was assured in either case, they did not express a strong desire for control. In short, subjects in Rodin's studies did not manifest any intrinsic need or desire for mastery and competence per se; they simply sought control when it was instrumental to good outcomes and ignored it when it was not.

## Learned Helplessness

The importance of perceived control in behavior is also highlighted by the study of learned helplessness, a phenomenon first shown in research on shock avoidance learning in dogs (Overmier & Seligman, 1967). Under ordinary conditions a dog learns to avoid shock that is preceded by a warning signal within a relatively small number of trials. In their study, however, Overmier and Seligman found that if dogs had been subjected to a series of uncontrollable shocks the day before training, they were virtually unable to learn shock avoidance when training was undertaken. The explanatory hypothesis—that the dogs had acquired a sense of helplessness that interfered with learning—became the basis for extensive study in both humans and lower animals of the conditions under which this debilitating effect occurs.

Most research on learned helplessness involves the use of a triadic (three condition) experimental design, in which the subject is first given a task and exposed to rewards or punishments that are either (1) contingent upon the subject's performance or (2) independent of what the subject does. Subjects in a third condition are (3) given no rewards or punishments. All subjects then perform a second task in which all outcomes are contingent on performance. Learned helplessness is assumed to have occurred if subjects that had received noncontingent feedback on the first task perform more poorly on the second task than subjects in the other two conditions.

**THE ORIGINAL THEORY.** It was hypothesized in the original theory of learned helplessness (e.g., Seligman, 1975) that any time the consequences of our behavior are not brought about by that behavior, whether they be good or bad consequences, the person will perceive that she or he is helpless in that situation. It is further assumed that this *subjective* feeling of helplessness may grow into a *generalized expectancy* that one's helplessness extends beyond the immediate situation and is truly a nonspecific state of learned helplessness.

Generalization from the specific conditions in which noncontingency of behavior is experienced to feelings of noncontingency in other situations is a critical element in the development of learned helplessness. A demonstration of the process requires the creation of objective noncontingency with one task followed by evidence of helplessness on a different task. A good example of this was provided by Hiroto and Seligman (1975), who used two different helplessness training tasks and two different subsequent test tasks. For both training tasks the usual triadic design was used. In one (called the instrumental training task), subjects were given training on a noise-escape procedure in which one third could terminate the noise by responding, one third could not, and a final third received no noise. In the other (the cognitive training task), a third of the subjects were given a solvable concept-formation task, one third an unsolvable task, and a third no task. Later all subjects were tested on either a noise-escape task or a task that involved the solving of anagrams, and in both performance was contingent on the subject's behavior. The critical comparisons for testing the generalization of learned helplessness were those in which (1) an instrumental training task was followed by the anagrams test and (2) the cognitive training task was followed by the noise-escape test.

The results of these two procedures are shown in Figure 5-7. It is clear that when the training task was such that subjects could not control the outcomes, whether the instrumental or the cognitive task was used, subsequent performance on a different task was inhibited relative to that of subjects in the other two training conditions. Thus helplessness generalized from the original situation to a second, unrelated situation.

When learned helplessness occurs, the person's behavior begins to suffer from three *deficits*. One is motivational and is manifested in a general state of apathy and inaction. A second is affective and consists of a lack of adaptive emotionality; the helpless person usually appears indifferent and even depressed. The third deficit is cognitive. The person's ability to process information normally breaks down, so that on later occasions when behavior *is* effective in determining outcomes, the person is unable to notice that the contingencies have changed and continues to function as if he or she lacked control.

*LATER DEVELOPMENTS.* The original theory of learned helplessness generated considerable enthusiasm among researchers and practitioners who dealt with the problems of how humans react to stressful events in everyday life. This enthusiasm led to the development of a theory of depression based on the three cognitive deficits noted above (Seligman, 1975). Hence depressives, who show motivational apathy, depressed affect, and what seems to be a relative inability to make accurate cognitive judgments (at least where their own actions are concerned; see Psyzczynski & Greenberg, 1987), show all the signs of people who have acquired generalized feelings of helplessness. In time, however, problems associated with the original theory of learned helplessness began to emerge. One was that sometimes people responded to lack of control over outcomes not with helplessness, but with increased efforts to gain control (Wortman & Brehm, 1975). Another concerned the conditions under which specific feelings of helplessness generalize from the situations in which they are acquired to a broader range of situations and become a characteristic

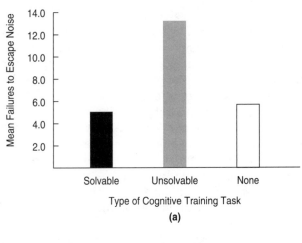

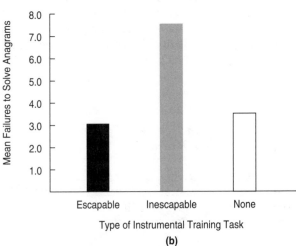

***Figure 5-7.*** (a) Effects of cognitive helplessness training on instrumental task performance and (b) effects of instrumental helplessness training on cognitive task performance. (Adapted from "Generality of Learned Helplessness in Man" by D. S. Hiroto and M.E.P. Seligman, *Journal of Personality and Social Psychology,* 1975, *31,* 311–327.)

response of the person to stressful encounters (e.g., Roth, 1980). Concerns such as these led to a reformulated theory of learned helplessness (Abramson, Seligman & Teasdale, 1978) which, though retaining lack of control as a central premise, placed its major emphasis on the reasons people hold for thinking that they lack control. In this way, attributional processes were introduced to the study of helplessness (see Weiner, 1985; Chapter 2).

It will be recalled from the discussion of attribution in Chapter 2 that Weiner (1985) emphasized the dimensions of locus, controllability, and stability in analyzing the effects of attributions on motivation and emotion. In their revised theory, Abramson and her associates (1978) utilized the dimensions of locus (internal versus external cause) and stability (stable versus changeable cause) and added another: *globality,* or the generalization of a cause across events. Just as the stability of a cause refers to its likelihood of repeating across time, globality refers to its likelihood of repeating across situations. Thus the revised theory goes, when a person experiences an aversive event, a cause will be assigned to that outcome that varies along three dimensions. Table 5-1 shows the combinations of attribution types that result when there are two levels of each of these three dimensions, along with a set of explanations that may be given in a hypothetical situation in which a woman has just been fired from her job in a company office.

The theory states that a *generalized* state of helplessness will result when attributions for a negative outcome are *stable and global.* In our example, the fired employee must feel that she is either generally incompetent (not merely unable to live up to the demands of *this* office) or the victim of a hostile environment (not just the animosity of *this* employer) before she will feel that

**TABLE 5-1**
**Major Dimensions of Attribution in Revised Theory**
**of Learned Helplessness and Some Examples**

*Event to be explained:* A woman is fired from her job.

| | **Specific** |
|---|---|
| **Internal** | |
| Stable | I couldn't master the computer software. |
| Unstable | I lost interest in the job. |
| **External** | |
| Stable | The boss was prejudiced against me. |
| Unstable | I got some bad breaks in the office. |
| | **Global** |
| **Internal** | |
| Stable | I am incompetent. |
| Unstable | I am exhausted. |
| **External** | |
| Stable | A lot of companies are sexist. |
| Unstable | I am an unlucky person. |

she is truly helpless to change her condition. This may cause, in turn, the general motivational apathy and cognitive deficits described by Seligman (1975). Note that the locus of the cause does not play a role in the development of the generalized feeling of helplessness: as long as her attributions are stable and global, the woman will feel helpless whether or not she also feels responsible for the outcome. What locus determines is her *affective* reaction to the situation. If her helplessness is accompanied by the idea that she was responsible, her sense of self-esteem will be diminished and she may become a candidate for depression. If, however, she believes that her helplessness is the result of a sexist policy practiced by most businesses, her affective response is likely to be anger. We may conclude, therefore, that the entire package of deficits outlined by Seligman (1975)—that is, cognitive, motivational, and affective—results when a person attributes a negative life event to an *internal, stable, and global cause.*

The reformulated learned helplessness theory of Abramson and colleagues (1978) is not the last word on the relationship of helplessness to depression. Even though an extensive amount of research on depression was based on the 1978 model (Sweeney, Anderson & Bailey, 1986), that model did not spell out a clear theory of depression. For that reason, Abramson, Metalsky, and Alloy (1989) developed a refinement that they call the theory of *hopelessness depression.* This theory was based on the 1978 model, but it goes beyond the scope of this chapter and is more appropriately related to issues of stress and health. It will be discussed in Chapter 11, when we turn to some applications of basic motivation theory to these problems.

## *The Desire for Noncontrol*

To this point we have consistently emphasized the positive aspects of being in control of situations, as if this were a universal feature of human behavior. It is not. Although having control may sometimes be useful and adaptive, at other times a person may find it more useful not to be in command of the situation. Whenever a person anticipates an unpleasant outcome, the desire *not* to be in control of that outcome can override the normal desire for control (Burger, 1989). At such times, as we observed in the last chapter, the person may seek to look helpless and thereby avoid blame, which is what transpires in self-handicapping. Control may also be avoided when one is convinced that relinquishing control to someone else will increase the likelihood of a desired outcome. This would be the case, for example, when the other person is seen as having greater expertise than oneself in the task at hand (e.g., Miller, 1980).

## *The Benefits of Illusory Control*

Earlier in the chapter we briefly noted that people sometimes maintain an illusion that they are in control of outcomes even when they are not. This phenomenon was cited as an extension of the idea that people have a basic motive for mastery. The illusion of control may be held for reasons other than a need for mastery, however. It may serve a useful purpose in helping the person adjust to painful or threatening circumstances.

As noted in Chapter 4, people often engage in ego-defensive behaviors when they perceive a discrepancy between their ideal and actual selves. Self-handicapping, excuse making, and symbolic self-completion are a few of the devices that we reviewed. Another such device is developing a false sense of being in control. This erroneous belief about the self serves the important function of buffering the person against the stresses of aversive events (Cohen & Edwards, 1989) and promoting adjustment and good mental health (Taylor & Brown, 1988). The person may, by forming the belief that she or he is a "good and in-control person," accomplish what Snyder (1989) has called a "negotiation of reality": a state in which one's experience of the world has been constructed in a way that allows the person to survive and to get along with self-esteem intact.

Does this mean that people should run away from reality and create dream worlds for themselves in order to achieve perfect happiness? One might think this would be the logical outcome of such motivated self-defensive processes. Such is not the case, however. Regardless of how many illusions we may form, including illusions of control, we still live in a world of real contingencies, and holding too many illusory beliefs about the self can create problems (e.g., Baumeister, 1989). Even those who have documented the benefits of defensive illusions about the self remind us that the self-concept is only one part of the person's total experience (e.g., Taylor & Brown, 1988). In addition to processing self-related information, we process a great deal of information about the world in a realistic way. It is the *balancing* of these two in our views of ourselves and the world that constitutes the negotiation process. In other words, we function best when we are basically in touch with reality but at the same time use some self-defensive strategies wisely in order to defend ourselves from being beaten about too much. Unrealistic, illusory, self-defensive behavior may, in fact, serve as a first line of defense against threatening or unpleasant events (such as failure to reach a goal), "buying us some time" in which to work out a better, more permanent solution to our problems (see Roth & Cohen, 1986). We will return to this topic in Chapter 11 when we take up in greater detail the matter of stress and how people cope with it.

# CHAPTER SUMMARY

1.   Personal control over one's immediate environment has long been considered by psychologists to be an important goal in life. The value of control as a mediator of stressful conditions has been documented in studies of both animals and humans. Control is typically preferred to helplessness.

**2.**  Explanations of the value of control among humans have reflected two theoretical approaches. One holds that humans have a motive for successful interaction with, and mastery of, their environments. The other is that control is simply useful and adaptive in most sitiuations and that having control maximizes the likelihood of obtaining good outcomes from one's actions.

**3.**  The effectance or mastery motive may be partly inherent in humans, but it has been studied most extensively as a product of the socialization process. Reinforcement for independent attempts at mastery in children forms the basis for development of the motive, which becomes internalized when the developing child becomes able to administer self-rewards. Punishment or non-reinforcement for independent attempts at mastery is a precursor of a motive system in which the child becomes dependent on others and seeks social approval.

**4.**  Other useful distinctions that have been made in describing the development of mastery are (a) between *internalization,* which is the personal acceptance of social values, and *introjection,* which is conformity to social values because of demands; and (b) between the mastery-oriented pattern of seeking *learning goals* and the helplessness-oriented pattern of seeking *performance goals.* All of these conceptual systems reflect a basic distinction between motivation for independence and competence and motivation for dependence on others.

**5.**  Motivation for mastery is manifested in several domains of life that are cognitive, physical, social, and broadly behavioral in nature. Judgments of one's competence are made by comparing one's performance in a domain with the recognized standard for that domain. The standards may involve the comparison of present performance with either one's past performance or the performance of others. Tendencies to use one or the other of these standards vary as a function of age, development, and level of ability. Discrepancies between the standard and the level of performance are associated with a lowered sense of self-worth.

**6.**  Competence plays a major role in intrinsic motivation and interest in tasks. Environmental events associated with motivation of behavior, such as rewards, surveillance, deadlines, and competition with others, have two effects. One is informational, in that meeting the demands set by such events informs the person about his or her level of competence. The other is controlling, in that each of these events can be regarded as an instance in which the behavior of the person is controlled by others. In general, to the extent that an environmental event, such as a reward, conveys competence information, it will enhance interest in the task. To the extent that it controls the person, it will decrease interest.

**7.** The value that a person places on competence also contributes to interest in tasks. Competence valuation, in turn, is determined by an interaction between environmental conditions (e.g., rewards) and personal variables such as achievement motivation. People who have high levels of achievement motivation place a higher value on competence in the absence of reward than when a reward is given. The opposite is true of people who have low levels of achievement motivation.

**8.** Motivation to have control and mastery over a situation is reflected in the finding that people sometimes have illusions of control when in fact they have no control. It also contributes to the personal variable of desire for control, which has several effects on motivation and behavior. Desire for control is related to control motivation, which is elicited by situations in which control is weakened or threatened and which is manifested in increased cognitive activity.

**9.** Epistemic motivation pertains to the need to seek and obtain information or knowledge. Often this serves the purpose of simplifying one's cognitive organization of the environment. Such organization facilitates the exercise of effective control. In a recent theory of epistemic motivation, Kruglanski has posited two antagonistic motives: the need for closure and the need for validity. High need for closure and low fear of invalidity promote the formation of simple and closed cognitive structures. The need for cognition is another epistemic motive that may be related to the need for control.

**10.** A belief in one's ability to exercise control is a central feature of self-efficacy. This state develops out of both personal and vicarious experiences of mastery, and it can be elicited by any stimulus that makes mastery and ability salient in the situation. Self-efficacy has a generally positive effect on motivation and has been shown to operate in such diverse areas as achievement, career choice, and health.

**11.** Learned helplessness is a generalized feeling of being out of control that develops from specific instances of noncontrol. This generalization is facilitated by the person's attributing specific instances to causes that are stable and global. The result is a general motivational and cognitive deficit. When internal attributions of cause are made, the person experiences negative affect and reduced self-esteem.

**12.** When being in control threatens to lead to either reduced self-esteem or other undesired outcomes, people may prefer not to have control.

**13.** Illusory control over outcomes can be adaptive in that it often promotes mental health and adjustment to negative events when balanced with other information about the real nature of those events.

## CHAPTER 6

# THE THEMATIC APPROACH: ACHIEVEMENT, AFFILIATION, AND POWER

## CHAPTER OUTLINE

The Thematic Approach to Motivation
Achievement Motivation
Affiliative Motivation
Power Motivation
Chapter Summary

## THE THEMATIC APPROACH TO MOTIVATION

In Chapter 2 an overall scheme was presented by which goals were described as a product of incentives, and incentives are produced by the activation of a need by situational stimuli such as important reference persons (see Table 2-1). In the three chapters that followed, we explored various aspects of the behavior of people when they are animated by goals. A detailed discussion of the nature and origins of needs was not undertaken. In this chapter we shall go back to the matters introduced in Chapter 2 and discuss needs—what they are, how they are measured, how they arise. This will be done in the context of a review of a major theory of motivation and research generated by that theory over the past 40 years.

This theory was introduced by David McClelland and his associates in 1953. In the first part of this chapter we will note some of the assumptions about motives on which this theory was based, the means by which motives are assessed in accordance with the theory, and the original version of the theory itself. We will then note some revisions of the original theory that have (1) modified the definition of a motive, and (2) defined the origins of basic human motives. In the three sections that follow the first section, we will review, in the general context of the theory, three specific human needs: achievement, affiliation, and power. Where applicable, we will introduce material from research that is designed to test theories and concepts other than the one that is central to this chapter, but that also addresses the analysis of the three needs.

## Murray's Concept of Needs

Ever since Henry Murray published his now-classic book *Explorations in Personality* (1938), there has been a strong link between motivation and personality psychology. This is because Murray defined personality in terms of individual differences in motive dispositions, with the latter conceptualized as a number of inherited and acquired *needs*. To some extent these needs, which have the status of persistent individual differences, have continued to play an important role in concepts of human motivation up to the present time. Most of the needs described by Murray are no longer studied, at least in the terminology that he used. Three have survived, however, and they will form the basis for the material to be discussed in this chapter. These three are the needs for achievement, affiliation, and dominance, the latter of which is now usually referred to as the need for power.

Murray (1938) assumed that many human needs are *non*conscious. This does not mean that they are *un*conscious, in the sense that psychoanalysts have defined human motives. Murray was not describing deep psychodynamic forces that relate ultimately to sex and aggression. Instead, he meant that often we satisfy our needs without being consciously aware of what we are doing. This is not a difficult idea to grasp given what we now know about "mindless" behavior. Much of what we do every day is not consciously thought out but is more or less routine and automatic. The reader will recall that these issues were brought up in Chapter 1. In addition, although Murray held that needs could be assessed in many ways, his major contribution to assessment was a test that he developed to measure nonconscious tendencies: the Thematic Apperception Test (TAT).

Because the thematic methodology for assessing nonconscious tendencies is basic to the assessment of motives that underlies most of the research discussed in this chapter, a brief description of the theoretical rationale for the method may be helpful. Needs, depending on their nature, activate either approach or avoidance behaviors: a situation will elicit either approach or avoidance depending on the dominant need that we feel when facing it. For example, a situation in which one is to be introduced to strangers will be approached by someone who has a strong need to be gregarious and to affiliate, but avoided by a shy person whose need is to protect a fragile sense of social esteem. Situations evoke more than approach and avoidance behaviors, however. They also elicit thoughts that are closely related to whatever behavior tendency is operating (see Chapter 2). These thoughts, in turn, form the basis for fantasy and imaginative activity. If a person is asked to fantasize and make up a story while he or she is in a particular need state, the story that is created should give some information about the parallel behavioral tendency and the underlying need.

The TAT is a series of pictures of human figures in situations that are not clearly meaningful. Persons who take the TAT are asked to describe the scenes shown in the pictures by making up stories. Because of the ambiguity of the scenes, it is assumed that the content of a story is based mainly on the fantasies and need-related thoughts in the person's mind at the time. The TAT, in other words, was alleged to provide a window into people's nonconscious need structures. It should also be noted that Murray (1938) argued that needs do not become active until they are evoked by appropriate situational conditions. It will be recalled that we made the same point in Chapter 1, where we proposed that needs and situational conditions (such as those involving reference persons) combine to form incentives.

## Motives as Conditioned Affect

An approach to human motivation similar to Murray's was later taken by David McClelland and his associates (McClelland, Atkinson, Clark & Lowell, 1953), who likewise utilized a TAT-like method of assessment but went beyond Murray by embedding their work within a general theory of motivation. This theory, which has undergone certain revisions between 1953 and the present, has represented a major tradition in the study of human motivation. Some of the ideas generated by it will make up the bulk of this chapter. One of the major tasks taken on by McClelland and his group was to explain the origins of motives. In their original theory they traced these origins to *affective* processes. To quote McClelland and his colleagues, *"a motive is the redintegration by a cue of a change in an affective situation.* The word *redintegration* in this definition is meant to imply previous learning. In our system, all motives are learned"* (McClelland et al., 1953, p. 28; italics original).

In other words, motives are built on conditioned, or learned, affect. On past occasions, changes in affect (such as one experiences during a feeling of anger or a surge of happiness) have been conditioned to specific stimuli in the situation. When these stimuli occur later in life, they act as cues for a "redintegration," or re-creation, of the original affective change. The cue has the power to elicit an affective state similar to the one that first occurred in its presence. If the newly elicited state of affect is different from the one that existed before the cue became manifest, it takes on the power of a motive. An example is a child who wins the praise of her parents for performing well in her first piano recital. Stimuli that surround the recital become associated with the increased pleasure that the child feels, so that on a subsequent occasion the thought of performing at another recital elicits an increase in pleasure. The child thus approaches the recital with confidence and anticipation of additional pleasure. If her initial experience with recitals had been an unpleasant one, however, the affective state elicited by cues related to recitals would represent a change in affect in a negative direction, and her tendency would later be to avoid recitals.

In the original theory, approach and avoidance were defined as manifest behaviors with specific objectives—namely, the continuation of positive stimulation in the case of approach and the termination of negative stimulation in the case of avoidance. Motives therefore have specific consequences for behavior. More precisely, motives *orient, select,* and *energize* behavior (McClelland, 1985). The affective-dispositional state that we are calling a motive directs attention toward certain stimuli in the environment rather than others, it promotes the learning of material relevant to the affective state, and it activates and powers responses that are efficacious in avoiding or approaching situations, depending on the nature of the affect involved.

What does all of this have to do with the needs and individual differences with which we began this chapter? Let us suppose that the child we noted earlier in our example regularly and recurrently receives praise and rewards for doing well in all of her activities. On each occasion she will associate increased positive affect with the challenges of taking on tasks and doing well at them. In time a generalized tendency to approach tasks will emerge from this, and it will be labeled as a *motive to achieve;* in the language of needs, we would say that the child has a relatively high *need for achievement.* If she had encountered recurrent failure and punishment, she would have developed instead, and in the same way, a need to avoid failure.

## Motives and Values

It is important to grasp the fundamentals of McClelland's original theory of motivation because its general features continue to guide research on achievement, affiliation, and power (see below). However, the idea that a motive is solely a nonconscious state assessed exclusively by means of the thematic method is no longer held (McClelland, Koestner & Weinberger, 1989). Before we can explore the implications of this revised theory, we must note one final feature of the original one: the distinction that it made between motives and values.

In the original version of the theory, McClelland (1984) drew an important distinction between motives, as defined above, and *values,* which are conscious states that a person recognizes and can articulate. One important difference between the two is how they are measured. Whereas motives require the use of the thematic method, values are assessed by means of self-report tests such as the Edwards Personal Preference Scale (Edwards, 1957), the Work and Family Orientation Questionnaire (Spence & Helmreich, 1983), the Rokeach Value Survey (Rokeach, 1973), and the Personality Research Form (Jackson, 1974).

Another important difference between motives and values in the original version of the theory is that the two are correlated with different aspects of behavior and performance. Because motives "orient, select, and energize" behavior, they predict such actions as sensitivity to goal-related stimuli and ability to learn goal-related material as well as performance on tasks such as verbal learning or mental arithmetic (McClelland, 1985). They also predict arousal during performance: subjects who score high in need for achievement, for example, have been shown to have higher levels of cardiovascular arousal than subjects low in achievement motivation (Beh, 1990). Values are better predictors of self-conscious behavioral choices, such as decisions to expend effort on tasks or to persist in the face of failure.

## Implicit and Self-Attributed Needs

In the revised theory, the distinction between motives and values is dropped in favor of a broader definition of motives. The nonconscious need state originally called a motive is now called an *implicit need;* like its original counterpart, it is assessed by means of the thematic method. In addition, McClelland and his associates (1989) now describe a second type of motive, called a *self-attributed need,* which is a conscious state that the person can describe and that is therefore assessed by self-report measures. In other words, the self-attributed motive is what was originally called a value.

The revision of the theory involves more than just changing the names of constructs, however. The two needs are defined as different kinds of human motivation, in that each influences a different class of behaviors. In general, it is proposed that implicit needs predict most accurately behavioral trends over a long period of time, whereas self-attributed needs best predict specific responses to immediate situational conditions. For example, fantasy-based measures of achievement motivation (i.e., implicit needs) predict achievement-related economic behavior over periods of several years, and thematically assessed intimacy motivation predicts happiness in marriage many years later (McClelland et al., 1989). Self-attributed needs, on the other hand, are especially good predictors of behavior in specific situations when powerful cues are present to evoke the behavior. These cues can be, and often are, social in nature.

What McClelland and colleagues (1989) call a self-attributed need appears to be similar to what we have described simply as a need in Chapter

2 (see Table 2-1). This is what we might expect, given the social emphasis that we have been placing on human motivation. In Chapter 2 we noted that a need becomes the basis for a specific incentive when one or more salient reference persons are present. The reference person provides a relevant standard for behavior (see Chapter 4). This invoked standard, if accepted by the person, becomes the guiding value for subsequent goal setting and behavior. In their conceptualization of the effects of self-attributed needs, McClelland and his associates make many of these same points.

## Natural Incentives and Motives

In its original version, the theory of McClelland and his associates, while being specific on how affect becomes conditioned to situational stimuli, did not go into great detail on what causes the initial affective reaction itself. In another major extension of the theory, McClelland (1985) provided this detail by introducing the concept of *natural incentives*. These incentives are affective reactions to specific stimuli in the environment, and they arise from mechanisms that are *innate and unlearned*. Once evoked, natural incentives elicit responses that are specifically related to the stimuli that originally set off the process. Such incentive processes have been widely studied in the past by specialists in behavioral biology, called *ethologists* (e.g., Lorenz, 1966). It is known, for example, that among certain species of fish, the appearance of a red spot on the body of a male automatically elicits an attack from other males (Tinbergen, 1951). The red spot is called a sign stimulus, or releaser, because it signals a certain response (attack) and then "releases" it from the attacking organism. The response is called consummatory because it satisfies a supposed "urge to attack" that is set off by the stimulus. McClelland (1985) in fact used the example of fighting fish to illustrate his revised theory of motivation, which, like the theory of the ethologists, is based on the concepts of sign stimuli and specific consummatory responses. The "urge to respond" that we can only imagine in some anthropomorphic way among lower animals is conceptualized as a central affective state in humans. Thus the sign stimulus activates this state, which in turn generates a stimulus-specific consummatory reaction.

How do we get from these innate reactions to what may be properly called motives? As in the original theory, a process of *learning* is involved. The consummatory response brings about a desired state of affairs that we will call the *consummatory experience:* for example, eating reduces hunger and causes a feeling of contentment, interacting with a loved one produces the pleasure of closeness, and fleeing from danger elicits feelings of security and safety. We might say, therefore, that the end result of this whole sequence of variables is the attainment of a *goal state*. When this goal state has become manifest, it becomes associated with events in the immediate situation. The sign stimulus is one such event, but there are others. Any stimulus that happens to be in the situation at the time the goal state is attained can become associated with that state. These latter stimuli become, therefore, cues for anticipation of the goal state that ordinarily follows a consummatory response. A motive, McClelland now states, is "a *learned, affectively charged anticipatory goal state* aroused by various cues" (McClelland, 1985, p. 132; italics original).

The process of motive formation is described schematically in Figure 6-1. This process applies to all human motives. Table 6-1 lists the sign stimulus, the affective state, and the consummatory response for some of the more common motives. For example, a situation in which one has an opportunity to have an impact on her or his environment is a sign stimulus for an affective state that produces the consummatory response of self-assertion (see Brehm, 1966). When this behavior results in the person having an impact, the resulting experience becomes conditioned to cues in the environment and becomes the basis for the power motive. To take another example, the demands made by a mildly difficult task, followed by successful completion of the task and a feeling of satisfaction over having met the challenge, establishes the origins of achievement motivation. In much the same way, the presence of other people

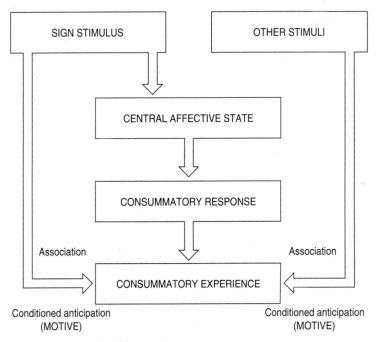

***Figure 6-1.*** Scheme of McClelland's theory of sign stimuli, natural incentives, and motives. (Adapted from *Human Motivation* by D. C. McClelland, 1985, Glenview, IL: Scott, Foresman.)

**TABLE 6-1**
**A Taxonomy of Common Natural Incentives**

| Sign Stimulus | Emotion | Consummatory Response | Motive |
|---|---|---|---|
| Interference with one's impact on the environment | Anger | Assertiveness | Power |
| Pain | Fear | Flight | Avoidance |
| Moderately hard task | Challenge | Effort | Achievement |
| Presence of other people | Social excitation | Seeking of contact | Affiliation |

*Source:* Adapted from *Human Motivation* by D. C. McClelland, 1985, Glenview, IL: Scott, Foresman.

causes a social excitement that elicits gregarious behavior and leads ultimately to affiliative motivation. The role of pain in generating avoidance motivation has already been discussed.

We now have a background in some of the theoretical premises that underlie the study of the three motives listed at the beginning of the chapter as the major descendants of Murray's system of needs: achievement, affiliation, and power. We will now review some of the ways in which these motives have been studied.

## ACHIEVEMENT MOTIVATION

In the preceding section we observed that motives grow out of the intrinsic pleasure that certain behaviors generate. In the case of achievement motivation, people should have an incentive to perform well on a task that is moderately challenging. This incentive can have various effects on behavior. An important one concerns the level of risk that a person should take when given an option. If tasks of moderate difficulty engender the natural incentive for achievement motivation, then people should choose such tasks over those of greater or lesser difficulty. Why is this so? Why, for example, is achievement motivation not set off by the demands of very difficult problems, or very easy ones? Certainly one would derive more pleasure and satisfaction from mastering a terribly hard task than from handling a moderately hard one. On the other hand, if success is the goal, one would be almost certain to succeed on a simple task. So why should a moderately challenging task be the natural incentive for achievement motivation?

# Tendencies to Approach Success and Avoid Failure

**THEORETICAL FORMULATIONS.**    Two answers have been given to this question. We will consider first the one given by J. W. Atkinson, a co-author of the initial theory of achievement motivation (McClelland et al., 1953). Atkinson (1974a) has described a hypothetical "tendency to approach success" ($T_s$) that is equal to the perceived expectancy of success on a task multiplied by the value of success. This concept should be familiar after our earlier discussion of how expectancies and values multiply to determine goal-seeking behavioral tendencies (see Chapter 1). Atkinson made one assumption in designing his theory: expectancy and value are not independent; as one increases, the other decreases. (A moment's thought shows why this is a safe assumption: one derives little satisfaction from succeeding at a task that is too easy but feels elated after overcoming a very difficult one.) Using the terms $P_s$ (probability of success) to indicate expectancy and $I_s$ (incentive value of success) to indicate value, Atkinson stated the relationship between the two as: $I_s = (1 - P_s)$, so that the tendency to approach success could be expressed as $T_s = P_s \times (1 - P_s)$.

A simple example illustrates numerically why a moderately hard task should be associated with the greatest approach tendency. Let us suppose that a person has a choice among a very easy task (where the probability of success is 0.7), a moderate task (with a probability of success of 0.5), and a hard task (having a probability of success of only 0.3). As Table 6-2 shows, the strength of $T_s$ is greatest when $P_s = 0.5$—that is, when the task is neither too hard nor too easy. We need not rely on number manipulations to understand this. Because $P_s$ and $I_s$ are inversely related, any decision that we make about them necessarily involves a tradeoff. If we choose a very easy task, there is little satisfaction to be had because the value of success is too low. If we choose too hard a task, the possible value of success is high but we will probably fail. It makes sense, therefore, to conclude that the best combination of $P_s$ and $I_s$ to choose for maximum satisfaction is the one in which they are about equal.

**TABLE 6-2**
**Tendency to Approach Success for Tasks That Vary in Difficulty**

| Task | $P_s$ | $I_s$ | $T_s$ |
|---|---|---|---|
| Task 1 (very difficult) | 0.3 | 0.7 | 0.21 |
| Task 2 (moderately difficult) | 0.5 | 0.5 | 0.25 |
| Task 3 (very easy) | 0.7 | 0.3 | 0.21 |

This tells only part of the story, however. According to Atkinson, the preference for moderate challenge illustrated in Table 6-2 is characteristic only of people who have relatively high achievement motivation. At this point we must consider another motive that frequently operates in task-related settings: the desire or need to avoid failing. People sometimes work very hard at tasks not so much to succeed as merely to avoid looking bad. Such a behavioral tendency Atkinson has labeled the tendency to avoid failure $(T_f)$. The strength of this tendency is equal to the person's expectancy, or perceived probability, of failure $(P_f)$ times the negative incentive value of failure $(I_f)$. The magnitude of $I_f$ is inferred from the magnitude of the probability of success: the greater the probability of success at a task (i.e., the easier the task is), the worse the person will look if he fails at it. This relationship is expressed in the theory by the equation $I_f = -P_s$.

We need now only remember that $P_s = 1 - P_f$ (because the two outcome probabilities must sum to 1.00), and we are able to calculate the strengths of the tendencies to avoid failure for the same three tasks described in Table 6-2. These outcomes appear in Table 6-3. Here we note that the strongest avoidance tendency (i.e., the greatest negative) is found when the task is of moderate difficulty, and the weakest avoidance tendencies are found when the task is either very difficult or very easy. The person who wants only to avoid looking bad when failing has two options: she can avoid failing by choosing a very easy task, or she can avoid embarrassment following failure by taking on a heroic challenge that is largely beyond her capabilities.

In every situation a person is probably motivated to some extent by both achievement and failure-avoidance motives. Likewise any given person is probably animated sometimes by one motive and sometimes by the other. Nevertheless—and this is where individual differences come into the picture—for most people, one or the other motive tends to be dominant most of the time. When we say that a person is a high achiever, we mean that his or her behavior is guided most of the time by achievement motivation and that in any situation the achievement motivation is likely to be stronger than the motive to avoid failure. Exactly the opposite is true of a person who we designate as being failure-avoidant in his or her approach. Atkinson used the term *resultant achievement motivation* (RAM) to express this balance between the

**TABLE 6-3**
**Tendency to Avoid Failure for Tasks That Vary in Difficulty**

| Task | $P_f$ | $I_f$ | $T_f$ |
|---|---|---|---|
| Task 1 (very difficult) | 0.7 | $-0.3$ | $-0.21$ |
| Task 2 (moderately difficult) | 0.5 | $-0.5$ | $-0.25$ |
| Task 3 (very easy) | 0.3 | $-0.7$ | $-0.21$ |

two motives. Theoretically RAM is equal to achievement motivation minus fear of failure. If the person's achievement motivation is stronger than the motive to avoid failure, the person's RAM is said to be positive; if fear of failure is higher than achievement motivation, RAM is negative.

***RESEARCH ON THE THEORY.*** Numerous studies have been conducted to test the theory of individual differences in risk taking on tasks. In these studies, achievement motivation is assessed by the thematic method described above, and fear of failure is measured by one of several available scales for assessing test anxiety (e.g., Sarason, 1972). Subjects are classified as being above or below the median in their scores on both measures. Two groups are then usually contrasted: subjects who are high (i.e., above the median) in achievement motivation and low in fear of failure (high RAM), and those who are low in achievement motivation and high in fear of failure (low RAM). The conclusions from these studies that seem to be most valid are (1) persons who are high in RAM do tend to prefer moderately difficult tasks, but (2) persons who are low in RAM do *not* show a strong tendency to choose easy and very difficult tasks over moderately difficult ones. What they do show in many instances is a tendency of failure-oriented people to avoid extremely easy

*A strong need to achieve within an academic setting produces an incentive for studying.*

tasks and to seek out very difficult ones (e.g., deCharms & Carpenter, 1968; Hamilton, 1974). The reason for this may be that most people would rather experience a "glorious failure" than succeed by adopting a low standard of success. In our competitive society, a certain amount of prestige seems to be associated with the risk-taking entrepreneur who takes chances in order to "make a bundle." On the other hand, people who compete below their level of ability are likely to attract criticism. Think, for example, of the scorn shown by sports writers for college football teams that play only weaker opponents. The tendency to avoid easy challenges may therefore be part of the fear of social ostracism shown by people who are generally afraid of failure.

We may, therefore, expect this avoidance tendency to be most pronounced among people who have the most to lose by looking as if they are operating below their levels of ability. Such a phenomenon was nicely demonstrated in a study by Isaacson (1964), which applied the Atkinson risk-taking model to an analysis of choices of major areas of study made by college students. Some of the students were in an honors program in which, presumably, they were expected to accept academic challenges. The remainder of the students were enrolled in normal curricula. The difficulty of the various majors had been estimated previously by analyses of how well students who varied in scholastic aptitude had performed in each one. The results of the study, shown in Figure 6-2, indicate that both honors and non-honors students who

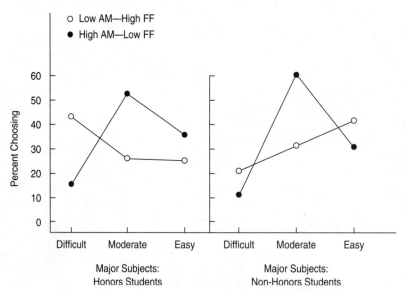

**Figure 6-2.** Percent of students who chose majors of varying difficulty. *Note:* AM = achievement motivation; FF = fear of failure. (Adapted from "Relation Between Achievement, Test Anxiety, and Curricular Choices" by R. L. Isaacson, *Journal of Abnormal and Social Psychology,* 1964, *68,* 447–452.)

were relatively high in achievement motivation opted for majors that were of moderate difficulty. Among students whose main motive was to avoid failure, however, the Atkinson hypothesis was not supported. Honors students showed a clear preference for very difficult majors, whereas non-honors students showed a similarly strong preference for the easiest majors.

## An Alternative Viewpoint

An alternative explanation of why people who are highly motivated to achieve seek out moderately difficult challenges has been derived from the premises of attribution theory. It will be recalled from Chapter 2 that people attribute their outcomes on tasks to various apparent causes, such as ability, effort, task difficulty, or luck. The alternative viewpoint that we are considering here begins with the assumption from attribution theory (e.g., Weiner, 1985) that people feel more positive about successes that are due to their ability than they do to similar successes that are the result of external causes such as luck or the efforts of others. It also holds that achievement-motivated people have a greater desire than their less motivated counterparts to find out how good they are at tasks and that they therefore seek out tasks that give them the greatest amount of informational feedback about their ability. This characteristic of tasks to provide information about a person's ability level has been called *diagnosticity* (Trope & Brickman, 1975) because tasks that have this characteristic are useful in diagnosing ability as a contributor to success or failure relative to other factors. Another way to look at diagnosticity is in the context of the desire that most people have to understand themselves—that is, their "underlying need to assess their own attributes accurately" (Trope, 1975, p. 1005).

Those who pursue this line of reasoning argue that tasks of intermediate difficulty are more diagnostic of ability level than are either very hard or very easy ones. On very easy tasks, success tells us very little about ability level because most people succeed; success is therefore more a function of task difficulty (an external factor) than of personal ability. Likewise, most people fail at very hard tasks, so once again the outcome tells us less about ability than it does about the nature of the task. Only when a task is moderately difficult, when the chance of success is close to 50–50, will individual ability rather than task difficulty play much of a role in determining the outcome, so that success will truly diagnose the person's ability level.

Trope (1975) verified the importance of diagnosticity in task selection through the ingenious device of manipulating subjects' perceptions of task difficulty and diagnosticity information independently. He found that subjects tended to choose highly diagnostic tasks more than less diagnostic ones, and that subjects who were high in achievement motivation made such a choice to a greater degree than did subjects low in achievement motivation. These results therefore support a cognitive attributional approach to achievement motivation.

# AFFILIATIVE MOTIVATION

The study of what motives lie behind interpersonal affiliation has been carried out by several investigators who take different theoretical positions. In this section we will review some of these investigations and the positions that inform them.

## Need for Affiliation

Those who have followed the approach first spelled out by McClelland and colleagues (1953) have studied a need for affiliation, which, like the need for achievement, is defined as a stable individual difference variable. Less attention has been paid to affiliation than to achievement and power. A thematic method of assessing the affiliative need was first developed by Shipley and Veroff (1952), and this need has been shown to have the properties of a true motive in that it energizes, selects, and guides behavior. For example, people who are high in the need for affiliation work harder than others to maintain interpersonal communicative networks; they make a greater number of non-business telephone calls, they write more letters, and they pay more visits to friends than do people who are low in the motive (Lansing & Heyns, 1959). The effects of affiliative needs on everyday behavior have also been shown in a study by McAdams and Constantian (1983) in which participants listed their activities each time they received a signal from paging devices that they carried with them during their daily routines. The study showed that need for affiliation was correlated positively with both talking to others and writing letters.

One reason that the need for affiliation has not attracted more attention may be that some investigators consider it to be mainly an avoidance motive—that is, a fear of rejection. Boyatzis (1973) tested this possibility by developing a projective measure that assessed separately the true need for affiliation and the fear of rejection. It was found that the two motives had different effects on behavior. For instance, need for affiliation was positively correlated with the number of close friends that a person had, whereas fear of rejection was correlated with the degree of similarity in beliefs between people and their close friends. The latter indicates that fear of rejection reflects a defensive desire to be accepted (and not rejected) by others, whereas need for affiliation leads to more active pursuit of good relationships. However, McClelland and Pilon (1983) found that mothers of people high in need for affiliation tended to report that they had been unresponsive to their children's crying during infancy. This suggests that fears of being rejected during childhood may carry over into similar fears in adulthood that influence measures of the need for affiliation.

## The Intimacy Motive

In order to avoid some of the problems associated with the construct of need for affiliation, McAdams (1980) developed an alternative that he labeled the *intimacy motive*, defined as "a recurrent . . . preference or readiness for a particular quality of interpersonal experience, an experience of warm, close, and communicative exchange with another or with others" (McAdams & Powers, 1981, p. 574). The motive is assessed by the thematic method, with intimacy motivation being inferred from story themes that include such items as pleasant interpersonal encounters, interpersonal dialogue leading to personal growth, and a sense of commitment to, and concern for, another person (McAdams, 1980).

Evidence for the effects of the intimacy motive on behavior comes from several studies by McAdams and his associates. In one such study, subjects were rated by their friends on a number of characteristics and these ratings were compared across levels of intimacy motivation in the subjects (McAdams, 1980). Subjects classified as relatively high in the motive were described as being more warm, sincere, loving, natural, and appreciative and as less dominant, outspoken, and self-centered than low scorers. In a subsequent study, McAdams and Powers (1981) used a psychodrama (role-playing) technique in which subjects' actions were videotaped and later scored by judges. The level of intimacy motivation of the actors was found to be positively correlated with the amount of physical proximity to the group that they established during the psychodrama, the number of times they used the pronoun *we* in their speech, their use of reciprocal dialogue with the group, and their willingness to surrender control to the group. In addition, as in the earlier study (McAdams, 1980), peer ratings of the subjects showed that those high in intimacy motivation were seen as being more sincere, loving, and natural than low scorers. In still another study, McAdams (1982) found that intimacy motivation influenced people's memories for events in their past. People who were high in this motive were more likely to recall past experiences in which they felt extreme elation and a sense of transcendence in connection with close interpersonal contacts than were people low in the motive.

In general, McAdams has found that intimacy motivation and need for affiliation are different motives with different behavioral effects. However, in their study of daily ongoing behavior described above, McAdams and Constantian (1983) found that the two motives converge and overlap to some extent. Perhaps the best conclusion to draw is that the two are different motives but they have some common effects. One of McAdams and Constantian's findings is worth noting, however, because it highlights an important difference between the two motives. Intimacy motivation was negatively related to wanting to be alone while interacting with someone, whereas need for affiliation was not. Thus people high in intimacy motivation desire to keep interactions going once they have begun. Need for affiliation was positively related to wanting to interact with others while alone, whereas intimacy motivation was not. In other words, people who are high in need for affiliation desire to start interactions when they are not interacting. This pattern suggests that need for affiliation may represent mainly a desire not to be alone, whereas intimacy motivation may be associated more with enjoyment of contact, and a desire to keep it alive, once it has been established.

## Attachment Theory and Motivation

The study of infant attachment behavior has long been familiar to students of developmental psychology. In several familiar studies involving both human babies and young primates, the importance of contact between infants and adult figures or their surrogates has been established (e.g., Harlow, 1958; Spitz, 1945). On the basis of these studies, a general theory of attachment has been developed (Bowlby, 1980), according to which infants are said to have a need for contact with the mother or mother-substitute. When such attachment is broken, the infant goes through three stages: protest (e.g., crying, searching), despair (sadness, passivity), and, in humans, detachment, which appears to be a defensive avoidance of the mother when she returns.

A model of individual differences in attachment style has been derived from this theoretical position (Ainsworth, Blehar, Waters & Wall, 1978). This model delineates three distinctive attachment styles that develop in children as a function of how they are treated by their mothers. One is the secure style. If the mother has been sensitive and responsive to the child's need for contact, the child comes to feel safe in the environment. She freely explores her surroundings, returning every so often to her mother to establish contact before venturing forth to explore further. The secure child manifests a general sense

*Children whose mothers are inconsistent in meeting their needs for contact when they are infants may later develop an anxious/ambivalent attachment style.*

of confidence and growing independence. Children whose mothers are inconsistent in meeting their needs for contact, sometimes ignoring them and at other times forcing affection on them, come to show the anxious/ambivalent attachment style. Such a child is anxious and fearful, and more concerned with attaching himself to his mother than he is with exploring the environment. Such a child becomes inhibited, dependent, and low in self-confidence. Finally, children who are rejected and avoided by their mothers learn to protect themselves against this loss of contact by ignoring and avoiding the mother in return. A child who displays such an avoidant attachment style may show what appears to be normal exploratory behavior, but this behavior is animated more by a need to escape from the mother than by a need to explore.

It has been proposed that the need for attachment is a prototype for adult motivation and behavior (Shaver, Hazan & Bradshaw, 1988). According to this line of reasoning, attachment styles developed in infancy underlie and help to determine some important adult motives and actions. In one study to test this idea, Hazan and Shaver (1987) found a connection between attachment style and love. Adults responded to a questionnaire that had three statements derived from the writings of the Ainsworth group. Each respondent chose one of the statements that best expressed his or her feelings about close relationships with others (Table 6-4). On the basis of this choice, the respondent was classified as secure, anxious/apprehensive, or avoidant in attachment style. In addition, the questionnaire contained items to assess

### TABLE 6-4
### *Self-Descriptor Prototypes of Attachment Styles*

**Secure Attachment Style**

I find it relatively easy to get close to others and am comfortable depending on them and having them depend on me. I don't often worry about being abandoned or about someone getting too close to me.

**Anxious/Ambivalent Attachment Style**

I find that others are reluctant to get as close as I would like. I often worry that my partner doesn't love me or won't want to stay with me. I want to merge completely with another person, and this desire sometimes scares people away.

**Avoidant Attachment Style**

I am somewhat uncomfortable being close to others; I find it difficult to trust them completely, difficult to allow myself to depend on them. I am nervous when anyone gets too close, and often love partners want me to be more intimate than I feel comfortable being.

*Source:* From "Romantic Love Conceptualized as an Attachment Process," by C. Hazan & P. Shaver, *Journal of Personality and Social Psychology,* 1987, *52,* 511–524.

feelings that occur in romantic relationships (e.g., trust, fear, happiness). Secure respondents expressed greater happiness, friendship, and trust in their relationships than did persons in the other groups. Anxious/ambivalent people scored higher than others on jealousy, expressed a greater mix of pain and joy in their relationships, and showed a more obsessive preoccupation with their loved ones. Avoidant respondents expressed the highest level of fear of close relationships. Results similar to these (which were obtained among Americans) have also been reported for respondents in Australia (Feeney & Noller, 1990). Thus a relationship appears to exist between attachment style and the ways people carry out romantic relationships.

A similar concordance between attachment style and work motivation has been shown by Hazan and Shaver (1990). Using a method similar to the study just described, these researchers found that secure persons showed the highest level of interest in their jobs, the greatest satisfaction with work, and the least fear or worry about being evaluated. People who were anxious/ambivalent, by contrast, tended to treat work mainly as a search for approval, to express feelings of not being appreciated on the job, and to prefer working with others to working alone. This distinction suggests that a secure attachment style developed during childhood may play a role in the development of intrinsic interest in work, whereas an anxious/ambivalent style may underlie to some degree an approval-centered approach (see Chapter 5). Finally, persons characterized by the avoidant style tended to regard work primarily as a means of getting away from undesired social relationships.

A third area of life to which infant attachment has been related is fear of personal death. Mikulincer, Florian and Tolmacz (1990) have reported finding that secure adults report less fear of death than insecurely attached ones and that the greatest fear of death is expressed by anxious/ambivalent persons. This finding seems to fit the general picture of the secure person as one who shows relatively little distress over separation in childhood and who carries this same style into adulthood.

## POWER MOTIVATION

In a formal sense, the power motive is similar to the achievement and affiliative motives; like the latter, it is engaged and activated by natural incentives. The scoring categories for inferring power motivation from stories were developed by Winter (1973) and consist of such themes as engaging in strong action, controlling and/or helping other people, inducing emotional responses such as happiness or fear in others, and having a concern for one's reputation as an effective individual. Taken together, these themes point to the natural incentive for the power motive: having impact on one's environment and appearing to be a competent and "in-control" person (see Table 6-1).

# Behavioral Correlates of Power Motivation

The power motive affects behavior in many ways. Winter (1973) found that young men with a high need for power are relatively likely to engage in competitive sporting events, and McClelland and Watson (1973) discovered that men with strong power needs placed more risky bets while playing roulette than did less power-motivated males, provided that the betting activity was observed by others. It would appear that the need for power generates specific behaviors only when people can thereby be seen as standing out and having impact on their surroundings. The power motive is also correlated with aggression among working class men (Boyatzis, 1973) and with spouse abuse among middle-class men (Mason & Blankenship, 1987).

# A Model of Power Orientation

McClelland, Davis, Kalin, and Wanner (1972) found four types of behavior to be correlated with high levels of power motivation: (1) power-oriented reading (i.e., a liking for literature about sexual and aggressive themes), (2) collection of prestige possessions like expensive automobiles, weapons, or stereo equipment, (3) participation in competitive sports, and (4) membership and officeholding in organizations. From these data McClelland (1975) designed a two-dimensional model of power motivation that describes four different power orientations. The model is shown in Table 6-5. Its two dimensions are the *source* of power (i.e., whether power comes from within the person or from outside the self) and the *object* of power (i.e., whether the power is directed toward the self or toward some other person or persons). As Table 6-5 shows,

**TABLE 6-5**
***Classification of Four Power Orientations***

| Object of Power | Source of Power | | | |
|---|---|---|---|---|
| | **External** | | **Internal** | |
| Self | I. | Power-based reading<br>Religious mysticism<br>Drug and alcohol use | II. | Collection of possessions<br>Body-building<br>Self-discipline |
| Other | IV. | Organization membership<br>Messianism<br>Bureaucratic style | III. | Competitive sports<br>Aggression, bullying<br>"Helping" to dominate |

*Note:* Roman numerals represent hypothetical stages in development (see text for details).
*Source:* Adapted from *Power: The Inner Experience,* by D. C. McClelland, New York: Irvington, 1975.

*Body building is sometimes motivated by a desire to feel a sense of inner power.*

each of the four behavioral correlates of power listed by McClelland and colleagues (1972) occupies a quadrant in this model.

When the person feels the source of his or her power to be some external agent but the object of power to be the self, the result is behavior through which some external source is used to make the person "feel strong." The power-oriented reading that McClelland found among men high in need for power may have such an effect, possibly by engendering hero worship and identification with strong characters. In the same manner a person may follow a dominating leader and draw personal strength from becoming absorbed in a mighty cause. McClelland has also shown that the need for power is closely allied with consumption of alcohol, and that feelings of strength can be elicited by mild intoxication (McClelland et al., 1972).

By collecting possessions that enhance one's prestige, the person derives power for the self from personal sources. The person who typifies this combination is the self-centered individual who exerts great personal discipline in order to discover the strength that lies within. Developing one's physical resources through body building or one's mental resources through study represents another avenue to power for people who take this orientation.

When the source of power is internal but the object is another person or persons, the classic case of the aggressive dominator is defined. Such a person will manifest a competitive, hard-driving style in which winning at the expense of others is the major incentive. Specific examples of the type of person who seeks power in this way are the bully and the rapist, both of whom seek to enhance personal power through acts of violence and domination of others.

Finally, the combination of an external source and an external object of power creates the sort of person who seeks membership in, and leadership of, organizations, hoping thereby to influence and control others for the sake of the organization's goals. An extreme example is the person who sees himself or herself as a messenger from God, deriving power from a higher authority for the purpose of converting others and saving the world. To a lesser extent, the typical bureaucrat, who manages other people within the context of a larger organization from which the power to manage is derived, shows the same sort of power orientation as the religious messiah.

McClelland (1975) has argued that these four basic ways in which people express power motivation match four successive stages in psychological maturity similar to the stages in ego development described by Erikson (1963). The progression from the first to the fourth quadrant in Table 6-5 (from Roman numerals I to IV) is hypothesized to establish this succession of stages. Thus McClelland proposes that the highest form in which the power motive may be expressed is through the belief that one is moved to do his or her duty to others by following some higher external source of authority. In effect, in this scenario the self drops out as both a source and an object of power.

This is an interesting speculation for which virtually no evidence has been produced. However, two studies by Winter have yielded results suggesting that certain "lower" forms of expressing the need for power can be eliminated by the introduction of "higher" social concerns. Winter was particularly interested in comparing people who exercise power through such means as holding office in organizations with people who do so through "profligate" behavior such as drinking, fighting, and sexual exploitation. In one study, Winter (1988) found that this difference in behaviors was related to whether or not the persons involved had younger brothers or sisters (Table 6-6); office-holding was positively related to having younger siblings, whereas fighting and generally profligate behavior were negatively related to the latter. Why should this be so? Winter and Barenbaum (1985) suggested an answer: having (and presumably caring for) younger brothers or sisters may make people adopt a greater sense of social responsibility. This may inhibit the less socially desirable forms of power expression and channel the motive into more socially responsible paths. To test this, Winter and Barenbaum developed a thematic TAT-type instrument for assessing responsibility. When they determined the degree of correlation between a need for power and a score reflecting antisocial and profligate behavior (consisting of such actions as drinking,

**TABLE 6-6**
**Correlations Between Power Motivation and Two Behavior Variables: Office Holding and Participation in a Physical Fight as a Function of Having/Not Having Younger Siblings**

|  | Younger Siblings | No Younger Siblings |
|---|---|---|
| Officeholding | .45 | .05 |
| Participation in fight | −.24 | .11 |

*Source:* Adapted from "The Power Motive in Women—and Men" by D. G. Winter, 1988, *Journal of Personality and Social Psychology, 54*, 510–519.

fighting, involvement in traffic accidents, and impulsive behavior), a significant positive correlation for both women and men was found only when the responsibility score was low. These findings suggest that the adoption of a sense of responsibility may underlie, in part, the transition from Stage III to Stage IV in the overall scheme of power orientation.


## Power Syndromes

Further light on the distinction between Stage III and Stage IV expressions of power is found in McClelland's discussion of two basic power syndromes, or general styles in which power is wielded. The first, which resembles the pattern seen in Stage III, is called the *conquistador* (McClelland, 1975) or Don Juan (Winter, 1973) syndrome. It is characterized by a generally tough and overbearing style in both men and women. Dynamically it is formed by the combination of a high need for power, a low need for affiliation, and a low sense of inhibition in expressing power. The latter resembles what Winter and Barenbaum (1985; see above) called low responsibility. In men this syndrome is usually called *machismo* and is typified by aggressiveness and sexual domination of women. In women it reveals itself in general toughness and argumentativeness. In both genders the behavior is consistent with that of the stereotyped masculine role.

The other major syndrome, which corresponds to Stage IV in Table 6-5, is the *imperial* syndrome. This results from the combination of a high need for power, a low need for affiliation, and a high sense of inhibition in expressing power. The person who manifests this syndrome expresses power only through socially approved channels and, as a consequence, exercises power through organizations and bureaucracies. As noted, the public servant who operates at this level exercises power for social, not personal, reasons.

## Power, Stress, and Illness

The combination of a high need for power with a low need for affiliation and a tendency to inhibit expressing power may also render a person relatively susceptible to stress-related physical disorders. It was shown by McClelland (1979), for example, to be associated with elevated blood pressure in men. Subsequent studies showed that subjects who manifested this same pattern of motives and activity inhibition also reacted to stressful situations with increased arousal, reduced immune activity, and a higher incidence of respiratory illness than shown by persons who did not fit this pattern (McClelland, Floor, Davidson & Saron, 1980; McClelland & Jemmott, 1980; McClelland, Alexander & Marks, 1982). From such findings, McClelland and his associates have developed a theoretical model that links power and affiliation motives and life stress to both physical illness and several intervening physiological processes (Figure 6-3).

This model is grounded in empirical evidence. The high need for power, relatively low need for affiliation, and inhibition of the expression of power combine with stressful life events to create what McClelland calls stressed power motivation. This combination, as already noted, has been shown to be correlated with the incidence and severity of respiratory illness and with hypertension. It has also been shown to be associated with an increased output of epinephrine by the adrenal glands (McClelland et al., 1980). Increased epinephrine output is commonly associated with increased stress through the

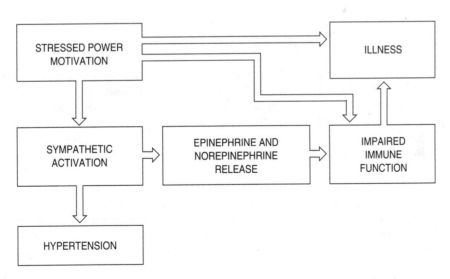

***Figure 6-3.*** Scheme of the theory that relates stressed power motivation to physiological stress and illness. (Adapted from *Human Motivation* by D. C. McClelland, 1985, Glenview, IL: Scott, Foresman.)

activation of the sympathetic branch of the autonomic nervous system. The inhibited power pattern has also been related to suppression of activity in the body's immune system. The increased output of norepinephrine, a biogenic substance like epinephrine, has likewise been associated with the inhibited power pattern. Finally, norepinephrine output has been shown to be associated with suppression of the body's immune system, causing McClelland and his associates to suspect that the former may help cause the latter (McClelland, Ross & Patel, 1985). Reduction of the immune function may in turn increase the likelihood of contacting infectious disease.

## Conclusions

Perhaps the most obvious characteristic of the power motive that emerges from recent research is that it influences people's lives mainly in combination with other variables. The development of the various manifestations of the power motivation across the four hypothesized stages appears to involve mixtures of the need for power with certain (as yet unstated) developmental variables, with an emerging sense of responsibility for others, and with a need for affiliation. The need for power is manifested in a wide range of specific behaviors, depending on the source and the object of power and on the interacting effects of the previously mentioned variables. Power motivation therefore has no simple and invariant effect on behavior. The recent discoveries that link power motivation to physiological stress and physical illness introduce an additional dimension to the study of the effects of this motive state.

# CHAPTER SUMMARY

**1.** The approach to human motivation begun by Murray and developed by McClelland and his associates in the 1950s is built on the idea that motives are nonconscious determinants of behavior. Because motives are not accessible to conscious awareness, their strength must be assessed from an analysis of fantasy behavior. Various projective measures modeled after Murray's Thematic Apperception Test have been used for such assessment.

**2.** McClelland has consistently defined motives as learned states of affect that select, guide, and energize behavior. Affect that is initially aroused by specific sign stimuli energizes consummatory responses that produce desired goals. The latter, which are natural incentives, become conditioned to stimuli in the situation. These stimuli thereby become cues for affectively charged conditioned anticipation of goal states.

**3.** In a more recent version of the theory, behavior is said to be guided and energized by either nonconscious implicit needs, measured thematically, or conscious self-attributed needs, assessed through self-report tests. As was noted in Chapter 2, self-attributed needs are especially likely to lead to the formation of specific incentives and goals by becoming manifest as values in specific social situations.

**4.** The study of achievement motivation has addressed to a large extent the choices that people make among tasks that vary in difficulty. People in whom achievement motivation is stronger than fear of failure generally prefer tasks of intermediate difficulty. Two explanations have been given for this finding. One emphasizes the maximum affective utility of an act that can be expected to lead to success 50% of the time. The other stresses the informational value of tasks in terms of the feedback that performance gives about the person's level of ability. Moderately difficult tasks, by maximizing such diagnosticity, are best able to satisfy the need for information about ability.

**5.** Affiliative motivation has traditionally been studied as a need to seek out and maintain human contact. Measures of this need have been criticized, however, on the grounds that they actually assess a need to avoid disapproval. The concept of intimacy motivation has been developed as an alternative to the need for affiliation. This motive is correlated with a loving nature, warmth, sincerity, and a lack of self-centeredness.

**6.** Attachment theory, originally developed to describe the contact between infants and their mothers, has been extended to the study of adult motives through the principle of adult attachment styles. Adults are accordingly classified as secure, anxious/ambivalent, or avoidant in their relationships with others. These styles are, in turn, correlated with motivation in love relationships and work.

**7.** Power motivation predicts four broad classes of behavior that can be located along dimensions related to the source and the object of power. These classes represent four orientations to power through which persons may proceed with increasing psychological growth and development. This sequence begins with the stage in which both the source and the object of power are the self and culminates in the stage in which both are external to the self.

**8.** Two basic syndromes describe how power is used. The conquistador syndrome, defined as the result of a high need for power, a low need for affiliation, and weak inhibitions in exercising power, is manifested in dominating, bullying, and aggressive behavior. The imperial syndrome, defined as the outcome of a high need for power, a low need for affiliation, and strong inhibitions in exercising power, leads to a controlled and bureaucratic manner of exercising power. Inhibition in exercising power may be related to a sense of social responsibility, which produces behavior consistent with the imperial syndrome.

**9.** The combination of high need for power, low need for affiliation, and strong inhibition disposes the individual to be relatively vulnerable to stressors. This motive pattern has been associated with hypertension, elevated epinephrine and norepinephrine levels, suppressed immune activity, and respiratory illness.

CHAPTER 7

# AROUSAL

## CHAPTER OUTLINE

In Chapter 1 we observed that at one time the concept of motivation was restricted to descriptions of the intensity of behavior, with the direction of behavior attributed to other variables. For this reason, the psychology of motivation consisted largely of theories related to drive and arousal. We also noted in Chapter 1 that current approaches take a broader and more holistic approach in which motivation involves an interplay of many variables. The material covered so far has thrown the blanket of "motivation" over a rich array of cognitive, affective, and activation-related concepts.

Constructs related to the intensity of behavior still play an important role in motivation, even though they no longer occupy the central role that they once did. In this chapter some of these constructs will be reviewed, beginning with a brief introduction to the earliest among them, drive theory. Following that, the current status of the concept of arousal will be described, with the focus mainly on the concept of optimal arousal levels and the physiological status of arousal. The last part of the chapter will be devoted to an examination of the relationship between arousal and performance.

## DRIVE THEORY

In Chapter 1 we reviewed the basic premises of drive theory as they were spelled out by Hull (1943). Although this theory eventually failed to provide a general explanation for behavior, it was a dominant viewpoint at one time, and we will review it briefly here. Hull taught that reducing drive is the basis of reinforcement and that through reinforcement a response becomes more habitual for the person. Thus Hull concluded that *habit strength* (*H*) for any behavior is a direct function of the number of times that behavior has been reinforced. But habit strength tells us only how likely it is that a response will occur in a given situation. The response must also be energized or intensified in order for a response potential to develop. Hull considered this *excitatory potential* (*E*), as he called it, to be equal to the habit strength for the response multiplied by the overall *drive* (*D*) level of the organism. Hence the multiplicative rule is $E = D \times H$.

From this basic premise, some predictions about human behavior could be derived. On tasks in which the correct response has the highest level of habit strength (i.e., easy or overlearned tasks), increased drive should lead to improved performance. For the same reason, on difficult tasks a high level of drive should impair performance by multiplying with (i.e., energizing) incorrect responses. Furthermore, as one works at a difficult task, drive should first impair performance (when the task is novel) but later facilitate performance after one has mastered the problem.

The study of drive in human behavior was carried out most extensively in connection with research on the Manifest Anxiety Scale (MAS). This scale was devised by Taylor (1953) to assess individual differences in tendencies to become aroused and anxious in potentially threatening settings. Taylor considered this anxious arousal to be a manifestation of drive. Thus, by assessing anxiety level with the MAS, one could predict how well or how poorly subjects should perform on easy and difficult tasks by invoking the multiplicative rule.

An example of this is seen in a study by Spielberger and Smith (1966). Subjects were given the task of memorizing a list of 12 nonsense syllables in order. These subjects had previously been classified into two groups according to whether they had scored relatively high or relatively low on the MAS. A well-documented characteristic of serial lists such as the one learned by Spielberger and Smith's subjects is the serial position effect: that items at the two ends of the list are learned more rapidly than those in the middle. Spielberger and Smith found that items 1, 2, 3, and 12 from their list were the least difficult to learn and items 6, 7, and 8 the most difficult; these two groups of items were therefore designated easy and hard, respectively, for further analysis. Figure 7-1 shows how many of these items were recalled in their correct positions across a total of 25 runs through the list (trials). Obviously the easy items at the two ends were learned relatively quickly, especially by subjects high in drive level as measured by the MAS. High drive initially hampered learning of the difficult midlist items, but once those items had become familiar (after the 15th trial), high drive facilitated learning. All of these findings are consistent with the predictions from drive theory.

The findings of the Spielberger-Smith experiment cannot be explained easily in terms of conscious striving for a goal, but they are accounted for without difficulty by drive theory. Perhaps the safest conclusion to draw from such results is that although the drive theoretical approach is no longer dominant, and although it does not account for most aspects of complex goal-related action, it still offers the most parsimonious explanation of at least *some* human behavior (see Brody, 1983).

# AROUSAL THEORY

## Arousal Versus Drive

Earlier in this chapter and elsewhere (Chapter 1), the theories of drive and arousal were discussed in terms of their similarities, in that both describe the nonspecific energization of behavior. However, the two theories are not

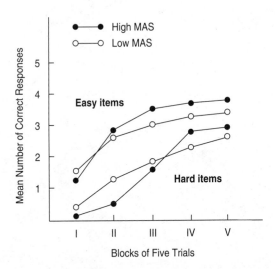

**Figure 7-1.** Number of times items were recalled in serial learning as a function of item difficulty and manifest anxiety. [From "Anxiety (Drive), Stress, and Serial-Position Effects in Serial-Verbal Learning" by C. D. Spielberger and L. H. Smith, *Journal of Experimental Psychology*, 1966, 72, 589–595.]

identical. The major premise of drive theory is that people are motivated to reduce or eliminate the effects of stimulating conditions. One of the reasons that drive theory failed to last as a major explanation for behavior was that human activity often does not reveal this tendency to reduce drive. People show strong proclivities to seek out and engage in activities that produce the *opposite* of reduced drive. Racing motorcycles, riding on roller coasters, sport parachuting, bungee jumping, and going to horror movies are just a few activities that elevate drive levels, yet many people regularly pursue such pastimes and enjoy them. Furthermore, the behavior of young children includes large amounts of time devoted solely to poking into cabinets, manipulating objects, and generally exploring their surroundings, motivated, apparently, only by curiosity. Even animals spend much of their time exploring their surroundings.

Research on curiosity and exploratory behavior was one of the major developments that caused many investigators to question the usefulness of drive theory. Another was the study of the effects of sensory deprivation carried out during the 1950s. These studies showed that there are definite limits to the amount of stimulus reduction that people can tolerate. When subjected to long periods of reduced stimulation, humans exhibit mounting stress (Persky, Zuckerman, Curtis & Perloff, 1965) and an increasing tendency to seek complex stimuli (Jones, 1966). What these studies appeared to show was that

People sometimes try to attain a high level of arousal through participation in exciting activities.

low levels of stimulation, which elicit little drive and should, according to drive theory, be attractive, are in fact drive inducing and aversive.

## *The Optimal Stimulation Level*

At first, drive theorists attempted to assimilate such findings to their viewpoint by inventing new drive states to which they gave names like the "boredom drive." In this way they argued that understimulation, instead of being a condition of low drive, is actually a high drive state, and that exploratory behavior is reinforced by a reduction in this condition (Berlyne, 1963). Gradually, however, the view began to emerge that drive reduction may not be the sole basis for reinforcement, and that under some conditions slight *increases* in stimulation may be reinforcing. Such conditions would be those in which the person is operating at a level of stimulation that is too low for efficient functioning (Hebb, 1955) or maximum pleasure (Berlyne, 1967). It was therefore concluded that people seek from their environments not a minimal level of stimulation, but a moderate *optimal* level.

The process of stimulation is directly related to certain characteristics, or properties, of stimuli. The most obvious are physical properties like intensity, duration, and frequency. Also important are the *collative* properties, which refer to such matters as the way in which stimuli are organized and the ways they relate to each other and to the environment. Among the major collative properties are novelty, changeability, complexity, meaningfulness, and surprise value. Variation along these dimensions elicits arousal in much the same way as do variations in intensity or rapidity of presentation (Berlyne, 1960). A novel stimulus, for instance, elicits more arousal than a familiar one and a complex stimulus is more arousing than a simple one. In the case of every collative property, there is some discrepancy between the stimulus and some expected or resting state (see Chapter 3).

Berlyne (1966) extended the idea of the optimal stimulation level to curiosity and exploratory behavior, proposing that such behavior can be of two types. Both are motivated by a need to bring stimulation nearer to the optimal level. One type, *diversive* exploration, is a reaction to understimulation. The individual becomes habituated to her surroundings, experiences boredom, and is uncomfortable. To raise her level of stimulation she seeks out new stimuli to replace the ones to which she has adapted. The other type of exploratory behavior, *specific* exploration, is a process by which an overstimulated person tries to bring his level of arousal down by seeking familiar or simple stimuli. This requires a selective scanning of the environment in order to find stimuli that reduce arousal.

Arousal theory, with its concept of the optimal level, offers an alternative to drive theory's explanation of the intensive aspects of behavior and at the same time avoids the pitfalls of the concept of drive reduction. The two theories have traditionally differed in other ways as well. Whereas drive is a purely hypothetical construct inferred from behavior, with no necessary links to physiology, arousal has usually been thought of in terms of physiological activation. It is often assessed indirectly through such measures as changes in heart rate, skin conductance, muscle tension, and blood pressure.

## Arousal and Stimulus Seeking

The principle of the optimal stimulation level leads to the conclusion that living beings are happiest and function best when they are moderately aroused. Any event that causes a person's arousal level to exceed or to drop below the optimal level is a cause for either negative affect or diminished positive affect; such an event will be experienced as aversive (Konecni, 1979). It is this aversive decrease in positive affect that motivates the person to either increase or decrease the arousal level so as to bring it nearer to the optimal level. The relationship of arousal to affect is therefore a curvilinear one, described by an inverted U curve commonly called Wundt's curve after the German psychologist Wilhelm Wundt, who first described it (see Figure 7-2).

The theory of motivation that arose from the idea of the optimal arousal level (e.g., Berlyne, 1967; Hunt, 1965; Walker, 1980) was a discrepancy theory similar to the one reviewed in Chapter 3 in connection with the process of goal seeking. The optimal level for maximum positive affect can be thought of as a constant goal that people seek. Deviations from this goal state, caused by either overstimulation or boredom, are discrepant from the goal and thereby induce relatively negative affect that, in turn, motivates either stimulus reduction or stimulus-seeking behavior. When a person wishes to relax after a day filled with problems on the job, for example, he will probably avoid both noisy parties and total solitude with nothing to do. The most comfortable level

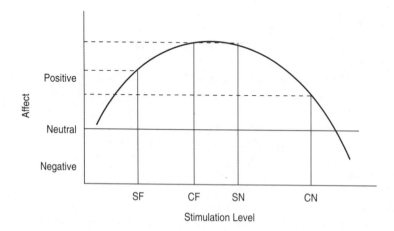

*Figure 7-2.* Wundt's curve. The four discrete points on the stimulation level axis represent four combinations of novelty and complexity: SF = simple familiar; CF = complex familiar, SN = simple novel, and CN = complex novel.

of stimulation is more likely to be found with a few friends over a quiet dinner.

The several collative properties have an additive effect on arousal. For example, if an event is both complex and novel, arousal from the two sources adds up to make this event more arousing than one that is either simple and novel or complex and familiar. The least arousing combination is found in a familiar and simple event. Four hypothetical events that combine novelty and complexity are superimposed on Wundt's curve in Figure 7-2. Some interesting phenomena can be explained by this curve. For example, the phenomenon of "acquired taste," whereby people start out disliking something but come to like it as they become more familiar with it, may represent a change in affect associated with a complex event (like eating exotic food or looking at modern art) that is initially unfamiliar (hence, complex and novel) but gradually becomes complex and familiar with increased experience. The result would be a shift from mild negative affect to fairly strong positive affect. The same

*Relaxing with a few friends is one way in which people achieve an optimal level of arousal after a stressful day.*

reasoning may explain why persons who have been trained in music enjoy atonal and complex music more than do untrained people (Crozier, 1974).

# PSYCHOLOGICAL REVERSALS

## The Theory

An alternative explanation for the relationship between arousal and affect is the theory of *psychological reversals* (Apter, 1989). This theory states that humans have not one optimal level of arousal, but two. Which of the two levels is optimal at any given time depends on which of two orientations toward the environment the person has taken. These orientations constitute what Apter calls *metamotivational* states.

One of these states characterizes the person who is serious, task centered, and engaged in working toward a goal. This is called the *telic* state, and it is characterized by decision, commitment, a focusing of attention on the goal, and the activity necessary to attain the goal. Note the similarity between the telic state and what Kuhl (1985) called action orientation (see Chapter 3). A person who is in the telic state takes pleasure in making progress toward a goal and in ultimately reaching it. A more extreme example of a telic state is evoked by the need for survival under threatening conditions; here, too, the person must be task centered and serious because the goal may be life itself.

The other state is called the *paratelic*. The person in this state is less concerned with reaching a goal than with whatever activity happens to be going on. This state is marked by a focus on the activity itself rather than in its instrumental purpose, and it can generate a playful attitude under some conditions. A person who is deeply immersed in a paratelic state may become so engrossed in activity (as creative artists sometimes do) that no thought is given to such mundane matters as eating or sleeping. This state is similar to what Csikszentmihalyi (1990) has called "flow" activity.

The person's metamotivational state and arousal state function jointly to determine the optimal level of arousal. Arousal, in this theory, is experienced in emotional terms; the specific emotion that is experienced depends on the metamotivational condition at the time the arousal occurs. The telic state can be thought of as an "arousal-avoidance" condition. The person who is expending effort in trying to carry out a difficult task performs best if the overall arousal level is relatively low. Too much arousal under these conditions will overload the person's information-processing capabilities, causing attentional difficulties and slowing progress toward completion of the task. The person experiences high arousal as anxiety and is motivated to avoid such a state. The telically oriented person prefers relatively low arousal, which is experienced as relaxation. This is shown in Figure 7-3.

The paratelic state is characterized by "arousal-approach" tendencies. When one is engaged in play, for example, or in creative activity, a high state

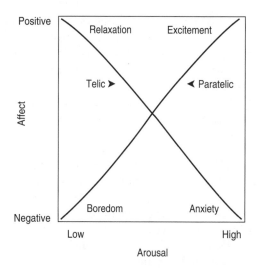

*Figure 7-3.* Relationship of affect to arousal for persons in telic or paratelic metamotivational states. (From *Reversal Theory: Motivation, Emotion and Personality* by M. J. Apter, 1989, London: Routledge.)

of arousal is usually exhilarating, not aversive, and experienced as pleasant excitement. The aversive condition for the person in the paratelic state is underarousal, which is experienced as boredom (see Figure 7-3). This theory therefore stipulates two optimal arousal levels: a low one associated with the telic state and a high one associated with the paratelic state. A person is motivated to strive for one or the other depending on his metamotivational state at the time.

The psychological reversals by which the theory is named are changes from one metamotivational state to the other. As noted in Chapter 3, behavior consists of frequent changes from one motive to another. Changing circumstances elicit different tendencies and strengthen some motives at the expense of others. This is what happens in psychological reversals. The change from one state to the other causes the experience elicited by one's level of arousal to change accordingly, with corresponding changes in one's motives and emotions. If, for example, a person suddenly leaves a paratelic state and enters a telic state, a high level of arousal will change from pleasant excitement to anxiety. Whereas she had previously been inclined to seek the high state of arousal, she will now be motivated to avoid it. A passenger on an exciting ride at an amusement park, for example, may find that her pleasant state of activation suddenly turns to fear and panic if she hears a loud sound of something snapping inside the mechanism.

Reversal theory predicts that as one changes between telic and paratelic states over time, so should one's tendencies to seek or avoid arousing conditions. This has been shown in a study by Walters, Apter, and Svebak (1982).

The subjects in this study were asked every 15 minutes over a period of four hours to make several ratings: their preferences among a number of colors, how arousing each color was, and how they felt at the time of the assessment. In the latter rating the subject chose one adjective from each of three pairs: playful-serious, spontaneous-planning ahead, and bored/excited–relaxed/anxious. The theory predicted that if a subject preferred at a given time an arousing color over less arousing ones, the self-description of feeling at that time should be playful, spontaneous, and excited because each of these is a characteristic of a paratelic orientation. On the other hand, if a subject preferred a less arousing color over more arousing ones, the self description should be expressed as serious, planning, and relaxed, all characteristics of a telic orientation. Significant effects were found for ratings of playful-serious and spontaneous-planning. Subjects who described themselves at the time as playful or spontaneous showed a clear preference for highly arousing colors (Figure 7-4), whereas subjects who described themselves as serious and planning showed an equally clear preference for less arousing colors.

## Causes of Psychological Reversals

The study by Walters and colleagues (1982) did not go into what caused subjects to experience psychological reversals over the four-hour period; it showed only the effects of the two states. What are some of the causes of

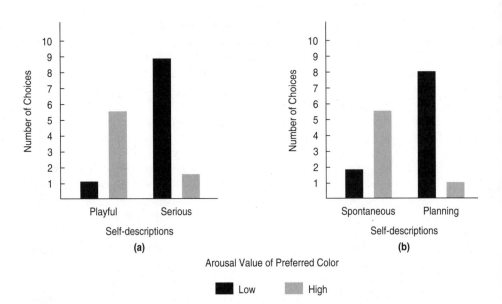

*Figure 7-4.* Choice of high- versus low-arousing colors in relation to playful-serious and spontaneous-planning moods. (From "Color Preference, Arousal, and the Theory of Psychological Reversals" by J. Walters, M. J. Apter, and S. Svebak, *Motivation and Emotion,* 1982, *6,* 193–215.)

reversals? Consider first some of the reasons why people change from a paratelic to a telic state. Salient cues in the environment may elicit such changes. For example, a person engaged in some enjoyable activity may be reminded by glancing at a calendar of an imminent deadline for some work that had been put off. Immediately the person's pleasant excitement will yield to an unpleasant feeling of anxiety. Needs may also intrude on a person in the paratelic state to cause a reversal. The artist who has been absorbed in creative activity, for example, will sooner or later experience hunger and other bodily demands that cannot be ignored. Nor does the intrusive need have to be biological to induce a reversal. Consider two people playing a game of tennis. What starts out as an occasion for fun and enjoyment may suddenly turn seriously competitive if the players think that their self-esteem is at stake. A paratelic orientation of tennis as fun may change into one of wanting to win at any cost. Recall also the discussion in Chapter 5 of studies in which intrinsic motivation for a task was undermined by extrinsic rewards and other circumstances that shifted the person from an autonomous to a control orientation. Possibly what Deci and Ryan (1985) call the autonomy orientation involves a measure of what Apter calls the paratelic state: in both conditions the person may derive some pleasure from feelings of self-determination that have nothing directly to do with the particular goal being sought. It would follow from reversal theory that the introduction of an extrinsic reward for behavior that has been intrinsically motivated may cause a person to shift from a paratelic to a telic state, which could cause the activity to become less attractive and more like a chore.

What conditions prompt the other type of reversal—from the telic to the paratelic? One might be the completion of a task. People often react to the end of an important job by feeling relaxed and seeking activity that will enhance and prolong the relaxation. Another could be failure to reach a goal; the person may respond by adopting an attitude of indifference and pleasure seeking, at least for a short time. Even the simple act of taking a break from a difficult task in order to seek some temporary diversion can bring about a brief interval of paratelic orientation. The point of all these examples is that neither metamotivational state is rigid; the person may pass from one to the other as conditions change.

# INDIVIDUAL DIFFERENCES IN STIMULUS SEEKING

## Extraversion-Introversion

The theory of optimal stimulation levels explains exciting behaviors such as going on frightening amusement park rides as diversionary behaviors aimed at bringing the arousal level nearer to the optimum. All people engage in stimulating behavior of some magnitude at some times, but there is considerable individual variation. The most highly developed approach to different

*Extroverts seek situations in which the surrounding level of noise is relatively high.*

individual desires for stimulation is the theory of introversion-extraversion proposed by Eysenck (1967). This theory states that introverts are more arousable than extraverts, so that at any level of stimulation they show greater physiological activation (Bullock & Gilliland, 1993). Accordingly, the optimal level of stimulation is lower for introverts than for extraverts. If, therefore, persons of the two personality types are placed in the same environment, the extravert is more likely than the introvert to be understimulated. In order to raise her or his level of stimulation to attain the optimal, the extravert typically seeks out exciting and arousing events. This is why introverts prefer quiet surroundings and avoid crowds of people, whereas extraverts make friends, go to parties, and avoid prolonged isolation.

Evidence of greater stimulus seeking by extraverts than by introverts has come from numerous studies (Eysenck, 1967). One question that arose in connection with these findings was whether extraverts and introverts, after choosing to expose themselves to different levels of stimulation, manifest approximately the same levels of arousal after having done so. In other words, is the optimal arousal level the same for both groups, with the only difference being that this level is achieved at a lower level of stimulation by one than by the other?

This problem was investigated in a study by Geen (1984). Subjects in this experiment were men who had been classified as extraverts or introverts on the basis of their scores on the Eysenck Personality Inventory, a scale commonly used to measure this trait. All subjects then took part in a learning task while exposed to noise presented at a constant intensity level. Half of the introverts and half of the extraverts were asked to adjust the noise generator until it produced a volume that was "just right" as a background while they worked at the task. For each introvert and extravert who chose a certain noise level, a person of the other type was assigned that level by the experimenter and was given no choice in the matter. This procedure is called a yoked control design; each introvert who selected the noise level that he received was "yoked" to an extravert who received that same noise arbitrarily, and vice versa.

As the subjects went through the task while hearing the noise, their levels of skin conductance were measured. The findings of the experiment are shown in Figure 7-5. The dependent variable is the number of skin resistance responses (SRRs) that occurred during the first two minutes of the task period. SRRs are specific short-term changes of a given magnitude followed by a rapid return to baseline. They reflect accurately the overall arousal level of the subject over time. Introverts chose, on the average, less intense noise than did extraverts (55 decibels versus 72 decibels). At both intensities, extraverts

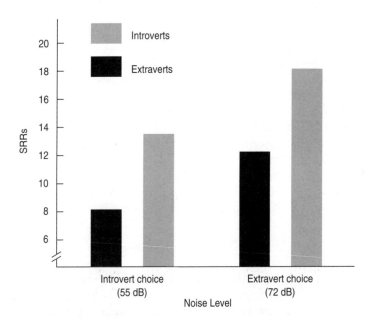

*Figure 7-5.* Number of SRRs among extraverts and introverts as a function of noise intensity. (Adapted from "Preferred Stimulation Levels in Introverts and Extraverts: Effects on Arousal and Performance" by R. G. Geen, *Journal of Personality and Social Psychology,* 1984, *46,* 1303–1312.)

were less aroused than introverts, as the theory predicts. Extraverts and introverts did *not* differ significantly in their arousal levels elicited by the chosen levels of stimulation. Introverts who received noise at 55-dB intensity showed an average of 13.85 SRRs, whereas extraverts who received noise at 72-dB intensity showed an average of 12.00 SRRs. The optimal arousal level is therefore approximately the same for extraverts as it is for introverts; what differs between the two personality groups is the level of stimulation at which that optimal level is reached.

## Sensation Seeking

Earlier in this chapter we noted that research done in the 1950s and 1960s on stimulus deprivation formed part of the basis for the emergence of the concept of optimal stimulation. Another outcome of that research was the discovery of individual differences in tendencies to search for situations that are stimulating and exciting. This discovery led to the development of the concept of sensation seeking (Zuckerman, 1990). The theory of sensation seeking predicts individual differences in both behavior and psychophysiological reactivity to situations. Sensation-seeking tendencies are measured by means of the Sensation Seeking Scale (SSS; Zuckerman, 1979). In addition to providing an overall score for the variable, the scale yields separate scores on the four subscales of (1) thrill and adventure seeking, (2) experience seeking, (3) disinhibition, and (4) boredom susceptibility.

Scores on the entire SSS and on various subscales correlate with a wide range of behaviors related to the search for stimulation. These include drug use, frequency of sexual experiences, tendencies to drive at high speeds and to take high risks in gambling and in personal health, and propensities for antisocial and criminal behavior (e.g., Zuckerman, 1979; Zuckerman, Ball & Black, 1990; Horvath & Zuckerman, 1993). In attempting to explain such individual differences, Zuckerman at one time adopted a theory of optimal levels of stimulation similar to that of Eysenck, but later he found that explanation insufficient for the phenomenon. More recently, Zuckerman (1990) has gone beyond the simple concept of an optimal stimulation level and has proposed underlying neural and chemical processes in the brain.

## Telic Dominance

Earlier we noted that Apter's theory of psychological reversals stipulates a number of situational variables that can cause a person to shift from the telic to the paratelic mode, or vice versa. In addition, people show individual tendencies to prefer one or the other mode most of the time, thereby manifesting either telic dominance or paratelic dominance. These are not to be thought of as stable personality traits, but instead as relatively stable *preferences* for one of the two states. Once a person has adopted one of the two states, he or she is affected by it in the same way, regardless of which type of mode dominance is characteristic (Apter, 1989). Telic/paratelic dominance is assessed by means of a self-report Telic Dominance Scale (Murgatroyd, Rushton, Apter & Ray, 1978).

People who are telic dominant tend, as we might expect, to be arousal avoiders, whereas those who are paratelic dominant are similar to what we have been calling sensation seekers. Mode dominance should be associated with a preference for being in that mode. For example, telic-dominant persons should be more likely than paratelic-dominant ones to seek activities that are serious and task centered, whereas paratelic-dominant people should prefer playful or recreational activity. This has been shown in a study by Lafreniere, Cowles, and Apter (1988) in which subjects spent two hours interacting with a microcomputer with freedom to select either statistics-teaching programs or video games for their activity. Subjects who had been found beforehand to be telic dominant spent most of their time on the teaching programs, whereas subjects who were more paratelic dominant spent most of their time playing video games.

There is some evidence that telic- and paratelic-dominant states may also be associated with mental health and adjustment. In a study by Martin, Kuiper, Olinger & Dobbin (1987), subjects were given both the Telic Domi- nance Scale and a questionnaire that assessed the stressfulness of their everyday lives (see Chapter 11). They also reported how much negative emo- tionality they usually experienced. In general, high levels of life stress are associated with high levels of negative feelings. However, Martin and col- leagues (1985) found that levels of negative emotionality experienced by telic- and paratelic-dominant people were differentially related to reported stress levels. Telic-dominant subjects showed a direct relationship between life stress and negative mood: the greater the stress, the worse the mood. Paratelic dominant subjects showed the highest level of negative mood when their lives were either highly stressful or relatively stress free; a *moderate* level of life stress was associated with maximum positive affect. Thus, although paratelic-dominant people do tend to enjoy some excitement and challenge in their lives, they stop short of levels that can lead to threat or danger.

# PHYSIOLOGICAL MODELS OF AROUSAL

As we noted, the concept of arousal has traditionally had a physiological basis, defined in terms of the person's level of activation in the central and autonomic nervous systems and the skeletal-muscular system. Beyond such a general conceptualization, however, physiological models of arousal vary considerably. In this section we will consider three theoretical models of underlying physiological processes that have been used to explain various aspects of arousal.

## The Reticular Formation and Limbic System

The reticular formation is a large bundle of neurons in the midbrain that ultimately activates the cells of the cerebral cortex. It serves two functions: to convey specific sensory information from the sense receptors to such areas as the auditory and visual cortex, and to carry nonspecific impulses that raise the general activation level of the entire cortical region. Any external stimulus elicits both types of impulse. For example, a sudden loud noise evokes a specific reaction carried by neurons in the auditory system as well as excitation in the nonspecific fibers. This is why such a noise causes one both to hear it and to be startled by it. The reticular formation can also be activated by internal emotional events that originate in the activity of still another brain area, the limbic system (Routtenberg, 1968). During the 1950s and 1960s, when the concept of general arousal was widely accepted in psychology, the moderating role of the reticular formation was considered a major factor in motivation and emotion. Since the decline of the idea of general arousal, of which more will be noted below, interest in the nonspecific reticular functions has likewise waned.

## The Behavior Activation and Inhibition Systems

A more recent physiological model of arousal is that of Gray (1981), who has described two antagonistic mechanisms within the brain: a Behavior Activation System (BAS) and a Behavior Inhibition System (BIS). These systems are activated by stimuli that signal or predict the onset of rewards and punishments. A warning signal, for example, telling the person that the situation poses a threat, sets off the BIS, causing a general inhibition of behavior. The person slows down, becomes vigilant and cautious, and takes measures to avoid harm. A signal that predicts the onset of a pleasant and rewarding state of affairs elicits activity in the BAS, with a consequent increase in activity level and reward-seeking behavior. Both the BAS and BIS also have inputs into a central arousal mechanism that intensifies both the approach and avoidance behaviors controlled by the respective systems.

In the motivational terminology that we are using, we might say that the conditions surrounding the setting of a positive goal (i.e., one to be approached) activate the BAS. Specific brain mechanisms underlie the goal-directed action that was described in behavioral terms in Chapter 3. Similarly, the conditions that surround the setting of a negative goal (avoiding or getting away from some aversive state) initiate activity in the BIS.

## *An Arousal-Activation-Effort Model*

A model that relates physiology to attention and problem solving has been proposed by Pribram and McGuinness (1975). This model states that two processes are elicited by a stimulus: a short-term increase in physiological activity that is called *arousal,* and a longer-lasting increase that is designated *activation.* The two differ in important ways. Arousal accompanies an orienting reaction to the stimulus that is necessary for the stimulus to be recognized; it can be thought of as a "What is it?" response. People do more than just react to stimuli, however. They also attend to the environment in the sense that they look for events, they anticipate, and they construct an internal representation of what is "out there" so that they can respond in certain adaptive and instrumental ways when certain events occur. Activation is defined as a state of *readiness to respond.* As noted above, this is a long-lasting physiological activity similar to that shown by a person who awaits a signal in an experiment on vigilance. This state is characterized by the question of how to respond when the awaited event occurs: "What is to be done?"

When a stimulus appears, therefore, the person not only recognizes it, but also enacts certain responses that he or she has been ready to make. Controlled behavior, which is what goes on during the instrumental, adaptive, problem-solving activities of everyday life, requires that these two processes— arousal and activation—be coordinated into a single behavioral sequence. We must first recognize the environmental condition and then respond to it in a controlled way. The coordination of the two systems requires the action of a third system, one that controls expenditure of the *effort* needed to bring stimulus recognition into line with instrumental behavior. Three areas of the brain control the three systems: the arousal system is controlled by the amygdala, the activation system by the basal ganglia of the forebrain, and the effort-coordination system by the hippocampus. The model is summarized in Figure 7-6.

A concrete example of everyday problem solving may illustrate these processes. Suppose a woman dislikes a certain man very much and is disposed to get away from him every time she sees him. One day as she is sitting in a restaurant, she sees the disliked man enter. Finishing her lunch quickly, she pays her bill and leaves, taking a route that keeps her at a distance from the man. In terms consistent with the model, the woman is ready to respond to the man by avoiding him or escaping from his presence. His appearance in the restaurant causes her to become suddenly aroused, in an unpleasant way, as she recognizes him. Recognition plus readiness to respond are then brought

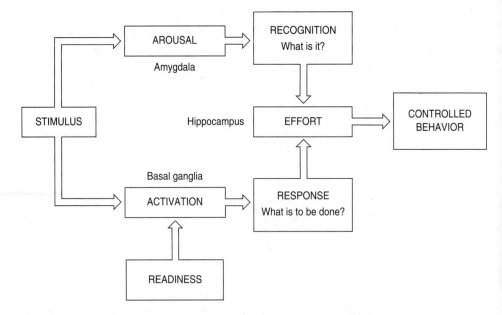

**Figure 7-6.** Schematic diagram of interrelationships among arousal, activation, and effort systems in controlled behavior. (Adapted from "Arousal, Activation, and Effort in the Control of Attention" by K. H. Pribram and D. McGuinness, *Psychological Review,* 1975, *82,* 116–149.)

together in a controlled, problem-solving activity: leaving the restaurant. The Pribram-McGuinness model explains the activities going on in the woman's brain that are controlling all of this activity that we can observe only as behavior.

# THE PSYCHOPHYSIOLOGY OF AROUSAL

## Psychophysiology and General Arousal

If a "general" state of arousal exists, as the early physiological models proposed, then this state should be manifest in much the same way across a number of the body's specific systems. We would expect, for example, that activity in the autonomic nervous system would lead to a number of highly intercorrelated reactions, such as heart rate, muscle tension, and electrical conductivity of the skin. These measures should, in turn, correlate highly with activation in the central nervous system, reflected in patterns of brain wave activity. Both types of nervous system arousal should also be correlated with skeletal-muscular and behavioral responding.

## Criticism of General Arousal

This theory of general arousal has received a good deal of criticism. Psychophysiologists have routinely reported that the various indicators of arousal correlate with one another only weakly. Lacey (1967) concluded from this that human behavior is characterized by three different arousal systems, with each only loosely related to the others. One is the cortical system, the operation of which is assessed by analyzing patterns of electrical activity in the cerebral cortex. The second is the autonomic system, manifested in the activity of organs innervated by the autonomic nervous system. The third is behavioral, measured through motor activity.

Moreover, even within each of these systems, the several indicators of arousal are not always closely related. Heart rate and skin conductance, for example, usually show only moderate correlations at best. Furthermore, Lacey's (1967) research has shown that people have clear and consistent individual differences in psychophysiological responding. In general, an individual tends to react to stimuli strongly in some ways and weakly in others. Some people are "skin conductance reactors," for example: given any one of a wide variety of exciting, threatening, or stressful conditions, these people tend to show large changes in electrodermal activity. At the same time they may show little or no change in heart rate. Other people may show the exact opposite pattern across the two measures. People tend, therefore, to show two things in their psychophysiological activity: *autonomic response specificity* (a tendency to react with some responses more than others) and *situational stereotypy* (a tendency to respond with the same pattern of responses across a wide range of eliciting conditions).

## Significance of Heart Rate Change

Lacey's work is important also because it demonstrates that psychophysiological activity may be sensitive to the demands for attention placed on the person. More specifically, certain systems of the body, such as muscle tension and skin conductance, react to all stimulus changes in mainly the same way: with increased activity. If one were to seek a physiological correlate of "general arousal," it would have to be such a unidirectional measure. Heart rate is different. Sometimes it accelerates in response to situational conditions, and at other times it decelerates. In general, when the situation is such that attention to the environment is called for, as when people are concentrating on the features of a problem or waiting for a signal, heart rate decelerates; when the situation gives rise to stimuli that startle the person or are aversive, heart rate accelerates. There are various theories of why this is so (Jennings, 1986), but one in particular has special significance for a motivational analysis of behavior: the direction of heart rate change may be linked to changes in the incentive for various courses of action (Obrist, 1976).

Evidence that the direction of cardiac change is related to incentive was shown first in studies that involved the avoidance of aversive stimuli. One by Elliott (1969) shows this effect clearly. Subjects awaited the onset of a painful electric shock that was to be delivered to the hand. Half of the subjects were told when to expect the shock and half were not; in addition, within each of these groups half were able to escape the shock when it came by pulling their hands away from the shock-delivery plate, whereas the other half of the subjects had their hands secured to this device, making escape impossible. Heart rate was measured before the instructions about shock were given, during the period in which the subjects waited, and again during the administration of the shock.

During the waiting period, subjects who knew when to expect the shock had higher heart rates than those who did not. In addition, Elliott found that when the shock was given, subjects who could escape it showed *higher* heart rates than those who were compelled to accept it passively. The latter finding runs directly counter to a common observation in the study of human stress: that controllable stressors are less stressful than uncontrollable ones (see Cohen, 1980, for a review of these studies). Obviously, the heart rates of Elliott's subjects showed more than just "stress" effects. In the late stages of the waiting period, the subjects who knew when to anticipate the shock apparently prepared themselves to make whatever defensive reactions they could. The increased heart rates of these subjects probably reflected a *preparation for responding* to the shock. Subjects who did not know when the shock would come could not mobilize their coping resources in the same way. For the same reason, subjects who could escape the shock (i.e., could make a response) showed higher heart rates than those who had to remain passive.

Thus heart rate increases occur when subjects have an incentive to respond in order to escape punishment. A series of studies by Fowles and his associates (Fowles, 1983) shows a similar incentive effect on heart rate when the person is motivated to seek a reward. In a study that measured reaction time, Fowles, Fisher, and Tranel (1982) gave subjects false feedback about their performance on a trial-by-trial basis so that subjects believed they were able to meet the criterion for reaction speed either 10% or 90% of the time. Half the subjects in each condition were given a small amount of money for each success and half were not. The subjects who were given money had higher heart rates than those who were given only feedback about their performance. The amount of success (10% or 90%) enjoyed by the subjects had no effect on heart rate. In addition, when subjects who had been receiving 10% success feedback were shifted to a 50% success condition late in the study, only those who were also given money revealed a corresponding shift upward in heart rate. A parallel finding has been reported by Tranel, Fisher, and Fowles (1982), who showed that subjects who were shifted from a monetary reward condition to a feedback-only condition showed a significant decrease in heart rate, whereas those who continued to receive the monetary incentive did not.

# THE YERKES-DODSON LAW

One of the oldest theoretical approaches to expressing a relationship between arousal and performance is the Yerkes-Dodson Law (Broadhurst, 1957). It consists of two premises: (1) the optimal level of arousal associated with maximum performance at any task is intermediate across the range of possible arousal levels, and (2) the optimal level is lower for difficult tasks than for easy ones. The result is several curves, one for every hypothetical level of task difficulty, all of them in the shape of an inverted U (Figure 7-7).

As an empirical generalization, the Yerkes-Dodson Law makes some sense. People undoubtedly perform better when they are moderately alert and aroused than when they are extremely relaxed or when they are excited and overwrought. The first premise of the law—the inverted U describes the relationship of arousal to performance—has been supported by numerous studies. The second premise—the optimal level is higher for easy tasks than for difficult ones—has received little support (e.g., Suedfeld & Landon, 1970; Bargh & Cohen, 1978).

Numerous methods have been used to manipulate arousal levels in studies of the Yerkes-Dodson Law, among them sensory deprivation, monetary incentives, induced muscle tension, and psychological stressors. A study by Revelle, Humphreys, Simon, and Gilliland (1980) shows clear support for the law using still another operational definition of high, low, and moderate arousal. The subjects for this study had been classified as high or low scorers on a scale that measured the trait of *impulsivity*. Half the subjects were tested during morning hours and half during the afternoon. In addition, half

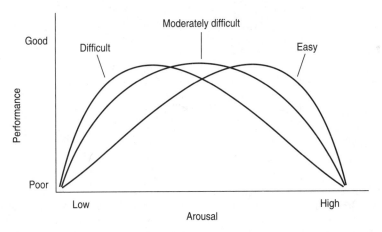

***Figure 7-7.*** The Yerkes-Dodson Law. Curves represent different functions for difficult, moderately difficult, and easy tasks.

the subjects in every condition were given a small dose of caffeine prior to the task and half were given a placebo. Those who got caffeine were obviously more aroused than those who received the placebo. Impulsivity and time of day are interacting variables: people who are low in impulsivity tend to be most highly aroused in the morning and less so in the afternoon, whereas high impulsives show their greatest arousal in the afternoon hours. By means of these operations, Revelle and his associates were able to create eight different combinations of level of personality, time of day, and drug.

Two groups of subjects were very highly aroused: high impulsives who received caffeine in the afternoon (because to their already high diurnal arousal they added more with the caffeine) and low impulsives who received caffeine in the morning (for the same reason). Two other groups were in a state of very low arousal: high impulsives who received the placebo in the morning and low impulsives who received the placebo in the afternoon. The other four combinations represented levels of arousal intermediate to the two extremes.

All subjects took a moderately difficult multiple-choice test after ingesting the caffeine or the placebo. According to the Yerkes-Dodson Law, the four groups that were moderately aroused should have performed better on this test than the groups at the higher and lower levels of arousal. As Figure 7-8 shows, this is what Revelle and his colleagues found.

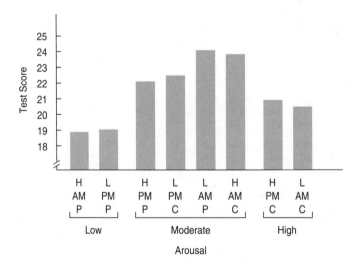

**Figure 7-8.** Test scores as a function of arousal level. *Note:* H = high impulsive subjects; L = low impulsive subjects; AM = morning; PM = afternoon; C = caffeine; P = placebo. (From "The Interactive Effect of Personality, Time of Day, and Caffeine: A Test of the Arousal Model" by W. Revelle, M. S. Humphreys, L. Simon, and K. Gilliland, *Journal of Experimental Psychology: General,* 1980, *109,* 1–31.)

## Overmotivation

Another situation that can evoke behavior consistent with the Yerkes-Dodson Law is one in which the person has been placed under strong demands to achieve. Such conditions produce *overmotivation* (Atkinson, 1974b), which occurs when people are so highly motivated to perform well that they exceed their optimal level of arousal for good performance. An interesting example is provided in an experiment by Heckhausen and Strang (1988). Male semiprofessional basketball players served as subjects. Each player was instructed to dribble the ball along a specific route that had been laid out on the floor, to take a shot, and then to repeat the procedure as many times as could be done in five minutes. For some five-minute periods the players were given the goal of trying to make as many baskets as they would when exerting themselves normally. At other times they were urged to set a personal record by making more baskets than they would under normal conditions. Several measures were made: the number of shots that the player took during each five-minute period, the number of shots made, and the number of dribbling errors committed. In addition, small blood samples were taken and analyzed for the level of lactates in the blood. Lactates are generated by the metabolism of blood sugar and are therefore an indirect indicator of how aroused the player was in each phase of the study.

The results of the study gave clear evidence of overmotivation. Following instructions to set a personal record, players took more shots than they did when performing normally, but their ratio of shots made to shots taken (i.e., their hit rate) was lower. They also committed more dribbling errors when they tried to set a record and revealed higher levels of blood lactates. Thus instructions to set a record produced a high level of arousal accompanied by an increased level of activity and a reduced level of efficiency. The latter is the overmotivation effect.

Heckhausen and Strang (1988) also reported that the overmotivation effect can be reduced or eliminated by the use of internal self-control mechanisms. In particular, players who manifested high levels of action orientation did not become overmotivated, whereas those who were high in state orientation did (see Chapter 3). Action-oriented players showed hit rates for shooting that were as high when they tried for records as when they performed normally; state-oriented subjects showed the expected lower hit rate under "record" conditions. It will be recalled from Chapter 3 that action orientation is a critical personality variable in the self-control that is necessary for protecting the intention to seek a goal and for following through to goal attainment. In the study of Heckhausen and Strang, action-oriented subjects revealed what the authors called *exertion control*—that is, a modulation and tempering of exertion that prevented them from becoming aroused beyond their optimal level for the task. Consistent with this conclusion, action-oriented subjects showed lower levels of blood lactates in the "record" condition than did state-oriented subjects.

## Theoretical Explanations of the Yerkes-Dodson Law

The Yerkes-Dodson Law is an empirical generalization, a statement of a relationship between arousal and performance that has been shown across a wide range of operations and measures. It does not give reasons for the inverted U curve. Various explanations have been offered, however, and we will consider two of these theoretical accounts.

*CUE UTILIZATION.*    The Yerkes-Dodson Law may reflect cognitive processes related to attention and the ways in which information from the environment is used. In everyday functioning we usually do not respond equally to all the stimuli that impinge upon us. Instead, we attend to some stimuli more than to others, so that the former become central in our cognitive structures and the latter remain peripheral. Our level of arousal at any given time influences the proportion of cues that form the central core of our cognitive structure. The more highly aroused the person is, the narrower is the range of cues that make up this central core and the larger the proportion of stimuli that are on the periphery. Another way of stating this general observation is that arousal restricts attention or the range of cues that are utilized in performance (Easterbrook, 1959). The attention-restricting function of increasing arousal has been shown in several ways. For example, stimulating a subject with noise during a learning task facilitates learning of the material, but hinders incidental recall of other matters that occur at the same time (e.g., Davies & Jones, 1975).

How does this explain the Yerkes-Dodson Law? To answer this question we must assume that in any problem-solving situation not all the stimuli available to the person are relevant to the task. Some of the stimuli are irrelevant and potentially distracting. When arousal is increased moderately, the effect may be a narrowing of attention down to the cues that are relevant to the task and the elimination of peripheral distractors. Continued increases in arousal may, however, narrow attention to such an extent that some of the central cues needed for problem solving are ignored. The result would be a progressive decline in performance.

*MULTIPLE PROCESSES.*    Humphreys and Revelle (1984) have explained the Yerkes-Dodson Law in terms of two processes that occur in performance. These processes have opposite effects, and a tradeoff between them is proposed as an explanation for the inverted U function. The first of these is *sustained information transfer,* in which the person takes in a stimulus, associates some response with it, and then executes the response. Much of this is virtually automatic. This is the sort of rudimentary processing that characterizes easy tasks like simple arithmetic, reaction time to a single stimulus, and crossing out specified letters from a printed text. The main requirement of such tasks is sustained attention over a period of time and not complex memory processing. The second process in Humphrey and Revelle's theory is *short-term memory.* On all tasks except the most simple, the person must maintain information in an available form so that it may be integrated for the solution. This requires occasional rehearsal. Eventually the person must retrieve this information in the course of recall, recognition, or memory scanning. Short-term memory incorporates sustained information transfer plus a great deal more. Tasks that require the use of short-term memory are therefore more complex than simple ones that require only information transfer.

Arousal is linked to each of the two processes. As arousal increases, sustained information transfer is progressively enhanced, but short-term memory is progressively hindered. When a task requires the enactment of both processes, performance at very low levels of arousal is poor because of impaired information transfer (e.g., inattention), whereas performance at high levels of arousal is impaired by an overload on short-term memory. Thus performance should be best when the combined levels of these two processes are maximal, and this occurs at intermediate levels of arousal (Figure 7-9).

## Critique of the Yerkes-Dodson Law

In spite of its long history, the Yerkes-Dodson Law has been criticized by some psychologists on several grounds (e.g., Naatanen, 1973; Neiss, 1988). One is the doubtful utility of any principle based on the concept of "general arousal"; reasons for questioning this concept have already been reviewed. A related argument is that by emphasizing arousal as a unidimensional phenomenon, we have obscured the real differences among the specific psychological states (e.g., fear, anger, anxiety, elation) from which arousal has been inferred (Neiss, 1988).

Instead of seeking a simple effect of arousal on performance, a more fruitful line of study might be to look for specific effects of these states. For

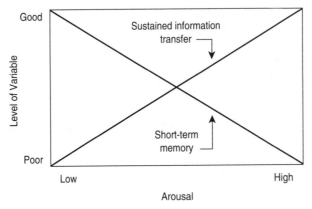

**Figure 7-9.** Theoretical relationships of arousal to sustained information transfer and short-term memory. (From "Personality, Motivation, and Performance: A Theory of the Relationship Between Individual Differences and Information Processing" by M. S. Humphreys and W. Revelle, *Psychological Review*, 1984, *91*, 153–184.)

example, one may define arousal in terms of a person's level of anxiety, and then show that a moderate level of anxiety facilitates performance on an examination when compared with a very low level or a very high one. The result will be an inverted U curve that relates anxiety level to performance, but does this indicate that differential arousal is causing the effect? It would seem as likely that very low anxiety is actually a condition of profound relaxation that could engender lack of involvement in the test, whereas very high anxiety could be a disorganizing state of panic that distracts the person from the test's demands.

This raises still another problem for arousal theory as an explanation for the inverted U. The effects of the operations used to induce arousal may in fact be caused by other processes, such as attention. This is shown in a study reported by Naatanen (1973). Subjects were given a simple reaction-time task to perform as they simultaneously pedaled a stationary exercise bicycle. The power level needed to pedal the machine was systematically manipulated by adjusting the resistance on the wheel. Subjects' heart rates were monitored continuously. Findings consistent with the Yerkes-Dodson Law were reported. As the subjects' heart rates increased, the speed of reaction in the reaction-time task first increased, but then decreased as the amount of exertion (and heart rates) became extreme. However, when the experiment was repeated with the reaction-time measure taken immediately *after* the subject had finished pedaling, speed of reaction and heart rate showed no relationship, even though the heart rates of the subjects were as high as they had been during the pedaling. The decrease in reaction speed during maximum exertion on the bicycle had not been caused directly by the arousal level generated by that exertion, or it would have continued to be so affected after the exercise had been completed. Instead, as the demands of the cycling task increased, the attention of the subjects was apparently diverted more and more to that task and away from the reaction-time problem.

The Yerkes-Dodson Law is, as noted above, an empirical generalization based on the observation of a particular relationship. As we have also seen, reasonable explanations for the law, based on the concept of arousal, have been formulated. Other explanations, such as the one in the study just cited, have not made arousal the major causal variable. Whether one accepts an interpretation of the law based on arousal will depend ultimately on the position that one takes regarding the usefulness of nonspecific energizers in explaining behavior. We will consider this in the final section of the chapter.

## CHANGING CONCEPTIONS OF AROUSAL

Certainly the construct of arousal no longer holds the commanding central position that it once did in motivational psychology. As we have seen, it has been criticized for two major reasons. One is that alternative concepts (e.g., specific emotions, attention) do a better job of explaining human action. The other is that the physiological infrastructure of the concept—the idea of general arousal—has been found wanting. However, in spite of these criticisms we may ask whether the construct of arousal still has any usefulness. The answer seems to be that arousal does serve a purpose, but in a different form from the one in which it was traditionally cast.

Arousal is not tied so closely to specific physiological processes as it once was. Instead it has assumed the status of a hypothetical construct. It still may have some physiological referents (for example, skin conductance measures seem to reflect a unidirectional "activation" process), but these no longer indicate the presence of an underlying system that drives or *determines* behavior. Instead, the concept now refers to a complex of processes, including behavioral and affective ones, that sometimes play an important role in concert with other processes (Anderson, 1990).

Arousal is a useful idea, in this modified form, because it follows from the obvious fact that all human functioning requires some level of energy. This viewpoint has been stated succinctly:

> *The primary role of the arousal functions in humans is to manage the selective and variable production, distribution, and use of the energy needed to fuel the organization and execution of behavior episodes (Ford & Ford, 1987, p. 19).*

Some level of activation must exist before the person can operate efficiently the mechanisms for selective attention and perception, the processing of information, the use of will, and the regulation of emotion that are all necessary for survival. All available evidence points to some optimal level or levels of arousal as necessary for this. The particular forms that such optimal-level approaches take have been the subject of much of this chapter.

## CHAPTER SUMMARY

**1.** The study of the role played by nonspecific energizers in human behavior has gone through several stages. Drive theory held that behavior is reinforced by the attainment of a low level of stimulation. Arousal theory, which arose partly as an alternative to drive theory, stipulated that a moderate level of stimulation is reinforcing. More recently, reversal theory has proposed the existence of two optimal levels.

**2.** Drive theory states that the potential level of any response is a joint function of that response's habit strength and the person's level of drive. High drive facilitates performance on simple or overlearned tasks but hampers performance on complex or novel ones. Although it has lost its former eminence among theories of motivation, drive theory still provides a parsimonious explanation for some behaviors.

**3.**   Arousal theory emerged in part because of the discovery of behaviors that are inconsistent with drive theory, such as exploration, sensation seeking, and intolerance of sensory restriction. Arousal theory proposes that moderate levels of stimulation are the most pleasant, and that both higher and lower levels are relatively aversive. Two types of exploratory behavior—diversive (stimulus seeking) and specific (stimulus restricting)—have been explained in terms of a moderate optimal level of stimulation.

**4.**   Arousal is determined in part by collative properties of stimuli, such as novelty, complexity, and incongruity. Arousal due to any of these properties of a stimulus combines with arousal due to other properties. Combinations of collative variables that generate moderate levels of stimulation are preferred over those that generate higher or lower levels.

**5.**   The theory of psychological reversals describes two states that characterize human orientations toward activity. In the telic state, people are problem centered, serious, and driven to make progress toward goals. In the paratelic state, people take pleasure from activity itself more than from goals toward which it may be directed. Situational variables cause reversals, so that the person shifts from one state to the other. This leads to changes in how arousal is experienced. For the person in the telic state, a low level of arousal is experienced as relaxing and desirable, whereas higher levels of arousal are felt as aversive sources of anxiety. For the person in the paratelic state, a low level of arousal is experienced as boring and undesirable, whereas higher levels of arousal are felt as pleasurable excitement.

**6.**   Individual differences play a role in moderating preferences for stimulation. Extraverts, for example, prefer higher levels of stimulation and engage in stimulus seeking more than do introverts. Sensation seeking is another variable that is correlated with preference for activities that increase excitement. Within the context of reversal theory, telic dominance is associated with a general preference for arousal avoidance and paratelic dominance with arousal seeking.

**7.**   Traditionally, arousal theory has had a physiological basis. Arousal was originally defined in terms of a single activating system in the reticular formation. More recent physiological models of arousal are more complex, proposing both activating and inhibiting systems as well as attention-regulating and coordinating ones.

**8.**   Theories of a single arousal system led to the conclusion that there is a general arousal state that involves activation of cortical, autonomic, and skeletal-muscular systems. These systems have, however, been found to be only weakly related. Even within the autonomic system, there is evidence of only a slight correlation across specific measures. Humans show instead a high degree of individual response patterning in autonomic activity, with considerable differences among persons.

**9.** Whereas some psychophysiological processes show a degree of generality across situations, heart rate does not. Situations that call for inhibition of responding and a high degree of sustained attention evoke decreases in heart rate, whereas situations that demand a readiness for and execution of a response elicit increases. Heart rate is responsive to cues for incentives in the situation; these cues may signal either avoidance of punishment or the possibility of a reward. In both cases, heart rate accelerates.

**10.** The Yerkes-Dodson Law is an empirical statement of a relationship between arousal and performance described by an inverted U curve. Moderate levels of arousal are associated with maximum performance. The law has been explained theoretically in terms of (a) a narrowing of attention to task-related cues produced by increasing arousal, and, alternatively, (b) a tradeoff between sustained information processing and short-term memory processes, which are affected by arousal in opposite ways.

**11.** The Yerkes-Dodson Law has been criticized as an oversimplification of the effects of specific psychological states, such as emotions, on behavior. It has also been argued that arousal produces the inverted U curve not in a direct manner, but indirectly through its effects on attention.

**12.** At the present time, the concept of arousal is considerably different from what it was when it was first formulated. It is no longer linked as closely to underlying physiological processes but has instead been broadened to describe a complex of behavioral, physiological, and affective components. It is no longer considered to have a direct and determining influence on behavior but is thought to be one of several interrelated variables, all of which contribute to human functioning.

CHAPTER $8$

# EMOTION

### CHAPTER OUTLINE

The importance of emotion in human life is a matter on which virtually everyone would agree, yet among the many constructs of psychology few have been the subject of as much disagreement. Motivation is sometimes treated like a natural companion of emotion. For example, college courses are sometimes entitled "Motivation and Emotion," and an influential journal also bears that title. Historically, the emotions have sometimes been placed at the center of behavior and assigned a critical role in motivation (e.g., McDougall, 1908; see Chapter 1), whereas at other times they have been described as forces that take people *out of* normal motivated behavior (Pribram, 1967). To the drive theorists, emotion was merely a convenient intervening variable to be interposed between manipulable stimuli and observable responses (Brown & Farber, 1951). Arousal theorists sought to eliminate the concept of emotion entirely and to replace it with general activation (Duffy, 1962). Today the idea of emotion is enjoying a revival of popularity among psychologists. The purpose of this chapter is to introduce some of the more important recent developments in emotion research and to relate them to older theoretical approaches where possible.

# THE COMPONENTS OF EMOTION

## Emotion: Central or Peripheral?

One old question that is still represented in some modern approaches is whether emotion is a product of activity in the central nervous system or whether it involves only activity in the periphery of the body (the skeletal muscles and internal organs that are innervated by the action of the autonomic nervous system). Is it a "brain" process or a "visceral" one? According to central theories, emotion is a state of consciousness that follows a change in some part of the brain elicited by appropriate stimuli. These theories describe complicated brain structures in the highly technical terminology of neuroscience. Peripheralist theories, on the other hand, have traditionally dominated the more "psychological" discussions of emotion. The peripheralist–centralist distinction underlies two of the earliest theories of emotion: those of William James and Walter Cannon.

**JAMES'S THEORY OF EMOTION.** The James-Lange theory, as it is called because it expresses the ideas of both James and the Danish physiologist Lange, states that emotion is aroused whenever a strong stimulus evokes a reflexive alteration in the internal organs and the skeletal muscles of the body. The particular form of this alteration is assumed to be specific to the stimulus that elicits it. When the change is experienced shortly thereafter, it "feeds back" to the brain and is experienced as a discernible emotion. It is this defining of emotion as the conscious counterpart of visceral and muscular processes that stamps the James-Lange theory as peripheralist: "My thesis," James (1890) wrote, ". . . is that *the bodily changes follow directly the perception of the exciting fact, and that our feeling of the same changes as they occur is the emotion*" (p. 449, italics original).

The James-Lange theory places emotion and behavior in a temporal relationship that is the exact opposite of what most people believe:

> *Common-sense says, we lose our fortune, are sorry, and weep; we meet a bear, are frightened, and run; we are insulted by a rival, are angry, and strike. The hypothesis here to be defended says that this order of sequence is incorrect, that one mental state is not immediately induced by the other, that the bodily manifestations must first be interposed between, and that the more rational statement is that we feel sorry because we cry, angry because we strike, afraid because we tremble (James, 1890, pp. 449–450).*

**CANNON'S CRITIQUE OF JAMES.** As one of the earliest critics of the James-Lange theory, Cannon (1929) proposed several reasons why he considered that theory to be inadequate:

1. Visceral changes are relatively slow and therefore cannot account for something as immediate as emotion.
2. Artificial stimulation of the viscera (e.g., with drugs) does not produce true emotion.
3. The viscera are relatively insensitive to stimulation.
4. Blocking or cutting off feedback from the periphery of the body to the brain does not eliminate emotional behavior.
5. Visceral changes are similar in all emotions and therefore cannot account for the rich diversity of emotion experienced by humans.

Evidence from modern research in psychophysiology and neuroscience has tended to undermine some of Cannon's points (e.g., Fehr & Stern, 1970; Ekman, Levenson & Friesen, 1983). Even so, a thoroughgoing peripheralistic approach to emotion does not agree well with most of what is known today. There can be little question that the peripheral parts of the body have some input into emotion. However, central processes also play an important role, as we will see later in this chapter. Cannon's own alternative to the James-Lange theory was that emotional *feelings* arise through stimulation of the dorsal thalamus, and that emotional *expression* arises through concomitant stimulation of the hypothalamus.

The James-Lange and Cannon theories are contrasted in Figure 8-1. Note that they offer alternative conceptualizations of the relationships among three variables: *physiological arousal, emotional experience,* and *motor behavior*. These three variables are the bases for all theories of emotion. Later in this chapter we will examine several contemporary studies that establish relationships among these same three variables.

## The Language of Emotion

Like any other construct of psychology, emotion cannot be observed or measured directly. An emotion is *inferred* from observable phenomena of the three types mentioned above: reports of experiences, expressive motor behavior, and physiological activity. Emotional experience is described in terms of the adjectives that people use to convey how they feel ("I am angry," "I feel happy," etc.). Expressive motor behavior may take the form of large muscle activity, such as stiffening when frightened, laughing when happy, and manifesting other forms of body language, but it is most commonly detected in the more subtle actions of the small muscles in the face (e.g., frowning, smiling). Activation consists of psychophysiological measures that were described in Chapter 7 and that constitute much of what James called the visceral basis of emotion. As we have noted, one of the problems that theorists of emotion have had to face, and have not yet settled, is the extent to which *specific* emotions can be detected from psychophysiological data.

To obtain some understanding of emotion, it is necessary to know not only the roles played by these three systems, but also how they relate to each

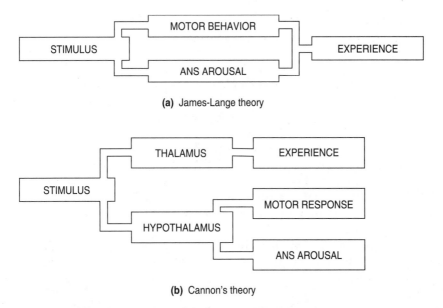

**(a)** James-Lange theory

**(b)** Cannon's theory

***Figure 8-1.*** Schematic diagrams of the James-Lange and Cannon theories of emotion, showing how each establishes relationships among experience, expression, and arousal in the autonomic nervous system (ANS).

other in the overall emotional process. To use a simple metaphor, emotion can be thought of as a stool resting on three legs. If these legs are free standing, the stool will be spindly and weak. If, however, rods can be secured to pairs of adjacent legs, the stool will be strong and sturdy. Theories of emotion such as those of James and Cannon were great because they linked the three underlying components of the construct (see Figure 8-1), and theories today still attempt to do this. We will consider some of these theories and how they link experience, arousal, and expression in the remainder of the chapter.

# COGNITION-AROUSAL THEORY

## Cognitive Labeling

As we have seen, the James-Lange theory was criticized by Cannon largely because it was too peripheralistic and did not assign enough importance to necessary central processes. This line of reasoning was taken up again by Schachter and Singer (1962) as the basis for a theory that sought to bring together the component of autonomic activation with a cognitive attribution of what the autonomic state signifies, and to define emotion as the result of that attribution. The theory can be summarized in four points:

1.  The body's immediate response to an exciting event is a general discharge in the autonomic nervous system. The resulting state of arousal is undifferentiated and the same for all eliciting events.
2.  If the source of arousal is correctly identified, the arousal state is attributed to it. The arousal is therefore given a cognitive label, and if any emotion is involved, it is appropriate to the event.
3.  If the source of arousal is not identified, the person conducts an attributional search of available information in the situation and makes a likely attribution on that basis. The emotion that follows this labeling process is appropriate to the perceived source of the arousal.
4.  Emotion is therefore always a joint product of a state of general arousal and a cognition in terms of which that arousal is understood.

Emotion requires that some rapid cognitive judgments be made in a context that is exciting. For example, suppose a woman who is walking along a sidewalk suddenly notices a man in front of her coming toward her quickly. Her initial reaction is a sudden rush of activation, which, according to this theory, is felt only as activation. If the man is looking at her in a menacing way, she will feel her arousal as fear. If, on second glance, she notices that she is at a bus stop, that a bus is approaching, and that the man's sudden move was not toward her at all but toward an approaching bus, her momentary rush of arousal will be felt as surprise and will soon subside.

In everyday life, the rush of arousal and the cognition by which the arousal is labeled are usually caused by the same event. For example, one hears a joke and feels amused because the funny story brings about a mild arousal that is quickly and accurately attributed to that event and felt as amusement. But the theory cannot be tested under such natural conditions because if both the arousal and the cognitive information arise from a single source, one can never be sure whether the amusement is actually the result of just one of these effects. Research to test the theory has therefore been largely based on a method in which arousal is elicited by one event but attributed to some other event that is independent of the source of arousal. If it can be shown that aroused subjects experience an emotion that is consistent with this second event to a greater degree than do unaroused subjects, then such a finding is considered to be evidence for the theory. This procedure is called the *misattribution* method.

For example, Schachter and Singer (1962) used an injection of epinephrine, a drug that excites the sympathetic division of the autonomic nervous system, to create arousal in some subjects, while other subjects received a placebo injection of saline solution. Some of the subjects who received epinephrine were told what to expect as a result of the drug: heart palpitations, hand tremors, and facial flushing. Others were deliberately misinformed, being told that the effects of the drug would be numbness in the feet, itching, and a headache. Still others were told nothing about drug effects. Each subject then had to spend some time with another person—an associate of the experimenter—who was either happy or angry and hostile about being in the experiment.

The theory predicted that subjects who were aroused by epinephrine and either kept ignorant of the true effects of the drug or deliberately misinformed about those effects would be less likely to attribute their arousal symptoms to the drug than would subjects who had been correctly informed. They would therefore be more likely to feel emotions consistent with the behavior of the other person in the situation because that behavior would be a salient cue by which arousal could be labeled. The findings gave partial support to the theory. Subjects who had been given epinephrine and had been either misinformed or told nothing about the effects of the drug and then were exposed to a happy model reported themselves to feel happier than those who had been accurately forewarned (Figure 8-2). Similar results were found among subjects who had observed a hostile and angry model; they behaved in a more angry manner after having received epinephrine and not been told about its effects than did those who had been informed.

Subsequent research found support for the Schachter-Singer theory under conditions that were more natural than the injection of an arousing drug. A study by Ross, Rodin, and Zimbardo (1969) provides one of the

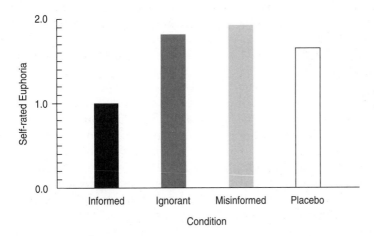

***Figure 8-2***. Subjects' self-ratings of euphoria as a function of drug administration and information about drug effects on the subject. (From data reported in "Cognitive, Social, and Physiological Determinants of Emotional State" by S. Schachter and J. A. Singer, *Psychological Review*, 1962, *69*, 379–399.)

strongest pieces of confirming evidence. Female subjects were first led to anticipate some painful electric shocks. This treatment, which presumably elicited fear in the subjects, was carried out contiguously with the onset of noise. Subjects were then informed about the effects they could expect from the noise. Half were told to anticipate the experiences that noise would actually produce (e.g., ringing in the ears, headache), whereas others were told to anticipate symptoms that are actually concomitant with fear (e.g., increased heart rate). Subjects who were given this latter treatment could, therefore, attribute the fear that arose from the threat of shock to the noise rather than to its true source. This should diminish somewhat the fear of the coming shock.

Subjects were then given a choice of two puzzles to solve. Success at one would be rewarded with an attractive prize; success at the other would grant avoidance of the threatened shocks. Fear of shock should, of course, cause subjects to prefer the latter task over the former. The results of the study showed that subjects who had not been led to attribute fear symptoms to the noise (and who therefore were presumably experiencing more fear) spent more time on the shock-avoidance task than they did on the reward-seeking one, as we might expect. However, subjects who *had* been led to attribute fear symptoms to the noise (and who therefore were presumably experiencing less fear) spent *less* time on the shock-avoidance task than they did on the reward-seeking one. Attribution of fear-generated arousal to a neutral source therefore lessened the fear of shock.

Other evidence tends to suggest certain weaknesses in the theory. It should be noted in Figure 8-2 that subjects who received a placebo, and who therefore should not have been aroused, showed at least as high a level of emotion as those who received epinephrine in at least one other condition. This finding has been reported by several other investigators who used arousing drugs in tests of the theory (see reviews by Manstead & Wagner, 1981, and Reisenzein, 1983), which leads to the conclusion that the findings of Schachter and Singer (1962) do not give unequivocal support to the theory. In addition, the theory also assumes that increased arousal should have no effect on emotion unless there are suitable cues for labeling the arousal. However, some researchers have shown that unexplained arousal is perceived as a cause of negative affect in and of itself (Marshall & Zimbardo, 1979; Maslach, 1979).

What are we to conclude from all this? The safest conclusion is that support for the Schachter-Singer theory is mixed. Some investigations provide support for the theory, whereas others report findings that are, in whole or part, inconsistent with the theory's predictions.

## Excitation Transfer

A viewpoint on the roles of cognition and arousal in emotion that is somewhat different from that of Schachter and Singer is Zillmann's (1978) theory of *excitation transfer*. The theory pertains to situations in which two arousing conditions occur in sequence. Autonomic arousal does not dissipate immediately upon termination of the condition that elicits it, so that if two arousing events are separated by a short amount of time, some of the arousal caused by one may be transferred to the other and, as a result, increase the intensity of emotion experienced in response to that setting.

The two events involved can be qualitatively quite different from each other. Two experiments show this. In one study, Zillmann (1971) first arranged for male subjects to be provoked to anger by another person and then showed these subjects one of three short sequences from commercial movies. One group saw an affectively neutral film involving travel, another saw a violent scene from a prize fight, and still others saw an erotic but nonviolent scenario. It had been established beforehand that the erotic film was more arousing than the violent film, which was in turn more arousing than the neutral one. After the film had been shown, each subject was given a chance to retaliate against the person who had provoked him by delivering a variable number of electric shocks. The aggressiveness of the retaliation was directly related to the arousal level of the film that had been seen. This was apparently because residual arousal from the film was labeled as anger at the time of retaliation, so that the greater the arousal, the more angry was the person.

Similar results following a different induction of arousal were found in a study by Zillmann, Katcher, and Milavsky (1972). Some subjects were provoked by another person, after which they engaged in vigorous physical exercise on a stationary bicycle. Other subjects took part in a quiet sedentary activity after having been provoked. When the subjects were later allowed to retaliate against the person who had provoked them, those who had performed the strenuous exercise were more aggressive than those who had done the physically less demanding task. Zillmann and his associates reasoned that arousal elicited by the exercise was still operative at the time of retaliation and was mistakenly labeled as anger.

The theory of excitation transfer is similar to that of Schachter and Singer in that both define emotion as an explanatory label that is attached to a state of general arousal. The major difference between the two theories is that the Schachter-Singer approach describes an aroused person who makes a deliberate search of the environment for information that explains the arousal, whereas Zillmann's theory presupposes a person who, somewhat passively, misreads his or her bodily state and its implications and mistakenly experiences emotion as a consequence.

It should be noted that excitation transfer can take place only under strictly limited conditions. The two events involved—the arousing one and the one to which residual arousal is transferred—cannot occur too closely together in time or the person will correctly attribute arousal to its true source. On the other hand, they cannot be too widely spaced either, or no residual arousal will remain to be mislabeled. A study by Cantor, Zillmann and Bryant (1975) established the importance of timing in excitation transfer. In a pre-experimental session, male subjects exercised vigorously on a stationary bicycle for one minute. Then measures of heart rate and blood pressure were made each minute for the next ten minutes, along with self-reports of how aroused the subject felt as a result of the exercise. On the basis of these measures, Cantor and her associates established that (1) after one minute, subjects were still aroused from the workout and reported still feeling aroused by it; (2) after five minutes, subjects were still physiologically aroused from the workout but reported themselves to be back to baseline levels of arousal; and (3) after nine minutes, subjects had returned to baseline arousal levels and reported this accurately. Thus, it was shown empirically that the conditions for excitation transfer (i.e., the presence of residual arousal that is not correctly attributed to its cause) were more likely to be found five minutes after exercise than after either one minute or nine minutes.

In the main experiment that followed, another group of male subjects was shown an erotic film either one, five, or nine minutes after terminating a one-minute exercise period. Those who saw this film five minutes after exercise, the period in which excitation transfer was most likely, reported themselves to be more sexually excited by the movie than were subjects who saw it after one minute or nine minutes. This experiment therefore illustrates the critical nature of the timing of events for the transfer process.

# PSYCHOEVOLUTIONARY THEORY

Ever since the 19th century, much of our thinking about emotion has been influenced heavily by Darwin's theory of evolution. This has led to the development of various psychoevolutionary approaches. The general assumption of these theories is that in the course of human evolution, certain emotions were part of larger patterns of adaptive behavior. They therefore acquired functional significance and were passed on from generation to generation through natural selection. For example, fear is part of our emotional repertoire because our distant ancestors experienced that state in the context of escaping from or avoiding danger. Any members of the species that did not experience fear in dangerous settings, for whatever reason, would be at relatively greater risk of being killed off. Thus the fear-experiencing organisms survived and the "fearless" ones perished.

## The Basic Emotions

Psychoevolutionary theory leads to the following conclusions:

**1.** The emotions that have the greatest significance for adaptation and survival are the so-called *basic emotions*. These represent a central core from which a large array of other emotions is formed.

**2.**   The basic emotions are universal among human beings. They transcend cultural differences. In addition, they are found, in some form, in other organisms that are phylogenetically related to humans.

**3.**   The basic emotions are grounded in biological processes. This assumption leads to two additional ones. The first is that each emotion includes its own distinctive pattern of physiological activity. The second is that each emotion includes a specific and universal patterning of expressive motor behavior that should be recognizable in humans across various cultures (see point 2 above).

We will refer to these three points later as we review some of what is known about emotion from modern research. First, however, we will consider the psychoevolutionary approach in greater detail by examining one such theory.

## Plutchik's Theory

Plutchik (1984) has developed a psychoevolutionary model built around eight basic emotions: *fear, anger, joy, sadness, acceptance, disgust, anticipation,* and *surprise.* Each is associated with a behavior pattern that has psychoevolutionary importance, as discussed above. In some cases, the link between the basic emotion and the behavior is clear and familiar. For example, the emotion of

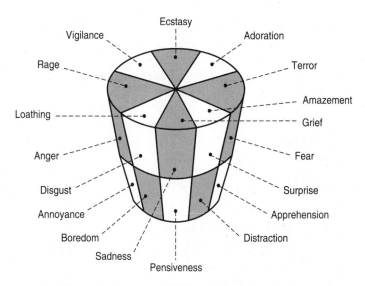

***Figure 8-3.***   Diagram of Plutchik's model of basic motives. (Adapted from "Emotions: A General Psychoevolutionary Theory" by R. Plutchik, in *Approaches to Emotion,* edited by K. S. Scherer and P. Ekman, 1984, Hillsdale, NJ: Erlbaum.)

fear is connected to the behavior pattern of *protection,* which Plutchik defines as behavior aimed at avoiding danger or harm, such as retreat, flight, or "any behavior that increases the distance between the organism and a source of danger" (Plutchik, 1984, p. 202). Anger is related to the behavior pattern of *destruction,* which is addressed to the breaking down and removal of barriers to satisfying important needs. Other connections are not so obvious. Sadness is connected to the pattern called *reintegration,* which is behavior in response to the loss of something of value, and its function is "to regain nurturant contact" (p. 202). Disgust is connected to behavior by which the person expels something harmful that has previously been incorporated. The adaptive value of each of these behavior patterns is what gives each associated emotion its evolutionary status.

We noted earlier that psychoevolutionary theory implies that all other emotions are constructed out of the basic ones in some way. Plutchik has proposed that these other emotions are variations of the basic ones along a dimension of intensity. Thus, for example, mild annoyance is a less intense version of anger, whereas rage is a more intense expression of anger. The resulting model, built from eight basic emotions and an intensity dimension, is shown in Figure 8-3. This model arranges the basics and their derivatives in four sets of opposing pairs—fear-anger, surprise-anticipation, sadness-joy, and acceptance-disgust—so that emotions that are close to each other are more similar than those that are farther apart or opposite each other.

## CONNECTIONS AMONG THE ELEMENTS OF EMOTION

The close connections among experience, arousal, and expressive motor behavior that are implied by biological and evolutionary approaches to emotion have been studied extensively. Individual studies are generally designed to show connections between experience and expressive behavior, between expressive behavior and arousal, and so forth. A few representative studies from this body of literature will be reviewed. Taken alone, none of these studies provides definitive evidence that experience, expressive behavior, and arousal covary to define the psychoevolutionary basis of emotion. Taken together, however, they give strong evidence for that approach.

### The Facial-Autonomic Connection

If basic emotions are rooted in the person's biological systems, and if this same biological substrate underlies the expressive motor behavior shown in facial displays, then there should be some connection between the actions of the facial musculature and the physiological activity associated with emotion. By manipulating facial expressions that show emotion, one should be able to produce distinct patterns of physiological activity for each specific emotional state. This problem was addressed in a study by Ekman and colleagues (1983).

Subjects in this study were either actors or scientists involved in the study of emotion. Each subject was trained to activate the muscles of the face on command so as to produce expressions (e.g., frowning, smiling, grimacing) associated with six basic emotions: *anger, fear, sadness, happiness, surprise,* and *disgust.* As this was being done, heart rate, finger temperature, skin resistance, and muscle tension in the forearm were measured. The results of the study showed some clear groupings of emotions along psychophysiological lines. Increases in heart rate above baseline levels were greater when the subjects expressed the facial action associated with anger, fear, and sadness than when they formed expressions associated with happiness, surprise, and disgust. Changes in finger temperature were greater in response to angerlike expressions than in response to the other five. Ekman and his colleagues summarized these findings by means of the scheme shown in Figure 8-4 and concluded from these findings that "it was contracting the facial muscles into the universal emotional signals that brought forth the emotion-specific autonomic activity" (Ekman et al., 1983, p. 1210). In other words, expressive motor behavior feeds back to the autonomic nervous system to produce specific arousal states.

## *Cerebral Lateralization and Emotional Experience*

If emotions have specific biological bases, this specificity could be represented in the central nervous system as well as in those organs of the body served by the autonomic system. There should, for instance, be certain types of activity in the brain during the experience of some emotions that would be different

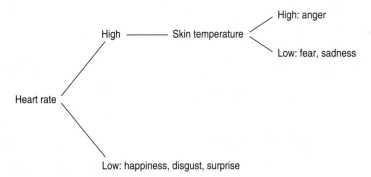

*Figure 8-4.* Branch diagram summarizing the relationship of six basic emotions to facial expressions found in emotion. (From "Autonomic Nervous System Activity Distinguishes Among Emotions" by P. Ekman, R. W. Levenson, and W. V. Friesen, *Science,* 1983, *221,* 1208–1210.)

from brain activity during other emotions. Davidson (1984) has proposed that differential activity in the two halves of the cerebral cortex underlies separate approach and withdrawal systems: the anterior (i.e., front) portion of the brain (consisting of the frontal lobe and the anterior portion of the temporal lobe) on the left side is active during approach behavior, such as moving toward desired goals, whereas the right anterior portion is active during withdrawal from undesirable events or conditions. Extending this finding to emotion, Davidson and his colleagues proposed that a stimulus that induces happiness should evoke more activity in the left anterior region than in the right, but that an unpleasant stimulus should produce more activity in the right anterior region (Davidson, Ekman, Saron, Senulis & Friesen, 1990).

Subjects were shown short films designed to induce feelings of happiness or disgust while recordings of the electroencephalogram were made from various sites in the brain, including the left and right anterior regions. The results showed greater activity in the left anterior temporal lobe during observation of the happy film than when the disgusting one was seen, whereas the disgusting film elicited greater activity in the right anterior temporal lobe than did the happy film. Thus activity in the left anterior region of the brain appears to subserve not only approach behavior but also happiness, whereas the right anterior region subserves both withdrawal tendencies and disgust.

## Critique of the Specificity Hypothesis

Studies such as the two reported above are usually offered as evidence that basic emotions are accompanied by specific underlying patterns of physiological activity. Not all students of emotion draw such a conclusion, however. Some critics of the specificity hypothesis argue instead that physiological specificity can be shown for only large response systems that include many different emotional states, and not for specific emotions (e.g., Panksepp, 1982). Others have questioned the whole concept of basic emotions that have developed through the evolutionary process (e.g., Ortony & Turner, 1990). The issue and the debate that it has engendered are far beyond the scope of this chapter. We should, however, be aware that the psychoevolutionary approach, with its corollary premise of basic emotions, is not without its detractors.

## The Experience-Facial Connection

The study by Davidson and colleagues (1990) sought to establish a connection from emotional experience to what we have called the arousal component. Others have attempted to discover a connection between experience and expressive motor behavior. In one such study, Cacioppo, Petty, Losch, and Kim (1986) induced different emotional experiences in women subjects by showing them photographs that depicted either pleasant or unpleasant scenes; within each category, some of the pictures were either moderate or relatively mild in the intensity of their depictions. As the pictures were being shown, electrical activity in the major facial muscles was simultaneously recorded. Among these were (1) the *corrugator supercilii* (which are located between the eyes in the mid-forehead region and which draw together in a typical "frowning" expression); (2) the *zygomaticus major* (which are located in the cheeks and which pull the corners of the mouth upward, as in a smile); and (3) the *orbicularis oculi* (the muscles around the eye sockets, which contract to form a "crinkled" expression during smiling). These muscle groups, as well as some other major ones in the face, are shown in Figure 8-5. Cacioppo and his associates found that pleasant stimuli evoked more muscle activity in the muscles associated with smiling (the *zygomaticus* and the *orbicularis oculi*) than did unpleasant ones, but that unpleasant stimuli elicited more activity in the corrugators (which are associated with frowning) than did the pleasant ones.

The measurement of electrical activity in the muscles of the face is only one method for studying a link between emotional experience and facial expressive motor behavior. Another method that has been used widely involves the "reading" of facial muscle actions by persons who have been trained in such a technique and the coding of such acts into patterns that are known to be closely correlated with the experience of specific emotions. Several such devices have been developed over the years, including the widely used Facial Affect Coding System (FACS) created by Ekman and his associates (Ekman, 1984). The underlying rationale of the FACS is closely related to our everyday experience of recognizing emotional displays in the faces of people around us. We are intuitively capable of considerable accuracy in

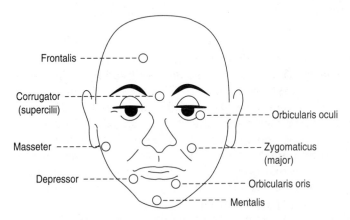

**Figure 8-5.** The major expressive muscles of the face.

recognizing the facial displays that accompany at least the basic emotions. Without necessarily knowing the underlying facial musculature, we can usually recognize an expression of happiness when we see it, especially if it is fairly strong, and we can distinguish between it and a look of fear or rage or disgust. The FACS takes the more scientific approach of training observers to recognize 44 specific patterns of underlying muscle activity in the face called *action units*. These involve the major facial muscles shown in Figure 8-5 as well as other muscles not shown in that diagram.

The action units are keys to the emotion being experienced at the time. In a study showing this, Ekman, Friesen, and Ancoli (1980) videotaped the faces of subjects as they watched either films that showed happy events (such as one of a puppy at play) or a stressful film that portrayed an accident in a workshop. The videotapes were later analyzed by trained raters who noted the action units manifested by the subjects. One action unit thought to reveal happiness (involving activity in the *zygomaticus major* muscles) was found to be closely related to experienced happiness: for example, the film that elicited the longest duration and the highest intensity of activity in this action unit was also rated by subjects as the one that caused them the most happiness. The unpleasant film was related to the occurrence of action units known to be associated with unpleasant emotions like fear, pain, and disgust.

## The Facial Feedback Hypothesis

One of the oldest approaches to the study of emotion is the general notion that our emotional experiences are an outgrowth of expressive motor behavior in the face. Often this approach has taken the form of a belief that we can regulate our emotional experiences by controlling our facial expressions. Thus we may feel that we can augment our feelings of grief at a funeral by assuming a somber aspect that befits the occasion, or we may try to cheer up a child who is crying by urging her to smile. This assumption that there is a link from the face to the central nervous system, where emotion is experienced, is known as the *facial feedback hypothesis*.

Research on the facial feedback hypothesis typically involves the artificial induction of a subject's facial expressions followed by assessment of how the subject feels. This research has been of two types, depending on the nature of the feelings that are assessed. The first type follows a *dimensional* approach, in which a relationship is sought between facial expression and changes in self-reports along a single dimension of positive and negative affect. It assumes that people are capable of describing whether they feel generally good or bad and approximately how intensely they feel either of these affective states. The second type follows a *categorical* approach, in which the relationship that is tested is between facial expressions and specific categories of emotion. This approach obviously presupposes a more highly developed system of afferent feedback from the face to the brain than does the less complex dimensional one.

*According to the facial feedback hypothesis, encouraging a sad person to smile may make the person feel happier.*

Most of the research that has been conducted to date involves the less complex dimensional procedure. For example, Laird (1974) instructed male subjects to assume one of two facial expressions by either contracting the eyebrows into a frown or lifting the corners of the mouth to smile. While holding the dictated expression, the subject looked at pictures likely to evoke either anger or joy, after which he described his feelings on an adjective checklist. In general, it made no difference what type of picture the subject saw; in both cases, self-descriptions of aggressiveness were higher as the subject frowned, whereas self-ratings of elation and surgency (e.g., words like *elated, carefree,* and *overjoyed*) were higher as the subject smiled.

Another interesting study that gives some evidence of dimensional facial feedback was conducted by Strack, Martin, and Stepper (1988). Subjects were instructed to hold a pen in their mouths while watching humorous cartoons. Some subjects held the pen with their lips, thereby activating "unpleasant" patterns of activity in the *depressor* and *orbicularis oris* muscles (see Figure 8-5). Others clenched the pen between the teeth, activating a "smile" expression by contracting the *zygomaticus major*. Ratings of the cartoons showed that subjects who watched while "smiling" were more amused than those who held the pen between the lips or than a group of controls who held a pen in one hand while watching.

Less has been done to test the categorical hypothesis. Laird, Wagener, Halal, and Szegda (1982) have reported finding that subjects were most able to recall verbal statements that were either angry, fearful, or sad in tone when they assumed facial expressions associated with these emotions. Other well-controlled studies have found no evidence for the experience of specific emotions following the manipulation of facial expressions (e.g., Tourangeau & Ellsworth, 1979). The status of the categorical hypothesis is still unclear (Buck, 1980). Part of the ambiguity that surrounds it is undoubtedly due to disagreements over what evidence of *any* sort of facial feedback—dimensional or categorical—really signifies. We will consider this matter next.

**COGNITIVE MEDIATION.**    How can we account for results that suggest the operation of feedback from the face in the experience of emotion? Several explanations have been offered. One is that the feedback process is mediated by cognitive processes: the person perceives that his or her face has taken on a particular expression and, knowing the significance of that expression for a given affective state, *infers* that this state is being experienced (Buck, 1985). This "I'm smiling, so I must be happy" phenomenon obviously depends on previous learning of the connection between the perceived facial expression and the associated emotion.

Laird has suggested that facial feedback may evoke feelings and percepts that initiate *memories* of the related affective state (Laird et al., 1982). This idea is related to the more fundamental one that thoughts and emotional moods are linked together in associative long-term memory networks. Thus it would follow from this idea that if a person perceives that he or she is expressing a particular emotion in the face and infers from this that an emotion is being experienced, certain associated thoughts and memories may be activated within the network. The inference "I'm smiling, so I must be happy" would, for example, then trigger memories of happy events in the past.

Does this happen? Laird and his associates (1982) have reported findings consistent with this idea. The subjects first read newspaper editorials that were chosen to activate feelings of anger (e.g., descriptions of how dolphins are killed during tuna fishing) and some humorous anecdotes by Woody Allen. Later the subjects were tested for their recall of the two sets of materials as they maintained frowning or smiling facial expressions. A clear interaction was found; subjects recalled more facts about the anger-inducing editorials when they frowned during recall than they did while smiling, whereas they recalled more facts about the humorous material when they smiled during recall than they did when frowning.

Thus feedback related to emotion from the face does evoke associated thoughts and memories. It is possible that the recall of past incidents involving emotional experience plays some role in the experience of emotion: the person experiences his or her expression, identifies the emotion associated with it, recalls past experiences of that emotion, and re-experiences some of those feelings as a result. We should note that this process does not require deliberate processing of the relevant information; the feeling of an affective state is not necessarily the cool and rational matter that this hypothesis seems to imply. Once a person has learned the connection between the facial expression and the accompanying affect, the process of drawing the inference may become habitual and virtually automatic. In the same way, the memorial process is not "voluntary"; it is associative and largely determined by the nature of the underlying memory network. Despite this, however, the process described here is still an *acquired* process that does not postulate any "wired-in" links between the face and the brain.

**BIOLOGICAL MEDIATION.** The alternative explanation is that facial feedback of affect requires just such innate biological connections. Most psychologists who advocate the facial feedback hypothesis take this point of view (e.g., Izard, 1990; Tomkins, 1984). Not every theorist who accepts the idea of direct physiological connections offers a detailed explanation of the mechanisms involved, but a recent theory makes an intriguing suggestion of one such mechanism.

Zajonc (1985; Zajonc, Murphy & Inglehart, 1989) has proposed a complex set of mechanisms that involve the facial muscles and the flow of blood in the head to account for the effects of facial expressions on experienced emotion. The structures involved in this process are (1) the veins of the face, (2) the internal carotid artery, which carries blood to the brain, (3) the cavernous sinus, a dilated chamber that receives blood from some of the facial veins and that, in turn, surrounds the internal carotid as it enters the brain, and (4) certain higher centers in the brain that are involved in the experience of emotion and are also warmed or cooled by the flow of blood into the cranium. Figure 8-6 schematizes the organization of these mechanisms.

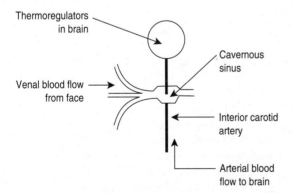

*Figure 8-6.* Schematic diagram of relationships among facial expression, venal blood flow, and brain blood temperature. (Adapted from "Feeling and Facial Efference: Implications of the Vascular Theory of Emotion" by R. B. Zajonc, S. T. Murphy, and M. Inglehart, *Psychological Review,* 1989, *96,* 395–416.)

The theory states that the facial muscles act on the facial veins in a mechanical way, by influencing their dilation and constriction. When this mechanical action on the facial veins produces dilation, the blood being carried by them is cooled. At the same time, facial expressions facilitate or inhibit the passage of air through the nasal cavity, and this passage of air also cools the blood in the facial veins (much as blowing on the back of one's hand causes a cool sensation). Thus the action of the facial muscles can, through either or both of these mechanisms, cause the blood that enters the cavernous sinus to be relatively cool or warm. The temperature of this blood in turn helps to cool (or not cool) the blood that is entering the brain through the internal carotid. Thus the blood that reaches the higher centers that control the temperature of the brain is relatively cool or warm, partly as an indirect result of facial activity. The final step in the theory is the proposition that changes in brain temperature are correlated with affective experiences. The mediating influences are assumed to be hormonal and neurotransmitter activities, which are affected by blood temperature and which in turn produce emotional and affective states.

The theory predicts that the facial expressions associated with emotions will evoke not only affective states but also measurable changes in blood temperature in the brain. The effects of the facial muscles on the facial vasculature do not necessarily depend on emotion, however. Facial muscle action that is enacted for any reason whatever should have the predicted effects. In a series of experiments designed to test the theory, Zajonc and his associates (1989) used a methodology that did not involve induced emotion. Facial muscle action was instigated by having subjects pronounce vowel sounds, some of which required intense constriction of certain facial muscles while others could be made with a relatively relaxed face. Blood temperature, which should be higher among subjects who made the sounds that demand the most strenuous muscle action, was measured by means of infrared photography of the forehead directly above a branch of the anterior cerebral artery. Subjects were asked to rate how much they liked the vowel sounds that they had uttered.

The results of these studies generally supported the theory. Blood temperature was higher during the formation of some vowels (such as the letter *u*, which requires pursing of the lips) than it was during the uttering of others (such as the *ah* and *o* sounds). The latter types of vowel were also generally rated as more pleasant and better liked than the former. Zajonc and his colleagues also found that cooler blood temperatures in the brain and higher ratings of positive affect were obtained when cool air was blown directly into the nose than when warm air was used. Altogether, therefore, the results of the several studies were consistent with the predictions of the theory.

**FEEDBACK AS INFORMATION.** Frijda (1986) has suggested an explanation of the function of facial feedback that makes the process essentially informational. It is based on a more general theory that defines emotion as a function of readiness and preparation for carrying out some action specific to the emotion and the situation that elicits it. Examples are the readiness to shout when joyful, to cry when sad, and to snarl when angry. States of *action readiness* are evoked by appraisals of the meaning of the situation, and they correlate highly with these appraisals (Frijda, Kuipers & ter Schure, 1989).

Applying this theory to the explanation of facial feedback effects, Frijda (1986) proposes that such feedback plays a role in the experience of emotion "if, and only if, it complements an action tendency or activation state" (p. 236). This implies that the person must first be motivated to carry out some act and that he or she has mobilized some energy toward that end. If the experience of facial activity is consistent with this tendency, it confirms that the intention has been fulfilled. For example, suppose a person sees an old friend for the first time in many months and is motivated to show her pleasure over the encounter. Feelings emanating from her face informing her that she is smiling serve to confirm and complement that action tendency. Expressive acts, in and of themselves, do not produce emotion; they produce only the image, or idea, of an emotion. Only when this idea combines with a readiness to act does a true emotion come into being.

# OTHER THEORIES OF EMOTION

Several other modern theories of emotion share certain features with the ones already discussed while adding some new elements as well. In this final section of the chapter we will briefly review two of these approaches.

## Perceptual-Motor Theory

Leventhal (1980) has developed a complex theory of emotion based on the fundamental premise that emotion is constructed out of both innate and learned elements. Human beings are endowed with two systems by which they process information from the environment. In one of these, the objective processing system, information is analyzed "coolly" and voluntary behavior is initiated. This system will not concern us. The other, the *emotional processing system,* accounts for the initial construction of the emotional experience and the activation, by this experience, of coping behaviors. We will consider only the way in which the emotion is constructed because this is the most basic element in the theory.

Emotion is an experience that results from three kinds of information processing. The first is *sensory-motor processing,* which takes place on the lowest and most primitive level. It follows a route that is innate and "wired into" the person, and it produces relatively simple motor responses (i.e., physical movement) to stimuli. The fussing of a newborn baby in response to physical discomfort is a case of such low-level processing. In fact, very young babies produce recognizable expressions of several emotions in reaction to appropriate situational cues; that they do this long before they have had the opportunity to learn such responses constitutes some of the strongest evidence for Leventhal's theory (e.g., Field, Woodson, Greenberg & Cohen, 1982). This sort of action Leventhal (1984) calls the "elementary core of emotional processing" (p. 274). It is not learned and it requires no cognitive judgments or understanding.

Over time, repeated experiences of such basic emotions become associated with specific settings and become conditioned to them. These settings later elicit memories of both emotional experiences and some of the motor responses that accompanied those experiences. At first, these memories are limited to single and concrete episodes, but with repeated experiences of these memories, they coalesce into prototypical or *schematic* experiences. For example, the sight of her mother will at first evoke in the child a memory of some past occasion on which she experienced love, but over many such occasions, the appearance of the mother will set off a generalized feeling of affection.

Finally, schematic processing leads the way to the still higher level of *conceptual processing*. At this level, the person reflects upon and understands past emotional experiences. The results of these reflections are then encoded in memory in the form of verbal propositions. This material can subsequently be retrieved from memory when the person wishes to ruminate on or to describe his emotional experiences, or to carry out some behavior that has implications for emotional behavior or control. Reflection on the motor-behavioral aspects of past emotional episodes is important in forming standards for further expression and control of emotions. For example, a person who is not certain what emotion to show at the funeral of a friend may search his memory for information from past experiences that has been encoded in conceptual memory.

In any person except a very young one who has not had time to form emotional associations, the experience of emotion in response to a situation is the sum of the inputs from all three processes. Emotion is therefore constructed out of both innate and learned elements, as we noted above. Although these three levels of processing are sequential in their development, once all three are operational, they usually occur virtually simultaneously. Thus, for instance, a person does not first experience the sensory-motor aspect of an emotion, then the schematic, and finally the conceptual. The person experiences a unified phenomenon to which all three processes are contributing at the same time.

This theory has some important implications for matters discussed earlier in the chapter. The first is the question of the role of cognition in emotion. Unlike the Schachter-Singer theory, the perceptual-motor theory does not require cognition as a necessary element in the differentiation of specific emotions. It is assumed that the sensory-motor processing system distinguishes among the emotions and leads to differential experiences. Nevertheless, it is obvious that cognition plays an important role in Leventhal's approach. The sensory-motor system accounts for only the most rudimentary emotional experiences. The full experience requires the added input from schematic and

*Some psychologists argue that smiling is an* effect *of happiness and not a cause.*

conceptual memory. Furthermore, in those aspects of the theory that come after the construction of emotional experience, and upon which we are not dwelling in this brief introduction, Leventhal describes the ways in which the person responds to his or her emotions with various coping stretegies and action plans, as well as the ways in which the results of those actions are appraised and evaluated. All of this cognitive activity is essential to emotion in the broadest sense.

The second matter for which the theory has implications is the facial feedback hypothesis. In this theory, expressive motor behavior in the face is considered to be an outward manifestation, or effect, of central emotional experience and not a cause. Thus Leventhal does not follow the facial feedback approach. In fact, he has suggested that actions that are deliberately undertaken to stimulate the experience of emotion (such as arranging the face in an "emotional" expression) are processed in the objective and voluntary system and not in the emotional one, and that such actions may actually *inhibit* true emotional experience (Leventhal, 1984). The reader may test this idea sometime by waiting until she or he feels amused by something and then *forcing* a laugh. This action will probably not increase the humor of the situation but terminate it instead.

## Cognitive Appraisal Theory

The centerpiece of the approach to emotion taken by Lazarus (1991) is a cognitive appraisal process that bears some similarity to the one described by Leventhal. For Lazarus, however, cognition is the most important element in the construction of emotions. In his view, in our interactions with the environment we make regular appraisals of events, of the significance of these events for ourselves, and of the outcomes of the strategies and devices that we use to cope with these events. Emotions come and go in this context.

Our first appraisal of an event that has emotional implications consists of making a judgment of the significance of the event for our well-being. The event, or, more precisely, the change in our surroundings produced by the event, is appraised as being (1) irrelevant and of no significance, so that it can be safely ignored; (2) positive and benign; or (3) stressful, in that it signals some harm or loss that has already happened, some threat of harm or loss that will soon occur, or some difficult challenge. The second and third of these appraisals create the conditions for another round of appraisals and for the experience of emotion. A benign primary appraisal obviously elicits positive affect, pleasant emotions, and behaviors aimed at allowing approach to the situation. An appraisal of the situation as one that has caused harm or loss (e.g., losing one's job) results in a state marked by emotions such as sadness, depression, and resignation. Appraisal of impending threat (e.g., being informed that one's job may be terminated in the future) evokes fear and anxiety, as well as watchfulness and possibly anger. When the appraisal signals challenge (e.g., being told that one can be promoted to a better job if one shows an increase in productivity), the dominant response consists of increased effort and persistence along with positive affect.

When the primary appraisal leads to the conclusion that the situation is stressful, a secondary appraisal is then made, by means of which the person assesses the availability of resources for coping with the stress. This generally takes one of two forms. In *problem-based coping,* the person concentrates his energies on eliminating the source of stress; that is, he takes a problem-centered approach. In *intrapsychic coping,* the person focuses her attention not on the problem, but on her own emotional response to the problem. This may include changing oneself in order to adapt to the stressful event, or it may involve a subjective withdrawal from the situation through repression and denial of the problem. The reader may note the similarity between Lazarus's two types of coping responses and Kuhl's constructs of action and state orientations from Chapter 3.

The theory of emotion of Lazarus and his colleagues is closely tied to their research on stress and coping, matters that will be discussed in Chapter 11. For now, however, a few characteristics of the theory should be noted. First, the theory assumes that the person is in a constant *transaction* with his environment. The relationships between person and environment are reciprocal; the environment impinges upon, and demands responses from, the person, but at the same time the person actively influences the environment through coping behavior. The view of human nature implicit in this model is different from the typical one taken by more behaviorally oriented psychologists. In Lazarus's theory the person is not a passive recipient of stimulation, reacting with specific emotions to specific conditions, but rather an active agent in her world, determining her emotional state by virtue of her cognitive activity.

Second, whether emotion is a cause or an effect is a moot question in this theory. Does cognition precede or follow emotion? The answer depends on where one enters the ongoing cycle of adaptive behavior. Emotions are not fixed and enduring states, but rather short-lived episodes that come and go. An emotion certainly results from a cognitive appraisal, but the emotion, once elicited, helps to determine subsequent action, which in turn is appraised, with consequences for subsequent emotion. For example, suppose a person quits his job because of stresses in the workplace and takes a new position elsewhere. The act of quitting is a means of coping with a stressor, and the unpleasant affect that had been associated with the job may be replaced by joy. However, the appraisal process may introduce other cognitions, such as loss of self-esteem over giving up on the first job, so that positive affect is tempered by negative. Subsequent appraisals may reveal that the second job is stressful for reasons of its own, so that negative affect is exacerbated, and so on. In an ongoing transactional system, the difference between causes and effects tends to become obscured.

Third, the study of the transactional nature of stress, appraisal, coping, and emotion requires methodologies that are suitable for that purpose. Methods that give a cross-section of behavior in time, such as controlled experiments, are not suited to this sort of approach. Research must be extended over a period of time to isolate the flow of the processes involved. Such research is also best carried out in natural settings rather than in the artificial ambience of the laboratory. Some examples of this type of research will be reviewed in Chapter 11.

## CHAPTER SUMMARY

1.   One of the oldest issues in the study of emotion is whether emotion is the effect of processes in the brain or of processes in the periphery of the body. The James-Lange theory defined emotion as the perception of changes in bodily states that involve the skeletal musculature and the autonomic nervous system. In criticizing the James-Lange theory, Cannon proposed that

emotional feelings arise in the thalamus and emotional expression in the hypothalamus.

2.   Emotional theories are based on inferences from three types of observable phenomena: subject reports of experiences, expressive motor behavior in the large muscles and in the face, and physiological activity. To a large extent, theories of emotion seek to explain relationships among these three phenomena.

3.   Schachter and Singer's cognition-arousal theory is similar to the James-Lange theory in that it links emotion to feedback from organs innervated by the autonomic nervous system. Unlike the earlier theory, however, the Schachter-Singer approach defines this feedback as generalized and undifferentiated arousal that is labeled as a specific emotion in terms of available cognitions about the immediate environment. This theory has been tested by numerous experiments that involve the misattribution of arousal to nonemotional stimuli. Although some of these studies support the theory, many others do not.

4.   Another cognition-arousal theory, Zillmann's theory of excitation transfer, rests on better empirical evidence. This approach accounts for emotion under a special set of circumstances in which arousal from one source is mistakenly attributed to another source that occurs within a short period of time. The residual arousal, after having been transferred, contributes to the emotional reaction to the second event. This happens only during the period in which (a) there is a residue of arousal from the first event and (b) that arousal is not correctly attributed to that event.

5.   Psychoevolutionary theories of emotion are based on the assumption that certain basic emotions have been part of larger patterns of adaptive behavior passed on through natural selection. These basic emotions are the central core from which other emotions are constructed. They are grounded in biological processes, so that each basic emotion includes a specific pattern of physiological activity and a specific pattern of expressive motor behavior.

6.   Empirical research has been addressed to discovering connections among emotional experience, arousal, and expressive motor behavior. One finding from this research is that manipulated facial expressions that mimic expressions shown during emotion are correlated with simultaneous changes in autonomic arousal. It is concluded from this that different emotions are accompanied by different arousal patterns. It has also been shown that activity in the anterior regions of the left cerebral hemisphere subserves both approach behavior and positive affect, whereas activity in the anterior right hemisphere subserves withdrawal behavior and negative affect. Induction of

emotional experiences also has been shown to elicit specific patterns of activity in the facial musculature.

**7.** The facial feedback hypothesis attributes at least some of the experience of emotion to processes that connect the facial muscles and vasculature to the brain. Evidence consistent with the hypothesis has shown that facial expression appears to be correlated with feelings of positive versus negative affect. Whether specific emotions are engendered by feedback from the face is still open to question. Theories of facial feedback are of two types: those that postulate cognitive intervening processes and those that specify physiological connectors, such as Zajonc's hypothesis that the temperature of the supply of blood to the brain mediates emotional experiences.

**8.** Leventhal's perceptual-motor theory describes emotion as an experience that is constructed from basic sensory-motor experiences and long-term memory that grows out of those experiences. Emotions are differentiated on the basis of sensory-motor processing. Cognition plays an important role in this theory in the elaboration of emotional experience through schematic and conceptual memory, but it is not necessary for the initial experience.

**9.** The theory of Lazarus and his associates is the most consistently cognitive of all the modern viewpoints. In this theory emotion is part of an ongoing person-environment transaction within which the person constantly appraises both the environment and his or her relationship to it. The individual is not a passive recipient of stimulation but an active and constructive agent who copes with situational changes and influences the emotions that those changes elicit.

CHAPTER *9*

# PROSOCIAL AND AGGRESSIVE MOTIVATION

### CHAPTER OUTLINE

Prosocial Motivation
Aggressive Motivation
Chapter Summary

People spend much of their time interacting in face-to-face relationships in which they either help or hurt one another. Such interactions may involve the operation of specific motives and incentives, which have been described elsewhere (see Chapter 2). In this chapter we will examine helping (prosocial) behavior and hurting (antisocial or aggressive) behavior within a motivational framework. In human interaction, persons serve as the cause of situations that call forth actions from each other. The actions thus evoked are directed toward others, and the ultimate source of these actions is basic motives or need states. To illustrate this, let us first consider a common prosocial act: a person who is relatively affluent encounters a homeless person on the street and responds to that person's request by giving him some money. Obviously the unfortunate person creates the social situation for the more comfortable one, and this situation engages a social motive in the latter. The result is an incentive to give money to the needy person.

This all seems simple. However, we still have not identified the basic motive that is engaged by the request of the homeless person. Is it a genuine desire to help that person or is it only a wish to buy him off and send him away? Assuming that the desire to help is genuine, what more do we know about it? Is it a selfless motive to help a needy person even though it costs the giver something, a motive that we call altruism, or is it calculated to obtain something for the giver, such as praise from others or a warm feeling of having done something good? Does a person do good only when others are watching and likely to approve?

As we will show later in the chapter, the study of prosocial behavior is often aimed at answering the basic question of underlying motives. In fact, the motivational analysis of all interactive behavior, both prosocial and antisocial, can be reduced to the question of the needs that are engaged by the actions of other people. In the case of aggression, the following example poses another question about motives. During a tense and hard-fought baseball game, a pitcher deliberately hits a batter with one of his fast balls and the batter responds by throwing down his bat, rushing to the pitching mound, and wrestling the pitcher to the ground. From the standpoint of the batter, the pitcher has created a situation that engages a motive or need. What is that need? Possibly the batter thinks that the pitcher is trying to intimidate him and must be resisted, lest the batter look weak and passive. Or possibly the batter thinks that the pitcher has violated a rule of good sportsmanship and that retaliation in kind must be taken. Perhaps the batter is merely trying to persuade the pitcher not to throw at him again. Only the batter is in a position to understand his motives. However, a person sitting in the grandstand and observing this little altercation on the field will be in a much better position to understand exactly what is going on if there is at least some idea of the underlying motive for the retaliatory action.

As we will show in this chapter, human aggression is seldom analyzed in terms of basic motives. Research on the subject has consisted mainly of pointing out the situational causes of aggression, the ways in which aggression is manifested in behavior, and, to some extent, the effects of aggressive behavior. We will review some of what this research has discovered. We will speculate from time to time on the motives that are probably operating, but until a more focused motivational approach to human aggression is taken, this is all that we can do.

# PROSOCIAL MOTIVATION
## Theories of Prosocial Behavior

**SPECIFIC REWARDS AND PUNISHMENTS.**   People do things for one another for a number of reasons, and the several theories of prosocial behavior that have been proposed are built around these reasons. Perhaps the oldest theory is that people are always motivated by a desire for the maximum pleasure and the miniumum pain. If giving aid to a person in need can bring direct rewards to the helper, whether they be material or social (e.g., praise and approval from others), the end result is pleasant and rewarding. Such direct rewards need not always be as direct and visible as social approval, however. They can be internalized through experience, so that a person may come to be helpful and prosocial in order to get such self-administered prizes as pride and a sense of satisfaction. Helping may also be motivated by a desire to avoid punishments that the person anticipates as a consequence of not helping, such as public disapproval and embarrassment or internal states of guilt and anxiety.

**EMPATHIC JOY.**    Smith, Keating, and Stotland (1989) have proposed that people help others in need so that they may share vicariously the joy that results from the other's relief from distress. In a sense this is variation of the notion of helping for specific rewards described above. Vicarious happiness brings pleasure to the helper and is therefore essentially a selfish incentive.

**AVOIDANCE OF DISTRESS.**    Helping another person who needs assistance may also be the result of feelings of distress caused by the other's plight. We call these feelings *empathy* because they are based on a shared suffering with the other person. One reason that the observer who is sharing suffering with the victim attempts to help the latter may be that, by terminating that person's distress, the observer likewise gets relief. For example, the person who becomes discomfited by the sight of a homeless person and who then drops some money into the hand of that person may walk away feeling relieved for having done a small act of kindness. It must be emphasized that the motivation of the helper in this case is purely selfish. The helpful act is animated not by a desire to make the recipient feel better but by the helper's need to avoid empathic pain.

**TENSION.**    A variant of the theory just described has been proposed by Reykowski (1982), who describes empathy as a state of tension evoked by a perceived discrepancy between the condition of another person and what one wishes were the state of that person. For example, learning that a friend has just lost her job and is in debt may be contrasted with the condition that one wishes for her friend: employment and financial solvency. To the extent that the wish and the reality are discrepant, the observer will experience unpleasant tension and a consequent need to reduce tension. Helping the other person may reduce the perceived discrepancy to some extent.

**ALTRUISM.**    All the theories of helping described so far have been hedonic and self-centered. In each case a person is thought to help someone else in order to obtain something: direct rewards, a good feeling about himself or herself, avoidance of censure, relief from personal distress, or vicarious happiness. There may be an additional motive for helping others, however: a selfless desire to secure the other person's good whether or not the helper receives anything in the bargain. This type of prosocial behavior we call altruism, and it, like the search for relief of personal distress, is a reaction to feelings of empathy. Thus shared suffering with another person may evoke helping either because it is an aversive condition that must be relieved or because it sensitizes the person to the other person's suffering and elicits a desire to end that suffering. Of course, there is no reason empathy cannot lead to both motives; the two are not mutually exclusive. In the two following sections, we will analyze studies that bear on these two possible responses to empathy for others in need: relief of personal distress and altruism.

## The Empathy-Distress Hypothesis

NORMATIVE AND ALTRUISTIC HELPING.    The hypothesis that helping behavior may be instrumental to the relief of negative affect is consistent with the findings of Weiss and his associates that the sight of a suffering person being relieved reinforces the helping response (e.g., Weiss, Boyer, Lombardo & Stitch, 1973). Helping behavior may therefore be acquired through instrumental learning. That being the case, it can also be argued, in the language of drive theory (see Chapter 7), that the helping response is reinforced through the reduction of the drive that had been elicited by empathy with the suffering person. The suffering of others and the negative affect that it produces become cues for the instrumental helping response. It would appear, therefore, that the gratifying nature of helping behavior is acquired through social learning.

A subsequent study by Cialdini and Kenrick (1976) supported this conclusion by showing that very young children, who have not yet become highly socialized, do not react to negative affect with helping behavior. Cialdini and Kenrick first manipulated negative affect by instructing children to think about either sad experiences or affectively neutral objects in their surroundings. The children were drawn from three age groups: school grades 1–3, 5–7, and 10–12. After this manipulation, all of the children were given an opportunity to contribute, privately and anonymously, some valuable coupons to other children. Whereas age had no effect on generosity following the induction of a neutral mood, giving was a direct function of age among children with an induced negative mood (Figure 9-1).

The Cialdini and Kenrick study does not prove that young children are incapable of helping others; it shows only that they have not yet learned that helping can reduce or eliminate negative affect. Any rewards that they receive from helping behavior must be more direct. To use a distinction made by Rosenhan (1969), young children are capable of "normative" helping—that is, helping behavior for which they receive direct rewards such as approval from adults. It is only after adequate social learning that children become capable of "autonomous" helping, which is the result of internalized values and occurs without external rewards (Cialdini, Baumann & Kenrick, 1981).

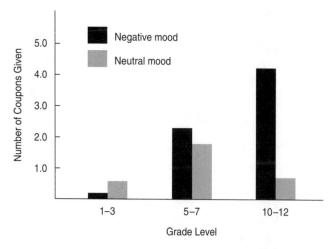

**Figure 9-1.** Helping by children in three age groups following induction of neutral or negative mood. (Adapted from "Altruism as Hedonism: A Social Development Perspective on the Relationship of Negative Mood State and Helping" by R. B. Cialdini and D. T. Kenrick, *Journal of Personality and Social Psychology,* 1976, *34,* 907–914.)

**THE AROUSAL: COST-REWARD MODEL.**    Sometimes helping others in distress can be so dangerous or difficult that even with the best of intentions an observer will not be willing to offer help. In such instances we would say that the costs of helping are so excessive that they outweigh the reward to be gained by relief from empathic distress. This concept is the basis for an *arousal: cost-reward model* of helping behavior (Dovidio, Piliavin, Gaertner, Schroeder & Clark, 1991). According to this model, helping behavior consists of two components. The first is arousal caused by the sight of another person in need and the attribution of the arousal state to that person's distress. The arousal state thus becomes a condition of negative affect, which the person is motivated to reduce. One response that may reduce negative affect is the prosocial one. However, before actually helping, the person analyzes the cost-benefit balance. This is the second component of the model.

That observing the suffering of others arouses the observer has been documented in several studies (e.g., Lazarus & Alfert, 1964; Gaertner & Dovidio, 1977). We also have considerable evidence that empathic arousal motivates helping behavior (Dovidio, 1984; Eisenberg & Miller, 1987). The evidence that pertains to the cost-reward aspects of the model is somewhat more complex because, for one thing, two types of cost are involved. The costs associated with helping are obvious: danger to the helper, time, effort, personal discomfort, and the possibility of lost rewards. As these costs increase, helping obviously becomes less likely. In addition, there are costs associated with *not* helping, such as loss of respect from others, self-blame, and guilt. The effects of these costs depend in large part on the costs of helping. As long as the costs of helping are relatively low, helping increases as the costs of not doing so increase. In general, we help others in order to avoid looking bad or incurring social disapproval only when we can do so without suffering too much for it. When the cost of helping is high, people give either indirect (i.e., relatively "cheap") help or no help at all. For example, whereas one may not jump into shark-infested water to save a stranger, one may still help by trying to find a rope to throw to the endangered victim. If the costs of helping are prohibitive, the observer may react to not helping by cognitively redefining the situation in a self-protecting way—by derogating the victim, by classifying the situation as "not serious," or by disavowing all personal responsibility. The interrelated effects of the cost of helping and the cost of not helping are summarized in Figure 9-2.

A study by Shotland and Heinold (1985) illustrates the principle that when the perceived costs of helping are high, the help that is given is at best indirect. Students in a class in first-aid training were exposed to a staged "accident" in which the victim appeared to be suffering arterial bleeding. The students had been selected so that some were relatively advanced and had received training in first aid, whereas the remainder were new to the class and untrained. Direct help to the victim (e.g., attempts to stop the bleeding) was given to a greater extent by trained students than by untrained ones; indirect help, such as seeking the assistance of others, was given to a greater extent by untrained students than by trained ones. The costs of direct help (e.g., the risk of unwittingly doing harm to the victim) were probably seen as higher by untrained subjects than by trained ones—hence, the high level of indirect aid.

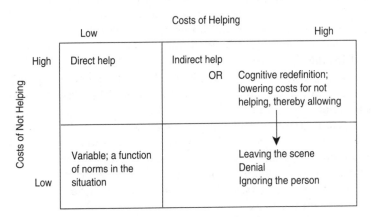

***Figure 9-2.*** Helping and nonhelping behaviors under conditions of high and low costs for helping and not helping. (From "The Arousal: Cost-Reward Model and the Process of Intervention: A Review of the Evidence" by J. F. Dovidio, J. A. Piliavin, S. L. Gaertner, D. A. Schroeder, and R. D. Clark, III, in *Prosocial Behavior,* edited by M. S. Clark, 1991, Newbury Park, CA: Sage.)

## *Transient Mood States*

In addition to reflecting the processes of arousal and cost-reward analysis, helping behavior can be influenced by temporary states of positive or negative affect (Salovey, Mayer & Rosenhan, 1991). Such conditions are usually studied experimentally, with positive or negative affect induced prior to the subjects' introduction to a situation in which prosocial behavior is an option. Affect has been induced in many ways, such as thinking pleasant or unpleasant thoughts, succeeding or failing at a task, or receiving a gift. The effects of induced positive moods, such as happiness, are fairly straightforward: persons whose happiness has been increased are more likely to engage in prosocial behavior when given the opportunity than are persons who have not been induced to feel positive affect. For example, in a study by Isen and Levin (1972), subjects who had found some money in a pay telephone were more likely later on to help a person retrieve some papers that had accidentally been dropped than were subjects who had not found any money. This effect is found even in young children. Isen, Horn and Rosenhan (1973) observed that fourth graders who had just won a game were more charitable in donating money to a toy fund for poor children than were children who had lost.

The evidence is somewhat less clear following the induction of negative affect. What happens depends to some extent on the nature of the negative state that is created. People who have been made to feel guilty about having done something wrong may be motivated to help others, possibly in hopes of expiating their guilt (Darlington & Macker, 1966). When the person feels sad, however, the outcome may depend on the direction in which the sadness is focused: if the focus is on the suffering of another person, helping behavior is facilitated by the sad mood, but when the focus of sadness is on the self and one's own problems ("feeling sorry for oneself"), sadness does not animate helping behavior (Thompson, Cowan & Rosenhan, 1980).

How can we account for these findings? One possibility is that the induced mood influences attention to, and thoughts about, oneself. Both positive and negative affective states have been shown to cause a person's attention to shift more to the self and less to external objects or persons (Salovey, 1992). This focus of attention on the self can have three effects when the mood is positive: (1) it can make the person aware of her or his good fortune, thereby triggering a social comparison with less fortunate others, (2) it can remind the person of a social norm that we should help others less fortunate than ourselves, and (3) it may amplify the original positive affective state, thereby intensifying the first two effects. The result of these outcomes should be increased prosocial behavior.

A study by Berkowitz (1987) indicates that self-awareness and induced positive affect may operate to influence helping in still another way. All subjects were first asked to think about pleasant, unpleasant, or neutral matters. Later, half of the subjects were made self-conscious by seeing their reflections in a mirror (this is a common method for increasing self-awareness; see Chapter 4). Finally, all were given an opportunity to help the experimenter catch up on a backlog of work by adding some columns of numbers on data sheets. Induced self-awareness and induced affect interacted to determine helping behavior (Figure 9-3): the effects of positive affect on helping were significantly greater among highly self-aware people than among those in whom self-awareness had not been induced. Berkowitz therefore showed that increased self-awareness magnifies the influence of positive affect on helping behavior, perhaps by heightening the person's perceptions of how good he or she is feeling.

Changing one's focus of attention is not the only effect of induced positive mood. It is also possible that a positive feeling improves one's perceptions of situations and of other people. It may cause one to perceive someone in need as a "good" person who is worthy of whatever help we may give. It may also lead one to see social relationships, such as the one with the person in need, as being more attractive than they would otherwise be (e.g., Manucia, Baumann & Cialdini, 1984). A third possibility is that giving help may enable one to maintain the positive mood that was originally induced. Williamson and Clark (1989) have shown, for example, that helping another person leads to an increase in positive affect and to a more favorable self-evaluation. People may therefore learn through experience that prosocial behavior enhances feelings of pleasure. If they wish to sustain such feelings (as might be the case after a pleasant experience), helping others might be one means to that end.

The direction of attentional focus (see above) may explain some of the effects of induced negative mood on helping behavior. If such a mood is

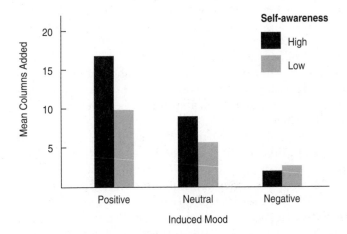

**Figure 9-3.** Helping behavior among subjects high and low in self-awareness following induction of positive, negative, or neutral mood. (After "Mood, Self-Awareness, and Willingness to Help" by L. Berkowitz, *Journal of Personality and Social Psychology,* 1987, *52,* 721–729.)

focused on the self rather than on the person who needs help, the result may often be feelings of helplessness and depression (Psyzczynski & Greenberg, 1987), and these states can interfere with thoughts about helping in all but the most compelling cases. If, however, the negative mood causes one to focus on the person in need, the subsequent reaction may be a desire to help. This desire could be animated by a need for relief from the aversive state, by altruistic motives, or by some combination of the two.

## Sense of Community

Help giving depends very much on the relationship between the donor and the receiver. The closer the observer is to the person in need—in the sense of being, for example, a friend, a relative, or a fellow member of some in-group—the more likely he or she is to give help. In part this is because the relationship influences the degree to which the observer experiences empathic arousal. In a related study, Lanzetta and Englis (1989) gave subjects a task that was supposedly being carried out simultaneously by a fellow subject. This other person was described as either a competitor or someone who was trying to cooperate with the subject. Following these instructions each subject observed a videotape that supposedly showed the other person—the cooperator or the competitor—performing in another room. The videotape, which was actually a standard one shown to all subjects, showed the other person smiling at times and at other times grimacing with pain. Meanwhile, the subject's level of skin conductance was measured to provide an index of empathic arousal.

Lanzetta and Englis reasoned that subjects should become more empathically aroused when they watched a cooperator express pain than when that person smiled because of their generally friendly attitude toward that person. The opposite should occur when a competitor was being watched. Because of the induced antagonistic relationship, subjects should be more upset and aroused when that person smiled than showed expressions of pain. Figure 9-4 shows that both of these results were obtained, and that empathic arousal in response to another person's suffering is affected by the closeness one feels toward the other.

People are more likely to give help to a person in need when the two share what Clark and Mills (1979) call a *communal relationship*—that is, one in which the persons feel responsible for each others' welfare and desire to help each other. Most of the other relationships that we form are *exchange relationships,* in which we interact with strangers, colleagues, fellow workers, or business associates. In such cases, help is usually given as a repayment for past assistance or in anticipation of future needs and requests. One implication of this distinction is that helping behavior should be more related to another person's suffering when one shares a communal relationship with the other than when the relationship is based on exchange. A study by Clark, Oulette, Powell, and Milberg (1987) showed this to be the case. Subjects were

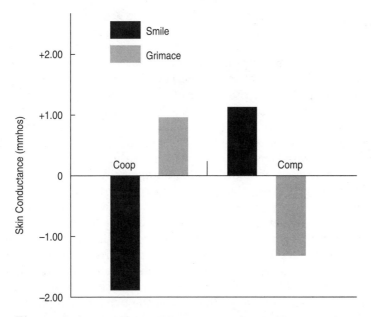

*Figure 9-4.* Increases and decreases in skin conductance during expressions of positive or negative affect by a cooperator or a competitor. (From "Expectations of Cooperation and Competition and Their Effects on Observers' Vicarious Emotional Responses" by J. T. Lanzetta and B. G. Englis, *Journal of Personality and Social Psychology, 1989,* 56, 543–554.)

found to be more helpful to another person who appeared to be sad when he or she had a communal relationship with that person than when there was only an exchange relationship.

## Helping as Coping

Helping others can have still another value: it can assist the help giver in coping with personal problems. For example, turning one's attention to assisting others can be an effective distractor from one's own difficulties. Prosocial behavior can promote coping in other ways as well (Midlarsky, 1991): (1) by enhancing one's belief that life has value and purpose, (2) by increasing feelings of competence and control (see Chapter 5), (3) by increasing positive affect and decreasing negative affect, and (4) by facilitating the integration of the person into the social system as a valuable member; such social integration may, among other things, extend and strengthen the person's social support network. In turn, all of these beneficial outcomes of prosocial behavior may increase the likelihood of the person's behaving prosocially again, so that the sequence of events may be cyclical and self-sustaining.

### Empathy and Altruism

Whether human beings are capable of ever being motivated solely by a concern for the good of others is a problem that has been debated by philosophers and religious thinkers for centuries. The belief that humans are inherently selfish and self-serving lies at the center of most rational and economic views of human behavior. In fact, some versions of this idea assert that society functions best when each of its members is motivated to accumulate as many resources as possible. This belief is the basis of the argument that all prosocial behavior is motivated by a wish for personal gain.

Others have argued that although humans may spend much of their time in self-serving activities, they have the capacity for unselfish service to others or the desire to perform such service. It should be emphasized at the outset that altruism is identified in prosocial behavior in terms of the *motive* of the help giver. If one person helps another for unselfish reasons, it does not matter whether he or she gets some individual gain from the activity as long as the *intent* is to help the other person unselfishly (Batson & Oleson, 1991).

Distinguishing between selfish and altruistic motives in prosocial behavior is usually difficult in everyday life because the two motives often generate identical behaviors. However, it is possible to design controlled experiments in which these motives predict different outcomes. Several studies of this type have been conducted, and overall they point to altruism as a real human

*The desire to help others may be motivated by empathy for those in need.*

motive independent of other considerations. In one such study Batson and his associates separated altruism from the selfish quest for personal satisfaction (Batson, Dyck, Brandt, Batson, Powell, McMaster & Griggitt, 1988). They argued that people who are truly motivated by altruism should place the other person's welfare ahead of any personal concern, whereas people who help others in order to feel personal satisfaction should place their own feelings first. In their study, Batson and his colleagues induced subjects to feel empathy for a fellow subject who was supposedly feeling fearful as he or she waited to receive some electric shocks. Some of the subjects were informed that if they performed well on an impending task, they could save the other person from being shocked; others were not told this. Then, just before the experiment was to begin, half of all subjects were told that shocks would not be delivered after all. One quarter of the subjects therefore performed the task even though it could no longer be considered prosocial behavior. At that point the mood state of all subjects was measured.

The reasoning behind the study was that if the subjects were motivated only to maximize their own satisfaction through helping the frightened person, then the only group that would express an increase in pleasant mood would be those who could actually allay the other person's fear by helping. On the other hand, if the subject was motivated by a genuine concern for the other person, the greatest increase in pleasant mood should occur in those conditions in which the other person was not shocked. The latter is in fact what was found. Subjects who learned that shock would not be given felt better than those who thought that it would be given, *regardless of whether they were the cause of the other person's avoiding the shock.* This finding is more consistent with an assumption that subjects were altruistically motivated than with the counterassumption that subjects wanted to help in order to feel self-satisfaction.

In another study, Toi and Batson (1982) distinguished between altruism and relief of personal distress as a motivator of helping. They reasoned that if such relief is the motive, then giving subjects easy access to escape from the situation might alleviate their distress and reduce helping. Thus, when ease of escape from the situation is varied, subjects should help more when escape is difficult than when it is easy. However, if altruism motivates helping in such a situation, it would be expected that subjects would help the person in need regardless of whether escape is easy or difficult, simply because they would not exercise the option to escape. Thus ease of escape should play no role in helping behavior. Toi and Batson's results supported the latter prediction (Figure 9-5).

The two experiments described here are typical of those carried out by Batson and his colleagues to show that helping behavior does occur under conditions in which motives other than altruism can be ruled out on logical grounds. Again, two points must be emphasized in considering Batson's research. First, it does not purport to show that all prosocial behavior is altruistic, but only that prosocial behavior can sometimes be motivated by selfless

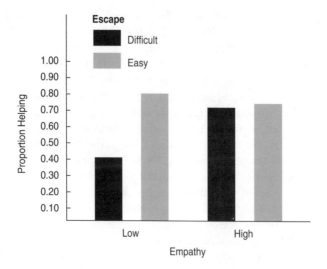

**Figure 9-5.** Helping behavior by subjects high and low in empathy when escape from situation is easy or difficult. (From "More Evidence That Empathy Is a Source of Altruistic Motivation" by M. Toi and C. D. Batson, *Journal of Personality and Social Psychology,* 1982, *43,* 281–292.)

concerns. Second, it does not state that a prosocial act must be entirely free of self-gain in order to be considered altruistic. As already noted, all that is required is that the help giver *intends* to be unselfish in his or her actions toward the other person. Overall, the studies reported by Batson and his associates appear to make their case.

## Motivational Analysis of the Models

Of the several theories that have been formulated to explain prosocial behavior, the two that have received the most attention have been the empathy-distress and the empathy-altruism alternatives. These are not mutually exclusive. People may sometimes behave according to one motive and at other times according to the other. Perhaps future studies will reveal the conditions under which people behave altruistically and those under which they practice a more self-serving type of behavior toward others. For now, we can only conclude from the evidence, some of which has been discussed in this chapter, that both motives have an effect.

Figure 9-6 contrasts the two approaches by summarizing their premises in terms of the motives, situations, and incentives that were introduced in Chapter 2. It should be noted that both theories propose that knowledge of

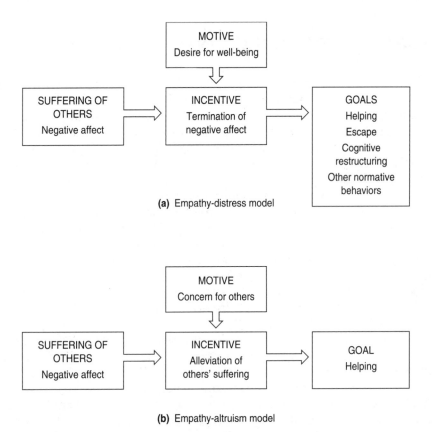

**Figure 9-6.** Schematic diagrams of the empathy-distress and empathy-altruism theories of helping.

the suffering of others elicits negative affect; this is the condition of empathy that provides the situational input to engage the dominant motive. Implicit in the empathy-distress model is the assumption that this motive is the need for personal well-being and positive affect. Thus, according to the theory the dominant incentive in the situation is associated with termination of the negative affect. From this point on, the actual behavioral goal depends on the interplay of cost-reward factors described above and illustrated in Figure 9-2. In contrast to this, the empathy-altruism approach specifies that the dominant motive is a concern for the welfare of the suffering others. The incentive that dominates behavior is the alleviation of this suffering, and the person's goal thus becomes attaining this alleviation through whatever means are available. This is what drives the desire to help the other person.

# AGGRESSIVE MOTIVATION

Much has been written over the past 30 years about the psychology of aggression. Most of this writing has been addressed to such questions as the ways in which aggressive behaviors are learned, the immediate social conditions that elicit aggression, the form that aggressive behavior takes, the consequences of this behavior, and strategies for controlling it. Little attention has been given, directly at least, to what *motivates* aggressive behavior. This is not to say that matters such as the ones listed above are not important for understanding aggressive motivation. It means only that aggression research has traditionally not emphasized motives in explaining the phenomenon. In this section we will concentrate mainly on a motivational analysis of aggressive behavior patterned after the scheme outlined in Chapter 2. We will attempt to identify and explore (1) the nature of situations that engage and activate motives related to aggression, (2) the specific motives that are thus engaged, (3) the resulting incentives that animate subsequent behavior, and (4) the specific goals of aggressive behavior when these incentives are translated into courses of action.

Geen (1990) has listed several situational conditions that have been shown to be linked to aggressive responses; among these are frustration of acts directed toward attaining a desired goal, deliberate provocations such as physical attacks or verbal insults, irritation and pain caused by stimuli in the environment, and the stresses of everyday interpersonal conflicts, such as those that arise when someone violates important communal standards. This list is of course not exhaustive. For purposes of analysis, these causes of aggression can be conveniently broken down into three categories: (1) situations in which a person is unpleasantly aroused, either by the acts of other people or by the intrusion of some unwelcome stimulus from the environment; (2) situations in which the person is caused some embarrassment or humiliation by the actions of others; and (3) situations in which the person's sense of justice and fairness is outraged by the actions of other people. In the sections that follow, we will explore three motivational approaches to aggressive behavior in which each of these types of situation is seen as engaging a specific motive and creating, along with the motive, a particular incentive.

The three situations are shown schematically in Figure 9-7. The general design of this scheme is derived from the discussion in Chapter 2. In each case a motive that is relevant to that situation has been suggested. It is further suggested that the engagement of each motive by the particular situation generates an incentive for action that becomes manifest in the setting of specific behavioral goals. The details of these processes will be explained in the three sections that follow.

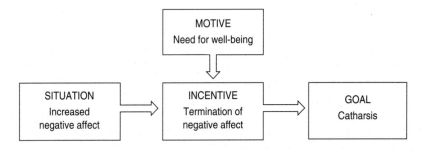

**(a)** Motive of need for well-being

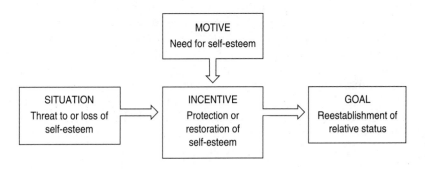

**(b)** Motive of need for self-esteem

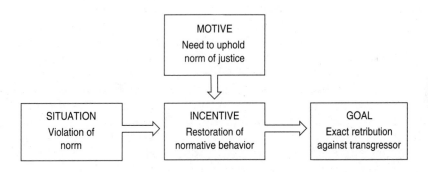

**(c)** Motive of need to uphold norm

***Figure 9-7.*** Diagram of motives for aggression.

## Negative Affect

ATTACK AND FRUSTRATION.   Situations that involve frustration of goal-directed activity, interpersonal provocations, and painful stimulation all have one thing in common: each leads to increases in negative affect, presumably by upsetting the person's normal need for well-being [see Figure 9-7(a)]. In every case, the victims feel unpleasant, they may become physiologically aroused, their levels of hostility and anger may increase, and they are more likely to aggress against people around them. Sometimes this aggression is easily explained: the person against whom the frustrated or provoked party aggresses is often responsible for the aggressor's discomfort and is therefore recognized as an antagonist. It is not surprising, therefore, that the most reliable and potent causes of interpersonal aggression are deliberate physical attacks and insulting and degrading verbalizations (Geen, 1968). This is especially likely when the provoked person judges the acts of the provocateur to be willful, malicious, and avoidable (Ferguson & Rule, 1983; Dodge, Murphy & Buchsbaum, 1984). When provocation is regarded as less malicious in intent, it elicits less anger and less subsequent aggression.

An example of attenuating aggression by reinterpreting the motives of the provoking person was shown in an experiment by Johnson and Rule (1986). Subjects were angered by receiving several bursts of loud and aversive noise from another person while performing a task. To some subjects it was explained that the person who delivered the noise was extremely distraught because of a personal problem, whereas others were told that this person was only mildly upset. It was assumed that subjects would be likely to forgive a provocation by a highly distraught person (by regarding the attack as less malicious) but not one by a less disturbed person. In addition, the information concerning the condition of the provocateur was given either before the noise was administered or afterward.

Subjects were then given an opportunity to retaliate against the other person. When this person had ostensibly been highly distraught and subjects had known this at the time of the attack, the subjects were less aggressive in their retribution than were those who learned about the mitigating circumstances later. The timing of the information had no effect on subjects' aggression when the provocateur had been only mildly upset. The results of this study suggest that when victims of an attack do not attribute malice to the attacker *during the attack*, they respond to that attack with less anger than they would ordinarily show, whereas if they make this attribution later, the anger originally incited by the attack tends to be relatively high.

Attributions of hostility and malice in others are influenced by more than the situation alone. To some extent they reflect individual differences in personality. These are especially likely to affect attributions when it is unclear exactly what is going on in the situation. In a study reported by Dodge (1980), boys who had been classified by teachers and peers as being either aggressive or nonaggressive were prevented from completing a puzzle by the intrusion of another boy. For some subjects the intruder acted out of a clearly hostile intent, whereas for others his interference was an accidental blunder. For still other subjects the intentions of the other boy were vague and ambiguous. All subjects were then given a chance to retaliate against the other by destroying a puzzle on which he was working. As was expected, the hostile boy invited more retribution than did the benign or ambiguous one. In addition, subjects who had been classified as aggressive were more aggressive toward the other boy than were nonaggressive subjects when the other boy's motives were ambiguous. When the motives of an attacker are clearly understood, people retaliate or do not retaliate on the basis of those motives. When an attacker's motives are not clear, individual differences in aggressiveness predict the victim's behavior. The tendency of aggressive people to attribute hostile intent to another when the latter's actions are ambiguous has been called the *hostile attribution bias* (Nasby, Hayden & DePaulo, 1979).

Aggression may also follow provocation for which nobody is obviously responsible. Geen (1968), for example, found that subjects who had been frustrated only by their inability to complete an unsolvable task were significantly more aggressive toward an innocent bystander than were subjects who had not been frustrated. In this study, some subjects worked at a solvable task but were prevented from completing it by the well-meaning intrusions of another subject. Others were unable to complete the task

*Conflict between people can lead to verbal, and sometimes physical, aggression.*

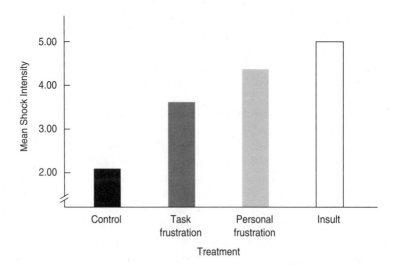

**Figure 9-8.** Aggression following insult and two types of frustration. (Drawn from data reported in "Effects of Frustration, Attack, and Prior Training in Aggressiveness upon Aggressive Behavior" in R. G. Geen, *Journal of Personality and Social Psychology,* 1968, *9,* 316–321.)

because they had been given a version of the task that, though looking like the solvable form, was actually impossible to complete. A third group of subjects completed the task but were insulted by the other subject (actually an assistant of the experimenter), who made several gratuitous comments about their performance. A fourth group was not provoked in any way. Subsequent aggression by the subject against the other person, in the form of electric shocks that were ostensibly given, varied as shown in Figure 9-8. Insults and personal frustrations both elicited more aggression than did task frustrations, but even task frustrations provoked more aggression than did no provocations at all.

**ENVIRONMENTAL STRESSORS.**    Unpleasant environmental conditions such as heat, smoke, and uncontrollable noise have been shown to promote aggression against others even when the victims are in no way the causes of those conditions (e.g., Geen, 1978; Zillmann, Baron & Tamborini, 1981; Anderson, 1989). In these cases, it is possible that negative affect alone, whatever its source, could be the underlying cause of the aggression. The central role of negative affect as an elicitor of human aggression has been documented and discussed in detail by Berkowitz (1989, 1992).

**CATHARSIS.**    How does increasing the level of negative affect in a situation provoke aggressive behavior? As we have noted, one way is by engaging a specific need or desire for well-being. When this motive is activated by conditions that threaten well-being, an incentive is created for terminating the negative affective state that the situation has evoked (see Dollard, Doob, Miller, Mowrer & Sears, 1939). Behaviors that might allow the person to attain this valued state are then activated. The ultimate goal of these behaviors has been called *catharsis*, or a reduction of aversive stimulation. The process is shown in Figure 9-7(a).

That aggressive behavior reduces activation previously elicited by provocation has been shown in numerous studies (e.g., Hokanson & Edelman, 1966; Geen, Stonner & Shope, 1975). To some extent the link between aggressing and tension reduction may be innate, but there is also evidence that it can be shaped by social learning. Research by Hokanson and his associates has shown that when people are reinforced for reacting to provocation with aggression, they subsequently experience a greater reduction in arousal after aggressing than after responding in a friendly way (Hokanson, Willers & Koropsak, 1968). However, following a history of reinforcement for responding to provocation prosocially, they experience greater catharsis after being friendly to the provocateur than after retaliating.

Expressing anger has been shown to have positive implications for health, whereas "holding anger in" and suppressing it can have opposite effects. Studies have shown, for example, that people whose normal tendency is to respond to provoking situations by suppressing anger have generally higher levels of blood pressure than those who respond by venting their anger (e.g., Johnson, Spielberger, Worden & Jacobs, 1987). This tendency to suppress anger, called the "anger-in" style, has also been found to contribute to coronary heart disease among people who tend to experience moderate to high levels of anger when provoked (Dembroski, MacDougall, Williams, Haney & Blumenthal, 1985; Jorgensen, Gelling & Kliner, 1992).

One final matter must be noted. Some theories of aggression state that catharsis of arousal through aggressive behavior reduces the intensity of subsequent aggression (e.g., Dollard et al., 1939). Actually the opposite happens: expression of aggression tends to *increase* the intensity of aggression that comes later (Geen et al., 1975). The simplest explanation for this is that the emotional catharsis produced by aggressing increases the person's expectancy that future aggression will be followed by similarly rewarding consequences.

## Threat to Self-Esteem

Another motive that may be engaged by provocation is the need for self-esteem. If a person is made to look weak or foolish, for example, this may be a serious embarrassment to that person, who may then retaliate in order to recover some of the lost esteem [Figure 9-7(b)]. This process is often observed in popular fiction, where the revenge of the humiliated person is a common theme. Protection or restoration of self-esteem is also cited as a cause of aggression by numerous social scientists (e.g., Felson, 1984). The evidence on the subject is mixed and inconclusive, however. Some studies have shown that people with high self-esteem react to provocation with more aggressiveness than those low in self-esteem, whereas others have shown the opposite.

More recent studies suggest that the relationships among provocation, self-esteem, and aggression are not the simple ones assumed in early studies, and that other variables may be involved. Maybe anger is not linked to self-esteem directly but is instead linked to other emotional states that attack and break down self-esteem. A study by Tangney, Wagner, Fletcher, and Gramzow (1992) has shown that people who are relatively likely to experience *shame* are also more likely to express anger and hostility and to blame others for bad things that happen to them. Shame is an aversive emotion that brings about a negative evaluation of the self and a temporary breakdown in self-esteem. The corresponding tendency to blame others shown by shame-prone people may cause them to become angry and hostile toward those whom they see as the cause of their poor self-esteem. Thus shame may be an intervening variable in the effects of provocation on self-esteem.

But even level of self-esteem may not in itself be an important cause of emotions related to aggression. A study by Kernis, Granneman, and Barclay (1989) indicates that level is not as important as *stability of self-esteem* in predicting anger and hostility. In this study subjects kept records of their feelings for one week by filling out questionnaires at various times during each day. At the end of this period, their daily reports formed the basis for the investigators' calculations of how high their average self-esteem had been during the week and also how much it had varied from one report to the next. At the end of the week, all subjects filled out a scale that measured anger and hostility. Stability of self-esteem correlated more highly than level of self-esteem with anger and hostility. In addition, the variables of level and stability interacted. This interaction indicated that among subjects low in self-esteem, the stability of self-esteem had no effect on the two aggression-related emotions. However, among subjects who were high in self-esteem, greater anger and hostility were shown among those who were also unstable. This finding suggests that the people who are most vulnerable to a loss of self-esteem when they are provoked are those who have a high but *fragile* sense of self-worth. Such people are not secure in their high self-esteem and are therefore in jeopardy of losing it when it is attacked.

## Violation of Norms

There is a third way in which we may consider the motivation of aggressive behavior. In most instances, aggression is not an isolated act. It arises in the context of an ongoing relationship in which all parties have certain expectations regarding normal behavior. Social behavior is carried out in accordance with social standards, or *norms*, that are agreed upon by the persons involved. In situations that involve interpersonal conflict, the usual norm prescribes that each person will cause only as much discomfort to others as is necessary for attaining his or her goals. Should any people exceed the normative level, their behavior will be considered by the others to be excessive and motivated by an intent to hurt. It will, in others words, be regarded as a malicious act of aggression (DaGloria & DeRidder, 1977; Ohbuchi, 1982).

In an example given at the beginning of this chapter, a pitcher was observed deliberately throwing a ball at a batter and being retaliated against by the victim. In the present theoretical context, we would say that the pitcher violated the norm of using only as much force as is necessary to win the baseball game. It is a commonly accepted practice in baseball for a pitcher to throw the ball *near* the batter—the so-called brush-back pitch—to prevent him from getting comfortably set in his batting stance (i.e., "digging in"). This action falls within the boundaries set by the norm. However, actually hitting the batter with the ball does not fall within these boundaries. Such an act is considered a violation of the norm and is therefore labeled malicious and excessive.

The initial response to such judgments of intent and malice is anger and a desire to retaliate. This may be, as we have seen, because a malevolent attack activates a basic motive such as a need for well-being or a need for high self-esteem. But it may also engage another motive: a need to uphold social standards in a fair and just way. Restoring a normative state of affairs becomes a valued outcome in such a situation. The behavior that is generated to bring about this valued state is exact retribution against the aggressor [see Figure 9-7(c)]. If the retaliation is exact and in kind, the normative state that existed before the malicious transgression will be restored (Mummendey & Mummendey, 1983). Of course, if the retaliation is regarded by the recipient as being excessive and more than the original crime deserved, then the norm will be considered violated again, this time by the other party, and another retaliation will occur. It is clear from this model that unless conflicting parties can agree at some point that retribution has been fair and exact, the cycle of attack and retaliation will continue to *escalate* (Mummendey, Linneweber & Lopscher, 1984).

## Conclusion: Two Kinds of Aggression or One?

It is customary to distinguish between two types of human aggression. The first, usually called angry or *affective* aggression, is characterized by anger or some other negative emotion, whereas the other, called *instrumental* aggression, is carried out in a less affectively charged way for purposes that have nothing to do with feelings for the victim. The first type is characteristic of a crime of passion in which one person kills another out of hatred or fury. The second type is exemplified by a professional killing conducted for a fee. This distinction has been commonly drawn (e.g., Bandura, 1973; Geen, 1990) and has some utility, but it may oversimplify or even distort the nature of aggression and the goals that aggression serves.

For one thing, there is no reason to make a sharp distinction between instrumentality and affect in aggression. Most acts of aggression are characterized by both. The aggression visited on a victim by an emotionally aroused perpetrator is not, except perhaps in cases of temporary insanity, without instrumental value. As we have seen, a person who has been insulted or humiliated by another may try to hurt the other in order to restore a sense of self-esteem. One who has been frustrated in her attempts to reach a goal by the meddling of a friend may aggress angrily, but also, in part at least, in order to reduce stress. Nor is instrumental aggression completely separable from affect. Generation of negative affect may facilitate the carrying out of aggression that is motivated mainly by instrumental concerns. For example, it is common during wartime for governments to encourage hatred toward the people against whom the war is being fought, even though most people on both sides have no real reason to hate their adversaries.

By blurring the traditional distinction between affective and instrumental aggression, we are in a better position to understand aggression as a more or less normative part of human interaction rather than as a pathological behavioral aberration (DaGloria, 1984). In most instances aggression is not an isolated act. It arises in the context of an ongoing relationship in which all parties have certain expectations regarding normal behavior. The point of view summarized in the third paradigm of Figure 9-7 is consistent with this approach. As the figure shows, a motivational analysis of aggression in terms of basic motives, incentives, and goals is indifferent to the actual content of these categories.

## CHAPTER SUMMARY

1.  Prosocial behavior has been explained in many ways; some involve the pursuit of personal desires or needs. Helping has been attributed to (a) seeking specific rewards, either material or social; (b) avoiding specific punishments for not helping; (c) experiencing empathic joy over another person's good fortune; (d) reducing tension by helping another person attain a state of well-being; and (e) alleviating one's distress over the discomfort of the victim.

2.  Another theoretical explanation for helping is that humans are capable of unselfish prosocial behavior, called altruism. Designating a prosocial act as altruistic does not require that the helper gets no personal gain from the act. What matters is that the person intends to help the victim for reasons that are unselfish. The basis of both altruism and relief of personal distress is empathy, which is a vicarious experience of another person's distress. Controlled laboratory experiments that isolate altruistic motives from selfish ones show that altruism is a motive for some prosocial behavior.

3.  Prosocial behavior is acquired through social learning. Knowing that another person has been relieved by one's help reinforces the helping

response. Thus the suffering of others and the negative affect that it produces become cues for the instrumental helping response. Young children do not respond to negative affect with helping behavior because they have not yet learned that helping reduces negative affect.

**4.** The arousal: cost-reward theory of helping defines prosocial behavior as the result of two processes: empathic arousal and an analysis of the costs and rewards involved in helping. Costs of helping include time, effort, personal discomfort, and loss of possible rewards. Balancing these are costs associated with not helping, mainly social disapproval and guilt. When the costs of helping are low, people are more prosocial. When the costs of helping are high, people are less likely to give direct help and more likely to give indirect help or no help at all.

**5.** Prosocial behavior is influenced by temporary changes in positive and negative affect. Happiness generally facilitates helping. Increases in helping caused by positive affect may be encouraged by a simultaneous increase in self-awareness. Unhappiness that is felt as guilt may promote helping as a means of expiation for wrongdoing. Sadness leads to enhanced helping if attention is focused on unfortunate others, but not if it is directed toward oneself.

**6.** Positive affect can cause a general tendency to perceive people more favorably, thereby rendering them more worthy of help. In addition, help giving may produce a sustained positive mood and good self-evaluation. For both of these reasons, positive mood can facilitate helping.

**7.** Empathy for a person in need is greater when one has a sense of community with the victim than when the relationship between the two is based on the exchange of goods or services. The costs of not helping and the rewards for helping are also relatively high when the victim shares a communal relationship with the actor. For these reasons, helping is more likely in a communal than in an exchange relationship.

**8.** Helping can be of value as a means of coping with one's personal problems. It can distract the person from these problems, enhance beliefs that life is meaningful and valuable, increase one's sense of competence and control, and promote integration of the person into social support networks.

**9.** Aggression is elicited by situations that engage specific motives. One such motive is a need for well being that is activated by aversive conditions and subsequent negative affect. Among these conditions are frustrations and interpersonal attacks. Physical or verbal assaults provoke more aggression than do interpersonal frustrations. Even frustration that arises from failure at a task evokes more aggression than does no provocation at all. Certain environmental stressors can also lead to aggression because of the negative affect that they engender.

**10.**   Aggression that follows interpersonal provocation can be attenuated by a cognitive judgment that the provocation was not malicious. When mitigating circumstances surround the provocation, it leads to less emotional arousal than when no such circumstances are present. Individual differences in hostility and aggressiveness can also contribute to the attributions of another person's maliciousness when the motivation for the latter is ambiguous.

**11.**   Expressing anger and hostility reduces the emotional arousal caused by provocation. This is the process of emotional catharsis. Even though aggression may lead to catharsis, it does not reduce subsequent aggression. Instead, aggression facilitates further expressions of aggressive behavior.

**12.**   Aggression also occurs when a threat to the self engages a motive to maintain and protect one's self-esteem. People who are likely to feel shame are especially likely to express anger following unpleasant experiences because shame undermines self-esteem. Stability of self-esteem interacts with level of self-esteem in determining anger and hostility. The people most likely to aggress when they are threatened are those who have high but insecure self-esteem.

**13.**   Aggression may represent behavior that is instrumental to upholding a norm of justice and equity. When one party to a social relationship uses more force than is considered necessary to gain a desired end, according to prevailing norms, the other party regards the behavior as malicious and contrary to agreed-upon rules. Exact retaliation in kind and degree is then taken as a means of restoring the normative relationship.

**14.**   From a motivational standpoint, in which behavior is analyzed in terms of motives, situations, incentives, and goals, the customary distinction between instrumental and affective aggression tends to lose much of its force. A common pattern of motivational processes accounts for both types of aggression.

# MOTIVATING EFFECTS OF SOCIAL SETTINGS

A major premise of this book has been that most human motivation takes place in social settings (see Chapter 1), and the material reviewed so far has shown the extent to which this is true. There is another sense in which motivation takes on a particularly social characteristic: the interpersonal element is both immediate and direct. Certain interpersonal situations create such an immediacy, so that the motivational forces that act on the individual arise from close, even face-to-face, encounters. Three such situations will be discussed in this chapter.

The first situation is one in which the person experiences discomfort and uneasiness in the presence of others with whom she or he interacts. This discomfort may be manifest in physiological symptoms such as blushing, muscle tension, and a racing heart. It may produce feelings of uneasiness, awkwardness, and self-criticism and a strong desire to flee from the setting. It can also have effects on behavior. The person may show disfluency in speech, nervous laughter, and a cautious, defensive style in relating to others. These various manifestations of discomfort are subsumed by the general designation of *social anxiety.* In the first section of this chapter we will examine some of the causes and consequences of this phenomenon.

The second situation is one in which the person must perform in the presence of other people who are either coworkers or a passive audience. In either case the individual must maximize his or her performance in some way independent of what the coworkers or the spectators may be doing. The question that we will ask in the second section of the chapter is whether the presence of others has an effect on the performance of the individual on tasks and, if so, whether that effect is beneficial or harmful. Such effects have usually been referred to as *social facilitation.*

In the third situation the individual is part of a group engaged in some common endeavor. Every member of the group is expected to contribute to the outcome. In the third section of this chapter we will pose the question: Do people give their maximum individual efforts under such conditions, or does each individual contribute less than he or she would contribute if acting alone? Is there, in other words, any loss of motivation to perform on a cooperative task in a group setting? These questions fall under the heading of a process called *social loafing.*

Each of these situations occurs often in everyday life. Social anxiety is a common response to social situations of all sorts, ranging from cocktail parties to job interviews. In any situation in which a person must create a certain impression on someone, there is the potential for social anxiety. Social facilitation and social loafing are especially likely to be observed in occupational settings. Some jobs are done in the company of other workers who are performing the same tasks, which raises the possibility that the workers in the group may have reciprocal effects on one another. In other situations, people work under the surveillance of supervisors who evaluate their product; then the observer is an audience for the worker. Sometimes workers are assigned tasks to be carried out collectively, so that the possibility of loafing by members of the group can have serious consequences for production. Later in this chapter we will examine an application of the social facilitation paradigm to a practical problem of occupational psychology. First, however, we must understand the underlying motivational processes that are set in motion by the presence of other people.

## SOCIAL ANXIETY

When someone wishes to make a good impression on another person with whom he or she is interacting, but doubts that such a favorable impression can be made, the result is social anxiety (Schlenker & Leary, 1982). This is a transitory state that is evoked only by certain interactive situations and that probably subsides when such situations end. However, some people are more likely than others to experience social anxiety in those situations, perhaps as a result of past experiences and learning. The relative tendency of a person to become socially anxious in interpersonal settings is called *social anxiousness*. It should be noted that whereas social anxiety is a condition, or *state*, into which people sometimes enter, social anxiousness is a relatively stable and permanent tendency to react to situations by assuming that state.

The outcomes of the state of social anxiety are varied. They include physiological arousal, such as increased heart rate, muscle tension, and blood pressure (Leary, 1983), and tense behavior, including disfluency in speech (such as the use of wrong words, hesitancy, and quivering of the voice). Socially anxious people also show a tendency to *disaffiliate* with interacting partners by saying less, avoiding eye contact, and, when possible, actually leaving the interaction altogether. When disaffiliation is difficult or impossible, social anxiety may lead to interaction that is guarded, shallow, and calculated only to protect the person from making mistakes that could lead to rejection or embarrassment. This behavior, called *innocuous sociability* (Leary, 1983), may consist of talking about only safe topics like the weather, or it may be manifested in superficial agreements with what the other person says, nodding of the head in agreement, and other such actions.

Subjects in a study by Leary, Knight, and Johnson (1987) spent five minutes in conversation with another person of the same gender, during which time their verbalizations were recorded on tape. Later these tapes were analyzed, and the verbal behaviors of the subjects were sorted into a number of categories. The speech of subjects who were high in social anxiousness, and therefore most likely to be socially anxious in that sitation, tended to include relatively large numbers of superficial questions (e.g., "Who is your roommate?"), simple ackowledgments of the other person's remarks (e.g., "Uh-huh"), and confirmations of what the other person said (e.g., "I didn't like the movie either"). Socially anxious people therefore avoided making statements that might disclose something about themselves.

The behavior of socially anxious people can be compared to what experimental psychologists have studied as *passive avoidance*—that is, an inhibition of responding in order to avoid undesired consequences. The socially anxious person withholds information about himself out of fear that the other person will dislike and reject him much as a rat in a Skinner box will inhibit pressing a bar when the barpress is followed by an electric shock. In a later section of this chapter, we will note that people who are made anxious about possible failure at a task also respond by withholding responses and becoming extremely cautious in their behavior.

## Impression Motivation

Social anxiety is related to what Leary and Kowalski (1990) have called *impression motivation*—that is, motivation to present oneself to other people in such a way that one can control the impressions that the others form. Impression motivation is a function of three variables. One is the *relevance* of the impression (assuming that it is the one desired) for the attainment of desired goals. It is assumed that one does not wish to impress others just for the sake of impressing them, but that some instrumental purpose is served by having the self accepted in a desired way. For example, making a good impression on an interviewer when applying for a job may help one to obtain the position. Believing that one's behavior is relevant to obtaining a goal is, of course, another way of saying that one holds a high *expectancy* that the behavior will produce the desired outcome (see Chapter 2). The second variable in impression motivation is the *value* of the goal that is sought; the more valued the goal (in our example, the job), the greater will be the person's desire to make a good impression (see Chapter 2). The third variable is the perceived *discrepancy* between the impression that one wants to make and the impression that one actually thinks is being made. This idea was discussed in Chapter 3. When the discrepancy is relatively large, it means that the person is not being accepted by others in the way that she or he wishes, so a concerted attempt at managing a different impression is undertaken. For example, a job applicant who has been expressing herself in a modest and accommodating way may, if she thinks that she is not making a good impression, switch to a more self-assertive style.

Obviously, the value of an impression and the size of the discrepancy between the actual and the desired impressions may contribute to social anxiety, especially in people who are high in social anxiousness. In addition, regardless of the size of the discrepancy, social anxiety will be a function of the extent to which the person feels unable to execute the correct self-presentational behaviors. If the person feels inadequate and not competent to make a good impression, he or she will have a low expectancy of doing so. This latter type of expectancy has been linked to feelings of personal competence and *self-efficacy* (see Chapter 5).

The actual process of believing that one will make a desired impression consists of two steps. First, the person must believe that he or she is capable of presenting the self in a way that *can* produce the desired impression. Second, the person must believe that this self-presentation *will* produce that impression. The first belief is the basis for a *self-presentation efficacy expectancy* (e.g., "I am capable of presenting myself in a way necessary to create the desired impression"). The second constitutes a *self-presentation outcome expectancy* (e.g., "If I present myself correctly, the other person will form the desired impression").

Of the two, it is the efficacy expectancy that makes the major contribution to social anxiety. In a study by Maddux, Norton, and Leary (1988), assessments were made of each type of expectancy—outcome and efficacy—along with social anxiousness and the amount of social anxiety that the respondent anticipated in response to a set of imaginary social scenarios. Social anxiousness was correlated to a moderate degree ($r = -0.32$) with self-presentation outcome expectancies; the more socially anxious the person was, the more he or she expected that effective self-presentations would not lead to desired impressions. However, efficacy expectancies were *highly* correlated with social anxiousness ($r = -0.65$), so that the greater the social anxious-ness, the more the person believed that making an adequate self-presentation was impossible. Furthermore, of the two expectancies, only the efficacy expectancy was correlated with the amount of anxiety that people thought they would experience in threatening social situations.

The exact relationship among self-presentation outcome and efficacy expectancies and social anxiety may actually be a complex one involving the ways in which people interpret instances in which expected outcomes do not materialize (Leary & Atherton, 1986). For example, a combination of high efficacy expectancy and low outcome expectancy might cause the person to conclude that effective impression management is not because of personal inadequacies but because of rejection by others (e.g., "I make a strong self-

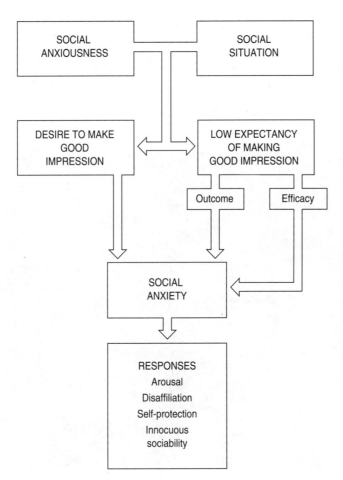

*Figure 10-1.* Schematic model of variables and processes in social anxiety.

presentation, but others refuse to recognize it"). Such an attribution would probably evoke anger rather than anxiety. The combination of low outcome and low efficacy expectancies (e.g., "I cannot present myself well, and even if I could, I would be rejected") is more likely to produce helplessness and depression than social anxiety. The only combination likely to produce anxiety is high outcome expectancy and low efficacy expectancy, which might cause the person to attribute failure in impression management to personal inadequacies (e.g., "I could make a good impression if I were able to present myself properly, but I cannot"). Feelings such as these could lead to anxiety and self-criticism.

Figure 10-1 summarizes the processes involved in the effects of social anxiety on behavior.

## Social Anxiety in Test Situations

Few people who have attended a conventional school or college have escaped at least some experience of test anxiety. The widespread use of tests and examinations, beginning in the earliest grades, along with the grading system and all that hangs on it, instills a fear of failure, at least to some degree, in virtually every student. As befits a subject of such wide notoriety, test anxiety

*Test anxiety can arise in any situation in which the possibility of failure is recognized.*

has been studied extensively since at least the 1950s. In the sense that we are using the term, it is not limited to classroom tests per se; test anxiety arises in any situation in which a person's performance is evaluated by others and in which the possibility of failure is clearly recognized. Its effects have been well documented: nervous tension and arousal, interference with ongoing activity, self-criticism and a tendency to blame oneself for failures, a desire to escape from the test situation, and increased cautiousness and conservatism in behavior (Geen, 1987; Sarason, 1984).

The symptoms of test anxiety resemble in many ways those of social anxiety described above. Test anxiety may, to a large extent, be considered a special case of social anxiety. If a person is motivated to perform well on a test, often one of the main reasons is to impress parents, friends, teachers, employers, or other people whose approval is important. Thus making an impression through good performance is highly valued. The person who suffers from test anxiety, however, tends to feel inadequate to the task and to anticipate failure, probably because of past failures, so that her or his efficacy expectancies are relatively low (Carver & Scheier, 1989).

## Motivational Basis
## for Self-Presentation

Social anxiety is therefore rooted in the process of self presentation, where it represents an undesirable by-product of failed impression management. Why is self-presentation so important that its failure causes such an undesirable outcome? Before we can answer this question it is necessary to consider some basic principles of human motivation. The literature on the subject lists a large number of identifiable human motives. Some of these motives produce behavior that brings the individual closer to other people and fosters a sense of community between the person and his or her social environment. Others are associated with behavior that tends to separate the individual from the immediate community and to emphasize individual gains that are either independent of or at the expense of other persons in the social environment.

These classes of motive correspond to a fundamental distinction between individualism and sociality that has been recognized by many psychologists (e.g., Wiggins, 1992). Bakan (1966) has identified these concepts as the two fundamental "modalities" of human existence. One, called *agency*, pertains to "the existence of the organism as an individual" and is manifested in such behaviors as self-defense and self-assertion. The other, described as *communion*, refers to "the participation of the individual in some larger organism of which the individual is part" (Bakan, 1966, p. 15). The distinction between these two modalities of life subsumes many of the familiar social motives. Those associated with communion go by such names as affiliation, intimacy, attachment, approval, empathy, and altruism. Motives associated with agency include assertiveness, independence, achievement, power, and dominance.

Some observers (e.g., Hogan, 1983) have proposed that these two classes of motives arise from the fact that humans have, from the beginning, lived in groups while organizing those groups according to a status hierarchy. Thus two basic human needs have evolved: the need for *status* and dominance and the need for *inclusion* and affiliation. These needs, in turn, give rise to the fear of social failure. People fear social failure because it threatens both their inclusion within the community and their social status and identity. Being disapproved of by others cuts the person off from his or her desired social identity. The person becomes a less-than-valued being. People work hard at making good impressions on others so that this will not happen.

**TERROR MANAGEMENT.**   One explanation of the need for inclusion is that people use society as a protection against having to face their personal mortality (Solomon, Greenberg & Psyzczynski, 1991). Human culture provides a context, or drama, within which each person can play an assigned role. Successful enactment of one's role allows integration into the society and some assurance of social support when it is needed, social approval, and maintenance of self-esteem. Failure to enact one's part brings the threat of social exclusion and loss of the social buffer against the terror of death and nonbeing.

The fear of death can have some powerful effects on interpersonal behavior. The person who is threatened by contemplation of his or her mortality reacts by identifying with and protecting the world view of the culture, and by rejecting others who do not share this view. Greenberg, Psyzczynski, Solomon, Rosenblatt, Veeder, Kirkland, and Lyon (1990) carried out a series of studies to show that when people are reminded of mortality they adopt an attitude that emphasizes differences between the in-group and the out-group. In each study, some of the subjects were given vivid reminders of their own mortality. In one study, people who had received such a reminder subsequently expressed greater preference for others of their own religious faith than for people who professed a different religion; subjects who had not been reminded of mortality did not express any preference between the two. In other studies, reminders of mortality prompted subjects to express a greater liking for those who held attitudes similar to their own and to reject others who held dissimilar attitudes. Greenberg and his associates concluded that people are liked or disliked according to whether they validate or undermine one's own world view. Thinking of death reminds one of the importance of the world view in fending off terror, and therefore increases tendencies to love one's own and reject those who differ.

**SOCIAL SURVIVAL.**   A related, but perhaps less existential, theory has been proposed by Baumeister and Tice (1990) and elaborated by Leary (1990). Both of these viewpoints emphasize social anxiety rather than fear of death as the consequence of social rejection. Anxiety may serve as a warning signal to the person that rejection is possible or even imminent, so that the person can avoid behaving in such a way that would make him or her appear unattractive or worthless. Becoming worthless to society poses serious dangers for adaptation and survival. Anxiety, therefore, may interrupt undesirable behavior, focus attention on that behavior, and motivate the person to seek alternative courses of action.

## SOCIAL FACILITATION

Near the end of the 19th century a social psychologist at Indiana University named Norman Triplett made an interesting observation. After watching some amateur bicycle racers practicing their sport, he concluded that individuals seemed to go faster when they were in the company of another rider than when they were cycling alone. After making numerous measurements of racing speeds, Triplett concluded that his impression had been correct. To explain this phenomenon, usually referred to as the *social facilitation* of individual performance, Triplett (1898) advanced several hypotheses. Some were commonsensical (e.g., that one rider "shelters" the other from a headwind), whereas others were fanciful (e.g., that riders become "hypnotized" by observing the circular motions of each other's wheels, and that while in this state they experience "muscular exaltation"). However, one of the other hypotheses was that the presence of a second rider introduced a "dynamogenic" factor by acting as a stimulus to, and thereby increasing the motivation of, the first.

The situation that Triplett described, in which individual performance is facilitated by the presence of another person or persons performing the same task, is called the *coaction* situation. Over the years following the discovery of

*Performance anxiety is sometimes manifested as stage fright.*

this effect, the study of social influences on performance was expanded in two ways. First, it was extended to situations in which other people are present as the individual performs, not as coactors, but as passive observers. This is called the *audience* situation, and it forms the basis for the common phenomena of performance anxiety and stage fright. Second, it was discovered through research that the presence of others facilitates performance only under certain conditions; under other conditions it has the opposite effect: it degrades performance.

## Drive and Arousal in Social Facilitation

The exact nature of these conditions was not spelled out for some time, but studies conducted over several decades suggested that one important factor seemed to be the difficulty of the tasks that the individual performed. Then in 1965 Zajonc published a theoretical article on social facilitation and inhibition of performance that explained many of the previously unexplained findings. Zajonc's (1965) analysis rested on three premises:

1. The presence of others, as coactors or observers, arouses the individual.
2. Increased arousal (drive) facilitates performance on easy or overlearned tasks.
3. Increased arousal inhibits or degrades performance on difficult or novel tasks.

The last two premises were derived from drive theory (see Chapter 7), according to which *drive energizes and intensifies responses that have a high probability of occurring.* On easy or overlearned tasks the most probable responses are the correct ones, whereas on difficult tasks they are more likely to be incorrect. Socially engendered arousal, therefore, intensifies correct responses on easy tasks, producing social facilitation, but intensifies incorrect responses on difficult ones, leading to performance decrements. In a demonstration of this, Hunt and Hillery (1973) gave subjects a finger maze through which they had to find their way without being able to see their hands. Some subjects were given a difficult maze and others an easy one. The results of the study showed that subjects who performed along with another subject who worked at his or her own maze task (i.e., a coactor) made fewer errors on the easy maze task than did subjects who worked alone, but they made more errors on the difficult one.

**EVALUATION APPREHENSION.**    Why does the presence of others increase the arousal of the person who is performing the task? Several answers have been suggested. One is related to the concept of social anxiety discussed above. Performing before an audience may make people anxious because they fear that poor performance will be evaluated unfavorably by the observers. Such an outcome would be similar to failing to make an impression in self-presentation, and the outcome would be social anxiety. In other words, the presence of an audience during the performance of a task is arousing because it evokes the fear of an unfavorable evaluation (Weiss & Miller, 1971).

If this is the case, then the presence of others should arouse the performer only when the others are believed to be judges of the performance. To some extent, subjects may experience the fear of being evaluated whenever they are observed, but fear should be felt especially when the observers are explicitly described as evaluators. Geen (1983) found evidence of this in a study in which subjects performed either an easy or a difficult learning task. Some subjects performed this task while alone, and others performed before an observer. To some subjects the observer was described as an evaluator of the subject's performance, whereas to others he was said to be interested in observing the subject only so that he could later give the subject some help on a future task. Because high arousal was expected to facilitate performance on easy tasks but hinder performance on difficult tasks, it was predicted that subjects who were evaluated would perform better (e.g., make fewer errors) on the easy task, but worse on the difficult one, than subjects who were observed for purposes of future help. This is what the findings of the study showed (Figure 10-2).

*UNCERTAINTY.* Another reason that people become aroused while working at a task in the company of other people is that they are not certain what those others might do (Zajonc, 1980). People often behave unpredictably, and their

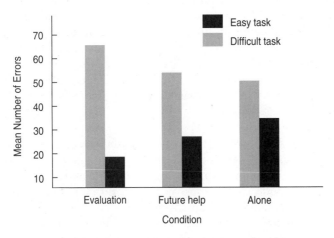

*Figure 10-2.* Effects of task difficulty and reasons for observation on social facilitation/inhibition of learning. (Drawn from data in "Evaluation Apprehension and the Social Facilitation/Inhibition of Learning" by R. G. Geen, *Motivation and Emotion*, 1983, 7, 203–212.)

actions may compel us to react even though we are not prepared to do so. It has long been recognized that uncertainty is potentially stressful and arousing (Weiss, 1971). In a major review of studies of social facilitation and inhibition, Guerin (1986) concluded that even when evaluation apprehension does not occur in social settings, the presence of others can still be arousing for this reason.

The uncertainty associated with the presence of others motivates behavior that Guerin (1983) has called *social monitoring.* In an attempt to control uncertainty, the individual watches other people who are present and seeks to predict their actions. This monitoring process reduces the arousal that would otherwise be elicited. To show this, Guerin conducted an experiment in which subjects performed a difficult learning task either alone or in the presence of another person who sat either within the subject's field of vision or behind the subject. When the other person was seen by the subject, either he was attentive to what the subject was doing or he ignored the subject. Guerin found that there was more social inhibition of performance on the difficult task among subjects who performed before an attentive observer than among those who were ignored, and that the poorest performance was that of subjects who did the task in the presence of a person who sat behind them and could not, therefore, be monitored. Subjects had no way of knowing whether this person was observing them or not; it was the uncertainty that produced the poor performance.

**DISTRACTION AND CONFLICT.**    Another reason the presence of others may lead to increased arousal during performance is that the other people may distract the performer from the task (Baron, 1986). Distraction leads to attentional conflict when the person is unable to attend to the other people and to the demands of the task at the same time. Attentional conflict causes the person to become agitated and aroused, and this condition, in turn, has effects on behavior that are predictable from drive theory. In support of this approach, Baron, Moore, and Sanders (1978) found that subjects who worked on a task before an audience not only showed the predicted social facilitation effects but also described themselves as more distracted by the situation than subjects who worked alone.

**CONCLUSION ON SOCIAL AROUSAL.**    It should be noted in conclusion that the three explanations for socially engendered arousal that have been reviewed here show some overlap. Each one is an explanation for the arousing effects of a social presence on individuals who are performing tasks. One states that the presence of others is arousing when these people are perceived as judges and evaluators; another holds that the arousal is due to uncertainty about what the others may do; the third proposes that the others arouse by distracting the individual. Obviously these are not mutually exclusive processes. For example, uncertainty about what others may do can itself be a distraction, fear of being negatively evaluated may increase uncertainty (i.e., the person will not know how the judge may respond to his or her performance), and being distracted from a task may increase the fear of failing. It is perhaps safest to conclude that each of these processes operates in social settings to some extent and that each contributes to the overall level of arousal felt by the individual (Geen, 1989).

## Impression Management

SELF-PROTECTIVE BEHAVIOR.   The presence of other people may also have effects on performance that are not linked to arousal processes but are related instead to the person's desire to make a good impression on others. If apprehension over being evaluated is what makes the audience setting so damaging to performance on difficult or complex tasks, then this audience effect may be thought of as a form of social anxiety. That being the case, it should also manifest some of the other properties of social anxiety, such as the defensive and cautious behavior that has been shown to characterize socially anxious people. People who are socially anxious as they perform should be motivated to express themselves in socially acceptable ways and to inhibit any behavior that is likely to embarrass them or make them look unattractive.

Several examples of this sort of impression management are found in the study of the social facilitation and inhibition of performance. For example, in a study by Blank, Staff, and Shaver (1976), subjects were required to give verbal associations to common words. The subjects emitted more common and familiar word associations when they were being observed than they did when performing alone. Of greater interest was the finding that the largest difference between the two conditions was found in the number of unique and idiosyncratic associations made (i.e., responses given by nobody else). Blank and his associates suggested that subjects who were observed restrained themselves from making unusual responses in order to avoid looking strange. Perhaps the reason they wished to avoid looking strange was to forestall implicit social rejection.

A second example is found in a study by Berger, Hampton, Carli, Grandmaison, Sadow, and Donath (1981). It was noted that subjects who were observed during a learning task suppressed outward signs of practicing more than did nonobserved ones. Outward signs of practice include such behaviors as moving the lips while reading, counting aloud, counting on one's fingers, and closing the eyes while rehearsing. Subjects may have inhibited such aids to learning while being observed because they considered these actions unlikely to be approved by the audience.

In a pair of studies, one involving an audience and the other involving coaction, Geen found more evidence that subjects whose peroformance is overtly evaluated react with greater conservatism and cautiousness than do those whose performance is merely being observed and those who work alone. In the first study Geen (1985) gave subjects a difficult task that required them to construct words out of anagram sets. The subjects attempted to solve the anagrams either in the company of the experimenter or alone. When the experimenter was present, he either observed the subject quietly or observed in such a way as to indicate that he was carrying on a constant evaluation of the performance, by looking carefully at what the subject was doing, checking a stopwatch occasionally, and writing comments on a pad of paper. Moreover, subjects in this condition, but not in the other two, were told that they were being tested. It was expected that cautiousness in performance would be shown in the number of anagrams the subjects attempted to solve.

It was also expected that social anxiety arising from the evaluation would be more intense in subjects who had a normal tendency to become anxious in such situations. All subjects had been classified before the experiment into groups made up of relatively high and low scorers on a test that assesses individual differences in the tendency (trait) to become anxious. The results of the study (Figure 10-3) showed that the conditions of observation and evaluation had different effects only on subjects who were high in trait anxiety. Among highly anxious subjects, the ones who were overtly evaluated attempted fewer anagrams than did those who were merely observed or alone. In addition, anxious-evaluated subjects experienced a greater increase in anxiety above pretest levels than did those in the other conditions. Finally, the number of anagrams attempted and the change in anxiety were significantly correlated in a negative direction: the greater the increase in anxiety, the fewer anagrams were attempted.

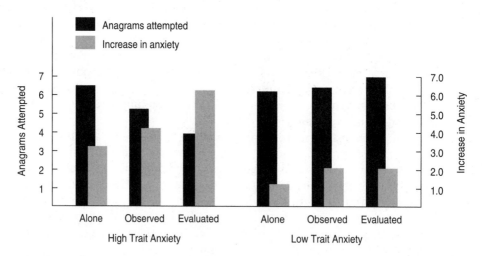

*Figure 10-3.* Effects of trait anxiety and observer status on response withholding and state anxiety. (Drawn from data in "Evaluation Apprehension and Response Withholding in Solution of Anagrams" by R. G. Geen, *Personality and Individual Differences,* 1985, *6,* 293–298.)

In the second of the two studies mentioned above, Geen, Thomas, and Gammill (1988) used a similar anagram task to examine the relationship between coaction and the presence or absence of the experimenter at the time of testing. A major purpose of this study was to examine the effects of coaction on performance within the theory of social anxiety. If social anxiety elicited by the situation is responsible for the social facilitation or inhibition of performance, why does such anxiety arise during coaction?

One possible answer is that people who perform the same task perceive themselves to be in competition for the approval that follows good performance. Competition may remind the subjects that failure (i.e., being outperformed by competitors) is a possible outcome of their efforts. In this way evaluation apprehension may enter into coaction settings much as it does in audience situations. Furthermore, it was reasoned that if this is the case, then the evaluation apprehension that is experienced in the coaction setting should be stronger if the experimenter is present than it would be if she were absent, because the presence of the experimenter, who dispenses implicit approval or disapproval, should serve as a reminder that failure is a feasible outcome.

Geen and his colleagues (1988) therefore expected that cautiousness would be greater (i.e., the anagrams attempted would be fewer) among coacting subjects when the experimenter was present than when she was absent. Figure 10-4 indicates that this expectation was borne out by the findings. In addition, the combination of coaction and experimenter presence created the largest increase in self-reported anxiety from before the task to immediately

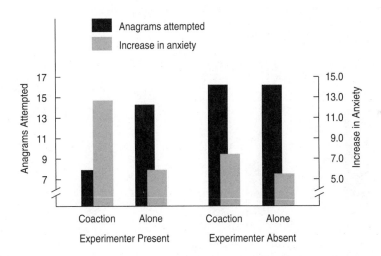

***Figure 10-4.*** Effects of presence of experimenter and coaction on response withholding and state anxiety. (Drawn from data reported in "Effects of Evaluation and Coaction on State Anxiety and Anagram Performance" by R. G. Geen, S. L. Thomas, and P. Gammill, *Personality and Individual Differences,* 1988, *9,* 411–415.)

after the task. This supports the idea that coacting subjects experienced their greatest apprehension when the experimenter was present.

**EFFORT.**    The desire to make a good impression in the socially evaluative setting has been found in several studies in which social facilitation and inhibition effects are not shown following a prior success experience. For example, Geen (1979) carried out an experiment in which subjects were first exposed to performance feedback on a preliminary verbal learning task that led them to believe that they had done either very well or very badly. After this, they worked at a second difficult verbal learning task either alone or while being observed. The observer knew how well or poorly the subject had done on the first task. The expected outcome—poorer performance while being observed than in isolation—was found *only when subjects had done poorly on the preliminary task.* Following a good performance on the first task, subjects who did the second task while being observed actually performed *better* (i.e., made fewer errors) than did those who worked alone (Figure 10-5).

   Additional data showed that the only condition in which subjects showed a significant increase in emotional arousal above baseline levels was the one in which they performed the second task in front of an observer after having performed poorly on the first task. This emotional arousal could indicate apprehension over being evaluated by an observer who was familiar with the subject's recent weak performance on a similar task. Performance in this condition was the worst of any in the experiment, probably because of the debilitating effects of evaluation anxiety. Subjects who were coming off a good performance on the first task probably experienced a different reaction when being observed. Having made a good impression on the observer by the initial

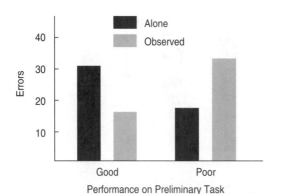

**Figure 10-5.** Errors on second task as a function of observation and performance on first task. (Drawn from data reported in "Effects of Being Observed on Learning Following Success and Failure Experiences" by R. G. Geen, *Motivation and Emotion,* 1979, *3,* 355–371.)

success, these subjects may have been motivated to expend greater effort on the second task in order to make another good impression.

In a subsequent study, Geen (1981) found evidence of this hypothesized effort. The experiment was similar to the one just described, with the exception that the second task was an unsolvable problem. It was expected that if subjects were motivated to put forth effort at a task, they would persist for a longer time before giving up on the problem than would less motivated subjects. The findings of the experiment showed that, following a good performance on an earlier task, subjects who were observed persisted at the unsolvable task longer than did those who worked alone. Their greater persistence can be taken as evidence of their desire to perform up to a level that they had attained earlier, and to sustain the good impression that they had made.

## Cognitive Overload

So far, we have noted that the social facilitation and inhibition effect has been explained as (1) a manifestation of increased arousal due to the presence of others and (2) behavior directed toward impression management. A third theoretical approach has been advanced by Baron (1986): other people in the situation are stimuli, which, when added to stimuli associated with the task and its context, overload the person's capacity for processing information about the environment. The immediate consequence of stimulus overload is a temporary strain on the person's ability to attend to important features of the situation. This approach to social facilitation is consistent with theories of attentional capacity. When stimuli that are irrelevant to performance are present (e.g., other people), capacity that is expended in attending to them is not available for the demands of the task (Kahneman, 1973). An immediate consequence of overtaxing the attentional system is a selective narrowing of attention to a relatively small number of stimuli (Geen, 1980). This can be thought of as a defensive reaction that lessens the cognitive overload by reducing the total amount of stimulation (Hockey, 1979).

How does this selective attention influence the social facilitation and inhibition of performance? We must begin by noting that when attention becomes more selective under conditions of overload, it does so by narrowing its focus in the direction of stimuli that are at the center of attention. Thus stimuli that are on the periphery are ignored first. As the magnitude of the stimulus overload increases, progressively more and more peripheral stimuli are eliminated from attention (Easterbrook, 1959). If we assume that easy tasks are those that involve the use of relatively little information from the environment—that is, information that is more or less central in attention—then the elimination of attention to peripheral stimuli should enhance performance because these peripheral cues are potential distractors. From this it follows that cognitive overload evoked by the presence of others should facilitate performance on easy tasks.

Difficult tasks are another matter. One reason they are difficult is because they demand that the person process a wider range of information than is the case with easy tasks. Peripheral stimuli that are only nuisance distractors for easy tasks may well provide necessary information on harder tasks. Cognitive overload that results from the presence of others may therefore cause attention to be too selective, so that social presence hinders performance on difficult tasks. This effect has been shown in a study by Geen (1976), in which subjects who were observed while performing a learning task were less able to utilize additional information given to them during the course of the task than were subjects who performed alone. This finding suggests that observed subjects were focusing their attention on stimuli directly related to the task and shutting out the additional material.

## *Computer Monitoring of Performance*

At the beginning of this chapter, we noted that the social facilitation paradigm is potentially important in the study and understanding of performance in work settings. In this section we will review some studies that have a bearing on such an application. They deal with a problem of interest to industrial-organizational psychologists: the effects of electronic monitoring of workers in their jobs. Surveillance of workers by supervisors has been a common industrial procedure, carried out to record rates of production, compare actual production with production goals, and give feedback to workers on their progress, or lack of progress, in meeting these goals. Until recently, such procedures were carried out through direct personal observation by immediate superiors, but more recently the use of centralized computer facilities has been replacing the older method. Electronic surveillance has been facilitated by the increasing use of computerized work stations for employees. Computer monitoring has been defined as "the use of computer hardware and software to collect, store, analyze, and report individual or group actions or performance on the job" (Nebeker & Tatum, 1993, p. 509).

Computer monitoring has been defended as a means of improving the efficiency of the surveillance process, allowing more rapid feedback to the worker, and increasing productivity. However, critics of the procedure have observed that it leads to increased feelings of stress among workers, increased dissatisfaction with the job, a lowering of morale, and an emphasis on the quantity of production at the expense of quality (Aiello, 1993). Until recently, investigation of these issues was hindered by the lack of an overall theory that encompasses both the behavioral (i.e., production) and the affective (e.g., stress) outcomes of computer surveillance. Now, however, we have several studies in which the effects of computer surveillance have been approached through the application of the theory of social facilitation.

Aiello (1993) has suggested that a worker whose behavior is being observed by a computer should behave in approximately the same way as one who is observed through more direct surveillance. In other words, computer

*A number of factories now monitor the performance of workers through electronic means like closed-circuit television.*

monitoring is a special case of the audience paradigm of social facilitation that was defined above. If this is so, then a good place to begin the analysis of the phenomenon is by observing the effects of computer monitoring on the performance of easy and difficult tasks. Aiello and Svec (1993) conducted an experiment in which subjects worked at a difficult anagrams task while their performance was monitored either directly by a nearby human observer or indirectly through the computer at which they worked. A group of control subjects (who were actually monitored through the computer) were told that they were *not* being observed in any way. The results of the study showed that subjects who did not think they were being monitored (i.e., who thought they were performing alone) solved more anagrams correctly than did those who thought they were being monitored. In addition, the type of monitoring used (computer or human observer) was irrelevant: computer monitoring had the same socially inhibiting effect on complex task performance as did direct human monitoring. This finding is consistent with the theory of social inhibition of performance on difficult tasks.

In a subsequent study that also involved the solution of difficult anagrams, Aiello, Shao, Chomiak, and Kolb (1993) found that computer-monitored subjects not only solved fewer anagrams than did nonmonitored subjects, but also attempted fewer solutions. This replicates a similar finding noted above (Geen, 1985), in which an inhibition of behavior was found when a human evaluator was present. Thus computer surveillance appears to create the same tendencies toward conservative responding as direct monitoring.

Does computer monitoring also have a socially *facilitating* effect on the performance of an easy task? The results of a second study in the report by Aiello and colleagues (1993) indicate that it does. Subjects were given the relatively easy task of keypunching sets of six-digit numbers from a worksheet into the computer. Some subjects had not been told that their work would be monitored, whereas others worked in the knowledge that their performance was being watched by a supervisor sitting at a master terminal. The results showed that subjects who knew that they were being monitored keypunched more digit sets than those who did not, and they also keyed in the numbers with fewer mistakes. Thus both the quantity and quality of production were enhanced by computer monitoring.

At the most fundamental level, therefore—the social facilitation and inhibition of easy and diffcult tasks—social facilitation theory can explain the effects of computer monitoring. In addition, the studies that have been conducted shed some light on intervening variables in the process by suggesting that certain conditions may moderate the effects of surveillance. For example, in the study by Aiello and Svec (1993), one group of computer-monitored subjects was informed that the monitoring could be terminated at any time by the subject's merely pushing a button on the computer. Even though none of these subjects in this condition actually stopped the surveillance, they solved more anagrams correctly than did those who had no control over the monitoring. They did not, however, solve as many as subjects who were not monitored. Thus the perception of being in control of the situation mitigates the socially inhibiting effects of computer monitoring without completely eliminating them.

Another variable that may influence the effects of computer surveillance is the degree to which the organization (i.e., the people doing the monitoring) threatens the worker, in contrast to the degree to which it gives the worker assistance and support. Recall that in the research on social facilitation reviewed above, evaluation apprehension in the presence of an evaluating observer was reduced when the evaluation was said to be preparatory to giving the subject helpful feedback about his or her performance (e.g., Geen, 1983). This same effect has been shown in the study by Aiello and coworkers (1993). Half of the subjects in that study (the "positive climate" condition) were told that their work was being monitored so that the subject might later be given assistance in improving his or her anagram-solving skills. The other half of the subjects (the "negative climate" condition) were told only that their performance was being closely watched and judged for its accuracy. The results showed that the performance of subjects in this latter condition got worse as the experiment went on, whereas the performance of subjects in the positive-climate condition improved significantly over the same period. In addition, monitored subjects who worked under the "helpful" condition reported being less anxious and less stressed than those in the negative-climate condition.

It is still too soon to draw more than tentative conclusions regarding the effects of computer monitoring on performance. However, the studies cited here indicate that the social facilitation paradigm accounts for many of the findings. Being monitored by indirect electronic means appears to generate evaluation apprehension (i.e., anxiety) in the same way as does direct surveillance. This state, in turn, facilitates the performance of easy tasks and inhibits the performance of more difficult ones. Circumstances that may reduce the anxiety and evaluation apprehension normally engendered by surveillance, such as gaining control over the aversive situation or converting evaluation into a means for helping the individual, reduce the performance-inhibiting effects of the surveillance on complex task performance. A good start has been made in the investigation of this issue, and more elaborate studies will undoubtedly be reported in the future.

## SOCIAL LOAFING

Another social phenomenon that can be traced back to studies done early in the 20th century is the apparent loss of motivation in groups of people who are working toward a common goal. It was first reported by Ringelmann in 1913 in connection with research that he was doing on the relative merits of human versus machine labor in agricultural work. Ringelmann noted that when groups of individuals are organized to perform collective tasks (such as rope pulling), the total output is less than we would expect if we added together the normal outputs of the individuals working alone. Moreover, as the size of the group was increased, the discrepancy between the sum of individual outputs and that of the group was greater (Kravitz & Martin, 1986). Although Ringelmann attributed this effect to less-than-perfect coordination among members of the group, so that some efficiency is lost with each new member added, he conceded that it may also have been due to motivation loss. In other words, each person may have "loafed" when involved in a task in which the responsibility for performance could be left to others. Interest in the effect was revived in 1979, when Latané and his colleagues reopened the question of apparent motivation loss in groups and called it social loafing.

Latané, Williams, and Harkins (1979) conducted an experiment in which subjects shouted or clapped their hands for five seconds in response to a signal from the experimenter. Each subject made both responses under four different conditions: sometimes alone, and sometimes as a member of a shouting or clapping group of one, three, or five additional people. In every condition the amount of noise made by the clapping or shouting was measured in sound pressure units (i.e., dynes per centimeter).

Figure 10-6 shows the amount of sound pressure generated per person in

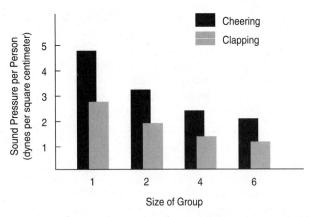

**Figure 10-6.** Intensity of noise produced by subjects alone and in groups of varying size. (Drawn from data reported in "Many Hands Make Light the Work: The Causes and Consequences of Social Loafing" by B. Latané, K. Williams, and S. G. Harkins, *Journal of Personality and Social Psychology,* 1979, *37,* 822–832.)

groups of two, four, and six persons as well as the average amount generated by subjects shouting and clapping alone. Clearly, as the group increased in size, each person, on the average, made less noise. In a second experiment Latané and his colleagues showed that whereas some of this performance decrement in groups could be traced to loss of coordination, another portion of it was due to a reduction in effort. The latter, of course, represented the apparent motivation loss that had been mentioned as a possibility by Ringlemann.

Subsequent studies showed that social loafing occurs across a broad range of tasks, including motor performance in a maze, creativity, attention, cognitive processing, and even swimming. It is therefore a robust and general phenomenon. The next question that we must ask is: If social loafing is the result of a loss of motivation in the social setting, what causes that loss? Three answers have been suggested. The first is that people loaf in groups when they think that others may be loafing. The second is that people loaf when they are not interested in the task and have a safe cover of anonymity. The third is that loafing occurs when the person has been given no standard of good performance against which to judge his or her production.

## Output Equity

When people work together on a common problem, each person probably wonders, at least part of the time, whether he or she is doing more than a "fair share" of the labor. This concern is part of a larger one for equity in social situations. Equity is not the same as equality. It is a condition that exists when each person reaps rewards from the situation that are proportional to his or

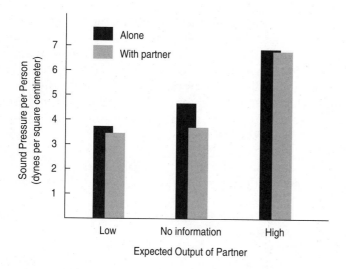

**Figure 10-7.** Intensity of noise produced by subjects alone or with a partner across three levels of expectancy of partner's efforts. (Drawn from data reported in "Equity in Effort: An Explanation of the Social Loafing Effect" by J. M. Jackson and S. G. Harkins, *Journal of Personality and Social Psychology,* 1985, *49,* 1199–1206.)

her costs and inputs. When the situation is such that everyone shares equally in whatever reward is given for the product (such as the approval of the experimenter for a good group performance), the norm of equity requires that nobody contribute more effort than anyone else. Social loafing may come about because the individual in the group thinks that others are not doing their fair share of the work. In order to avoid being imposed upon, the individual then reduces her or his own effort. Kerr (1983) has appropriately called this the "sucker effect."

An experiment by Jackson and Harkins (1985) produced results that suggest the sucker effect. Subjects in this study manifested social loafing by shouting more loudly when alone than when in pairs only after they had first been given no information about their partners' intended level of effort. After having been informed that the partner intended to expend either a high or a low amount of effort on the task, subjects likewise expended high or low effort (Figure 10-7). In other words, when subjects had not been specifically informed of the partner's intention, they appear to have concluded that the partner was loafing.

## "Hiding in the Crowd"

Another theoretical explanation for social loafing is that the desire to loaf is a reaction to tasks that are boring, tiresome, or otherwise unlikely to engage the subject's involvement, and that loafing will occur unless something is done to stop it. Kerr and Bruun (1981) have called this the "hide in the crowd" effect to indicate that the presence of other group members provides a cover of anonymity for the unmotivated person. Anonymity is facilitated by the usual practice in social loafing experiments of pooling subjects' outputs. For example, one typical procedure calls for subjects to make objects that are then thrown into a common box so that the extent of any individual's contributions cannot be known. If anonymity was taken away by making possible the identification of each person's contribution to the group product, social loafing should be mitigated or eliminated. This approach was taken in a study by Williams, Harkins, and Latané (1981); when subjects were told that individual responses could be detected, they shouted as loudly in a group as they did when alone.

Findings such as this introduce the possibility that evaluation apprehension plays a part in social loafing (Harkins, 1987). Subjects whose contributions can be identified run the risk of incurring disapproval if they give less than their fair share of the effort to the group. The fact that each member of the group is working on a common task also introduces an element of coaction and competitiveness into the situation. Loafing that can be detected will lead not only to possible social disapproval but also to looking bad in comparison to other members of the group. Harkins and Jackson (1985) found evidence for this by showing that subjects in a group of four whose products could be identified indulged in less social loafing when they all worked on the same task than when each did a different one.

Social loafing, therefore, may not represent a loss of motivation in the social setting as much as a response to an already low level of motivation to perform. It originates in tiresome or uninvolving tasks that generate no intrinsic interest, so that unless some other motive is supplied, such as the need to avoid disapproval, the person will not expend normal effort. Social loafing should not, therefore, occur when the group is assigned an involving task. Brickner, Harkins, and Ostrom (1986) found this to be true. Subjects, all of whom were college students, were instructed to list their thoughts about general comprehensive examinations as a requirement for graduation. A high level of involvement was incited in some subjects by telling them that these examinations were going to be given at their school in the following semester. The remaining subjects were told either that the new examinations would come at some later time or that they were being implemented at another college. When the thought-listing task was introduced in a relatively uninvolving way (as in the latter two conditions), subjects generated fewer thoughts when their individual ideas could not be identified than when they could; that is, they loafed. However, when the topic was highly involving, there was no evidence of loafing.

## Matching a Standard

Szymanski and Harkins (1987) have suggested still another explanation for social loafing. When individuals in a group are given no standard definition of what constitutes acceptable performance, they are more likely to loaf than when they are given such a standard. Szymanski and Harkins assigned subjects the task of inventing uses for common objects, and they informed one group of subjects about "the average number of uses generated by students in (previous) research." Simply giving this information eliminated social loafing, even when subjects had complete anonymity. Why should providing a standard for performance reduce social loafing? One possible answer is that when subjects are given a standard, they monitor their own performance and, in effect, evaluate themselves; thus the matching-to-standard may simply be a special case of an internalized evaluation apprehension effect. Another

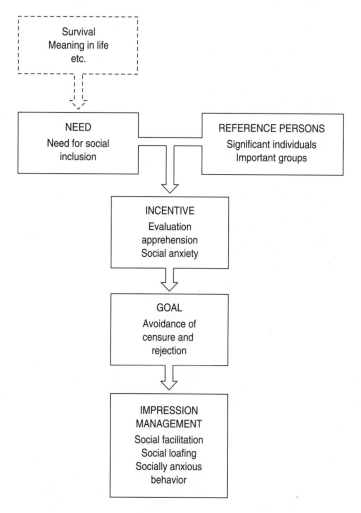

**Figure 10-8.** Scheme of motivational antecedents of impression management processes in social anxiety, social facilitation, and social loafing.

possibility is that by defining the task in terms of a standard, the experimenters made it more interesting and involving for the subjects. Whatever the explanation, the provision of a performance standard was sufficient to prevent social loafing.

## CONCLUSION

Several causal variables have been identified in the social facilitation or inhibition of individual performance and in social loafing, but one important one that is common to both phenomena is apprehension over being evaluated by other people. Evaluation apprehension is a negative incentive that can motivate self-presentation strategies in such a way that performance before an audience is enhanced, even when difficult tasks are undertaken. It can also motivate people to perform at their best on uninvolving tasks and not to loaf when they have the opportunity to do so. As we have noted in this chapter, evaluation apprehension and social anxiety are closely related. Each is a manifestation of a larger and more basic motive for social inclusion (Figure 10-8). Thus a number of distinct social behaviors appear to be subsumed by a fundamental need to belong to a collective and not to be cut off from other people.

## CHAPTER SUMMARY

**1.** A large part of human life takes place in settings in which social influence is immediate and direct. Such settings give rise to social anxiety, the social facilitation and inhibition of individual performance, and social loafing.

**2.** Social anxiety is a state that arises when a person desires to make a favorable impression on someone but doubts that such an impression can be made. This state is most likely to be found in people who have strong dispositional tendencies to become anxious.

**3.** Social anxiety has several effects on behavior. Overt nervousness is one such effect. Another is disaffiliation: a breaking of contact with other people. When disaffiliation is not feasible, socially anxious people are likely to become cautious and defensive in their interactions.

**4.** Impression motivation underlies the processes that lead to social anxiety. People wish to make good impressions in order to make progress toward important goals. Impression motivation varies with the importance of those goals and the person's expectancy that making a good impression will lead to attaining the goals. The latter expectancy has two components: an efficacy expectancy (that one is capable of making the desired impression) and an outcome expectancy (that the desired impression will be followed by attainment of the goal). Social anxiety is primarily the result of a low efficacy expectancy.

**5.**   Anxiety in testing situations is similar in many ways to social anxiety. It follows from a desire to do well on the test, it is most likely to occur when the person doubts that the desired performance on the test will occur, and it evokes cautiousness and conservatism in responding to the test items.

**6.**   The motive for self-presentation is related to a more basic underlying motive for being accepted and included within a larger social collective. The fear of social exclusion is the motive for impression management.

**7.**   Social facilitation is the enhancement of individual performance by the presence of other people, as either observers or coactors. Its counterpart, social inhibition, is the impairment of performance under similar social conditions. Whether social facilitation or inhibition will occur depends largely on the difficulty of the task being performed. The presence of others generally facilitates performance on easy tasks but inhibits performance on more difficult ones.

**8.**   One explanation of social facilitation and inhibition is based on the assumption that the presence of others increases the performer's drive level. The immediate antecedents of increased drive have been described by various theorists as evaluation apprehension, uncertainty, and distraction from the task.

**9.**   Social facilitation and inhibition may also be related to impression management. Subjects who perform following the experience of doing well on a preliminary task perform better on a difficult subsequent task when they are observed than when performing alone. The prior experience of success evokes an expenditure of effort on the next task, the aim of which is to achieve continued success and approval.

**10.**   Social facilitation and inhibition are also related to cognitive overloads caused by the addition of other people to the task setting. Cognitive overload may selectively narrow attention that can facilitate performance on easy tasks but hinder performance on complex tasks.

**11.**   Recent studies of the computer monitoring of performance suggest that the social facilitation paradigm may explain some of the effects of this procedure. Social facilitation and inhibition of easy and difficult tasks, respectively, are found in studies of computer monitoring as in studies of direct audience observation.

**12.**   Studies of social loafing have shown that people often expend less effort when they are part of a coacting group than they do when acting alone. One explanation for this effect is that people loaf when they think that others in the group are loafing. Another explanation is that on most experimental tasks people are not motivated to expend effort, and that they loaf when they are safely anonymous in a coacting group.

**13.**    Social loafing can be reduced or eliminated by several procedures. Making the contribution of each group member identifiable greatly reduces loafing by introducing the possibility of unfavorable evaluation. Giving the person a performance standard also reduces loafing, probably by making the task more interesting and involving than it would otherwise be.

CHAPTER

# STRESS AND MOTIVATION

## CHAPTER OUTLINE

In the course of a normal day's activities people encounter many situations that upset their routine and require an adjustment in behavior. Most of the time the demands imposed by such situations are slight and the amount of adjustive behavior minimal. Responses are readily available to handle the requirements, and behavior flows more or less smoothly. But such is not always the case. Sometimes the situation changes so much or so suddenly that one has no easily summoned set of responses for adapting to it. Being fired from one's job, failing an important course, or losing a relative through sudden death are changes that cause severe dislocation of normal behavior. At other times, changes in life are not catastrophic, but they come in such profusion and in such a short period of time that they overwhelm a person through their sheer collective weight. Little everyday irritants like getting stalled in traffic, breathing someone else's cigarette smoke, and being subjected to the noise from a radio are not much in themselves, but they can have a powerful cumulative effect on one's sense of well-being. In both of these situations—big changes and little hassles—the person is said to be under stress.

The term *stress* is another example of a well developed and widely used metaphor of psychology (see Chapter 1). In this case the metaphor is from the physical and engineering sciences. To a physicist, for example, the word describes the application of force to materials in order to find out how much is needed to bend an iron bar or to snap a bolt. Psychologists use the term in an analogous way. The "force" arises from intense or closely spaced deviations from the normal flow of life, and the "break" occurs when the person can no longer cope with, and adapt to, the new conditions. Stress, therefore, may be defined as a response to a discrepancy between the normal, steady state of the person and some changed condition in the environment. This latter condition need not be physically concurrent with the stress that it produces. Memories of such changes and anticipations of changes yet to come can sometimes be as stressful as ones that actually occur. In this chapter we will review some of what is known about stress, beginning with a broad overview of how the concept has changed over the past 50 years. We will next consider a general working model of the stress process that takes into account much of the evidence that has been accumulated. Finally, we will examine in detail some of the variables described by that model.

# CHANGING CONCEPTIONS OF STRESS

The stress concept has undergone some changes since it first appeared. In general, these changes have revealed a shift from early emphases on stress as a biological reaction to changing physical conditions in the environment to a more psychological viewpoint at both the input and the output levels; that is, both the causes and the effects of stress are now sought in psychological variables as well as in physical ones. In addition, the importance of what people can do to reduce or modify stress is now widely recognized. These changing emphases have led to a new model of stress that we will describe in detail.

## Stress as Physical Reaction

Modern interest in stress can be traced back to the pioneering work of Selye (1956) on the manifold effects of physical stressors, such as harmful chemicals or enforced immobilization, on the physiology and body chemistry of laboratory animals. These effects could be quite severe: enlargement of the adrenal glands, shrinking of the thymus gland and lymph nodes, ulceration of the gastrointestinal tract, and even death. After extensive study of these effects over time, Selye discovered that the stress reaction could be divided into three discrete periods: an initial stage of *alarm*, in which the body mobilizes its resources to resist the stressor; a subsequent stage of *resistance*, in which the processes initiated in the first stage promote the beginning of recovery; and a final stage of *exhaustion*, during which continued exposure to the stressor overcomes the resistance, leading to serious physical damage and even death. This overall process was labeled the *general adaptation syndrome*. The effects described by Selye are called nonspecific stressor effects because they occur in more or less the same way in response to any stressful stimulus. In addition, of course, stressors cause effects that are specific to the stimulus and to the part of the body that is involved. For example, prolonged exposure to chemical fumes will cause specific damage to the respiratory system as well as evoke the nonspecific stress syndrome. It was, however, the nonspecific reaction that attracted the attention of stress researchers.

In the general adaptation syndrome, as we have noted, the body's systems respond to the stressor during the resistance stage. The process is not, therefore, entirely passive. Nevertheless, the resistance of the body described by Selye is an automatic one similar to the better known process of homeostasis. The theory therefore describes an animal that is mainly passive and reactive, not one that actively seeks to adapt to or control the situation. As we will see later, this view of a passive stress process was ultimately replaced by one that recognizes the active nature of adaptation.

## *Psychological Variables in Stress*

During the late 1950s psychologists began to find that stress is a function of more than just the physical properties of stressful events and that psychological variables play a large role in the process. In addition to experiencing stress because of the intensity, frequency, and duration of aversive events, people were shown to respond to such variables as the degree to which they could expect the stressor to occur, predict the time of its onset, and exert control over it. These psychological variables were shown to be antecedents of the same sort of physical deterioration in animals that Selye had observed (Mason, 1968, 1975). During the 1960s extensive research was carried out under controlled laboratory conditions in order to isolate and define the exact effects of psychological variables on stress in both animal and human subjects.

At about the same time, some studies by Lazarus and his colleagues were beginning to show that stress could be affected by the ways in which people encoded information about unpleasant or threatening events. In a series of experiments, these investigators showed that if motion pictures of stressful events were shown along with instructions to the subject to deny or otherwise reinterpret the events in a less stress-inducing fashion, physiological reactions to the film could be attenuated. For example, Lazarus, Opton, Nomikos, and Rankin (1965) showed subjects a short film in which men who were working in a mill suffer several especially gory accidents. Some subjects simply watched the movie as their skin conductance levels and heart rates were monitored. Subjects in another condition were led to deny the stressfulness of the situation by being told before seeing the film that the accidents were only realistic simulations. In a third condition, subjects were led to think that the accidents were real, but they were encouraged to take an objective, noninvolved, and intellectual point of view in observing them. Lazarus and his associates found that in both of the latter conditions, subjects were less aroused by the film, in terms of their levels of heart rate and skin conductance, than were subjects who saw the film without additional instructions.

Although the early research expanded and extended our understanding of how the stress process works, it suffered from two shortcomings inherent in its methodology. First, it involved artificial stressors such as electric shocks and loud noise; this procedure allowed the precise degree of control necessary for experimental investigation but left open the question as to whether responses to these conditions would be the same as reactions to everyday events. Second, the cross-sectional, one-shot laboratory approach was not suited to studying the possible effects that individual reactions might have on subsequent dealings with the stressful event. Experimental procedures called for measurement of the subject's immediate response to a stressor and no more. In short, the experimental method left little room for the study of long-term coping behaviors.

## Toward a New Stress Model

By the early 1970s three developments had taken place in the study of stress that turned research away from the purely experimental method and toward a more naturalistic approach. Largely as a result of these developments, a new model for stress, which will be described below, became the one most preferred for research.

One of these developments was the recognition that stress need not be the result of catastrophic changes in one's life, but that the ordinary trials and tribulations of the human condition might accumulate in such a way that the person becomes overwhelmed by them. The study of stress therefore moved away from the laboratory, with its manipulated conditions, and into the everyday lives of people. The study of the effects of *life events* was the result. A second development during this period was the abandonment of the cross-sectional approach in favor of a *transactional* one. Instead of assessing the immediate effects of single applications of a stressor, this approach involves the long-range observation of the person as she or he deals with the immediate environment both actively and reactively. In other words, it presupposes an active individual who is influenced by the environment but who also influences the environment through his or her actions. Finally, because this new transactional approach involves people who do not just react to events but who also interpret, appraise, and think about them, it followed that *individual differences* in such intervening processes would play an important part in the overall effects of stress. Individual variables therefore are a key element in the newer approach to stress that will be described in the next section.

## A Model of Stress

A working model for the stress process is shown in Figure 11-1. The elements of this model are drawn from several sources. The reader will recognize the basic format as a variation on the comparator-discrepancy theme that was presented in Chapter 3. This model also draws on the work of Lazarus (Lazarus & Folkman, 1984), Rahe and his colleagues (e.g., Rahe & Arthur, 1978), Schonpflug (1986), and others. These will be discussed in greater detail below. It is essentially a feedback model that involves continuous processes of appraisal and coping in the context of changes that occur in everyday life.

A life event happens against a backdrop of the way the person is just prior to the event; it therefore stands in contrast to this preexisting, or steady,

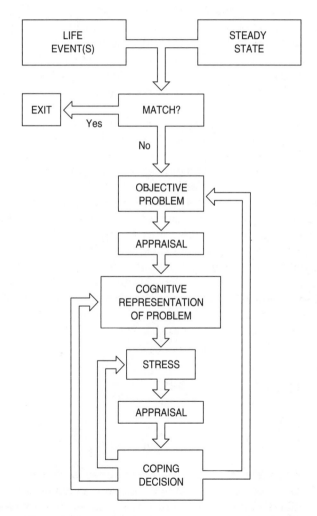

**Figure 11-1.** Model of stress, appraisal, and coping.

state, and it represents a change because of this contrast. Breaking up a relationship with a close friend, for example, has an impact only because the post-
breakup state is contrasted with the happier state that had existed before the
event. If there is no contrast, or very little contrast, between the new state
and the old, as in the case of a single minor annoyance, we quickly exit from
the system and go on about our business. As we noted above, however, either
a major life change or an accumulation of otherwise little annoyances can
cause sufficient contrast with the steady state to disrupt the normal flow of
behavior. When such a disruption happens, it constitutes a problem in the
objective sense. The person then makes a cognitive appraisal of the situation
and defines it as either harmless or harmful. If this *primary appraisal* leads
to a judgment that the new situation is harmful or potentially harmful, then
the person will experience stress.

At this point a *secondary appraisal* (actually a *reappraisal*) of the situation is made. The person now perceives the immediate situation as at least
potentially stressful and reacts by taking stock of resources that are available
for contending with, or adapting to, the new demands. On the basis of the
reappraisal, the person forms a strategy for coping with the situation. Details
of the two appraisal processes will be spelled out in a subsequent section of
this chapter.

This model actually reduces a highly complex process to a few essentials.
The processes of appraisal and coping can actually be considerably more
involved than this model suggests, for the simple reason that they must usually operate on more than one set of life events or changes at a time. In addition, the process of adjusting to one situation usually creates a new one with
its own demands and stressors (Schonpflug, 1986). For example, a woman
who hates her job may adapt by quitting and getting a new position (thereby
altering the life-event element in the model), only to discover that her new job
has bad features that the old one did not have. Or a young man may cope with
stress that arises from doubts about his sexual capability by engaging in
promiscuous behavior, only to find new problems brought on by the fear of
contracting AIDS. It should also be noted that the important variable of individual differences does not appear in Figure 11-1. These enter in at several
places in the process and will be discussed in that context.

# CAUSES OF STRESS
# IN HUMANS

### Catastrophes

The most obvious, if not the most frequent, source of stress is the sort of major
catastrophe, either natural or of human invention, that occasionally befalls
people. The stressful effects of one such event have been studied extensively
by psychologists. On March 28, 1979, an accident at the Three Mile Island

*Environmental disasters like the San Francisco earthquake of 1989 not only destroy property but also produce high levels of stress among the people affected by them.*

(TMI) nuclear power plant near Harrisburg, Pennsylvania, caused a drop in the level of coolant water and the consequent exposure of part of the reactor core. The heat generated by the uncovering of the atomic material may have caused a partial meltdown or explosion, which resulted in additional breakdowns. In the aftermath of the accident a large amount of radioactive water remained inside the reactor and equally dangerous krypton gas was trapped inside the containment building. Both the gas and the water became sources of radiation danger to people who lived nearby. Obviously, the shock of such a disaster was a severe stressor for these people.

In a series of studies, Baum and his associates studied several indicators of stress in a sample of people who lived within five miles of the TMI reactor. Baum, Gatchel, and Schaeffer (1983) measured psychological stress with self-reports of anxiety and depression, and physical stress in the form of both reported symptoms and elevated levels of epinephrine and norepinephrine in the urine. Both of these substances are secreted by the body in greater amounts during stressful periods than during periods of calm. Effects of the stress were also measured through performance on two cognitive-perceptual tasks. On every measure, people who lived near the TMI reactor showed evidence of greater stress than people in control groups who lived near either an undamaged nuclear facility or a coal-powered generator. This study was carried out one year after the accident, showing that the stressful effects were long lasting. Fifteen months after the accident, the krypton gas that had been trapped inside the containment building was vented into the atmosphere, and this event, like the original disaster, was followed by an increase in physical stress among people who lived near TMI (Gatchel, Schaeffer & Baum, 1985).

In other studies, Baum and his colleagues showed that stress among people who lived near TMI was mitigated by certain other variables. One such variable was the amount of personal control that people believed they had. Davidson, Baum, and Collins (1982) found that people who lived near TMI showed more symptoms of stress—both psychological and physical—and poorer task performance than did people who lived 80 miles away only if they also expressed strong feelings of personal helplessness. Among those who expressed a belief in personal control over their lives, those in the TMI sample showed no more stress than those who lived far from the damaged reactor. Fleming, Baum, Gisriel, and Gatchel (1985) also observed that social support had a mitigating effect on psychological stress (e.g., anxiety, depression, and performance on tasks) in the TMI sample, but not on physical stress (i.e., epinephrine and norepinephrine levels). Apparently social support served mainly to help people cope with stress so that it did not become manifest in emotional disorder.

## Major Life Events

Disasters such as the one that occurred at Three Mile Island are, fortunately, rare. Most stress arises from more mundane events that surround most of us in our normal lives. Interest in everyday events as antecedent conditions for mental and emotional disorders can be traced back to the noted American psychiatrist Adolf Meyer (1866–1950). In attempting to understand the causes of psychological disturbances, Meyer regularly had his patients keep diaries in which they recorded seemingly mundane events from their lives. Consistent with the biopsychological theory that he followed, Meyer believed that the analysis of patterns of life events over time was an important key to understanding mental problems. He was assisted in this effort by his wife, Mary Meyer, who frequently visited patients in their homes in order to learn about their daily routines and, in so doing, became the first American psychiatric social worker (Hilgard, 1987).

In more recent times the tradition begun by Meyer has been carried on in the development and use of self-report measures of life events as a basis for predicting both psychological stress and stress-related physical illnesses. One of the earliest to be developed was the Social Readjustment Rating Scale (Holmes & Masuda, 1974), which was a list of 43 events drawn from everyday life, with instructions to respondents to check off any event from the list that had occurred in their lives in a specified period of time. Pretesting had established a numerical value (called a Life Change Unit, or LCU) for each event proportional to its degree of severity (e.g., "death of a spouse" had a value of 100 LCUs, whereas the less serious "trouble with in-laws" had a value of just 29). The total amount of stress experienced by the person over the stipulated period of time was defined as the sum of the LCUs for all events checked. The rationale for this procedure is the belief, noted above, that stress accumulates from discrete events amassed in a short period of time.

Obviously, the more life changes that a person experiences and the more stressful the events are, the higher will be the person's LCU score. The theory underlying this work predicts that subjects with high LCU scores will experience a greater incidence and/or severity of stress-related illness over some period of time following the test than will persons with lower LCU scores. For example, Holmes and Masuda (1974) found a positive relationship between accumulated life stress in university students over an 18-month period and illnesses reported at a university health center over the 9 months that followed. Life changes have also been shown to predict such problems as heart disease (Theorell & Rahe, 1975) and stomach ulcers (Stevenson, Nabseth, Masuda & Holmes, 1979).

Not all of the items on the Social Readjustment Rating Scale represent undesirable changes. Included among the items, for example, are "marital reconciliation," "outstanding personal achievement," and "vacation," none of which would probably be considered unpleasant by most people. The theory behind the scale is that life changes per se are stressful, whether their affective consequences are positive or negative. This assumption is not entirely without merit inasmuch as even changes for the better sometimes require an investment of effort as the person must adjust to changed circumstances. It is also questionable whether anything that happens in normal life is an unmixed blessing. Taking a vacation, for example, is enjoyable for the most part, but it may also involve tedious preparations, discomfiting travel, jet lag, and other inconveniences that must be survived so that the enjoyment is possible.

Nevertheless, most of the evidence from the study of stress points to the conclusion that negative life events are far more stressful than positive ones. Taylor (1991) has reviewed the literature across several areas of research and concluded that the occurrence of negative events evokes a large-scale mobilization of the individual's physiological and cognitive resources, whereas positive events do not. Negative events evoke autonomic activation and intense affect. In addition, they have clear effects on cognitive processes, causing attention to become focused and cognitive processing to become more involved and complex.

This analysis is consistent with the findings of investigators who have separated life events into those that are mainly positive and those that are mainly negative and have found that only accumulations of negative life events predict psychological distress and emotional disturbance (Sarason, Johnson & Siegel, 1978; Vinokur & Selzer, 1975). It is also consistent with the concept of primary appraisals, which is elaborated upon below, according to which there should be little or no stress following an event that is appraised as benign.

## *Daily Hassles*

Stressful events that we call "hassles" (Lazarus & Cohen, 1978) differ from major life changes in several ways: they are more numerous and occur more often, they are less serious in objective terms, and, because of their immediacy, they are felt more keenly. For that reason, they are more likely than major changes to be represented in cognition as stressful. For example, getting caught in a traffic jam may not be as harmful to a person's well-being as learning that her son is on drugs, but at the time it is experienced it is more maddening. As we will see, the ways in which major life changes and smaller hassles relate to each other is a matter of importance for understanding stress.

Daily hassles were first measured by a scale that lists 117 annoying events (e.g., misplaced or lost things, auto maintenance, insufficient money for clothing) that most people experience at one time or another. Persons respond to the scale by indicating whether an event has happened to them within the past month and, if so, how much it upset them. Subsequent research on the effects of hassles has involved refinements of this original scale (e.g., DeLongis, Folkman & Lazarus, 1988).

In studies involving hassle scales, the frequency and intensity of hassles have been important contributors to stress. Kanner, Coyne, Schaefer, and Lazarus (1981) administered the scale along with two measures of psychological distress and, for purposes of comparison, a scale for measuring major life changes. The frequency of hassles was found to correlate with the distress measures more strongly than did the score derived from the scale that measured major changes. A study by DeLongis, Coyne, Dakof, Folkman, and Lazarus (1982) found that the frequency and intensity of hassles were more closely related to physical illness than was the measure of major life changes.

In both of these studies, the investigators concluded that small hassles have effects on both psychological stress and physical health that are independent of the effects of major life stressors. To a large extent, this conclusion is warranted by their data. However, in both studies a small but significant correlation was found between hassles and stressful life events. Kanner and coworkers (1981) found a correlation of 0.21 between frequency of hassles and incidence of stressful life events prior to the study. DeLongis and her associates (1982) found a correlation of 0.19 between hassle intensity and the life change measure. It is possible, therefore, that some of the influence of major life changes is mediated by smaller everyday hassles. People can become terribly annoyed by minor matters just after a major piece of bad luck has befallen them. Couples who are going through a divorce, for example, are often upset and depressed by little things that previously had not bothered them, and failure on an important examination may cause a student to become sensitive to little shortcomings in a friend that had not been noticed before. In a study that has some bearing on this discussion, Eckenrode (1984) studied the effects of major stressful events on mood and found that the immediate effect of such events is on the amount of stress evoked by smaller everyday annoyances. Therefore one interpretation of the relationship between major life events and hassles is that major events become sources of negative mood to the extent that they exacerbate the effects of hassles.

An alternative view of the relationship between the two variables is suggested by a study by Cohen, Tyrrell, and Smith (1993). Volunteer subjects were injected with common cold viruses under controlled conditions, after which the course of infections was assessed. Three measures of psychological stress were studied as possible correlates of illness. One was a measure of stress caused by major life events. Another measured the degree to which the person thought that current demands exceeded his or her ability to cope. The third was a measure of general negative affectivity (i.e., how bad the person usually feels). The results showed that the two measures of feelings of stress—perceptions of being overtaxed by demands and negative affectivity—were both positively correlated with the development of *infections*, defined as the growth of the viruses following injection. However, only the measure of stress due to negative life events was positively correlated with the development of the *symptoms* of the common cold.

Cohen and his colleagues have suggested an intriguing explanation for these findings. Possibly feelings of negative affectivity and perceived stress are dispositional states that form a baseline level of stress on a day-to-day

basis. It could also be suggested that these dispositional states are the immediate results of everyday hassles. Their effect on the person may be to inhibit
the operation of mechanisms that defend against the development of an infection following exposure to the virus, such as the body's natural immune system. In this way, background stress levels may dispose the person to develop
infections. The symptoms of the common cold, according to this hypothesis,
are inflammatory reactions to the newly developed infection, triggered by the
release of chemicals such as histamines into the circulatory system. The
occurrence of these reactions to infection is facilitated by acute stress following major life changes (Figure 11-2). This is only a hypothesis that awaits further study. It is, however, interesting to speculate on whether everyday hassles create the conditions—in this case, an infection—that can be translated
into full-blown symptoms of a disorder by subsequent major events.

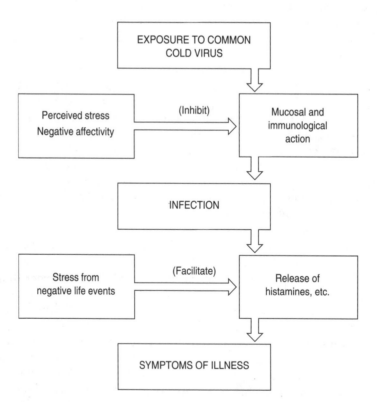

*Figure 11-2.* Hypothesized connections among dispositional affect, acute response to
life events, and development of the common cold. (Adapted from a discussion in
"Negative Life Events, Perceived Stress, Negative Affect, and Susceptibility to the
Common Cold" by S. Cohen, D. A. J. Tyrrell, and A. P. Smith, *Journal of Personality
and Social Psychology,* 1993, *64,* 131–140.)

# COGNITIVE APPRAISALS AND THE COPING PROCESS

## Primary and Secondary Appraisals

The heart of the model shown in Figure 11-1 is the two appraisals that precede the process of coping with the situation. The primary appraisal leads to the judgment of whether the situation is harmful, benign, or irrelevant to the person (Lazarus & Folkman, 1984). If it is either benign or irrelevant, and therefore harmless, a cognitive representation of the situation is formed in these terms, and the person experiences no stress. Furthermore, the emotional state of the person will be relaxed, free of worry, or even joyful. Stress and the experience of negative emotions result from a more negative primary appraisal. Such appraisals are of three types: *harm-loss*, which results from the judgment that some aversive event has already occurred and done its damage; *threat*, which follows the appraisal that the aversive event has not yet happened but is impending; and *challenge*, which results from the judgment that the situation is potentially dangerous but controllable with sufficient effort. Harm-loss appraisals are accompanied by feelings of sadness, depression, or helplessness; threat by feelings of fear, anxiety, or anger; and challenge by the experience of excitement and watchfulness. These emotional states are the immediate sources of stress.

The secondary appraisal, which comes after the initial stress has occurred, is the person's review of his or her resources for coping with the situation or with the state of stress itself. These resources are in part internal, such as feelings of competence and personal control over the situation (e.g., Thompson, Sobolew-Shubin, Galbraith, Achwankovsky & Cruzen, 1993), and in part a function of the external situation, such as social support and the availability of means for controlling the symptoms of stress. Out of this secondary appraisal emerges a coping strategy, which is the selection of one or more methods of dealing with the situation. In general terms, the means of coping fall into three classes: (1) attacking the problem itself in order to modify stress at its source, (2) modifying the meaning of the experience in a way that removes some or all of its aversive character, and (3) controlling the emotional consequences of the problem—that is, attacking the state of stress per se instead of its causes. The first of these methods of coping is usually called *problem focused* because it deals directly with the problem, and the latter two are *emotion focused* because they deal with the emotional effects of the problem without changing the objective situation at all.

Several instruments have been developed for the assessment of coping decisions. Perhaps the most widely used has been the Ways of Coping checklist (Folkman & Lazarus, 1985). It consists of a number of statements that describe actions carried out under stressful conditions, which the person reports either doing or not doing. These items are put into eight scales, one of which assesses problem-focused coping, six of which assess emotion-focused coping, and one of which measures a combination of the two. These eight scales are described in Table 11-1. This checklist and subsequent revisions of it have served as prototypes for numerous later measures of coping strategies (e.g., Carver, Scheier & Weintraub, 1989).

Some of the processes involved in coping with stress were shown in a study carried out by Folkman and Lazarus (1985) in connection with a naturally stressful situation: an important midterm examination in a university class. Students were given a stress questionnaire on three occasions. The first was two days before the examination, the second was five days after the exam but before grades had been announced, and the last came five days after grades had been posted. Included in this questionnaire was the Ways of Coping checklist (Table 11-1).

The preferred coping strategies varied across the phases of the study, suggesting that strategies were based on the changing demands of the situation. For example, problem-focused coping was used during the first period more than in either of the other periods, probably in the form of studying. Problem-focused coping then declined sharply from the first period to the second, when the exam had been completed and more studying could do no good.

## TABLE 11-1
### Scales from the Ways of Coping Checklist

*Problem-focused coping:* Attempting to analyze the problem and form a plan of action to deal with it

*Emotion-focused coping:*

    *Wishful thinking.* Wishing that the situation could be changed or would go away

    *Distancing.* Trying to forget the problem or detaching oneself from it

    *Emphasizing the positive.* Looking on the bright side; making the best of a bad arrangement

    *Self-blame.* Self-criticism; taking personal responsibility for the problem

    *Tension reduction.* Seeking relief through eating, drinking, drugs, exercise, and so on

    *Self-isolation.* Avoiding social contact; keeping problems to oneself

*Mixed problem- and emotion-focused coping:*

    *Seeking social support.* Obtaining information from others in order to work on the problem; seeking emotional support and comfort

*Source:* Adapted from "If It Changes, It Must Be a Process: Study of Emotion and Coping During Three Stages of a College Examination" by S. Folkman and R. S. Lazarus, *Journal of Personality and Social Psychology,* 1985, *48,* 150–170.

This decline in problem-focused coping during the second period was accompanied by an increase in some of the emotion-focused means, such as distancing, which represented a fatalistic "wait and see" attitude as the exam grade was being awaited. "Emphasizing the positive" was also used more during the pre-exam than the post-exam phase, probably because once the exam was over such cheerful attitudes would be replaced by realism.

A further analysis of problem- and emotion-focused coping was carried out by Folkman and her associates among a sample of middle-class married couples who experienced a range of stressful situations in their everyday lives (Folkman, Lazarus, Dunkel-Schetter, DeLongis & Gruen, 1986). The participants were studied over a six-month period, during which wives and husbands were interviewed separately once per month. On each occasion the person was asked to describe the most stressful encounter in her or his life during the preceding week. The person then made a secondary appraisal of the stressor by judging the extent to which the situation (1) could be changed, (2) had to be accepted, (3) was one about which more information was needed, and (4) was one in which the person had to hold back from doing what she or he wanted to do. The results of the primary and secondary appraisals therefore defined both the harm, threat, or challenge in the situation and the person's perception of his or her options in dealing with it. The respondent then completed a revised form of the Ways of Coping scales in order to indicate how he or she actually coped with the situation.

The means of coping that were used reflected the secondary appraisals made by the respondents. In situations thought to be changeable, people used various problem-focused means. In situations judged as having to be accepted, they used more distancing and escape avoidance (a coping strategy that combines elements of wishful thinking, tension reduction, and self-isolation; see Table 11-1). In situations perceived as requiring more information, the preferred means of coping were seeking social support and problem-focused approaches.

## Coping Effectiveness

Whether or not the model described at the beginning of this chapter and in Figure 11-1 has any validity or utility depends in the final analysis on whether coping is effective in reducing or terminating stress. Research on the use of coping strategies sometimes fails to go into the effectiveness of coping, but in recent years several studies on the subject have been reported, with mixed results. The clearest finding to emerge from these studies is that problem-focused coping appears to be more effective in reducing stress than do the emotion-focused types. The latter, in fact, have been shown to be counterproductive in that they sometimes *increase* the negative consequences of stress.

In a clear demonstration of the latter, Aldwin and Revenson (1987) analyzed the incidence of a range of symptoms associated with mental health as a function of the type of coping used. The participants in the study were asked first to recall the most stressful event in their lives during the past month, and then to report how they coped with the event. Another scale was used to assess the number of stress symptoms they experienced in the past month. The results of the study showed that the only means of coping that inhibited the development of stress symptoms were those that involved direct action against the stress-producing problem. Methods of coping that involved either escapism, such as wishful thinking, or the seeking of emotional support from others were associated with relatively *high* levels of symptom formation.

Other studies have shown, however, that some types of emotion-focused coping may have beneficial effects on *some* stress-related disorders. A study by Rohde, Lewinsohn, Tilson, and Seeley (1990) shows that emotion-focused coping can have mixed effects, depending on the method used. Participants in the study were middle-aged men and women who responded to a questionnaire that included items to assess major life events, daily hassles, and preferred ways of coping. From these data the investigators were able to derive measures of how much stress each respondent was experiencing and how he or she coped with it. Finally, the respondent's level of depression was measured both by means of questionnaire items and through a followup diagnostic interview. From the responses to the items that measured coping strategies, three major dimensions of coping were extracted through factor analysis. One was labeled Cognitive Self-Control, and it reflected a tendency to use a rational approach to the problems of life—that is, problem-focused coping. The second was called Ineffective Escapism, and it covered such behaviors as avoidance of people, passivity, and sensation-seeking behavior. The third, Solace Seeking, was derived from reports of actions aimed at taking one's mind off the problem. These latter two means of coping are therefore largely emotion focused.

Depression was assessed twice. The first measurement was made at the time that stress and the means of coping were measured, and the second was made two years later. Means of coping could therefore be analyzed in terms of both their concurrent effects of depression (at time 1) and their usefulness in predicting future depression (two years later). It is somewhat suprising that Cognitive Self-Control had no relationship to depression at either the first or second assessment of the latter. Ineffective Escapism was positively related to concurrent depression, and it also led to higher levels of future depression following stressful events that occurred over the next two years. Solace Seeking, however, led to more beneficial outcomes by buffering the effects of stressors over the two-year period and promoting lower levels of depression as a result. Thus, whether emotion-focused coping buffers one against the stressors of life or renders one vulnerable to such stressors may depend in part on what type of emotion-focused coping is used.

Emotion-focused coping may also have greater value at certain times than at others, and then it may augment the beneficial effects of problem-focused coping. Roth and Cohen (1986) have suggested that in the early stages of a traumatic episode, or in situations that are especially likely to overwhelm the person, emotion-focused coping may hold down the level of stress for a time so that the person can survive. It buys the person some time, during which information can be assimilated and more effective long-range coping strategies devised. It also provides hope and some feeling of mastery over the situation that can sustain the person until other arrangements can be made. Later, after the initial trauma has been weathered by these means, more problem-focused approaches can be taken.

## Social Support and Stress

As was noted, secondary appraisals of stressful situations include an assessment of not only coping options but also the availability of social support. Support from other people can take many forms: reassurance, guidance and advice, sympathy, direct assistance through the provision of goods and services. Social support has a generally beneficial effect on health and well-being. The reasons for this have not always been clear, however. One reason is that social support has two effects on health: a *general* effect and a *buffering* effect (Cohen & Wills, 1985). The general effect is a quality of life that is provided by the integration of the person into a social network, regardless of whether or not life is stressful. The buffer effect describes the help that is provided by social support to the person who is going through a stressful experience. This support either reduces the aversiveness of the stressor or fortifies

*Social support can be helpful to people going through stressful events in their lives.*

the person against it. This latter type of support is especially relevant to the subject of this chapter.

Most of the beneficial buffering effects of social support arise from the person's belief in the availability of such support. The actual receipt of social support is less related to well-being under stressful conditions than is the *perceived availability* (e.g., Wethington & Kessler, 1986; Heller, Swindle & Dusenbury, 1986). Just knowing that one has supportive friends who can be called upon can alleviate much of the person's stress. Received support does have some influence on stress, however, especially if it matches the particular demands of the situation (Cohen & Wills, 1985; Cutrona & Russell, 1990). For example, giving reassurance and acceptance to a person who is going through a difficult divorce may help the person feel better, whereas giving advice under such circumstances may be inappropriate and counterproductive.

# PERSONALITY, STRESS, AND COPING

As is the case in most aspects of human behavior, individual differences play an important role in the processes of stress and coping. Some people experience high levels of stress in situations that have weaker effects on other people. In addition, individuals obviously differ in the ways in which they cope with stressors, as the large body of research on ways of coping shows. Personality variables may have some influence on the coping methods that people choose. In this section we will review some of the personality variables that have been shown to influence the effects of stress on individuals.

Personality may, theoretically, moderate any of the steps in the process described in Figure 11-1. In terms of the research and theorizing that have been done to date, however, effects of personality have been studied mainly at two points. The first is at the beginning, where personality can exert an important influence on the types of situations that people select for themselves (Buss, 1987). There is evidence that some people are more likely than others to become embroiled in situations that create high levels of stress. If they experience a greater number of stressful situations than other people, they should naturally experience more stress as a result. The second place in the process at which the effects of personality have been studied is the one at which people react to the stressful situation and cope with it. In this sense, personality may interact with situational variables either to reduce or to exacerbate the intensity of the resulting stress.

## *Personality and Exposure to Situations*

The evidence is mixed regarding the first of these possibilities. In a study of women who lived in New Zealand, Fergusson and Horwood (1987) found some evidence that certain individual factors predisposed their subjects to become vulnerable to exposure to stressful life situations. Vulnerability was the product of a number of social disadvantages (e.g., low education, low socioeconomic status) and the personality variable of neuroticism, which is roughly equivalent to anxiety (Eysenck, 1967). Women who were high in neuroticism and also socially disadvantaged fell victim to a greater number of stressful events in their lives than did women who were low in neuroticism and free of social disadvantages. Fergusson and Horwood (1984), in another study with women from the same population, found that the number of stressful life events experienced was influenced to some degree by depression, with depressed women experiencing more such events than nondepressed ones.

One of the most coherent arguments for the hypothesis that personality affects the selection of life situations was made by Smith and Rhodewalt (1986) in connection with the personality variable known as the Type A Behavior Pattern. The typical Type A person has been described as one who manifests high levels of competitive striving, impatience, aggressiveness and hostility, and physiological reactivity to stressful situations (Rosenman & Chesney, 1982; Houston, 1983). Smith and Rhodewalt have reviewed a substantial body of evidence showing that Type A people "select, perceive, react to, and influence their social environment in ways that dramatically contribute to the stressfulness of their lives" (p. 234). For example, Type A's typically choose to work on problems of greater difficulty than do their opposite numbers, called Type B's, and show higher levels of physiological stress while doing so (Holmes, McGilly & Houston, 1984).

Type A's also tend in general to perceive situations as more stressful and challenging than do Type B's. For example, they set higher standards for themselves (Grimm & Yarnold, 1984) and are also more ready to recognize threats to their personal freedom (Rhodewalt & Comer, 1982). Thus Type A's tend to view any and all situations in which they must perform as more challenging than Type B's. This general tendency to regard situations in this light is another way in which Type A's place themselves under greater stress than do Type B's.

## *Personality as a Moderator of Stress Effects*

Studies of personality variables as moderators of the effects of stressful events are much more numerous than those that test the selection hypothesis. As we noted above, personality variables interact with situational variables to promote or to reduce stress. We will consider a few examples in this section.

***The Type A Behavior Pattern.*** In the previous section, the Type A Behavior Pattern (TABP) was discussed as a variable in the type of situations that people choose. The TABP has long been recognized as having a relationship with cardiovascular disease. Although the exact nature of that relationship is not clear, one possible link may be an interaction between the TABP and stressful life events. Given this pattern, the Type A person may be more likely than the Type B to experience high levels of stress in response to unpleasant life events; this stress, in turn, may be a precursor of heart trouble.

A study by Rhodewalt, Hays, Chemers, and Wysocki (1984) has shown such results. Male and female administrators at a large university completed a questionnaire that included measures of recent major life changes, physical health, psychological distress, and the TABP. Analysis of the results showed that among persons who had recently been under high levels of life stress, those who were also extreme Type A's showed higher levels of both cardiovascular symptoms and psychological distress than those who were either moderate Type A's or Type B's (Figure 11-3). Why does the TABP dispose people to develop higher levels of stress than are experienced by others? One possibility is that Type A's, while they experience greater physical stress than Type B's in difficult situations, are also more likely to deny this experience and to report themselves as being less strained than Type B's. Type A persons, in other words, may use mainly the relatively ineffective emotion-focused means of coping.

**ANXIETY AND NEUROTICISM.** The TABP is not the only personality variable that exacerbates the relationship of stressful events to stress. Two other such

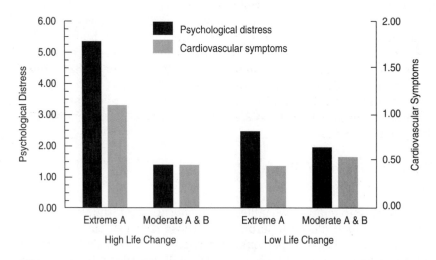

**Figure 11-3.** Psychological distress symptoms and cardiovascular symptoms of extreme Type A's, moderate Type A's, and Type B's under conditions of high and low life stress. (Drawn from data reported in "Type A Behavior, Perceived Stress, and Illness: A Person-Situation Analysis" by F. Rhodewalt, R. B. Hays, M. M. Chemers, and J. Wysocki, *Personality and Social Psychology Bulletin,* 1984, *10,* 149–159.)

variables are anxiety and neuroticism, the latter referring to a generalized tendency to feel bad and to look at the dark side of things, regardless of the objective nature of the situation. Kohn, Lafreniere, and Gurevich (1991) used a daily hassles scale to identify stress levels in the lives of a group of subjects, along with measures of trait anxiety and a psychiatric checklist used to detect stress-related symptoms. Their findings revealed an interaction between the amount of daily hassles and anxiety in predicting symptoms. The accumulation of daily hassles was positively related to the incidence of symptoms for all subjects, but especially so for those who were also high in trait anxiety.

Anxiety is also related to neuroticism. Bolger and Schilling (1991), for example, had subjects keep daily diaries for 42 days, recording both the occurrences of everyday stressors and the amount of distress that they experienced as a consequence. Subjects who had previously been classified as high in neuroticism experienced more emotional distress following stressful life changes than did subjects classified as low in neuroticism. It is interesting that Bolger and Schilling also tested for a possible effect of neuroticism on the self-selection of stressful life events (which was discussed in a previous section of this chapter), and they found virtually no effect. The influence of this variable on stress is therefore due to individual differences in reactions to stressors once they have occurred.

In a related study that involved a different methodology, Marco and Suls (1993) outfitted their subjects, who were all men, with "beepers" worn on the wrist that emitted randomly timed signals each day for eight days. At each signal the subject recorded any problems going on at the time and how distressed he felt. Subjects who were high in neuroticism were more distressed by daily problems at the time they occurred, and also slower to recover from problems experienced on the previous day, than were subjects who were low in neuroticism.

**HARDINESS.**    The variable of *hardiness* has been proposed to help explain the observation that some people, though exposed to high levels of daily stress, do not show the expected signs of psychological discomfort and poor physical health. It was introduced by Kobasa (1979), who identified three characteristics of hardy, stress-resistant people. These characteristics pertain to their primary appraisals of potentially stressful events. First, they appraise such events as being *controllable*. They are likely, therefore, to attach less harm or threat to these situations than are less hardy people. Second, hardy people tend to be highly *committed* to a positive view of themselves and their work. They therefore appraise everyday changes as normal events within a worthwhile and enjoyable situation. As a consequence, these changes are less likely to be felt as stressful than they would by a less committed person. Finally, hardy people look upon such changes not as threats but as *challenges* to be overcome, and therefore as opportunities for personal growth.

Hardiness is measured on a scale that contains items relevant to these three conceptual dimensions, and research on the effects of hardiness

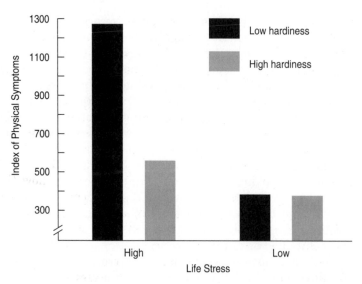

**Figure 11-4.** Reported physical illness as a function of hardiness and stressful life events. (Drawn from data reported in "Hardiness and Health: A Prospective Study" by S. C. Kobasa, S. R. Maddi, and S. Kahn, *Journal of Personality and Social Psychology,* 1982, *42,* 168–177.)

typically involves predicting illness on the basis of scores from this scale. In one such study (Kobasa, Maddi & Kahn, 1982), upper-level corporation managers completed three questionnaires separated by one-year intervals. The questionnaires contained the hardiness scale, a measure of major life events during the preceding year, and a self-report inventory of physical symptoms experienced over the past year. The results of the study showed that the respondents who had experienced relatively high levels of life stress also reported more physical illness than did those who had experienced lower levels of stress. However, respondents who scored high on the hardiness scale were less affected by stressful life events than were low scorers (Figure 11-4). A high level of hardiness did not completely obliterate the harmful effects of stress on health, but it did significantly reduce those effects.

Other studies of hardiness have taken into account the constituent factors of control, commitment, and challenge by assessing these three tendencies separately. Hull, Van Treuren, and Virnelli (1987) analyzed the three factors separately. They concluded that the three processes underlying these factors are independent phenomena that should be studied by themselves. Of the three factors, commitment and a belief in personal control were significantly related to low anxiety, optimism, and high self-esteem, whereas the challenge factor was not. However, subjects' reports of the extent to which they feel anxious in emergency situations were negatively correlated with all three factors, suggesting that the challenge factor may be related to the ways in which people react to specific situations.

Hardiness has been shown to have some relationships with coping processes, and these show some complexity. In a study of a sample of lawyers, Kobasa (1982) found that nonhardy persons tended not only to be pessimistic in their appraisals of life changes, but also to avoid serious attempts at problem solving. Belief in personal control has also been shown to affect the type of coping that people practice. Parkes (1984) has reported a study that clearly links belief in control to problem-focused coping. Subjects, who were all female student nurses, recalled an episode that occurred within the previous month and had been especially stressful; then they reported how they had appraised the event and also how they coped with it. The subject was also given a scale used to differentiate those who believe in personal control from those who tend to believe that their lives are not self-controlled. Figure 11-5 shows part of the findings from the study. Subjects reported using both problem-focused coping and "suppression," a strategy by which the stressful consequences of the event are denied and not recognized. Appraisals of the stressful situations were also classified according to how changeable the person thought the situation was versus how much she thought it could be changed with some attention and effort. Subjects who held strong beliefs in personal control (internals) responded to the appraised changeability of the situation with the appropriate coping methods. In situations that they considered changeable, they used more problem-focused coping than they did

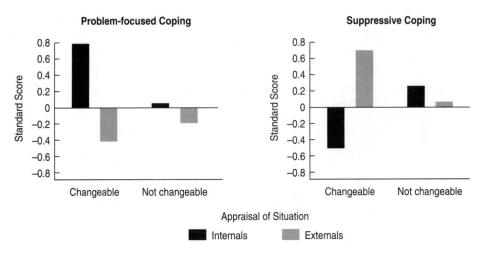

***Figure 11-5.*** Problem-focused and suppressive coping by internals and externals as a function of the appraisal of a situation as changeable or not changeable. (Adapted from "Locus of Control, Cognitive Appraisal, and Coping in Stressful Episodes" by K. R. Parkes, *Journal of Personality and Social Psychology,* 1984, 46, 655–668.)

in situations that were not considered changeable. In the latter, they opted more for suppressive coping. Persons who did not have strong beliefs in personal control (externals) did not match their coping strategies to their appraisals of the situation.

The tendency of persons with strong beliefs in personal control to use coping methods that are appropriate to the situation suggests that their coping will be more effective than that of externals. This may account for the finding reported by Shepperd and Kashani (1991) that high levels of control reduce the stressful effects of daily stressors with respect to both psychological distress and physical symptoms, and for the further finding that a belief in personal control is positively related to the effective functioning of the body's immune system (Okun, Zautra & Robinson, 1988).

***SELF-ESTEEM.***    High levels of self-esteem have a generally beneficial effect on a person's reactions to negative life events (Pearlin & Schooler, 1978). The question of why self-esteem helps a person to resist stress has been addressed in various ways. For example, self-esteem may be related to the ways in which people appraise potentially stressful changes in their lives. Campbell, Chew, and Scratchley (1991) have found that people with low self-esteem tend to rate the normal changes in their lives in more negative terms—that is, as more stressful—than do people who are high in self-esteem, and also to describe negative events as having a greater influence on they way they feel.

In addition to influencing the appraisal process, self-esteem is related to the ways in which people cope with certain kinds of negative events: those in which the person suffers a blow or threat to his or her sense of self-worth (e.g., Brown, Collins & Schmidt, 1988). When this happens, the person is motivated to restore or enhance the lost sense of self-appreciation. For various reasons, this leads the person not only to have self-aggrandizing thoughts about himself or herself, but also to derogate other people so that the self looks even better by comparison to these others (Wills, 1981). This sort of self-aggrandizing vis-á-vis other people is related to the processes of symbolic self-completion and downward social comparison that were described in Chapter 4. As was the case with those self-defense mechanisms, the person assumes desirable attributes as a defense against a loss in self-worth precipitated by some undesirable event.

Brown and Gallagher (1992) have shown that self-enhancement, relative to other people, following failure at a task is more likely to be practiced by people who are normally high in self-esteem than by people low in self-esteem. Success and failure at an experimental task were manipulated so that half of the subjects were informed that they had performed badly. Shortly after this had been done, subjects were asked to indicate the extent to which each of 48 adjectives described themselves. Half of these adjectives denoted socially desirable characteristics (e.g., imaginative, smart), and half described undesirable ones (e.g., foolish, lazy).

The overall self-ratings and other-ratings (ratings on positive adjectives minus ratings on negative adjectives) are shown in Table 11-2, along with the differences between self- and other-ratings. The strongest tendency to enhance the self relative to others was shown among subjects who were high in self-esteem and who had just failed at the task. Subjects low in self-esteem showed a slight amount of self-aggrandizement, but significantly less than that of subjects high in self-esteem. Thus coping with failure by inflating one's sense of self-worth is moderated by one's characteristic level of self-esteem.

Low self-esteem may, in fact, actually work *against* effective coping. Kernis, Brockner, and Frankel (1989) found that people who are low in self-esteem engage in *overgeneralization* of self-criticism following failure more than do those high in self-esteem. Overgeneralization is defined by Kernis and his colleagues as "the tendency for negative outcomes to make salient other feelings of personal inadequacy, possibly along dimensions that are seemingly unrelated to the initial negative outcome" (1989, p. 707). The study involved self-reports made by students in a class following an examination. Among students who did poorly on the examination, those who were low in self-esteem experienced more negative affect and a greater loss of motivation to perform well on the next test than did subjects who were high in self-esteem. In addition, self-esteem and tendencies to overgeneralize self-criticism, which were assessed by means of another scale, were significantly and negatively correlated. Kernis and his colleagues also determined that the effects of self-esteem on negative feedback from a stressful event (i.e., higher negative affect with low self-esteem) are *mediated* by the overgeneralization variable. In other words, self-esteem evokes discontent with the self because it causes the person to be more *generally* critical of the self than he or she might otherwise be.

**TABLE 11-2**
***Ratings of Self and Others Following Task Success***
***or Failure as a Function of Self-Esteem***

| | Prior Experience | | | |
| | Success | | Failure | |
| Rating | High SE* | Low SE | High SE | Low SE |
|---|---|---|---|---|
| Self | 4.35 | 3.97 | 4.41 | 4.19 |
| Other | 3.96 | 3.39 | 2.90 | 3.52 |
| Difference | 0.39 | 0.58 | 1.51 | 0.67 |

*SE = self-esteem.
*Source:* From "Coming to Terms with Failure: Private Self-Enhancement and Public Self-Effacement" by J. D. Brown and F. M. Gallagher, *Journal of Experimental Social Psychology,* 1992, *28,* 3–22.

*OPTIMISM AND HOPELESSNESS.*    Another variable that is generally associated with good outcomes for psychological and physical health is *optimism.* Scheier, Weintraub, and Carver (1986) administered the Ways of Coping checklist to subjects who had been asked to recall an especially stressful event from the recent past. Subjects had previously been tested for their level of optimism by means of a self-report scale. Optimism was related to the ways of coping preferred by the subjects; those who scored high in optimism used problem-focused coping more than did pessimists, especially when the stressful life event was considered to be controllable. Optimism was negatively related to denial and to "distancing" from the problem. Optimists tend to use problem-focused coping and to accept life stress in a realistic way as a general coping style across all stressful situations (Carver, Scheier & Weintraub, 1989).

The findings of a study by Aspinwall and Taylor (1992) agree with those of the studies cited above and also show that optimism plays a role in psychological and physical health. Optimists again were more likely to use active, problem-focused coping than were pessimists, and less likely to use defensive coping. As expected, the use of active coping was significantly related to good psychological adjustment. In addition, Aspinwall and Taylor showed that psy-

*Depending on their attributes of cause, people may react to negative life events with hopelessness and despair.*

chological well-being, which was affected by optimism, was in turn linked to physical health. Thus a tendency to be optimistic predicted good health, with psychological adjustment as an intermediary link in the relationship.

Just as optimism may attenuate the aversive effects of negative life events, feelings of *hopelessness* may dispose a person to react to such events in maladaptive ways. In Chapter 5 we noted the phenomenon of learned helplessness, which was described as a generalized feeling of lack of control in situations in which outcomes were felt not to be contingent on behavior. Learned helplessness was described as an antecedent of depression. In a revision of that theory, Abramson, Metalsky, and Alloy (1989) have downgraded the importance of noncontingency and focused on the impact of negative life events on depression. The new theory proposes a new subtype of depression based on generalized hopelessness, which is a product of both situational and personal factors. In general, the theory states that when people undergo a negative life event, they make certain judgments about the causes and consequences of that event and about themselves. To some extent these judgments are the result of situational factors that cause certain attributions to be made, and to some extent they reflect a personal tendency toward a particular attributional style.

Generalized hopelessness may come about in any of three ways: (1) when negative life events are attributed to stable and global causes (i.e., are enduring and likely to affect many aspects of one's life) and are also considered to be important, (2) when it is thought that the negative life event will have consequences that are unlikely to change or to be remediated, and to affect a large part of one's life, and (3) when the person believes that he or she is personally worthless and not likely to become any better. Regardless of which of these conditions leads to hopelessness, the development of hopelessness depression is facilitated.

## STRESS IN THE WORKPLACE

We will conclude this discussion of stress by examining briefly one of the ways in which some of the principles outlined above have been applied to a practical problem. The increased interest in stress in the 1950s and 1960s led a number of industrial and organizational psychologists to use the construct in studying the effects of working conditions on employees. Early research on the problem led to the conclusion that occupational stressors, which arise from interpersonal conflicts, physical work conditions, and certain features of organizational structure (e.g., time pressures and work overload), are associated with a range of employee disorders, among them coronary heart disease, mental health disorders, and negative emotionality and low employee morale (e.g., Kasl, 1973). The causal links between the several antecedent conditions and the observed outcomes were not always specified, but as evidence of the relationship continued to mount, the commonly accepted viewpoint was that the occupational conditions in some way caused the undesirable symptoms and affective states.

## Processes in Work Stress

In a review of the literature on occupational stress and health published in 1976, Cooper and Marshall proposed that outcomes related to negative affect and health problems are a function of two major antecedents: the conditions that prevail in the workplace and the personality of the worker. Cooper and Marshall (1976) therefore recognized that a certain set of working conditions might have undesirable effects on some workers but not on others, and that personal variables are moderators of these effects. This two-factor approach to work stress continues to be widely accepted and is, in one form or another, the basic model for more recently published ones (e.g., Arsenault & Dolan, 1983; Motowidlo, Packard & Manning, 1986).

OCCUPATIONAL STRESSORS.   Recent studies of work stress have clarified to some extent the nature of the antecedent conditions that lead to stress, the stressful outcomes, and the personality variables that moderate the connection between the two. Descriptions of the work conditions that lead to job stress vary from study to study, but a typical one has been reported by Spector, Dwyer, and Jex (1988). These researchers found that stress on the job (defined in terms of both negative affect and physical symptoms) was related to (1) a high level of ambiguity (e.g., not knowing what is expected of one by one's supervisor); (2) a low level of autonomy (i.e., a lack of decision-making power); (3) a high level of constraint (e.g., poor availability of supplies, highly restrictive rules, interruptions, equipment breakdowns); (4) a high level of conflict with other workers; and (5) a heavy workload (e.g., high demands for production, small amounts of free time). It seems clear that, to use the terminology introduced earlier in this chapter, these stressors are primarily daily hassles and not major life changes.

STRESS EFFECTS.   The main dependent variables of interest in contemporary research tend to be employees' reports of frustration, dissatisfaction, and physical symptoms (e.g., Spector, 1987), but some studies report behavioral outcomes. One example is a study by Chen and Spector (1992), which showed that antisocial actions such as aggression, theft, and sabotage were correlated with occupational stressors.

PERSONAL VARIABLES.   Among several personality variables that have been studied, two that emerge as important moderators of the effects of job stressors are (1) anxiety and (2) the Type A Behavior Pattern. Exactly how these personality variables enter into the relationship of antecedents to outcomes is not always specified (Ganster, Sime & Mayes, 1989), but the model reported by Motowidlo and coworkers (1986) suggests one interesting possibility. These investigators found that the Type A pattern was positively correlated with the *frequency* of stressful events on the job, whereas self-reported fear of negative evaluation (i.e., anxiety) was positively correlated with the *intensity* of stressful events. The first of these findings suggests that Type A persons, because of their competitiveness and impatience, are more likely to act in ways that provoke stressful events than are their less agitated Type B counterparts. The second finding suggests that after a stressful event has occurred, its intensity is moderated by the person's level of anxiety; the more anxious and fearful the person is, the more stressed he or she becomes when things go wrong.

### Coping with Work Stressors

The role of coping in occupational stress has received less attention than the processes described above; yet it would seem reasonable to assume that work stress, like any other, would vary as a function of the individual's efforts to cope with occupation-related stressors. Some studies have shown this to be the case. Schonfeld (1990), for example, reported that the use of coping strategies reduced symptoms of stress in a sample of public school teachers in a large city. This study was interesting because it examined the types of coping that were used by teachers. These tended to fall into two groups: strategies that were directed toward solving problems (e.g., seeking advice from others and taking positive action to settle problems with students), and strategies aimed at denying problems or reducing negative affect (selectively ignoring classroom problems or taking the attitude that the problems are less serious than they seem to be). Schonfeld found greater resistance to depression and psychosomatic problems in connection with problem-focused coping than with strategies designed to deny or reduce negative affect. This finding is consistent with others noted earlier (p. 285).

## CHAPTER SUMMARY

**1.** *Stress* is a term used to describe the emotional, physiological, cognitive, and behavioral reactions to either major aversive changes in one's life or an accumulation of smaller aversive events. Modern experimental research on the problem can be traced back to the work of Selye. The general adaptation syndrome in lower animals described by Selye consists of an initial alarm reaction followed by resistance to the stressor and eventual breakdown and death. Later studies of stress involved psychological variables such as predictability, control, and cognitive appraisal, all of which were shown to influence stress reactions in humans.

**2.** Modern approaches to stress are based on the assumption of a transactional relationship between humans and their environments. People react to stressful life events but also exercise some control over those events by first interpreting them and then using various strategies to cope with them.

**3.** Major catastrophes are one source of stress. The accident at the nuclear reactor at Three Mile Island (TMI) has been the subject of several studies on human stress. People who lived near TMI have shown higher levels of stress in terms of emotional, cognitive, and physiological reactions than people in comparison groups, even long after the accident. Even among people who lived near TMI, however, those who believed in personal control over events or had a high level of social support showed less severe stress than those who did not.

**4.** Everyday life events that cause a departure from ordinary routines are another source of stress. The preponderance of stress from life events is evaluated as aversive and unpleasant. Although the stress that arises from a single life change event may not be sufficient to produce stress, the effects of stressors may aggregate over a short period of time to have a collective influence.

**5.** Small everyday "hassles" also have an accumulative effect on stress. Because of their immediacy, hassles are usually felt more acutely than major life changes and are more closely linked to both psychological well-being and physical health than the latter. Hassles and major life changes tend to be moderately correlated, suggesting that the two may work together to influence stress. Major changes may generate negative affect to the extent that they generate smaller hassles or make the hassles more irritating than they would otherwise be.

**6.** The initial response to a potentially stressful situation is a primary appraisal of its subjective meaning. Events are judged to be either irrelevant, benign, or stressful. The precise nature of the latter judgment depends on whether the stressor has already been experienced, in which case the reaction is one of harm and loss, or the stressor is impending, in which case it is appraised as a either a threat or a challenge. Each of the several appraisals is accompanied by a related emotional state.

**7.** If the response to the primary appraisal is stressful, a secondary appraisal is made, whereby the person reviews his or her available resources for coping. Means of coping fall into three major categories: focusing on attacking the problem, modifying the primary appraisal in such a way as to reduce its stressful character, and controlling the emotional consequences of the problem. Several Ways of Coping scales have been devised to assess coping strategies. The coping strategy that is adopted depends to a large extent on the secondary appraisal that the person makes. Situations that are judged to be controllable, for example, tend to evoke problem-focused approaches, whereas situations considered to be unchangeable elicit emotion-focused or denial strategies.

**8.** The evidence is mixed as to what sort of coping is the most effective in the management of stress. Many studies have shown that problem-focused coping is more effective than emotion-focused, which is often associated with increased levels of stress. Other studies suggest that some types of emotion-focused coping may have some utility under certain conditions. Seeking reassurance from others, for example, may reduce depressive reactions to stressful events. Emotion-focused coping may also be especially valuable early in traumatic episodes, by protecting the person until more problem-focused coping can be carried out.

**9.** Secondary appraisals of stressful events may include considerations of available social support. A belief that such support is available has a buffering effect on situations so that people experience less stress than they would without such perceptions of support. Social support is most helpful when the type of support received matches the demands of the situation.

**10.** Individual differences in personality play two roles in the elicitation of stress by events. Certain personality characteristics predispose people to become involved in stressful situations. Persons classified as Type A's, for example, are especially likely to select situations that are stressful. Other variables either mitigate or exacerbate the stressful impact of events. The Type A Behavior Pattern, anxiety, and neuroticism all tend to be positively related to stress under harmful or threatening conditions. High levels of hardiness buffer the person against stress, mainly because hardy people have a strong sense of personal control that promotes the used of problem-focused coping. High levels of self-esteem and optimism also help to reduce stress reactions to harmful or threatening situations, whereas hopelessness contributes to the development of depression.

**11.** Some of the concepts from research on stress have been applied to work situations. Most models of work stress emphasize the interaction of occupational variables, such as job ambiguity, lack of control, conflict, constraints, and workload, with personal variables in causing stress. Anxiety and the Type A pattern have often been shown to be important moderators of job stress. As is the case with other stressors, work stress can be mitigated by coping behaviors, especially if these are problem focused.

CHAPTER **12**

# CONCLUDING COMMENTS

As the reader is well aware by now, the material covered in this book does not fit into a neat pattern. The emphasis has been on setting forth a tentative point of view about human motivation that accounts for at least much of what is known at the present time. This material comes from widely diverse research programs and theoretical positions, so that the final product lacks the coherence that might have been obtained if we had restricted our attention to one particular theory or set of assumptions.

We began in Chapter 2 with an approach to motivation organized around the construct of goals as the central element in motivation. In Chapters 3 and 4 we observed how the consideration of strategies and action control devices allows us to go beyond goal setting and to describe how goals are actually attained. In Chapters 5 and 6 we examined several basic human needs out of which incentives are constructed. Some of these have been familiar for some time: achievement, affiliation, and power. The others—competence and control—have come to the attention of motivation theorists more recently. In Chapters 7 and 8 we noted that two topics that have long been of interest to motivation theory—arousal and emotion—still generate new paradigms for investigation and prove useful in analyzing behavior. With Chapters 9, 10, and 11 we observed how some of the principles set forth in earlier chapters may extend the concept of motivation to such areas as social psychology, personality, and health psychology.

A few broad conclusions may be drawn from these matters. The first is that "energy" theories of motivation, which emphasize nondirective processes involving the activation and intensity of behavior, may not enjoy the dominant position that they once did, but are still alive and well. This does not mean, however, that we are headed back to the old days of drive theory or the concept of generalized arousal. Instead, we seem to have rediscovered, as it were, the old hedonic concept of *affect*, especially negative affect, and to have assigned to it many of the functional properties formerly subsumed by the once-favored concept of drive. Two good examples of this were seen in Chapter 9. One of the major approaches to prosocial behavior, as we observed, accounts for such behavior in terms of its utility in reducing feelings of empathic distress (Dovidio, Piliavin, Gaertner, Schroeder & Clark, 1991). According to this viewpoint, the person is "driven" to help others by the negative affect that he or she feels as a result of empathizing with the others' distress, and the behavior is terminated when this affect is reduced. In much the same way, a leading contemporary theory of aggression (Berkowitz, 1989) emphasizes negative affect in response to provoking conditions, thereby reformulating in different terminology the basic argument of the drive-centered frustration-aggression hypothesis.

The change in interest from drive to negative affect involves more than simply a shift in terms. The concept of drive described a *mechanism* of behavior that did not require, and was indeed often inimical to, any assumption of conscious awareness. As deprivation increased, drive increased, and with it the intensity of any behaviors that happened to be in progress at the time. Negative affect, on the other hand, is an *experience*, and the behavior that it motivates bears some relationship to that experience. This presupposes some level of awareness of how one feels and guarantees that cognition, at some level, is involved in motivation from the beginning. The theory of psychological reversals articulated by Apter (1989) and described in Chapter 7 is one example of a theory according to which objective conditions are translated into experiences in conscious awareness, and thence into motivated behavior. The same principle is observed in other phenomena described in the preceding chapters: stress and health, evaluation apprehension and social anxiety, altruism, and aggression, among others.

This leads us to the second conclusion that we can draw from the chapters of this book: the concept of *need* has maintained a central position in motivational psychology while changing somewhat in meaning over the years. As will be recalled from Chapter 6, Murray (1938) thought that some human needs are not part of consciousness and that we react to such needs without being aware of what we are doing. Other needs are conscious in the sense that we can describe them verbally and have a fairly good idea of how they affect our lives. As we have also noted, for many years McClelland and his associates tended to describe needs in nonconscious terms, and to relegate those motivational influences that can be described verbally to the realm of values.

More recently, however, these investigators have identified certain needs that are indeed susceptible to self-description, and they have argued that these needs are aroused primarily by social situations (Koestner, Weinberger & McClelland, 1991). This is an interesting development because it suggests that social motives are linked to certain specific needs of which people are consciously aware and which are activated by social stimuli. The model proposed in Chapter 2 outlines much the same sort of process without necessarily making a distinction between conscious and nonconscious needs. In both cases, however, the important operating element in motivated behavior is a state that results from the activation of a need by a specific social stimulus, and that then serves as an incentive for subsequent goal setting.

The older and more familiar needs for achievement, affiliation, and power are still defined in primarily affective terms (McClelland, 1985). The same may be true of the newer concepts of competence and control motivation (see Chapter 5). As we have seen, human beings appear to desire at least some degree of control over most of the situations in which they live. Being in control is desirable primarily because not being in control is aversive. Other human needs appear to be related to cognition as much as to affect. The need for cognitive structure that was reviewed in Chapter 5 is such a need. Here we see a basic need that pertains to understanding and interpretation of the environment and is therefore cognitive in nature, serving the purpose of forestalling negative affect by making the world a more orderly and less uncertain place.

The third conclusion to be drawn from this book is that the old and honorable concept of voluntarism has been brought back to a central position within the study of human motivation. We once again recognize the important role played by the will in behavior. As we noted in Chapter 1, voluntarism dominated the thinking about human action in Western society for most of its history, but it lost its privileged place with the rise of mechanistic theories in the 20th century. The development of the theory of action control, described in Chapter 3, brings volition back into the picture, along with the related concept of strategy in pursuing and striving for goals.

As was suggested in the historical review in Chapter 1, the history of human motivation (or of what has passed for the study of motivation in ages past) has reflected an interplay of two forces: affect and volition. From ancient times these have been construed as alternatives and, at some points in history, as antagonists. The tendency has been to concentrate on one more than the other, even to the point of excluding the other from consideration. The fourth conclusion to be drawn from the material reviewed in the preceding chapters is that *a complete theory of motivation must include both affect and volition.* The model presented in Chapter 2, the discussion of feedback models in Chapter 3, and the review of the principles of action control in that same chapter have together shown how volition and strategy complete the goal-setting process that was initially driven by affective variables.

We began this book by noting in the preface the many problems that have been associated with the concept of motivation in recent years. Despite all this, the idea has persisted and survived. The study of human motivation once again commands respectful attention within psychology. In this book we have examined one aspect of the revival of human motivation as an area of specialization, one that has placed a heavy emphasis on social psychology and, to a lesser degree, on organizational psychology. As was also stated in the preface, this book was not written to be a comprehensive survey of all that is known about human motivation, but instead to present a particular partisan viewpoint. Some important developments lie ahead in the field of social motivation, and we are happy just to think that we were around when it all started.

# REFERENCES

Abramson, L. Y., Metalsky, G. I., & Alloy, L. B. (1989). Hopelessness depression: A theory-based subtype of depression. *Psychological Review, 96*, 358–372.

Abramson, L. Y., Seligman, M. E. P., & Teasdale, J. D. (1978). Learned helplessness in humans: Critique and reformulation. *Journal of Abnormal Psychology, 87*, 49–74.

Aiello, J. R. (1993). Computer-based work monitoring: Electronic surveillance and its effects. *Journal of Applied Social Psychology, 23*, 499–507.

Aiello, J. R., Shao, Y., Chomiak, A., & Kolb, K. J. (1993). Social facilitation and electronic presence: Performance and stress under computer-based work monitoring. Unpublished study, Department of Psychology, Rutgers University.

Aiello, J. R., & Svec, C. M. (1993). Computer monitoring of work performance: Extending the social facilitation framework to electronic presence. *Journal of Applied Social Psychology, 23*, 537–548.

Ainsworth, M. D. S., Blehar, M. C., Waters, E., & Wall, S. (1978). *Patterns of attachment: A psychological study of the strange situation.* Hillsdale, NJ: Erlbaum.

Albert, S. (1977). Temporal comparison theory. *Psychological Review, 84*, 485–503.

Aldwin, C. A., & Revenson, T. A. (1987). Does coping help? A reexamination of the relation between coping and mental health. *Journal of Personality and Social Psychology, 53*, 337–348.

Amabile, T. M., DeJong, W., & Lepper, M. R. (1976). Effects of externally imposed deadlines on subsequent intrinsic motivation. *Journal of Personality and Social Psychology, 34*, 92–98.

Anderson, C. A. (1989). Temperature and aggression: The ubiquitous effects of heat on the occurrence of human violence. *Psychological Bulletin, 106*, 74–96.

Anderson, K. J. (1990). Arousal and the inverted-U hypothesis: A critique of Neiss's "Reconceptualizing arousal." *Psychological Bulletin, 107*, 96–100.

Apter, M. J. (1989). *Reversal theory: Motivation, emotion and personality.* London: Routledge.

Aronson, E. (1969). The theory of cognitive dissonance: A current perspective. In L. Berkowitz (Ed.), *Advances in experimental social psychology* (Vol. 4, pp. 1–34). New York: Academic Press.

Arsenault, A., & Dolan, S. (1983). The role of personality, occupation and organization in understanding the relationship between job stress, performance and absenteeism. *Journal of Occupational Psychology, 56*, 227–240.

Aspinwall, L. G., & Taylor, S. E. (1992). Modeling cognitive adaptation: A longitudinal investigation of the impact of individual differences and coping on college adjustment and performance. *Journal of Personality and Social Psychology, 63*, 989–1003.

Assor, A., Aronoff, J., & Messé, L. A. (1981). Attribute relevance as a moderator of the effects of motivation on impression formation. *Journal of Personality and Social Psychology, 41*, 789–796.

Atkinson, J. W. (1974a). The mainsprings of achievement-oriented activity. In J. W. Atkinson & J. O. Raynor (Eds.), *Motivation and achievement* (pp. 13–41). Washington, DC: Winston.

Atkinson, J. W. (1974b). Strength of motivation and efficiency of performance. In J. W. Atkinson & J. O. Raynor (Eds.), *Motivation and achievement* (pp. 193–218). Washington, DC: Winston.

Atkinson, J. W., & Birch, D. (1970). *The dynamics of action.* New York: Wiley.

Bakan, D. (1966). *The duality of human existence.* San Francisco: Jossey-Bass.

Bandura, A. (1973). *Aggression: A social learning analysis.* Englewood Cliffs, NJ: Prentice-Hall.

Bandura, A. (1977). Self-efficacy: Toward a unifying theory of behavioral change. *Psychological Review, 84,* 191–215.

Bandura, A. (1982). Self-efficacy mechanism in human agency. *American Psychologist, 37,* 122–147.

Bandura, A., Adams, N. E., Hardy, A. B., & Howells, G. N. (1980). Test of the generality of self-efficacy theory. *Cognitive Therapy and Research, 4,* 39–66.

Bandura, A., O'Leary, A., Taylor, C. B., Gauthier, J., & Gossard, D. (1987). Perceived self-efficacy and pain control: Opioid and nonopioid mechanisms. *Journal of Personality and Social Psychology, 53,* 563–571.

Bandura, A., Reese, L., & Adams, N. E. (1982). Microanalysis of action and fear arousal as a function of differential levels of perceived self-efficacy. *Journal of Personality and Social Psychology, 43,* 5–21.

Bandura, A., Taylor, C. B., Williams, S. L., Mefford, I. N., & Barchas, J. D. (1985). Catecholamine secretion as a function of perceived coping self-efficacy. *Journal of Consulting and Clinical Psychology, 53,* 406–414.

Bargh, J. A. (1990). Auto-motives: Preconscious determinants of social interaction. In E. T. Higgins & R. M. Sorrentino (Eds.), *Handbook of motivation and cognition* (Vol. 2, pp. 93–130). New York: Guilford.

Bargh, J. A., & Cohen, J. L. (1978). Mediating factors in the arousal-performance relationship. *Motivation and Emotion, 2,* 243–257.

Barnett, R. C., & Baruch, G. K. (1985). Women's involvement in multiple roles and psychological distress. *Journal of Personality and Social Psychology, 49,* 135–145.

Baron, R. S. (1986). Distraction-conflict theory: Progress and problems. In L. Berkowitz (Ed.), *Advances in experimental social psychology* (Vol. 19, pp. 1–40). New York: Academic Press.

Baron, R. S., Moore, D. L., & Sanders, G. S. (1978). Distraction as a source of drive in social facilitation research. *Journal of Personality and Social Psychology, 36,* 816–824.

Batson, C. D., Dyck, J. L., Brandt, J. R., Batson, J. G., Powell, A. L., McMaster, M. R., & Griggitt, C. (1988). Five studies testing two new egoistic alternatives to the empathy-altruism hypothesis. *Journal of Personality and Social Psychology, 55,* 52–77.

Batson, C. D., & Oleson, K. C. (1991). Current status of the empathy-altruism hypothesis. In M. S. Clark (Ed.), *Prosocial behavior* (pp. 62–85). Newbury Park, CA: Sage.

Battistich, V. A., & Aronoff, J. (1985). Perceiver, target and situational influences on social cognition: An interactional analysis. *Journal of Personality and Social Psychology, 49,* 788–798.

Baum, A., Gatchel, R. J., & Schaeffer, M. A. (1983). Emotional, behavioral, and physiological effects of chronic stress at Three Mile Island. *Journal of Consulting and Clinical Psychology, 51,* 565–572.

Baumeister, R. F. (1989). The optimal margin of illusion. *Journal of Social and Clinical Psychology, 8*, 176–189.

Baumeister, R. F., & Tice, D. M. (1990). Anxiety and social exclusion. *Journal of Social and Clinical Psychology, 9*, 165–195.

Beckmann, J., & Kuhl, J. (1984). Altering information to gain action control: Functional aspects of human information processing in decision making. *Journal of Research in Personality, 18*, 224–237.

Beh, H. C. (1990). Achievement motivation, performance and cardiovascular activity. *International Journal of Psychophysiology, 10*, 39–45.

Berger, S. M., Hampton, K. L., Carli, L. L., Grandmaison, P. S., Sadow, J. S., & Donath, C. H. (1981). Audience-induced inhibition of overt practice during learning. *Journal of Personality and Social Psychology, 40*, 479–491.

Berglas, S., & Jones, E. E. (1978). Drug choice as an internalization strategy in response to noncontingent success. *Journal of Personality and Social Psychology, 36*, 405–417.

Berkowitz, L. (1987). Mood, self-awareness, and willingness to help. *Journal of Personality and Social Psychology, 52*, 721–729.

Berkowitz, L. (1989). The frustration-aggression hypothesis: An examination and reformulation. *Psychological Bulletin, 106*, 59–73.

Berkowitz, L. (1992). *Aggression*. New York: McGraw-Hill.

Berlyne, D. E. (1960). *Conflict, curiosity and arousal*. New York: McGraw-Hill.

Berlyne, D. E. (1963). Motivational problems raised by exploratory and epistemic behavior. In S. Koch (Ed.), *Psychology: A study of a science* (Vol. 5, pp. 284–364). New York: McGraw-Hill.

Berlyne, D. E. (1966). Exploration and curiosity. *Science, 153*, 25–33.

Berlyne, D. E. (1967). Arousal and reinforcement. In D. Levine (Ed.), *Nebraska symposium on motivation* (Vol. 15, pp. 1–110). Lincoln, NE: University of Nebraska Press.

Betz, N. E., & Hackett, G. (1983). The relationship of mathematics self-efficacy expectations to the selection of science-based college majors. *Journal of Vocational Behavior, 23*, 329–345.

Betz, N. E., & Hackett, G. (1984). Applications of self-efficacy theory to understanding career choice behavior. *Journal of Social and Clinical Psychology, 4*, 279–289.

Biner, P. M., & Hammond, S. (1988). Effects of task difficulty and interruption on goal valence. *Journal of Research in Personality, 22*, 496–512.

Biner, P. M., Hua, D. M., Kidd, H. J., & Spencer, P. M. (1991). Incentive strength, need state, instrumental task difficulty, and the magnitude of goal valence. *Personality and Social Psychology Bulletin, 17*, 442–448.

Blank, T. O., Staff, I., & Shaver, P. (1976). Social facilitation of word associations: Further questions. *Journal of Personality and Social Psychology, 34*, 725–733.

Bock, M., & Klinger, E. (1986). Interaction of emotion and cognition in word recall. *Psychological Research, 48*, 99–106.

Bolger, N., & Schilling, E. A. (1991). Personality and the problems of everyday life: The role of neuroticism in exposure and reactivity to daily stressors. *Journal of Personality, 59*, 355–386.

Bolles, R. (1972). Cognition and motivation: Some historical trends. In B. Weiner (Ed.), *Cognitive views of human motivation* (pp. 1–20). New York: Academic Press.

Bowlby, J. (1980). *Attachment and loss: Vol. 3. Loss*. New York: Basic Books.

Boyatzis, R. E. (1973). Affiliation motivation. In D. C. McClelland & R. S. Steele (Eds.), *Human motivation: A book of readings* (pp. 53–81). Morristown, NJ: General Learning Press.

Bradley, G. W. (1978). Self-serving biases in the attribution process: A reexamination of the fact or fiction question. *Journal of Personality and Social Psychology, 36*, 56–71.

Brehm, J. W. (1966). *Response to loss of freedom: A theory of psychological reactance.* New York: Academic Press.

Brehm, J. W., & Self, E. A. (1989). The intensity of motivation. *Annual Review of Psychology, 40*, 109–131.

Brehm, J. W., Wright, R. A., Solomon, S., Silka, L., & Greenberg, J. (1983). Perceived difficulty, energization, and the magnitude of goal valence. *Journal of Experimental Social Psychology, 19*, 21–48.

Brickner, M. A., Harkins, S. G., & Ostrom, T. (1986). Effects of personal involvement: Thought-provoking implications for social loafing. *Journal of Personality and Social Psychology, 51*, 763–769.

Broadhurst, P. L. (1957). The interaction of task difficulty and emotion: The Yerkes-Dodson Law revived. *Acta Psychologica, 16*, 321–338.

Brody, N. (1980). Social motivation. *Annual Review of Psychology, 31*, 143–168.

Brody, N. (1983). *Human motivation: Commentary on goal-directed action.* New York: Academic Press.

Brown, J. D., Collins, R. L., & Schmidt, G. W. (1988). Self-esteem and direct versus indirect forms of self-enhancement. *Journal of Personality and Social Psychology, 55*, 445–453.

Brown, J. D., & Gallagher, F. M. (1992). Coming to terms with failure: Private self-enhancement and public self-effacement. *Journal of Experimental Social Psychology, 28*, 3–22.

Brown, J. S., & Farber, I. E. (1951). Emotions conceptualized as intervening variables—with suggestions toward a theory of frustration. *Psychological Bulletin, 48*, 465–495.

Buck, R. (1980). Nonverbal behavior and the theory of emotion: The facial feedback hypothesis. *Journal of Personality and Social Psychology, 38*, 811–824.

Buck, R. (1985). Prime theory: An integrated view of motivation and emotion. *Psychological Review, 92*, 389–413.

Bullock, W. A., & Gilliland, K. (1993). Eysenck's arousal theory of introversion-extraversion: A converging measures investigation. *Journal of Personality and Social Psychology, 64*, 113–123.

Burger, J. M. (1985). Desire for control and achievement-related behaviors. *Journal of Personality and Social Psychology, 48*, 1520–1533.

Burger, J. M. (1989). Negative reactions to increases in perceived personal control. *Journal of Personality and Social Psychology, 56*, 246–256.

Burger, J. M. (1991a). Personality and control. In V. J. Derlega, B. A. Winstead & W. H. Jones (Eds.), *Contemporary research in personality* (pp. 285–312). Chicago: Nelson-Hall.

Burger, J. M. (1991b). The effects of desire for control in situations with chance-determined outcomes: Gambling behavior in lotto and bingo players. *Journal of Research in Personality, 25*, 196–204.

Burger, J. M. (1992). *Desire for control: Personality, social, and clinical perspectives.* New York: Plenum.

Burger, J. M., & Hemans, L. T. (1988). Desire for control and the use of attribution processes. *Journal of Personality, 56*, 531–546.

Buss, A. H., & Plomin, R. (1984). *Temperament: Early developing personality traits.* Hillsdale, NJ: Erlbaum.

Buss, D. M. (1987). Selection, evocation, and manipulation. *Journal of Personality and Social Psychology, 53*, 1214–1221.

Cacioppo, J. T., & Petty, R. E. (1982). The need for cognition. *Journal of Personality and Social Psychology, 42*, 116–131.

Cacioppo, J. T., Petty, R. E., Kao, C. F., & Rodriguez, R. (1986). Central and peripheral routes to persuasion: An individual difference perspective. *Journal of Personality and Social Psychology, 51*, 1032–1043.

Cacioppo, J. T., Petty, R. E., Losch, M. E., & Kim, H. S. (1986). Electromyographic activity over facial muscle regions can differentiate the valence and intensity of affective reactions. *Journal of Personality and Social Psychology, 50*, 260–268.

Campbell, J. D., Chew, B., & Scratchley, L. S. (1991). Cognitive and emotional reactions to daily events: The effects of self-esteem and self-complexity. *Journal of Personality, 59*, 473–505.

Cannon, W. B. (1929). *Bodily changes in pain, hunger, fear, and rage* (2nd ed.). New York: Appleton-Century-Crofts.

Cannon, W. B. (1939). *The wisdom of the body* (rev. ed.). New York: Norton.

Cantor, J. R., Zillmann, D., & Bryant, J. (1975). Enhancement of experienced sexual arousal in response to erotic stimuli through misattribution of unrelated residual excitation. *Journal of Personality and Social Psychology, 32*, 69–75.

Carver, C. S. (1974). Facilitation of physical aggression through objective self-awareness. *Journal of Experimental Social Psychology, 10*, 365–370.

Carver, C. S. (1975). Physical aggression as a function of objective self-awareness and attitudes toward punishment. *Journal of Experimental Social Psychology, 11*, 510–519.

Carver, C. S., Antoni, M., & Scheier, M. F. (1985). Self-consciousness and self-assessment. *Journal of Personality and Social Psychology, 48*, 117–124.

Carver, C. S., Blaney, P. H., & Scheier, M. F. (1979). Reassertion and giving up: The interactive role of self-directed attention and outcome expectancy. *Journal of Personality and Social Psychology, 37*, 1859–1870.

Carver, C. S., & Scheier, M. F. (1989). Expectancies and coping: From test anxiety to pessimism. In R. Schwartzer, H. M. van der Ploeg & C. D. Spielberger (Eds.), *Advances in test anxiety research* (Vol. 6, pp. 3–11). Amsterdam: Swets & Zeitlinger.

Carver, C. S., & Scheier, M. F. (1990a). Origins and functions of positive and negative affect: A control-process view. *Psychological Review, 97*, 19–35.

Carver, C. S., & Scheier, M. F. (1990b). Principles of self-regulation: Action and emotion. In E. T. Higgins & R. M. Sorrentino (Eds.), *Handbook of motivation and cognition* (Vol. 2, pp. 3–52). New York: Guilford.

Carver, C. S., Scheier, M. F., & Weintraub, J. K. (1989). Assessing coping strategies: A theoretically based approach. *Journal of Personality and Social Psychology, 56*, 267–283.

Cervone, D. (1989). Effects of envisioning future activities on self-efficacy judgments and motivation: An availability heuristic interpretation. *Cognitive Therapy and Research, 13*, 247–261.

Cervone, D., & Peake, P. K. (1986). Anchoring, efficacy, and action: The influence of judgmental heuristics on self-efficacy judgments and behavior. *Journal of Personality and Social Psychology, 50*, 492–501.

Chen, P. Y., & Spector, P. E. (1992). Relationships of work stressors with aggression, withdrawal, theft and substance abuse: An exploratory study. *Journal of Occupational and Organizational Psychology, 65*, 177–184.

Chesney, A. A., & Locke, E. A. (1991). Relationships among goal difficulty, business strategies, and performance on a complex management simulation task. *Academy of Management Journal, 34,* 400–424.

Cialdini, R. B., Baumann, D. J., & Kenrick, D. T. (1981). Insights from sadness: A three-step model of the development of altruism as hedonism. *Developmental Review, 1,* 207–223.

Cialdini, R. B., & Kenrick, D. T. (1976). Altruism as hedonism: A social development perspective on the relationship of negative mood state and helping. *Journal of Personality and Social Psychology, 34,* 907–914.

Cialdini, R. B., & Richardson, K. D. (1980). Two indirect tactics of image management: Basking and blasting. *Journal of Personality and Social Psychology, 39,* 406–415.

Clark, M. S., & Mills, J. (1979). Interpersonal attraction in exchange and communal relationships. *Journal of Personality and Social Psychology, 37,* 12–24.

Clark, M. S., Oulette, R., Powell, M., & Milberg, S. (1987). Recipient's mood, relationship type, and helping. *Journal of Personality and Social Psychology, 53,* 94–103.

Cofer, C. (1980). The history of the concept of motivation. *Journal of the History of the Behavioral Sciences, 17,* 48–53.

Cohen, S. (1980). Aftereffects of stress on human performance and social behavior: A review of research and theory. *Psychological Bulletin, 88,* 82–108.

Cohen, S., & Edwards, J. R. (1989). Personality characteristics as moderators of the relationship between stress and disorder. In R. W. J. Neufeld (Ed.), *Advances in the investigation of psychological stress* (pp. 235–283). New York: Wiley.

Cohen, S., Tyrrell, D. A. J., & Smith, A. P. (1993). Negative life events, perceived stress, negative affect, and susceptibility to the common cold. *Journal of Personality and Social Psychology, 64,* 131–140.

Cohen, S., & Wills, T. A. (1985). Stress, social support, and the buffering hypothesis. *Psychological Bulletin, 98,* 310–357.

Cooper, C. L., & Marshall, J. (1976). Occupational sources of stress: A review of the literature relating to coronary heart disease and mental ill health. *Journal of Occupational Psychology, 49,* 11–28.

Cooper, J., & Fazio, R. H. (1984). A new look at dissonance theory. In L. Berkowitz (Ed.), *Advances in experimental social psychology* (Vol. 7, pp. 229–262). New York: Academic Press.

Crozier, J. B. (1974). Verbal and exploratory responses to sound sequences varying in uncertainty level. In D. E. Berlyne (Ed.), *Studies in the new experimental aesthetics* (pp. 27–90). New York: Wiley.

Csikszentmihalyi, M. (1990). *Flow: The psychology of optimal experience.* New York: Harper & Row.

Cutrona, C. E., & Russell, D. W. (1990). Type of social support and specific stress: Toward a theory of optimal matching. In B. R. Sarason, I. G. Sarason & G. R. Pierce (Eds.), *Social support: An interactional view* (pp. 319–366). New York: Wiley.

DaGloria, J. (1984). Frustration, aggression, and the sense of justice. In Mummendey, A. (Ed.), *Social psychology of aggression: From individual behavior to social interaction* (pp. 127–141). New York: Springer-Verlag.

DaGloria, J., & DeRidder, R. (1977). Aggression in dyadic interaction. *European Journal of Social Psychology, 7,* 189–219.

Darlington, R. B., & Macker, C. E. (1966). Displacement of guilt-produced altruistic behavior. *Journal of Personality and Social Psychology, 4,* 442–443.

Darwin, C. (1859/1936). *The orgin of species.* New York: Modern Library.

Davidson, L. M., Baum, A., & Collins, D. L. (1982). Stress and control-related problems at Three Mile Island. *Journal of Applied Social Psychology, 12,* 349–359.

Davidson, R. J. (1984). Hemispheric asymmetry and emotion. In K. R. Scherer & P. Ekman (Eds.), *Approaches to emotion* (pp. 39–57). Hillsdale, NJ: Erlbaum.

Davidson, R. J., Ekman, P., Saron, R. D., Senulis, J. A., & Friesen, W. V. (1990). Approach-withdrawal and cerebral asymmetry: Emotional expression and brain physiology. *Journal of Personality and Social Psychology, 58,* 330–341.

Davies, D. R., & Jones, D. M. (1975). The effects of noise and incentive upon attention in short-term memory. *British Journal of Psychology, 66,* 61–68.

deCharms, R., & Carpenter, V. (1968). Measuring motivation in culturally disadvantaged school children. In H. J. Klausmeier & G. T. O'Hearn (Eds.), *Research and development toward the improvement of education* (pp. 31–41). Madison, WI: Educational Research Services.

Deci, E. L. (1971). Effects of externally mediated rewards on intrinsic motivation. *Journal of Personality and Social Psychology, 18,* 105–115.

Deci, E. L. (1975). *Intrinsic motivation.* New York: Plenum.

Deci, E. L., Betley, G., Kahle, J., Abrams, L., & Porac, J. (1981). When trying to win: Competition and intrinsic motivation. *Personality and Social Psychology Bulletin, 7,* 79–83.

Deci, E. L., & Ryan, R. M. (1985). *Intrinsic motivation and self-determination in human behavior.* New York: Plenum.

Deci, E. L., & Ryan, R. M. (1987). The support of autonomy and the control of behavior. *Journal of Personality and Social Psychology, 53,* 1024–1037.

DeLongis, A., Coyne, J. C., Dakof, G., Folkman, S., & Lazarus, R. S. (1982). Relationships of daily hassles, uplifts, and major life events to health status. *Health Psychology, 1,* 119–136.

DeLongis, A., Folkman, S., & Lazarus, R. S. (1988). The impact of daily stress on health and mood: Psychological and social resources as mediators. *Journal of Personality and Social Psychology, 54,* 486–495.

Dembroski, T. M., MacDougall, J. M., Williams, R. B., Haney, T. L., & Blumenthal, J. A. (1985). Components of Type A, hostility, and anger-in: Relationship to angiographic findings. *Psychosomatic Medicine, 47,* 219–233.

Dewey, J. (1897). The psychology of effort. *Psychological Review, 6,* 43–56.

Diener, C. I., & Dweck, C. S. (1978). An analysis of learned helplessness: Continuous changes in performance, strategy and achievement cognitions following failure. *Journal of Personality and Social Psychology, 36,* 451–462.

Dodge, K. A. (1980). Social cognition and children's aggressive behavior. *Child Development, 51,* 162–170.

Dodge, K. A., Murphy, R. R., & Buchsbaum, K. (1984). The assessment of intention-cue detection skills in children: Implications for developmental psychopathology. *Child Development, 55,* 163–173.

Dollard, J., Doob, L. W., Miller, N. E., Mowrer, O. H., & Sears, R. R. (1939). *Frustration and aggression.* New Haven, CT: Yale University Press.

Dovidio, J. F. (1984). Helping behavior and altruism: An empirical and conceptual overview. In L. Berkowitz (Ed.), *Advances in experimental social psychology* (Vol. 17, pp. 361–427). New York: Academic Press.

Dovidio, J. F., Piliavin, J. A., Gaertner, S. L., Schroeder, D. A., & Clark, R. D., III. (1991). The arousal: cost-reward model and the process of intervention: A review of the evidence. In M. S. Clark (Ed.), *Prosocial behavior* (pp. 86–118). Newbury Park, CA: Sage.

Duffy, E. (1962). *Activation and behavior*. New York: Wiley.

Duval, S., Duval, V. H., & Neely, R. (1979). Self-focus, felt responsibility, and helping behavior. *Journal of Personality and Social Psychology, 37*, 1769–1778.

Duval, S., & Wicklund, R. A. (1972). *A theory of objective self-awareness*. New York: Academic Press.

Dweck, C. S., & Elliott, E. S. (1983). Achievement motivation. In E. M. Hetherington (Ed.), *Handbook of child psychology: Vol. 4. Socialization, personality, and social development* (4th ed. pp. 643–691). New York: Wiley.

Dweck, C. S., & Leggett, E. L. (1988). A social-cognitive approach to motivation and personality. *Psychological Review, 95*, 256–273.

Easterbrook, J. A. (1959). The effect of emotion on cue utilization and organization of behavior. *Psychological Review, 66*, 187–201.

Eckenrode, J. (1984). Impact of chronic and acute stressors on daily reports of mood. *Journal of Personality and Social Psychology, 46*, 907–918.

Edwards, A. L. (1957). *The social desirability variable in personality assessment and research*. New York: Dryden Press.

Eibl-Eibesfeldt, I. (1970). *Ethology*. New York: Holt, Rinehart & Winston.

Eisenberg, N., & Miller, P. A. (1987). The relation of empathy to prosocial and related behaviors. *Psychological Bulletin, 101*, 91–119.

Ekman, P. (1984). Expression and the nature of emotion. In K. R. Scherer & P. Ekman (Eds.), *Approaches to emotion* (pp. 319–344). Hillsdale, NJ: Erlbaum.

Ekman, P., Friesen, W. V., & Ancoli, S. (1980). Facial signals of emotional experience. *Journal of Personality and Social Psychology, 39*, 1125–1134.

Ekman, P., Levenson, R. W., & Friesen, W. V. (1983). Autonomic nervous system activity distinguishes among emotions. *Science, 221*, 1208–1210.

Ellenberger, H. (1970). *The discovery of the unconscious*. New York: Basic Books.

Elliott, E. S., & Dweck, C. S. (1988). Goals: An approach to motivation and achievement. *Journal of Personality and Social Psychology, 54*, 5–12.

Elliott, R. (1969). Tonic heart rate: Experiments on the effects of collative variables lead to a hypothesis about its motivational significance. *Journal of Personality and Social Psychology, 12*, 211–228.

Emmons, R. (1986). The personal striving approach to personality. In L. Pervin (Ed.), *Goal concepts in personality and social psychology* (pp. 87–126). Hillsdale, NJ: Erlbaum.

Emmons, R. A., & King, L. A. (1988). Conflict among personal strivings: Immediate and long-term implications for psychological and physical well-being. *Journal of Personality and Social Psychology, 54*, 1040–1048.

Erdelyi, M. H. (1974). A new look at the new look: Perceptual defense and vigilance. *Psychological Review, 81*, 1–25.

Erez, M. (1977). Feedback: A necessary condition for the goal setting-performance relationship. *Journal of Applied Psychology, 62*, 624–627.

Erez, M., & Zidon, I. (1984). Effect of goal acceptance on the relationship of goal difficulty to performance. *Journal of Applied Psychology, 69*, 69–78.

Erikson, E. (1963). *Childhood and society*. New York: Norton.

Ewart, C. K., Taylor, C. B., Reese, L. B., & Debusk, R. F. (1984). Effects of early post-myocardial infarction exercise testing on self-perception and subsequent physical activity. *American Journal of Cardiology, 51*, 1076–1080.

Eysenck, H. J. (1967). *The biological basis of personality*. Springfield, IL: Thomas.

Feeney, J. A., & Noller, P. (1990). Attachment style as a predictor of adult romantic relationships. *Journal of Personality and Social Psychology, 58,* 281–291.

Fehr, F. S., & Stern, J. A. (1970). Peripheral physiological variables and emotion: The James-Lange theory revisited. *Psychological Bulletin, 74,* 411–424.

Felson, R. B. (1984). Patterns of aggressive social interaction. In A. Mummendey (Ed.), *Social psychology of aggression: From individual behavior to social interaction.* (pp. 107–126). New York: Springer-Verlag.

Feltz, D. L., & Mugno, D. A. (1983). A replication of the path analysis of the causal elements in Bandura's theory of self-efficacy and the influence of autonomic perception. *Journal of Sport Psychology, 5,* 263–277.

Ferguson, T. J., & Rule, B. G. (1983). An attributional perspective on anger and aggression. In R. G. Geen & E. Donnerstein (Eds.), *Aggression: Theoretical and empirical reviews. Vol. 1: Theoretical and methodological issues* (pp. 41–74). New York: Academic Press.

Fergusson, D. M., & Horwood, L. J. (1984). Life events and depression in women: A structural equation model. *Psychological Medicine, 14,* 881–889.

Fergusson, D. M., & Horwood, L. J. (1987). Vulnerability to life events exposure. *Psychological Medicine, 17,* 739–749.

Festinger, L. (1954). A theory of social comparison processes. *Human Relations, 7,* 117–140.

Festinger, L. (1957). *A theory of cognitive dissonance.* Evanston, IL: Row Peterson.

Field, T. M., Woodson, R., Greenberg, R., & Cohen, D. (1982). Discrimination and imitation of facial expression by neonates. *Science, 218,* 179–181.

Fiske, S. T., & Pavelchak, M. A. (1986). Category-based versus piecemeal-based affective responses. In R. M. Sorrentino & E. T. Higgins (Eds.), *Handbook of motivation and cognition* (Vol. 1, pp. 167–203). New York: Guilford.

Fleming, L., Baum, A., Gisriel, M. M., & Gatchel, R. J. (1985). Mediating influences of social support at Three Mile Island. *Journal of Human Stress, 8,* 14–22.

Folkman, S., & Lazarus, R. S. (1985). If it changes, it must be a process: Study of emotion and coping during three stages of a college examination. *Journal of Personality and Social Psychology, 48,* 150–170.

Folkman, S., Lazarus, R. S., Dunkel-Schetter, C., DeLongis, A., & Gruen, R. J. (1986). Dynamics of a stressful encounter: Cognitive appraisal, coping, and encounter outcomes. *Journal of Personality and Social Psychology, 50,* 992–1003.

Ford, D. H., & Ford, M. E. (1987). Humans as self-constructing living systems: An overview. In M. E. Ford & D. H. Ford (Eds.), *Humans as self-constructing living systems: Putting the framework to work* (pp. 1–46). Hillsdale NJ: Erlbaum.

Fowles, D. C. (1983). Motivational effects on heart rate and electrodermal activity: Implications for research on personality and psychopathology. *Journal of Research in Personality, 17,* 48–71.

Fowles, D. C., Fisher, A. E., & Tranel, D. T. (1982). The heart beats to reward: The effect of monetary incentive on heart rate. *Psychophysiology, 19,* 506–513.

Freud, S. (1915/1963). Instincts and their vicissitudes. In P. Reiff (Ed.), *Sigmund Freud: General psychological theory.* New York: Collier Books.

Freud, S. (1920/1959). *Beyond the pleasure principle.* New York: Bantam Books.

Frey, K. S., & Ruble, D. N. (1990). Strategies for comparative evaluation: Maintaining a sense of competence across the life span. In R. J. Sternberg & J. Kolligian, Jr. (Eds.), *Competence considered* (pp. 167–189). New Haven, CT: Yale University Press.

Frijda, N. H. (1986). *The emotions.* Cambridge, U. K. : Cambridge University Press.

Frijda, N. H., Kuipers, P., & ter Schure, E. (1989). Relations among emotion, appraisal, and emotional action readiness. *Journal of Personality and Social Psychology*, *57*, 212–228.

Furedy, J. J., & Biederman, G. B. (1976). Preference for signaled shock phenomenon: Direct and indirect evidence for modifiability factors in the shuttlebox. *Animal Learning and Behavior*, *4*, 1–5.

Gaertner, S. L., & Dovidio, J. F. (1977). The subtlety of white racism, arousal, and helping. *Journal of Personality and Social Psychology*, *35*, 691–707.

Ganster, D. C., Sime, W. E., & Mayes, B. T. (1989). Type A behavior in the work setting: A review and some new data. In A. W. Siegman & T. M. Dembroski (Eds.), *In search of coronary-prone behavior: Beyond Type A* (pp. 169–194). Hillsdale, NJ: Erlbaum.

Gardner, H. (1985). *The mind's new science: A history of the cognitive revolution*. New York: Basic Books.

Gatchel, R. J., Schaeffer, M. A., & Baum, A. (1985). A psychophysiological field study of stress at Three Mile Island. *Psychophysiology*, *22*, 175–181.

Geen, R. G. (1968). Effects of frustration, attack, and prior training in aggressiveness upon aggressive behavior. *Journal of Personality and Social Psychology*, *9*, 316–321.

Geen, R. G. (1976). Test anxiety, observation, and the range of cue utilization. *British Journal of Social and Clinical Psychology*, *15*, 253–259.

Geen, R. G. (1978). Effects of attack and uncontrollable noise on aggression. *Journal of Research in Personality*, *12*, 15–29.

Geen, R. G. (1979). Effects of being observed on learning following success and failure experiences. *Motivation and Emotion*, *3*, 355–371.

Geen, R. G. (1980). Test anxiety and cue utilization. In I. G. Sarason (Ed.), *Test anxiety: Theory, research, and applications* (pp. 43–61). Hillsdale, NJ: Erlbaum.

Geen, R. G. (1981). Effects of being observed on persistence at an insoluble task. *British Journal of Social Psychology*, *20*, 211–216.

Geen, R. G. (1983). Evaluation apprehension and the social facilitation/inhibition of learning. *Motivation and Emotion*, *7*, 203–212.

Geen, R. G. (1984). Preferred stimulation levels in introverts and extraverts: Effects on arousal and performance. *Journal of Personality and Social Psychology*, *46*, 1303–1312.

Geen, R. G. (1985). Evaluation apprehension and response withholding in solution of anagrams. *Personality and Individual Differences*, *6*, 293–298.

Geen, R. G. (1987). Test anxiety and behavioral avoidance. *Journal of Research in Personality*, *21*, 481–488.

Geen, R. G. (1989). Alternative conceptions of social facilitation. In P. Paulus (Ed.), *Psychology of group influence* (2nd ed., pp. 15–51). Hillsdale, NJ: Erlbaum.

Geen, R. G. (1990). *Human aggression*. Pacific Grove, CA: Brooks/Cole.

Geen, R. G., Stonner, D., & Shope, G. L. (1975). The facilitation of aggression by aggression: Evidence against the catharsis hypothesis. *Journal of Personality and Social Psychology*, *31*, 721–726.

Geen, R. G., Thomas, S. L., & Gammill, P. (1988). Effects of evaluation and coaction on state anxiety and anagram performance. *Personality and Individual Differences*, *9*, 411–415.

Geer, J. H., Davison, G. C., & Gatchel, R. I. (1970). Reduction of stress in humans through nonveridical perceived control of aversive stimulation. *Journal of Personality and Social Psychology*, *16*, 731–738.

Gibbons, F. X. (1986). Social comparison and depression: Company's effect on misery. *Journal of Personality and Social Psychology, 51,* 140–148.

Gibbons, F. X., & Gerrard, M. (1989). Effects of upward and downward social comparison on mood states. *Journal of Social and Clinical Psychology, 8,* 14–31.

Gibbons, F. X., & McCoy, S. B. (1991). Self-esteem, similarity, and reactions to active versus passive downward comparison. *Journal of Personality and Social Psychology, 60,* 414–424.

Goethals, G. R. (1986). Social comparison theory: Psychology from the lost and found. *Personality and Social Psychology Bulletin, 12,* 261–278.

Goethals, G. R., & Darley, J. M. (1987). Social comparison theory: Self-evaluation and group life. In G. R. Goethals & B. Mullen (Eds.), *Theories of group behavior* (pp. 21–47). New York: Springer-Verlag.

Gollwitzer, P. M. (1990). Action phases and mind-sets. In E. T. Higgins & R. M. Sorrentino (Eds.), *Handbook of motivation and cognition* (Vol. 2, pp. 53–92). New York: Guilford.

Gollwitzer, P. M., Heckhausen, H., & Steller, B. (1990). Deliberative and implemental mind-sets: Cognitive tuning toward congruous thoughts and information. *Journal of Personality and Social Psychology, 59,* 1119–1127.

Gollwitzer, P. M., & Kinney, R. F. (1989). Effects of deliberative and implemental mind-sets on illusion of control. *Journal of Personality and Social Psychology, 56,* 531–542.

Gollwitzer, P. M., & Wicklund, R. A. (1985). Self-symbolizing and neglect of others' perspectives. *Journal of Personality and Social Psychology, 48,* 702–715.

Gollwitzer, P. M., Wicklund, R. A., & Hilton, J. L. (1982). Admission of failure and symbolic self-completion: Extending Lewinian theory. *Journal of Personality and Social Psychology, 43,* 358–371.

Greenberg, J., & Musham, C. (1981). Avoiding and seeking self-focused attention. *Journal of Research in Personality, 15,* 191–200.

Greenberg, J., Psyzczynski, T., Solomon, S., Rosenblatt, A., Veeder, M., Kirkland, S., & Lyon, D. (1990). Evidence for terror management theory II: The effects of mortality salience on reactions to those who threaten or bolster the cultural worldview. *Journal of Personality and Social Psychology, 58,* 308–318.

Greenwald, A. G., & Ronis, D. L. (1978). Twenty years of cognitive dissonance: Case study of the evolution of a theory. *Psychological Review, 85,* 53–57.

Grimm, L., & Yarnold, P. (1984). Performance standards and the Type A behavior pattern. *Cognitive Therapy and Research, 8,* 59–66.

Guerin, B. (1983). Social facilitation and social monitoring: A test of three models. *British Journal of Social Psychology, 22,* 203–214.

Guerin, B. (1986). Mere presence effects in humans: A review. *Journal of Experimental Social Psychology, 22,* 38–77.

Hamilton, J. O. (1974). Motivation and risk-taking behavior. *Journal of Personality and Social Psychology, 29,* 856–864.

Harackiewicz, J. M., Abrahams, S., & Wageman, R. (1987). Performance evaluation and intrinsic motivation: The effects of evaluative focus, rewards, and achievement orientation. *Journal of Personality and Social Psychology, 53,* 1015–1023.

Harackiewicz, J. M., & Manderlink, G. (1984). A process analysis of the effects of performance-contingent rewards on intrinsic motivation. *Journal of Experimental Social Psychology, 20,* 531–551.

Harackiewicz, J. M., Manderlink, G., & Sansone, C. (1985). Rewarding pinball wizardry: Effects of evaluation and cue value on intrinsic interest. *Journal of Personality and Social Psychology, 47*, 287–300.

Harkins, S. G. (1987). Social loafing and social facilitation. *Journal of Experimental Social Psychology, 23*, 1–18.

Harkins, S. G., & Jackson, J. M. (1985). The role of evaluation in eliminating social loafing. *Personality and Social Psychology Bulletin, 11*, 456–465.

Harlow, H. F. (1958). The nature of love. *American Psychologist, 13*, 673–685.

Harter, S. (1981). A model of mastery motivation in children: Individual differences and developmental change. In W. A. Collins (Ed.), *Aspects of the development of competence: The Minnesota symposia on child psychology* (Vol. 14, pp. 215–255). Hillsdale, NJ: Erlbaum.

Harter, S. (1990). Causes, correlates, and the functional role of global self-worth: A life-span perspective. In R. J. Sternberg & J. Kolligian, Jr. (Eds.), *Competence considered* (pp. 67–97). New Haven, CT: Yale University Press.

Hazan, C., & Shaver, P. (1987). Romantic love conceptualized as an attachment process. *Journal of Personality and Social Psychology, 52*, 511–524.

Hazan, C., & Shaver, P. (1990). Love and work: An attachment-theoretical perspective. *Journal of Personality and Social Psychology, 59*, 270–280.

Hebb, D. O. (1955). Drives and the C.N.S. (conceptual nervous system). *Psychological Review, 62*, 243–254.

Heckhausen, H., & Gollwitzer, P. M. (1987). Thought contents and cognitive functioning in motivational versus volitional states of mind. *Motivation and Emotion, 11*, 101–120.

Heckhausen, H., & Strang, H. (1988). Efficiency under record performance demands: Exertion control—an individual difference variable? *Journal of Personality and Social Psychology, 55*, 489–498.

Heider, F. (1958). *The psychology of interpersonal relations*. New York: Wiley.

Heller, K., Swindle, R. W., Jr., & Dusenbury, L. (1986). Component social support processes: Comments and integration. *Journal of Consulting and Clinical Psychology, 54*, 466–470.

Herrnstein, R. S. (1972). Nature as nurture: Behaviorism and the instinct doctrine. *Behaviorism, 1*, 23–52.

Higgins, E. T. (1987). Self discrepancy: A theory relating self and affect. *Psychological Review, 94*, 319–340.

Higgins, E. T. (1989). Self-discrepancy theory: What patterns of self-beliefs cause people to suffer? In L. Berkowitz (Ed.), *Advances in experimental social psychology* (Vol. 22, pp. 93–136). New York: Academic Press.

Higgins, E. T., Bond, R. N., Klein, R., & Strauman, T. (1986). Self-discrepancies and emotional vulnerability: How magnitude, accessibility, and type of discrepancy influence affect. *Journal of Personality and Social Psychology, 51*, 5–15.

Hilgard, E. R. (1980). The trilogy of mind: Cognition, affection, and conation. *Journal of the History of the Behavioral Sciences, 16*, 107–117.

Hilgard, E. R. (1987). *Psychology in America: A historical survey*. San Diego: Harcourt Brace Jovanovich.

Hiroto, D. S., & Seligman, M. E. P. (1975). Generality of learned helplessness in man. *Journal of Personality and Social Psychology, 31*, 311–327.

Hockey, R. (1979). Stress and cognitive components of skilled performance. In V. Hamilton & D. M. Warburton (Eds.), *Human stress and cognition: An information-processing approach* (pp. 141–177). New York: Wiley.

Hogan, R. (1983). A socioanalytic theory of personality. In M. Page & R. Dienstbier

(Eds.), *Nebraska symposium on motivation* (Vol. 31, pp. 55–89). Lincoln, NE: University of Nebraska Press.

Hokanson, J. E., & Edelman, R. (1966). Effects of three social responses on vascular processes. *Journal of Personality and Social Psychology, 3,* 442–447.

Hokanson, J. E., Willers, K. R., & Koropsak, E. (1968). The modification of autonomic responses during aggressive interchanges. *Journal of Personality, 36,* 386–404.

Hollenbeck, J. R., & Klein, H. J. (1987). Goal commitment and the goal-setting process: Problems, prospects, and proposals for future research. *Journal of Applied Psychology, 72,* 212–220.

Hollenbeck, J. R., Williams, C. R., & Klein, H. J. (1989). An empirical examination of the antecedents of commitment to difficult goals. *Journal of Applied Psychology, 74,* 18–23.

Holmes, D., McGilly, B., & Houston, B. K. (1984). Task-related arousal of Type A and Type B persons: Level of challenge and response specificity. *Journal of Personality and Social Psychology, 46,* 1322–1327.

Holmes, T. H., & Masuda, M. (1974). Life change and illness susceptibility. In B. S. Dohrenwend & B. S. Dohrenwend (Eds.), *Stressful life events: Their nature and effects* (pp. 45–72). New York: Wiley.

Horvath, P., & Zuckerman, M. (1993). Sensation seeking, risk appraisal, and risky behavior. *Personality and Individual Differences, 14,* 41–52.

Houston, B. K. (1983). Psychophysiological responsivity and the Type A behavior pattern. *Journal of Research in Personality, 17,* 22–39.

Hull, C. L. (1943). *Principles of behavior.* New York: Appleton Century.

Hull, J. G., Levenson, R. W., Young, R. D., & Sher, K. J. (1983). Self-awareness-reducing effects of alcohol consumption. *Journal of Personality and Social Psychology, 44,* 461–473.

Hull, J. G., Van Treuren, R. R., & Virnelli, S. (1987). Hardiness and health: A critique and alternative approach. *Journal of Personality and Social Psychology, 53,* 518–530.

Hull, J. G., & Young, R. D. (1983). Self-consciousness, self-esteem, and success-failure as determinants of alcohol consumption in male social drinkers. *Journal of Personality and Social Psychology, 44,* 1097–1109.

Hull, J. G., Young, R. D., & Jouriles, E. (1986). Applications of the self-awareness model of alcohol consumption: Predicting patterns of use and abuse. *Journal of Personality and Social Psychology, 51,* 790–796.

Humphreys, M. S., & Revelle, W. (1984). Personality, motivation, and performance: A theory of the relationship between individual differences and information processing. *Psychological Review, 91,* 153–184.

Hunt, J. McV. (1965). Intrinsic motivation and its role in psychological development. In D. Levine (Ed.), *Nebraska symposium on motivation* (Vol. 13, pp. 189–282). Lincoln, NE: University of Nebraska Press.

Hunt, P. J., & Hillery, J. M. (1973). Social facilitation in a coaction setting: An examination of the effects over learning trials. *Journal of Experimental Social Psychology, 9,* 563–571.

Hyland, M. E. (1987). Control theory interpretation of psychological mechanisms of depression: Comparison and integration of several theories. *Psychological Bulletin, 102,* 109–121.

Hyland, M. E. (1988). Motivational control theory: An integrative framework. *Journal of Personality and Social Psychology, 55,* 642–651.

Ickes, W. J., Wicklund, R. A., & Ferris, C. B. (1973). Objective self-awareness and self-esteem. *Journal of Experimental Social Psychology, 9,* 202–219.

Isaacson, R. L. (1964). Relation between achievement, test anxiety, and curricular choices. *Journal of Abnormal and Social Psychology, 68,* 447–452.

Isen, A. M., Horn, N., & Rosenhan, D. L. (1973). Effects of success and failure on children's generosity. *Journal of Personality and Social Psychology, 27,* 239–247.

Isen, A. M., & Levin, P. F. (1972). Effects of feeling good on helping: Cookies and kindness. *Journal of Personality and Social Psychology, 21,* 384–388.

Izard, C. E. (1990). Facial expressions and the regulation of emotions. *Journal of Personality and Social Psychology, 58,* 487–498.

Jackson, D. L. (1974). *Manual for the Personality Research Form.* Goshen, NY: Research Psychology Press.

Jackson, J. M., & Harkins, S. G. (1985). Equity in effort: An explanation of the social loafing effect. *Journal of Personality and Social Psychology, 49,* 1199–1206.

Jackson, S. (1986). *Melancholia and depression.* New Haven, CT: Yale University Press.

Jacoby, L. L., & Kelley, C. M. (1990). An episodic view of motivation: Unconscious influences on memory. In E. T. Higgins & R. M. Sorrentino (Eds.), *Handbook of motivation and cognition* (Vol. 2, pp. 451–481). New York: Guilford.

James, W. (1890). *Principles of psychology.* New York: Holt.

Janoff-Bulman, R., & Timko, C. (1987). Coping with traumatic events: The role of denial in light of people's assumptive worlds. In C. R. Snyder & C. E. Ford (Eds.), *Coping with negative life events: Clinical and social psychological perspectives* (pp. 135–159). New York: Plenum.

Jennings, J. R. (1986). Bodily changes during attending. In M. G. H. Coles, E. Donchin & S. W. Porges (Eds.), *Psychophysiology: Systems, processes and applications* (pp. 268–289). New York: Guilford.

Johnson, E. H., Spielberger, C. D., Worden, T. J., & Jacobs, G. A. (1987). Emotional and familial determinants of elevated blood pressure in black and white adolescent males. *Journal of Psychosomatic Research, 50,* 537–542.

Johnson, T. E., & Rule, B. G. (1986). Mitigating circumstance information, censure, and aggression. *Journal of Personality and Social Psychology, 55,* 642–651.

Jones, A. (1966). Information deprivation in humans. In B. Maher (Ed.), *Progress in experimental personality research* (Vol. 3, pp. 241–307). New York: Academic Press.

Jones, E. E., & Berglas, S. (1978). Control of attributions about the self through self-handicapping strategies: The appeal of alcohol and the role of underachievement. *Personality and Social Psychology Bulletin, 4,* 200–206.

Jorgensen, R. S., Gelling, P. D., & Kliner, L. (1992). Patterns of social desirability and anger in young men with a parental history of hypertension: Association with cardiovascular activity. *Health Psychology, 11,* 403–412.

Kagan, J., Reznick, J. S., & Snidman, N. (1988). Biological bases of childhood shyness. *Science, 240,* 167–171.

Kahneman, D. (1973). *Attention and effort.* Englewood Cliffs, NJ: Prentice-Hall.

Kanfer, F. H., & Hagerman, S. (1987). A model of self-regulation. In F. Halisch & J. Kuhl (Eds.), *Motivation, intention, and volition* (pp. 293–307). New York: Springer-Verlag.

Kanner, A. D., Coyne, J. C., Schaefer, C., & Lazarus, R. S. (1981). Comparisons of two modes of stress measurement: Daily hassles and uplifts versus major life events. *Journal of Behavioral Medicine, 4,* 1–39.

Kasl, S. V. (1973). Mental health and the work environment: An examination of the evidence. *Journal of Occupational Medicine, 15,* 509–518.

Kernis, M. H., Brockner, J., & Frankel, B. S. (1989). Self-esteem and reactions to failure: The mediating role of overgeneralization. *Journal of Personality and Social Psychology, 57,* 707–714.

Kernis, M. H., Granneman, B. D., & Barclay, L. C. (1989). Stability and level of self-esteem as predictors of anger arousal and hostility. *Journal of Personality and Social Psychology, 56,* 1013–1022.

Kernis, M. H., Granneman, B. D., & Mathis, L. C. (1991). Stability of self-esteem as a moderator of the relation between level of self-esteem and depression. *Journal of Personality and Social Psychology, 61,* 80–84.

Kerr, N. L. (1983). Motivation losses in small groups: A social dilemma analysis. *Journal of Personality and Social Psychology, 45,* 819–828.

Kerr, N. L., & Bruun, S. E. (1981). Ringelmann revisited: Alternative explanations for the social loafing effect. *Personality and Social Psychology Bulletin, 7,* 224–231.

Klein, H. J. (1989). An integrated control theory model of work motivation. *Academy of Management Review, 14,* 150–172.

Klinger, E. (1977). *Meaning and void.* Minneapolis: University of Minnesota Press.

Klinger, E., Barta, S. G., & Maxeiner, M. (1980). Motivational correlates of thought content frequency and commitment. *Journal of Personality and Social Psychology, 39,* 1222–1237.

Kobasa, S. C. (1979). Stressful life events, personality, and health: An inquiry into hardiness. *Journal of Personality and Social Psychology, 37,* 1–11.

Kobasa, S. C. (1982). Commitment and coping in stress resistance among lawyers. *Journal of Personality and Social Psychology, 42,* 707–717.

Kobasa, S. C., Maddi, S. R., & Kahn, S. (1982). Hardiness and health: A prospective study. *Journal of Personality and Social Psychology, 42,* 168–177.

Koestner, R., Weinberger, J., & McClelland, D. C. (1991). Task-intrinsic and social-extrinsic sources of arousal for motives assessed in fantasy and self-report. *Journal of Personality, 59,* 57–82.

Kohn, P. M., Lafreniere, K., & Gurevich, M. (1991). Hassles, health, and personality. *Journal of Personality and Social Psychology, 61,* 478–482.

Kolditz, T. A., & Arkin, R. M. (1982). An impression management interpretation of the self-handicapping strategy. *Journal of Personality and Social Psychology, 43,* 492–502.

Konecni, V. J. (1979). Determinants of aesthetic preference and effects of exposure to aesthetic stimuli: Social, emotional, and cognitive factors. In B. A. Maher (Ed.), *Progress in experimental personality research* (Vol. 9, pp. 149–197). New York: Academic Press.

Kravitz, D., & Martin, B. (1986). Ringelmann rediscovered: The original article. *Journal of Personality and Social Psychology, 50,* 936–941.

Kruglanski, A. (1989). *Lay epistemics and human knowledge: Cognitive and motivational bases.* New York: Plenum.

Kruglanski, A. W., & Freund, T. (1983). The freezing and unfreezing of lay-inferences: Effects on impressional primacy, ethnic stereotyping, and numerical anchoring. *Journal of Experimental Social Psychology, 19,* 448–468.

Kuhl, J. (1981). Motivational and functional helplessness: The moderating effect of state versus action orientation. *Journal of Personality and Social Psychology, 40,* 155–170.

Kuhl, J. (1982). Action- vs. state-orientation as a mediator between motivation and action. In W. Hacker, W. Volpert & M. von Cranach (Eds.), *Cognitive and motivational aspects of action* (pp. 67–85). Amsterdam: North-Holland.

Kuhl, J. (1984). Volitional aspects of achievement motivation and learned helplessness: Toward a comprehensive theory of action control. In B. A. Maher (Ed.), *Progress in experimental personality research* (Vol. 13, pp. 99–171). New York: Academic Press.

Kuhl, J. (1985). Volitional mediators of cognition-behavior consistency: Self-regulatory processes and action versus state orientation. In J. Kuhl & J. Beckmann (Eds.), *Action control: From cognition to behavior* (pp. 101–128). New York: Springer-Verlag.

Kuhl, J., & Beckmann, J. (Eds.). (1985a). *Action control: From cognition to behavior.* New York: Springer-Verlag.

Kuhl, J., & Beckmann, J. (1985b). Historical perspectives in the study of action control. In J. Kuhl & J. Beckmann (Eds.), *Action control: From cognition to behavior* (pp. 89–100). New York: Springer-Verlag.

Kuhl, J., & Helle, P. (1986). Motivational and volitional determinants of depression: The degenerated-intention hypothesis. *Journal of Abnormal Psychology, 95,* 247–251.

Lacey, J. I. (1967). Somatic response patterning and stress: Some revisions of activation theory. In M. H. Appley & R. Trumbull (Eds.), *Psychological stress: Issues in research* (pp. 14–37). New York: Appleton-Century-Crofts.

Lafreniere, K., Cowles, M., & Apter, M. J. (1988). The reversal phenomenon: Reflections on a laboratory study. In M. J. Apter, J. H. Kerr & M. Cowles (Eds.), *Progress in reversal theory* (pp. 247–254). Amsterdam: North-Holland.

Laird, J. D. (1974). Self-attribution of emotion: The effects of expressive behavior on quality of emotional experience. *Journal of Personality and Social Psychology, 29,* 475–486.

Laird, J. D., Wagener, J. J., Halal, M., & Szegda, M. (1982). Remembering what you feel: effects of emotion on memory. *Journal of Personality and Social Psychology, 42,* 646–657.

Langer, E. J. (1975). The illusion of control. *Journal of Personality and Social Psychology, 32,* 311–328.

Langer, E. (1989). Minding matters: The consequences of mindlessness-mindfulness. In L. Berkowitz (Ed.), *Advances in experimental social psychology* (Vol. 22, pp. 137–173). New York: Academic Press.

Lansing, J. B., & Heyns, R. W. (1959). Need affiliation and frequency of four types of communication. *Journal of Abnormal and Social Psychology, 58,* 365–372.

Lanzetta, J. T., & Englis, B. G. (1989). Expectations of cooperation and competition and their effects on observers' vicarious emotional responses. *Journal of Personality and Social Psychology, 56,* 543–554.

Lassiter, G. D., Briggs, M. A., & Slaw, R. D. (1991). Need for cognition, causal processing, and memory for behavior. *Personality and Social Psychology Bulletin, 17,* 694–700.

Latané, B., Williams, K., & Harkins, S. G. (1979). Many hands make light the work: The causes and consequences of social loafing. *Journal of Personality and Social Psychology, 37,* 822–832.

Latham, G. P., Erez, M., & Locke, E. A. (1988). Resolving scientific disputes by the joint design of crucial experiments by the antagonists: Application to the Erez-Latham dispute regarding participation in goal setting. *Journal of Applied Psychology, 73,* 753–772.

Latham, G. P., & Lee, T. W. (1986). Goal settings. In E. A. Locke (Ed.), *Generalizing from laboratory to field studies* (pp. 101–117). Lexington, MA: Lexington Books.

Lazarus, R. S. (1991). *Emotion and adaptation.* New York: Oxford University Press.

Lazarus, R. S., & Alfert, E. (1964). Short-circuiting of threat by experimentally altering cognitive appraisal. *Journal of Abnormal and Social Psychology, 69,* 195–205.

Lazarus, R. S., & Cohen, J. B. (1978). Environmental stress. In I. Altman & J. F. Wohlwill (Eds.), *Human behavior and the environment: Current theory and research* (pp. 89–127). New York: Plenum.

Lazarus, R. S., & Folkman, S. (1984). *Stress, appraisal, and coping.* New York: Springer-Verlag.

Lazarus, R. S., Opton, E., Nomikos, M., & Rankin, N. (1965). The principle of short-circuiting of threat: further evidence. *Journal of Personality, 33,* 622–634.

Leary, D. E. (Ed.) (1990). *Metaphors in the history of psychology.* New York: Cambridge University Press.

Leary, D. E. (1990). Psyche's muse: The role of metaphor in the history of psychology. In D. E. Leary (Ed.), *Metaphors in the history of psychology* (pp. 1–78). New York: Cambridge University Press.

Leary, M. R. (1983). *Understanding social anxiety: Social, personality and clinical perspectives.* Beverly Hills, CA: Sage.

Leary, M. R. (1990). Responses to social exclusion: Social anxiety, jealousy, loneliness, depression, and low self-esteem. *Journal of Social and Clinical Psychology, 9,* 221–229.

Leary, M. R., & Atherton, S. C. (1986). Self-efficacy, social anxiety, and inhibition in interpersonal encounters. *Journal of Social and Clinical Psychology, 4,* 256–267.

Leary, M. R., Knight, P. D., & Johnson, K. A. (1987). Social anxiety and dyadic conversation: A verbal response analysis. *Journal of Social and Clinical Psychology, 5,* 34–50.

Leary, M. R., & Kowalski, R. M. (1990). Impression management: A literature review and two-component model. *Psychological Bulletin, 107,* 34–47.

Lee, T. W., Locke, E. A., & Latham, G. P. (1989). Goal setting theory and job performance. In L. Pervin (Ed.), *Goal concepts in personality and social psychology* (pp. 291–326). Hillsdale, NJ: Erlbaum.

Leventhal, H. (1980). A perceptual-motor theory of emotion. In L. Berkowitz (Ed.), *Advances in experimental social psychology* (Vol. 17, pp. 117–182). New York: Academic Press.

Leventhal, H. (1984). A perceptual motor theory of emotion. In K. S. Scherer & P. Ekman (Eds.), *Approaches to emotion* (pp. 271–291). Hillsdale, NJ: Erlbaum.

Lewin, K. (1935). *A dynamic theory of personality.* New York: McGraw-Hill.

Little, B. R. (1983). Personal projects: A rationale and method for investigation. *Environment and Behavior, 15,* 273–309.

Locke, E. A., Latham, G. P., & Erez, M. (1988). The determinants of goal commitment. *Academy of Management Review, 13,* 23–39.

Locke, E. A., Shaw, K. N., Saari, L. M., & Latham, G. P. (1981). Goal setting and task performance: 1969–1980. *Psychological Bulletin, 90,* 125–152.

Lorenz, K. (1966). *On aggression.* New York: Harcourt Brace.

Maddux, J. E., Norton, L. W., & Leary, M. R. (1988). Cognitive components of social anxiety: An investigation of the integration of self-presentation theory and self-efficacy theory. *Journal of Social and Clinical Psychology, 6,* 180–190.

Manstead, A. S. R., & Wagner, H. L. (1981). Arousal, cognition, and emotion: An appraisal of two-factor theory. *Current Psychological Reviews, 1,* 35–54.

Manucia, G. K., Baumann, D. J., & Cialdini, R. B. (1984). Mood influences in helping: Direct effects or side effects? *Journal of Personality and Social Psychology, 46,* 357–364.

Marco, C. A., & Suls, J. (1993). Daily stress and the trajectory of mood: Spillover, response assimilation, contrast, and chronic negative affectivity. *Journal of Personality and Social Psychology, 64,* 1053–1063.

Markus, H. (1977). Self-schemata and processing information about the self. *Journal of Personality and Social Psychology, 35,* 63–78.

Markus, H., & Nurius, N. (1986). Possible selves. *American Psychologist, 41,* 954–969.

Markus, H., & Ruvolo, A. (1989). Possible selves: Personalized representations of goals. In L. Pervin (Ed.), *Goal concepts in personality and social psychology* (pp. 211–241). Hillsdale, NJ: Erlbaum.

Marshall, G. D., & Zimbardo, P. G. (1979). Affective consequences of inadequately explained physiological arousal. *Journal of Personality and Social Psychology, 37,* 970–988.

Martin, R. A., Kuiper, N. A., Olinger, J., & Dobbin, J. (1987). Is stress always bad? Telic versus paratelic dominance as a stress-moderating variable. *Journal of Personality and Social Psychology, 53,* 970–982.

Maslach, C. (1979). Negative emotional biasing of unexplained arousal. *Journal of Personality and Social Psychology, 37,* 953–969.

Mason, A., & Blankenship, V. (1987). Power and affiliation motivation, stress, and abuse in intimate relationships. *Journal of Personality and Social Psychology, 52,* 203–210.

Mason, J. W. (1968). Organization of psychoendocrine mechanisms. *Psychosomatic Medicine, 30,* 565–791.

Mason, J. W. (1975). A historical view of the stress field. *Journal of Human Stress, 1,* 6–12, 22–36.

Matsui, T., Okada, A., & Mizuguchi, R. (1981). Expectancy theory predictions of the goal theory postulate, "The harder the goals, the higher the performance." *Journal of Applied Psychology, 66,* 54–58.

McAdams, D. P. (1980). A thematic coding system for the intimacy motive. *Journal of Research in Personality, 14,* 413–432.

McAdams, D. P., & Constantian, C. A. (1983). Intimacy and affiliation motives in daily living: An experience sampling analysis. *Journal of Personality and Social Psychology, 45,* 851–861.

McAdams, D. P., & Powers, J. (1981). Themes of intimacy in behavior and thought. *Journal of Personality and Social Psychology, 40,* 573–587.

McArthur, L. Z., & Baron, R. M. (1983). Toward an ecological theory of social perception. *Psychological Review, 90,* 215–238.

McBride, A. B. (1990). Mental health effects of women's multiple roles. *American Psychologist, 45,* 381–384.

McClelland, D. C. (1975). *Power: The inner experience.* New York: Irvington.

McClelland, D. C. (1979). Inhibited power motivation and high blood pressure in men. *Journal of Abnormal Psychology, 88,* 182–190.

McClelland, D. C. (1985). *Human motivation.* Glenview, IL: Scott, Foresman.

McClelland, D. C., Alexander, C., & Marks, E. (1982). The need for power, stress, immune function, and illness among male prisoners. *Journal of Abnormal Psychology*, *91*, 61–70.

McClelland, D. C., Atkinson, J. W. , Clark, R. A., & Lowell, E. L. (1953). *The achievement motive*. New York: Appleton-Century-Crofts.

McClelland, D. C., Davis, W. B., Kalin, R., & Wanner, E. (1972). *The drinking man: Alcohol and human motivation*. New York: Free Press.

McClelland, D. C., Floor, E., Davidson, R. J., & Saron, C. (1980). Stressed power motivation, sympathetic activation, immune function, and illness. *Journal of Human Stress*, *6*(2), 11–19.

McClelland, D. C., & Jemmott, J. B., III. (1984). Power motivation, stress and physical illness. *Journal of Human Stress*, *6*(4), 6–15.

McClelland, D. C., Koestner, R., & Weinberger, J. (1989). How do self-attributed and implicit motives differ? *Psychological Review*, *96*, 690–702.

McClelland, D. C., & Pilon, D. A. (1983). Sources of adult motives in patterns of parent behavior in early childhood. *Journal of Personality and Social Psychology*, *44*, 564–574.

McClelland, D. C., Ross, G., & Patel, V. (1985). The effect of an academic examination on salivary norepinephrine and immunoglobulin levels. *Journal of Human Stress*, *11*(1), 52–59.

McClelland, D. C., & Watson, R. I., Jr. (1973). Power motivation and risk-taking behavior. *Journal of Personality*, *41*, 121–139.

McDougall, W. (1908). *Introduction to social psychology*. London: Methuen.

McReynolds, P. (1990). Motives and metaphors: A study in scientific creativity. In D. E. Leary (Ed.), *Metaphors in the history of psychology* (pp. 133–172). New York: Cambridge University Press.

Mento, A. J., Steel, R. P., & Karren, R. J. (1987). A meta-analytic study of the effects of goal setting on task performance: 1966–1984. *Organizational Behavior and Human Decision Processes*, *39*, 52–83.

Midlarsky, E. (1991). Helping as coping. In M. S. Clark (Ed.), *Prosocial behavior* (pp. 238–264). Newbury Park, CA: Sage.

Mikulincer, M., Florian, V., & Tolmacz, R. (1990). Attachment styles and fear of personal death: A case study of affect regulation. *Journal of Personality and Social Psychology*, *58*, 273–280.

Miller, G. A., Galanter, E., & Pribram, K. H. (1960). *Plans and the structure of behavior*. New York: Holt.

Miller, S. (1980). Why having control reduces stress: If I can stop the roller coaster, I don't want to get off. In J. Garber & M. E. P. Seligman (Eds.), *Human helplessness: Theory and applications* (pp. 71–95). New York: Academic Press.

Mineka, S., & Hendersen, R. W. (1985). Controllability and predictability in acquired motivation. *Annual Review of Psychology*, *36*, 495–529.

Mischel, H. N., & Mischel, W. (1983). The development of children's knowledge of self-control strategies. *Child Development*, *54*, 603–619.

Mischel, W., & Moore, B. (1980). The role of ideation in voluntary delay for symbolically presented rewards. *Cognitive Therapy and Research*, *4*, 211–221.

Mitchell, T. R. (1974). Expectancy models of job satisfaction, occupational preference and effort: A theoretical, methodological, and empirical appraisal. *Psychological Bulletin*, *81*, 1053–1077.

Motowidlo, S. J., Packard, J. S., & Manning, M. R. (1986). Occupational stress: Its causes and consequences for job performance. *Journal of Applied Psychology, 71,* 618–629.

Mowrer, O. H., & Viek, P. (1948). An experimental analogue of fear from a sense of helplessness. *Journal of Abnormal and Social Psychology, 43,* 193–200.

Mummendey, A., Linneweber, V., & Lopscher, G. (1984). Actor or victim of aggression: Divergent perspectives—divergent evaluations. *European Journal of Social Psychology, 14,* 297–311.

Mummendey, A., & Mummendey, H. D. (1983). Aggressive behavior of soccer players as social interaction. In J. H. Goldstein (Ed.), *Sports violence* (pp. 111–128). New York: Springer-Verlag.

Murgatroyd, S., Rushton, C., Apter, M. J., & Ray, C. (1978). The development of the Telic Dominance Scale. *Journal of Personality Assessment, 42,* 519–528.

Murray, H. A. (1938). *Explorations in personality.* New York: Oxford University Press.

Naatanen, R. (1973). The inverted-U relationship between activation and performance: A critical review. In S. Kornblum (Ed.), *Attention and performance* (Vol. 4, pp. 155–174). New York: Academic Press.

Nasby, W., Hayden, B., & DePaulo, B. M. (1979). Attributional bias among aggressive boys to interpret unambiguous social stimuli as displays of hostility. *Journal of Abnormal Psychology, 89,* 459–468.

Nebeker, D. M., & Tatum, B. C. (1993). The effects of computer monitoring, standards, and rewards on work performance, job satisfaction, and stress. *Journal of Applied Social Psychology, 23,* 508–536.

Neiss, R. (1988). Reconceptualizing arousal: Psychobiological states in motor performance. *Psychological Bulletin, 103,* 345–366.

Nikula, R., Klinger, E., & Larson-Gutman, M. K. (1993). Current concerns and electrodermal reactivity: Responses to words and thoughts. *Journal of Personality, 61,* 63–84.

Obrist, P. A. (1976). The cardiovascular-behavioral interaction—as it appears today. *Psychophysiology, 13,* 95–107.

Ogilvie, D. M. (1987). The undesired self: A neglected variable in personality research. *Journal of Personality and Social Psychology, 52,* 379–385.

Ohbuchi, K. (1982). On the cognitive integration mediating reactions to attack patterns. *Social Psychology Quarterly, 45,* 213–218.

Okun, M. A., Zautra, A. J., & Robinson, S. E. (1988). Hardiness and health among women with rheumatoid arthritis. *Personality and Individual Differences, 9,* 101–107.

O'Leary, A. (1992). Self-efficacy and health: Behavioral and stress-physiological mediation. *Cognitive Therapy and Research, 16,* 229–245.

Ortony, A., & Turner, T. J. (1990). What's basic about basic emotions? *Psychological Review, 97,* 315–331.

Overmier, J. B., & Seligman, M. E. P. (1967). Effects of inescapable shock upon subsequent escape and avoidance responding. *Journal of Comparative and Physiological Psychology, 63,* 28–33.

Oyserman, D., & Markus, H. R. (1990). Possible selves and delinquency. *Journal of Personality and Social Psychology, 59,* 112–125.

Panksepp, J. (1982). Toward a general psychobiological theory of emotions. *Behavioral and Brain Sciences, 5,* 407–467.

Parkes, K. R. (1984). Locus of control, cognitive appraisal, and coping in stressful episodes. *Journal of Personality and Social Psychology, 46,* 655–668.

Peake, P. K., & Cervone, D. (1989). Sequence anchoring and self-efficacy: Primacy effects in the consideration of possibilities. *Social Cognition, 7,* 31–50.

Pearlin, L. I., & Schooler, C. (1978). The structure of coping. *Journal of Health and Social Behavior, 19,* 2–21.

Pennebaker, J. W. (1985). Traumatic experience and psychosomatic disease: Exploring the roles of behavioural inhibition, obsession, and confiding. *Canadian Psychology, 26,* 82–95.

Pennebaker, J. W., & O'Heeron, R. C. (1984). Confiding in others and illness rates among spouses of suicide and accidental death. *Journal of Abnormal Psychology, 93,* 473–476.

Persky, H., Zuckerman, M., Curtis, G., & Perloff, W. (1965, April). *Anterior pituitary functions in three emotional states.* Paper presented at the meeting of the American Psychosomatic Society, Philadelphia.

Pervin, L. A. (1963). The need to predict and control under conditions of threat. *Journal of Personality, 31,* 570–587.

Pittman, T. S., & D'Agostino, P. R. (1985). Motivation and attribution: The effects of control deprivation on subsequent information processing. In J. H. Harvey & G. Weary (Eds.), *Attribution: Basic issues and applications* (pp. 117–141). New York: Academic Press.

Pittman, T. S., Davey, M. E., Alafat, K. A., Wetherill, K. V., & Kramer, N. A. (1980). Informational versus controlling verbal rewards. *Personality and Social Psychology Bulletin, 6,* 228–233.

Pittman, T. S., & Heller, J. F. (1987). Social motivation. *Annual Review of Psychology, 38,* 461–489.

Pleban, R., & Tesser, A. (1981). The effects of relevance and quality of another's performance on interpersonal closeness. *Social Psychology Quarterly, 44,* 278–285.

Plutchik, R. (1984). Emotions: A general psychoevolutionary theory. In K. S. Scherer & P. Ekman (Eds.), *Approaches to emotion* (pp. 197–219). Hillsdale, NJ: Erlbaum.

Polivy, J. (1990). Inhibition of internally cued behavior. In E. T. Higgins & R. M. Sorrentino (Eds.), *Handbook of motivation and cognition* (Vol. 2, pp. 131–147). New York: Guilford.

Porter, L. W., & Lawler, E. E. (1968). *Managerial attitudes and performance.* Homewood, IL: Dorsey.

Powers, W. T. (1973). Feedback: Beyond behaviorism. *Science, 179,* 351–356.

Pribram, K. H. (1967). Emotion: Steps toward a neuropsychological theory. In D. C. Glass (Ed.), *Neurophysiology and emotion* (pp. 3–40). New York: Russell Sage Foundation.

Pribram, K. H., & McGuinness, D. (1975). Arousal, activation, and effort in the control of attention. *Psychological Review, 82,* 116–149.

Psyzczynski, T., & Greenberg, J. (1983). Determinants of reductions in intended effort as a strategy for coping with anticipated failure. *Journal of Research in Personality, 17,* 412–422.

Psyzczynski, T., & Greenberg, J. (1987). Self-regulatory perseveration and the depressive self-focusing style: A self-awareness theory of reactive depression. *Psychological Bulletin, 102,* 122–138.

Psyzczynski, T., Greenberg, J., & LaPrelle, J. (1985). Social comparison after success and failure: Biased search for information consistent with a self-serving conclusion. *Journal of Experimental Social Psychology, 21,* 195–211.

Rahe, R. H., & Arthur, R. J. (1978). Life change and illness studies. *Journal of Human Stress, 4,* 3–15.

Reisenzein, R. (1983). The Schachter theory of emotion: Two decades later. *Psychological Bulletin, 94,* 239–264.

Revelle, W., Humphreys, M. S., Simon, L., & Gilliland, K. (1980). The interactive effect of personality, time of day and caffeine: A test of the arousal model. *Journal of Experimental Psychology: General, 109,* 1–31.

Reykowski, J. (1982). Motivation of prosocial behavior. In V. J. Derlega & J. Grzelak (Eds.), *Cooperation and helping behavior: Theories and research* (pp. 352–375). New York: Academic Press.

Rhodewalt, F., & Comer, R. (1982). Coronary-prone behavior and reactance: The attractiveness of an eliminated choice. *Personality and Social Psychology Bulletin, 8,* 152–158.

Rhodewalt, F., Hays, R. B., Chemers, M. M., & Wysocki, J. (1984). Type A behavior, perceived stress, and illness: A person-situation analysis. *Personality and Social Psychology Bulletin, 10,* 149–159.

Rhodewalt, F., Morf, C., Hazlett, S., & Fairfield, M. (1991). Self-handicapping: The role of discounting and augmentation in the preservation of self-esteem. *Journal of Personality and Social Psychology, 61,* 122–131.

Rholes, W. S., Michas, L., & Shroff, J. (1989). Action control as a vulnerability factor in dysphoria. *Cognitive Therapy and Research, 13,* 263–274.

Rodin, J., Rennert, K., & Solomon, S. K. (1980). Intrinsic motivation for control: Fact or fiction. In A. Baum & J. E. Singer (Eds.), *Advances in environmental psychology. Vol. 2: Applications of personal control* (pp. 131–148). Hillsdale, NJ: Erlbaum.

Rohde, P., Lewinsohn, P. M., Tilson, M., & Seeley, J. R. (1990). Dimensionality of coping and its relation to depression. *Journal of Personality and Social Psychology, 58,* 499–511.

Rokeach, M. (1973). *The nature of human values.* New York: Free Press.

Rosenblatt, A., & Greenberg, J. (1991). Examining the world of the depressed: Do depressed people prefer others who are depressed? *Journal of Personality and Social Psychology, 60,* 620–629.

Rosenfield, D., & Stephan, W. G. (1978). Sex differences in attributions for sex-typed tasks. *Journal of Personality, 46,* 244–259.

Rosenhan, D. (1969). Some origins of concern for others. In P. Mussen, J. Langer & M. Covington (Eds.), *Trends and issues in developmental psychology* (pp. 134–153). New York: Holt, Rinehart & Winston.

Rosenman, R. H., & Chesney, M. A. (1982). Stress, Type A behavior, and coronary disease. In L. Goldberger & S. Breznitz (Eds.), *The handbook of stress: Theoretical and clinical aspects* (pp. 547–565). New York: Macmillan.

Ross, L. D., Rodin, J., & Zimbardo, P. G. (1969). Toward an attribution therapy: The reduction of fear through induced cognitive-emotional misattribution. *Journal of Personality and Social Psychology, 12,* 279–288.

Roth, S. (1980). A revised model of learned helplessness in humans. *Journal of Personality, 48,* 103–133.

Roth, S., & Cohen, L. J. (1986). Approach, avoidance, and coping with stress. *American Psychologist, 41,* 813–819.

Routtenberg, A. (1968). The two-arousal hypothesis: Reticular formation and limbic system. *Psychological Review, 75,* 51–80.

Ruble, D. N., & Flett, G. L. (1988). Conflicting goals in self-evaluative information seeking: Developmental and ability level analyses. *Child Development, 59,* 97–106.

Ryan, R. M., & Connell, J. P. (1989). Perceived locus of causality and internalization:

Examining reasons for acting in two domains. *Journal of Personality and Social Psychology, 57,* 749–761.

Salovey, P. (1992). Mood-induced self-focused attention. *Journal of Personality and Social Psychology, 62,* 699–707.

Salovey, P., Mayer, J. D., & Rosenhan, D. L. (1991). Mood and helping: Mood as a motivator of helping and helping as a regulator of mood. In M. S. Clark (Ed.), *Prosocial behavior* (pp. 215–237). Newbury Park, CA: Sage.

Sarason, I. G. (1972). Experimental approaches to test anxiety: Attention and the uses of information. In C. D. Spielberger (Ed.), *Anxiety: Current trends in theory and research* (Vol. 2, pp. 381–403). New York: Academic Press.

Sarason, I. G. (1984). Stress, anxiety, and cognitive interference: Reactions to tests. *Journal of Personality and Social Psychology, 46,* 929–938.

Sarason, I. G., Johnson, J. H., & Siegel, J. M. (1978). Assessing the impact of life changes: Development of the Life Experiences Survey. *Journal of Consulting and Clinical Psychology, 46,* 932–946.

Schachter, S. (1959). *The psychology of affiliation.* Palo Alto, CA: Stanford University Press.

Schachter, S., & Singer, J. A. (1962). Cognitive, social, and physiological determinants of emotional state. *Psychological Review, 69,* 379–399.

Scheier, M. F., & Carver, C. S. (1983). Self-directed attention and the comparison of self with standards. *Journal of Experimental Social Psychology, 19,* 205–222.

Scheier, M. F., & Carver, C. S. (1988). A model of behavioral self-regulation: Translating intention into action. In L. Berkowitz (Ed.), *Advances in experimental social psychology* (Vol. 21, pp. 303–346). New York: Academic Press.

Scheier, M. F., Carver, C. S., & Gibbons, F. X. (1981). Self-focused attention and reactions to fear. *Journal of Research in Personality, 15,* 1–15.

Scheier, M. F., Weintraub, J. K., & Carver, C. S. (1986). Coping with stress: Divergent strategies of optimists and pessimists. *Journal of Personality and Social Psychology, 51,* 1257–1264.

Schlenker, B. R., & Leary, M. R. (1982). Social anxiety and self-presentation: A conceptualization and a model. *Psychological Bulletin, 92,* 641–669.

Schonfeld, I. S. (1990). Coping with job-related stress: The case of teachers. *Journal of Occupational Psychology, 63,* 141–149.

Schonpflug, W. (1986). Behavior economics as an approach to stress theory. In M. H. Appley & R. Trumbull (Eds.), *Dynamics of stress: Physiological, psychological, and social perspectives* (pp. 81–98). New York: Plenum.

Schunk, D. H. (1984). Self-efficacy perspective on achievement behavior. *Educational Psychologist, 19,* 48–58.

Seligman, M. E. P. (1975). *Helplessness: On depression, development, and death.* San Francisco: Freeman.

Selye, H. (1956). *The stress of life.* New York: McGraw-Hill.

Seta, J. (1982). The impact of comparison processes on coactors' task performance. *Journal of Personality and Social Psychology, 42,* 281–291.

Shaver, P., Hazan, C., & Bradshaw, D. (1988). Love as attachment: The integration of three behavioral systems. In R. Sternberg & M. Barnes (Eds.), *The psychology of love* (pp. 69–99). New Haven, CT: Yale University Press.

Shepperd, J. A., & Arkin, R. M. (1989). Determinants of self-handicapping: Task importance and effects of pre-existing handicaps on self-generated handicaps. *Personality and Social Psychology Bulletin, 15,* 101–112.

Shepperd, J. A., & Kashani, J. H. (1991). The relationship of hardiness, gender, and stress to health outcomes in adolescents. *Journal of Personality, 59,* 747–768.

Sherman, S. J., Skov, R. B., Hervitz, E. F., & Stock, C. B. (1981). The effects of explaining hypothetical future events: From possibility to probability to actuality and beyond. *Journal of Experimental Social Psychology, 17,* 142–158.

Shipley, T. E., & Veroff, J. (1952). A projective measure of need for affiliation. *Journal of Experimental Psychology, 43,* 349–356.

Shotland, R. L., & Heinold, W. D. (1985). Bystander response to arterial bleeding: Helping skills, the decision-making process, and differentiating the helping response. *Journal of Personality and Social Psychology, 49,* 347–356.

Showers, C., & Cantor, N. (1985). Social cognition: A look at motivated strategies. *Annual Review of Psychology,* 36, 275–305.

Silver, M. (1985). "Purposive behavior" in psychology and philosophy: A history. In M. Frese & J. Sabini (Eds.), *Goal directed behavior: The concept of action in psychology* (pp. 3–17). Hillsdale, NJ: Erlbaum.

Slovic, P., Fischoff, B., & Lichtenstein, S. (1977). Behavior decision theory. *Annual Review of Psychology, 28,* 1–39.

Smith, E. R., & Manard, B. B. (1980). Causal attributions and medical school admissions. *Personality and Social Psychology Bulletin, 6,* 644–650.

Smith, K. D., Keating, J. P., & Stotland, E. (1989). Altruism revisited: The effect of denying feedback on a victim's status to empathic witnesses. *Journal of Personality and Social Psychology, 57,* 641–650.

Smith, T. W., & Rhodewalt, F. (1986). On states, traits, and processes: A transactional alternative to the individual difference assumptions in Type A behavior and physiological reactivity. *Journal of Research in Personality, 20,* 229–251.

Smith, T. W., Snyder, C. R., & Handelsman, M. M. (1982). On the self-serving function of an academic wooden leg: Test anxiety and a self-handicapping strategy. *Journal of Personality and Social Psychology, 42,* 314–321.

Smith, T. W., Snyder, C. R., & Perkins, S. C. (1983). The self-serving function of hypochondriacal complaints: Physical symptoms as self-handicapping strategies. *Journal of Personality and Social Psychology, 44,* 787–797.

Snyder, C. R (1989). Reality negotiation: From excuses to hope and beyond. *Journal of Social and Clinical Psychology, 8,* 130–157.

Snyder, C. R., & Higgins, R. L. (1988). Excuses: Their effective role in the negotiation of reality. *Psychological Bulletin, 104,* 23–35.

Snyder, C. R., Higgins, R. L., & Stucky, R. J. (1983). *Excuses: Masquerades in search of grace.* New York: Wiley/Interscience.

Solomon, S., Greenberg, J., & Psyzcynski, T. (1991). A terror management theory of social behavior: The psychological functions of self-esteem and cultural world views. In M. P. Zanna (Ed.), *Advances in experimental social psychology* (Vol. 24, pp. 93–159). San Diego: Academic Press.

Spector, P. E. (1987). Interactive effects of perceived control and job stressors on affective reactions and health outcomes for clerical workers. *Work and Stress, 1,* 155–162.

Spector, P. E., Dwyer, D. J., & Jex, S. M. (1988). Relation of job stressors to affective, health, and performance outcomes: A comparison of multiple data sources. *Journal of Applied Psychology, 73,* 11–19.

Spence, J. T., & Helmreich, R. L. (1983). Achievement-related motives and behaviors.

In J. T. Spence (Ed.), *Achievement and achievement motives: Psychological and sociological approaches* (pp. 7–74). San Francisco: Freeman.

Spielberger, C. D., & Smith, L. H. (1966). Anxiety (drive), stress, and serial-position effects in serial-verbal learning. *Journal of Experimental Psychology, 72,* 589–595.

Spitz, R. (1945). Hospitalism: An inquiry into the genesis of psychiatric conditions in early childhood. *Psychoanalytic Study of the Child, 1,* 53–74.

Stagner, R. (1977). Homeostasis, discrepancy, dissonance: A theory of motives and motivation. *Motivation and Emotion, 1,* 103–138.

Stahl, M. J., & Harrell, A. M. (1981). Effort decisions with behavioral decision theory: Toward an individual differences model. *Organizational Behavior and Human Performance, 27,* 303–325.

Staub, E., Tursky, B., & Schwartz, G. E. (1971). Self-control and predictability: Their effects on reactions to aversive stimulation. *Journal of Personality and Social Psychology, 18,* 157–162.

Steele, C. M. (1988). The psychology of self-affirmation: Sustaining the integrity of the self. In L. Berkowitz (Ed.), *Advances in experimental social psychology* (Vol. 21, pp. 261–302). New York: Academic Press.

Stevenson, D. K., Nabseth, D. C., Masuda, M., & Holmes, T. H. (1979). Life events and postoperative course of patients with duodenal ulcers. *Journal of Human Stress, 5,* 19–28.

Strack, F., Martin, L. L., & Stepper, S. (1988). Inhibiting and facilitating conditions of facial expressions: A nonobtrusive test of the facial feedback hypothesis. *Journal of Personality and Social Psychology, 54,* 768–777.

Strauman, T. J., & Higgins, E. T. (1987). Automatic activation of self-discrepancies and emotional syndromes: When cognitive structures influence affect. *Journal of Personality and Social Psychology, 53,* 1004–1014.

Suedfeld, P., & Landon, P. B. (1970). Motivational arousal and task complexity: Support for a model of cognitive changes in sensory deprivation. *Journal of Experimental Psychology, 83,* 329–330.

Sweeney, P. D., Anderson, K., & Bailey, S. (1986). Attributional style in depression: A meta-analytic review. *Journal of Personality and Social Psychology, 50,* 974–991.

Szymanski, K., & Harkins, S. G. (1987). Social loafing and self-evaluation with a social standard. *Journal of Personality and Social Psychology, 53,* 891–897.

Tangney, J. P., Wagner, P., Fletcher, C., & Gramzow, R. (1992). Shame into anger? The relation of shame and guilt to anger and self-reported aggression. *Journal of Personality and Social Psychology, 62,* 669–675.

Taylor, J. A. (1953). A personality scale of manifest anxiety. *Journal of Abnormal and Social Psychology, 48,* 285–290.

Taylor, S. E. (1991). Asymmetrical effects of positive and negative events: The mobilization-minimization hypothesis. *Psychological Bulletin, 110,* 67–85.

Taylor, S E., & Brown, J. D. (1988). Illusion and well-being: A social psychological perspective on mental health. *Psychological Bulletin, 103,* 193–210.

Taylor, S. E., & Fiske, S. T. (1978). Salience, attention, and attribution: Top of the head phenomena. In L. Berkowitz (Ed.), *Advances in experimental social psychology* (Vol. 11, pp. 249–288). New York: Academic Press.

Taylor, S. E., & Lobel, M. (1989). Social comparison activity under threat: Downward evaluation and upward contacts. *Psychological Review, 96,* 569–575.

Tennen, H., & Herzberger, S. (1987). Depression, self-esteem, and the absence of self-protective attributional biases. *Journal of Personality and Social Psychology, 52,* 72–80.

Tesser, A. (1988). Toward a self-evaluation maintenance model of social behavior. In L. Berkowitz (Ed.), *Advances in experimental social psychology* (Vol. 21, pp. 181–227). New York: Academic Press.

Tesser, A., Millar, M., & Moore, J. (1988). Some affective consequences of social comparison and reflective processes: The pain and pleasure of being close. *Journal of Personality and Social Psychology, 54,* 49–61.

Tesser, A., & Smith, J. (1980). Some effects of friendship and task relevance on helping: You don't always help the one you like. *Journal of Experimental Social Psychology, 16,* 582–590.

Theorell, T., & Rahe, R. H. (1975). Life change events, ballistocardiography, and coronary death. *Journal of Human Stress, 1,* 18–24.

Thompson, E. P., Chaiken, S., & Hazlewood, J. D. (1993). Need for cognition and desire for control as moderators of extrinsic reward effects: A person $\times$ situation approach to the study of intrinsic motivation. *Journal of Personality and Social Psychology, 64,* 987–999.

Thompson, S. C. (1980). Will it hurt less if I can control it? A complex answer to a simple question. *Psychological Bulletin, 90,* 89–101.

Thompson, S. C., Sobolew-Shubin, A., Galbraith, M. E., Achwankovsky, L., & Cruzen, D. (1993). Maintaining perceptions of control: Finding perceived control in low-control circumstances. *Journal of Personality and Social Psychology, 64,* 293–304.

Thompson, W. C., Cowan, C. L., & Rosenhan, D. L. (1980). Focus of attention mediates the impact of negative affect on altruism. *Journal of Personality and Social Psychology, 38,* 291–300.

Thorndike, E. L. (1898). Animal intelligence: An experimental study of the associative processes in animals. *Psychological Review Monograph Supplements, 2* (Number 8).

Tinbergen, N. (1951). *The study of instinct.* Oxford: Clarendon.

Toi, M., & Batson, C. D. (1982). More evidence that empathy is a source of altruistic motivation. *Journal of Personality and Social Psychology, 43,* 281–292.

Tolman, E. C. (1932). *Purposive behavior in animals and men.* New York: Appleton.

Tolman, E. C. (1959). Principles of purposive behavior. In S. Koch (Ed.), *Psychology: A study of a science* (Vol. 2, pp. 92–157). New York: McGraw-Hill.

Tomkins, S. S. (1984). Affect theory. In K. S. Scherer & P. Ekman (Eds.), *Approaches to emotion* (pp. 163–195). Hillsdale, NJ: Erlbaum.

Tourangeau, R., & Ellsworth, P. C. (1979). The role of facial response in the experience of emotion. *Journal of Personality and Social Psychology, 37,* 1519–1531.

Tranel, D. T., Fisher, A. E., & Fowles, D. C. (1982). Magnitude of incentive effects on heart rate. *Psychophysiology, 19,* 514–519.

Triplett, N. (1898). The dynamogenic factors in pacemaking and competition. *American Journal of Psychology, 9,* 507–533.

Trope, Y. (1975). Seeking information about one's own ability as a determinant of choice among tasks. *Journal of Personality and Social Psychology, 32,* 1004–1013.

Trope, Y., & Brickman, P. (1975). Difficulty and diagnosticity as determinants of choice among tasks. *Journal of Personality and Social Psychology, 31,* 918–926.

Tubbs, M. E. (1986). Goal setting: A meta-analytic examination of the empirical evidence. *Journal of Applied Psychology, 71,* 474–483.

Veroff, J. (1969). Social comparison and the development of achievement motivation.

In C. P. Smith (Ed.), *Achievement-related motives in children* (pp. 46–101). New York: Russell Sage Foundation.

Vinokur, A., & Selzer, M. L. (1975). Desirable versus undesirable life events: Their relationship to stress and mental distress. *Journal of Personality and Social Psychology, 32,* 329–337.

Vroom, V. H. (1964). Work and motivation. New York: Wiley.

Wadsworth, M. W., & Ford, D. H. (1983). The assessment of personal goal hierarchies. *Journal of Counseling Psychology, 30,* 514–526.

Wagner, J. A., III, & Gooding, R. Z. (1987). Shared influence and organizational behavior: A meta-analysis of situational variables expected to moderate participation-outcome relationships. *Academy of Management Journal, 30,* 524–541.

Walker, E. L. (1980). *Psychological complexity and preference: A hedgehog theory of behavior.* Pacific Grove, CA: Brooks/Cole.

Walters, J., Apter, M. J., & Svebak, S. (1982). Color preference, arousal and the theory of psychological reversals. *Motivation and Emotion, 6,* 193–215.

Waterman, A. (1984). *The psychology of individualism.* New York: Praeger.

Weidenfeld, S. A., O'Leary, A., Bandura, A., Brown, S., Levine, S., & Raska, K. (1990). Impact of perceived coping efficacy on components of the immune system. *Journal of Personality and Social Psychology, 59,* 1082–1094.

Weiner, B. (1985). An attributional theory of achievement motivation and emotion. *Psychological Review, 92,* 548–573.

Weiner, B. (1986). *An attributional theory of motivation and emotion.* New York: Springer-Verlag.

Weiner, B., Amirkhan, J., Folkes, V. S., & Verette, J. A. (1987). An attributional analysis of excuse-giving: Studies of a naive theory of emotion. *Journal of Personality and Social Psychology, 52,* 316–324.

Weiss, J. M. (1971). Somatic effects of predictable and unpredictable shock. *Psychosomatic Medicine, 32,* 397–408.

Weiss, R. F., Boyer, J. L., Lombardo, J. P., & Stitch, M. H. (1973). Altruistic drive and altruistic reinforcement. *Journal of Personality and Social Psychology, 25,* 390–400.

Weiss, R. F., & Miller, F. G. (1971). The drive theory of social facilitation. *Psychological Review, 78,* 44–57.

Wethington, E., & Kessler, R. C. (1986). Perceived support, received support, and adjustment to stressful life events. *Journal of Health and Social Behavior, 27,* 78–89.

Wheeler, L., Koestner, R., & Driver, R. E. (1982). Related attributes in the choice of comparison others: It may be there, but it isn't all there is. *Journal of Experimental Social Psychology, 18,* 489–500.

Wheeler, L., & Zuckerman, M. (1977). Commentary. In J. Suls & R. Miller (Eds.), *Social comparison processes* (pp. 335–357). Washington, DC: Hemisphere.

White, R. W. (1959). Motivation reconsidered: The concept of competence. *Psychological Review, 66,* 297–333.

Wicklund, R. A. (1975). Objective self-awareness. In L. Berkowitz (Ed.), *Advances in experimental social psychology* (Vol. 8, pp. 233–275). New York: Academic Press.

Wicklund, R. A., & Brehm, J. W. (1976). *Perspectives on cognitive dissonance.* Hillsdale, NJ: Erlbaum.

Wicklund, R. A., & Gollwitzer, P. M. (1982). *Symbolic self-completion.* Hillsdale, NJ: Erlbaum.

Wiggins, J. S. (1992). Agency and communion as conceptual coordinates for the under-. standing and measurement of interpersonal behavior. In W. M. Grove & D. Cicchetti (Eds.), *Thinking clearly about psychology* (pp. 89–113). Minneapolis: University of Minnesota Press.

Williams, K. D., Harkins, S. G., & Latané, B. (1981). Identifiability as a deterrent to social loafing: Two cheering experiments. *Journal of Personality and Social Psychology, 40,* 303–311.

Williamson, G. M., & Clark, M. S. (1989). Providing help and desired relationship type as determinants of changes in mood and self-evaluations. *Journal of Personality and Social Psychology, 56,* 722–734.

Wills, T. A. (1981). Downward comparison principles in social psychology. *Psychological Bulletin, 90,* 245–271.

Wills, T. A. (1991). Similarity and self-esteem in downward comparison. In J. Suls & T. A. Wills (Eds.), *Social comparison: Contemporary theory and research* (pp. 51–78). Hillsdale, NJ: Erlbaum.

Winter, D. G. (1973). *The power motive.* New York: Free Press.

Winter, D. G. (1988). The power motive in women—and men. *Journal of Personality and Social Psychology, 54,* 510–519.

Winter, D. G., & Barenbaum, N. B. (1985). Responsibility and the power motive in women and men. *Journal of Personality, 53,* 335–355.

Wood, R. E., Mento, A. J., & Locke, E. A. (1987). Task complexity as a moderator of goal effects: A meta-analysis. *Journal of Applied Psychology, 72,* 416–425.

Woodworth, R. S. (1918). *Dynamic psychology.* New York: Columbia University Press.

Wortman, C. B., & Brehm, J. W. (1975). Responses to uncontrollable outcomes: An integration of reactance theory and the learned helplessness model. In L. Berkowitz (Ed.), *Advances in experimental social psychology* (Vol. 8, pp. 277–336). New York: Academic Press.

Wright, R. A., & Brehm, J. W. (1989). Energization and goal attractiveness. In L. A. Pervin (Ed.), *Goal concepts in personality and social psychology* (pp. 169–210). Hillsdale, NJ: Erlbaum.

Wright, R. A., Brehm, J. W., & Bushman, B. J. (1989). Cardiovascular responses to threat: Effects of the difficulty and availability of a cognitive avoidance task. *Basic and Applied Social Psychology, 10,* 161–171.

Wright, R. A., Contrada, R., & Patane, M. J. (1986). Task difficulty, cardiovascular response, and the magnitude of goal valence. *Journal of Personality and Social Psychology, 51,* 837–843.

Wright, R. A., & Gregorich, S (1989). Difficulty and instrumentality of imminent behavior as determinants of cardiovascular response and self-reported energy. *Psychophysiology, 26,* 586–592.

Zajonc, R. B. (1965). Social facilitation. *Science, 149,* 269–274.

Zajonc, R. B. (1980). Compresence. In P. Paulus (Ed.), *Psychology of group influence* (pp. 35–60). Hillsdale, NJ: Erlbaum.

Zajonc, R. B. (1985). Emotion and facial efference: A theory reclaimed. *Science, 228,* 15–21.

Zajonc, R. B., Murphy, S. T., & Inglehart, M. (1989). Feeling and facial efference: Implications of the vascular theory of emotion. *Psychological Review, 96,* 395–416.

Zedeck, S. (1977). An information processing model and approach to the study of motivation. *Organizational Behavior and Human Performance, 18,* 47–77.

Zillmann, D. (1971). Excitation transfer in communication-mediated aggressive behavior. *Journal of Experimental Social Psychology, 7,* 419–434.

Zillmann, D. (1978). Attribution and misattribution of excitatory reactions. In J. H. Harvey, W. J. Ickes & R. F. Kidd (Eds.), *New directions in attribution research* (Vol. 2, pp. 335–368). Hillsdale, NJ: Erlbaum.

Zillmann, D., Baron, R. A., & Tamborini, R. (1981). Social costs of smoking: Effects of tobacco smoke on hostile behavior. *Journal of Applied Social Psychology, 11,* 548–561.

Zillmann, D., Katcher, A. H., & Milavsky, B. (1972). Excitation transfer from physical exercise to subsequent aggressive behavior. *Journal of Experimental Social Psychology, 8,* 247–259.

Zuckerman, M. (1979). *Sensation seeking: Beyond the optimal level of arousal.* Hillsdale, NJ: Erlbaum.

Zuckerman, M. (1990). The psychophysiology of sensation seeking. *Journal of Personality, 58,* 313–345.

Zuckerman, M., Ball, S., & Black, J. (1990). Influences of sensation-seeking, gender, risk appraisal, and situational motivation on smoking. *Addictive Behaviors, 15,* 209–220.

Zuckerman, Mi. (1979). Attribution of success and failure revisited, or: The motivational bias is alive and well in attribution theory. *Journal of Personality, 47,* 245–287.

# PHOTO CREDITS

# NAME INDEX

# Subject Index

TO THE OWNER OF THIS BOOK:

I hope that you have found *Human Motivation* useful. So that this book can be improved in a future edition, would you take the time to complete this sheet and return it? Thank you.

School and address: _____

Department: _____

Instructor's name: _____

1. What I like most about this book is: _____

_____

_____

2. What I like least about this book is: _____

_____

_____

3. My general reaction to this book is: _____

_____

4. The name of the course in which I used this book is: _____

_____

5. Were all of the chapters of the book assigned for you to read? _____

   If not, which ones weren't? _____

6. In the space below, or on a separate sheet of paper, please write specific suggestions for improving this book and anything else you'd care to share about your experience in using the book.

_____

_____

_____

_____

_____

Optional:

Your name: _____ Date: _____

May Brooks/Cole quote you, either in promotion for *Human Motivation* or in future publishing ventures?

Yes: _____ No: _____

Sincerely,

*Russell G. Geen*

FOLD HERE

FOLD HERE